CHEAP EATS
IN LONDON

timeout.com

Published by Time Out Guides Ltd, a wholly owned subsidiary of Time Out Group Ltd
Time Out and the Time Out logo are trademarks of Time Out Group Ltd

© **Time Out Group Ltd 2007**
Previous editions 2003, 2004, 2005

10 9 8 7 6 5 4 3 2 1

This edition first published in Great Britain in 2007 by Ebury Publishing
Ebury Publishing is a division of The Random House Group Ltd,
20 Vauxhall Bridge Road, London SW1V 2SA

Random House Australia Pty Limited 20 Alfred Street, Milsons Point, Sydney, New South Wales 2061, Australia
Random House New Zealand Limited 18 Poland Road, Glenfield, Auckland 10, New Zealand
Random House South Africa (Pty) Limited Isle of Houghton, Corner Boundary Road & Carse O'Gowrie, Houghton 2198, South Africa

Random House UK Limited Reg. No. 954009

Distributed in USA by Publishers Group West
1700 Fourth Street, Berkeley, California 94710

Distributed in Canada by Publishers Group Canada
250A Carlton Street, Toronto, Ontario M5A 2L1

For further distribution details, see www.timeout.com

ISBN 10: 1-904978-96-7
ISBN 13: 978-1-904978-96-1

A CIP catalogue record for this book is available from the British Library

Colour reprographics by Wyndeham Icon, 3 & 4 Maverton Road, London E3 2JE

Printed and bound in Germany by Appl

Papers used by Ebury Publishing are natural, recyclable products made from wood grown in sustainable forests

Edited and designed by
Time Out Guides Limited
Universal House
251 Tottenham Court Road
London W1T 7AB
Tel + 44 (0) 20 7813 3000
Fax + 44 (0) 20 7813 6001
Email guides@timeout.com
www.timeout.com

Editorial

Editor Tom Lamont
Deputy Editor Edoardo Albert
Listings Checkers Jill Emeny,
Cathy Limb, Fiona Shield
Proofreader Mandy Martinez
Indexer Cathy Limb

Managing Director Peter Fiennes
Editorial Director Sarah Guy
Deputy Series Editor Cathy Phillips
Financial Director Gareth Garner
Guides Co-ordinator Holly Pick
Accountant Kemi Olufuwa

Design

Art Director Scott Moore
Art Editor Pinelope Kourmouzoglou
Senior Designer Josephine Spencer
Graphic Designer Henry Elphick
Digital Imaging Simon Foster
Ad Make-up Jenni Prichard

Picture Desk

Picture Editor Jael Marschner
Deputy Picture Editor
Tracey Kerrigan
Picture Researcher
Helen McFarland

Advertising

Sales Director Mark Phillips
Sales Manager Alison Wallen
Advertising Sales Ben Holt, Jason Trotman
Advertising Assistant Kate Staddon
Copy Controller Baris Tosun

Marketing

Group Marketing Director John Luck
Marketing Manager Yvonne Poon
Marketing & Publicity Manager, US
Rosella Albanese

Production

Group Production Director Mark Lamond
Production Manager Brendan McKeown
Production Coordinator Caroline Bradford

Time Out Group

Chairman Tony Elliott
Financial Director Richard Waterlow
TO Magazine Ltd MD David Pepper
Group General Manager/Director
Nichola Coulthard
Managing Director, Time Out International
Cathy Runciman
TO Communications Ltd MD David Pepper
Group Art Director John Oakey
Group IT Director Simon Chappell

Contributors
Reviews in this guide were written by: Esther Adams, Ismay Atkins, Joseph Bindloss, Peterjon Cresswell, Guy Dimond, Alexi Duggins, Jill Emeny, Jan Fuscoe, Sarah Guy, David Jenkins, Neon Kelly, Tom Lamont, Cathy Limb, Jenny Linford, Natalie Moore, Rebecca Omonira, Tom Peel, Emma Perry, Charlotte Rumsey, Andrew Shields, Sammie Squire, Andrew Staffell, Sejal Sukhadwala, Elizabeth Winding.

The Editor would like to thank all contributors to the *Time Out Eating & Drinking Guide 2007*, whose work forms the basis for parts of this book.

Maps john@jsgraphics.co.uk.

Cover photography by Britta Jaschinski, taken at Carluccio's (www.carluccios.com).

Openers photography by Jitka Hynkova.

Photography by pages 6, 7, 9, 10, 15, 38, 39, 76, 114, 161, 166, 169, 170, 177, 180, 184, 191, 196, 199, 204, 207, 212, 215, 217, 229, 232, 238, 257 Heloise Bergman; pages 6, 44, 45, 64, 65, 79, 104, 105, 108, 110, 111, 119, 124, 125, 129, 132, 139, 141, 142, 144, 153, 188 Tricia de Courcy Ling; pages 6, 17, 80, 83, 246, 247 Britta Jaschinski; pages 30, 31, 90, 96, 97, 236, 242 Agnese Sanvito; pages 71, 172, 250, 251 Ming Tang Evans.

About the guide

What is cheap?

Cheap is, of course, relative – London is one of the world's most expensive cities, after all. And yet, hidden among its many fine and fancy restaurants, is a galaxy of lower-priced eateries. So arm yourself with a twenty quid note and a hearty appetite, and tuck in.

In all of the **more than 500** places reviewed within this guide you should be able to get two courses (starter + main or main + dessert), plus half a bottle of house wine (or a couple of beers) plus service (we've assumed ten per cent when it is not automatically added) for no more than **£20 per person**.

Where restaurants allow you to bring your own booze, we've estimated the cost as £5 for a bottle of wine from an off-licence plus any corkage charged by the restaurant. In places that don't allow any alcohol, we've assumed you'll have a couple of soft drinks.

We have indicated in the relevant reviews those restaurants where only certain items on the menu fall within the 'budget' category.

Average

In the listings for each restaurant, you'll see one to three £ signs. These indicate average per person prices as follows:

£	= **under £14**
££	= **£14-£17**
£££	= **£17-£20**

Meal deals

At the end of each area chapter you'll find a section headed 'Meal deals'. The restaurants listed here would normally be too expensive to qualify as 'cheap eats', but offer menus at certain times or on certain days that would bring in a meal at less than £20 a person.

In the area

After 'Meal deals' comes 'In the area', which gives basic listings of branches that appear within that area but are affiliated to places that are reviewed elsewhere in the guide. Look in the index to find the review of the main branch.

Stars

Those restaurants that we particularly like are marked ★ in this guide. These are not necessarily the cheapest places, but all are outstanding in some way.

New

Those restaurants added since last year are marked NEW . These aren't necessarily new businesses, but are new to the guide.

Telephone numbers

All phone numbers listed in this guide assume you are calling from within London. From elsewhere in the UK, prefix each number with **020**. From abroad, dial your international access code, then **44** for the UK, and then **20** for London.

Unbiased reviews

The reviews in *Cheap Eats in London* are based on the experiences of Time Out restaurant reviewers. Restaurants and cafés are always visited anonymously, and Time Out pays the bill. No payment or PR invitation of any kind has secured or influenced a review. The editors select which places are listed in this guide, and are not influenced in any way by the wishes of the restaurants themselves. Restaurants cannot volunteer or pay to be listed; we list only those we consider to be worthy of inclusion. Advertising and sponsorship has no effect whatsoever on editorial content. An advertiser may receive a bad review, or no review at all.

Disclaimer

While every effort has been made to ensure the accuracy of information within this guide, the publishers cannot accept responsibility for any errors it may contain. Details can change, and it's always advisable to phone to check before setting out.

Contents

Better brekkies

Breakfasting at some of London's best
restaurants needn't be a budget-breaker.
Tom Lamont finds some surprisingly cheap
morning eats.

The advice to eat a good breakfast is repeated relentlessly
from the time of our first solid meal. Parents, teachers,
dieticians and doctors have long bored us with one of the
weariest maxims out there, 'breakfast is the most important
meal of the day'. Others have pitched in over the centuries:
Victorian moralists, who believed a hot breakfast was ample
protection against alcoholism ('when a breakfast sustains
us properly, we do not have that sinking feeling, compelling
us towards the dram-shop'), to a modern-day chef like Fergus
Henderson of St John, who asks, with characteristic foodie

Dorchester Grill Room.
See p13.

eccentricity: 'What could prepare you better for the adventures the day holds than a plate of devilled kidneys on toast and a glass of black velvet?' It is agreed: a warm, nourishing breakfast is critical.

Where to get it? Despite their slow decline, London still has a clutch of wonderful caffs – E Pellicci (see p176) foremost among them. And the sandwich chains cater for a morning hunger pretty well: ham and cheese croissants at Pret a Manger, excellent bircher museli (museli soaked in fruit juice then mixed with yoghurt) at Eat, and surprisingly good Marmite and cheese toasties at Starbucks. But there's another option, even for the money-conscious. Breakfast is the ideal meal-time at which to take advantage of a high-end restaurant – one that might otherwise be prohibitively expensive.

In this guide, we list the best places to eat in London for £20 a head or less; obviously, many of the capital's smart brasseries and posh hotels don't match this criteria. Breakfast is the solution, and often it's the most hassle-free way to experience London's grander addresses: prices are lower, tables easier to collar without booking.

Londoners are catching on to the notion of a slap-up feast for £15 a head. According to the wonderfully titled 'head of breakfast' at the **Wolseley** in Piccadilly, 'breakfast business has just gone up and up and up'. We saw it for ourselves on a recent weekday morning visit: the Wolseley's cavernous, multi-domed brasserie was full to capacity. Many were enjoying a simple breakfast like the mixed pâtisserie basket (£6.50). Others breakfasted more substantially: omelette Arnold Bennett (a dished, creamy omelette made with smoked haddock, £8.75), grilled kipper with mustard butter (£8.50), or a Wolseley english (£12.50), the full works featuring bacon, sausage and black pudding. Smoked salmon and scrambled eggs (£11.50) was a rich marriage of intensely flavoured salmon, creamy yellow scramble and sweet toasted brioche. With cutlery, tableclothes and accoutrements that exude bygone charm – a pot of tea comes with a dainty tea-strainer – we came away feeling like a character from PG Wodehouse.

A few doors down on Piccadilly, in its ground floor Fountain restaurant, **Fortnum & Mason** offer a similarly lavish breakfast at wallet-neutral (if not wallet-friendly) prices. There's wheat-free museli with own-made fruit purée (£6), grilled kippers (£8), corned beef hash (£8), or an english breakfast (£10), which features a choice of two black puddings, one a blood pudding from west Yorkshire, the other a variety made with barley from southern Ireland. A pot of rich Assam Hazelbank tea made a fine accompaniment to eggs benedict (£10). Serving with just as much splendour across town, try breakfast at the **Dorchester Grill Room**. Befitting the enormous mural in which a tartan-clad Scotsman looks pensively into the distance, try smoked haddock kedgeree (£12). Otherwise, there's sumptuous eggs Benedict with crispy bacon (£16).

Modern mornings

Breakfasts like these, in majestic settings, evocative of a bygone era, are a must-tick experience – as much for the atmosphere they afford as the quality of food. But there are a host of modern restaurants putting just as much effort in to their breakfast service, pushing fry-ups towards the posh without quite so much show and swagger. Morning meals are a particular treat at British restaurant **Roast** which hangs over Borough Market. Enjoy a 'Full Borough' fry-up (£12) in a zen-like restaurant with crisp linen and unstressed staff, looking out at the morning activity of the market. Elsewhere on the menu there's 'tattie scone' with Ayrshire streaky bacon, mushrooms and egg (£8.50), smoked trout with scrambled eggs (£10),

Automat 33 Dover Street,
W1S 4NF (7499 3033).
Breakfast served 7-11am
Mon-Fri. Brunch served 11am-
4pm Sat, Sun. Map p269.
Christopher's 18 Wellington
Street, WC2E 7DD (7240
4222). Brunch served
11.30am-3pm Sat, Sun.
Map p273.
Inn The Park St James's
Park, SW1A 2BJ (7451
9999). Breakfast served
8-11am Mon-Fri; 9-11am
Sat, Sun.
1 Lombard Street
1 Lombard Street, EC3V 9AA
(7929 6611). Breakfast
served 7.30-11am Mon-Fri.
Map p271.
Quality Chop House 92-94
Farringdon Road, EC1R 3EA
(7837 5093). Breakfast
served 7.30-10am Mon-Fri.
Map p270.
Roast The Floral Hall,
Borough Market, Stoney
Street, SE1 1TL (7940
1300). Breakfast served
7-10am Mon-Fri; 8-11am
Sat. Map p289.

or roast tomatoes on toast with Worcestershire sauce and celery salt (£5.50).

If morning views appeal, head to St James' Park for Oliver Peyton's **Inn The Park**: its modern wooden structure fits perfectly into a lakeside slot, and every table looks out over the water. Breakfasts here include granola with yoghurt and pomegranate (£5.50), a toastie of Rhug Estate bacon and tomato (£6), eggs florentine (£6), or cinnamon pancakes with bananas and maple syrup (£5.50).

Pancakes, a classically American breakfast, are a popular order at **Christopher's** in Covent Garden. Choose from blueberry with fruit compote, or buttermilk with bacon and syrup. Two courses here cost £14.50, so follow pancakes with huevos rancheros (a Tex-Mex breakfast featuring fried eggs, salsa and cheese on soft tortilla) or french toast with roast peach and marscapone. Leave a week or more to digest before trying an American roadside diner-style brekkie at **Automat** in Mayfair. They also serve pancakes (£8 with various toppings), as well as ham muffin with egg (£8) and the 'Automat big breakfast' (£10), which, quite incredibly, includes steak as well as the usual bacon and sausage. For equally artery-clogging British fare, try Farringdon's **Quality Chop House** offer a meat-intensive breakfast menu, including grilled calves liver,

Inn The Park

bacon and egg £12.50; in the City, the brasserie at **1 Lombard Street** do a similar dish for £14.50, as well as lamb kidney 'diable' (made with strong mustard, £9.75) and lemony grilled kipper (£9.95). If you can only manage something small (perhaps you've recently been to Automat) order gentlemen's relish on toast (£3.75).

Breakfasts abroad

London's breakfast gamut spreads further than English classics like bacon and eggs or gentlemen's relish. For a European slant, the **Zetter** in Shoreditch serve up cool, Med-style breakfasts; try avocado bagel with crispy pancetta and mozarella (£5.50). Allez for a French spin on Sunday brunch to Bethnal Green's **Bistrotheque**. Best are croque monsieur (£5), and lardons, sautéed potatoes and fried egg (£5.50). Further abroad, munch on Danish pastries (£2.25 for a selection) at Danish brasserie **Lundum's** in South Kensington, or spicy scrambled eggs on layered rice pancakes (£14) at South Indian restaurant the **Cinnamon Club** in Westminster. In the tapa room at Marylebone's **Providores & Tapa Room**, we particularly like 'Turkish eggs' (poached, with whipped yoghurt and chilli, £5), as well as grilled sardine bruschetta (£5.80) and miso porridge, made with brown rice, apple and syrup (£4.50).

Bistrotheque 23-27 Wadeson Street, E2 9DR (8983 7900). Brunch served 11am-4pm Sat, Sun.
Cinnamon Club The Old Westminster Library, 30-32 Great Smith Street, SW1P 3BU (7222 2555). Breakfast served 7.30-9.30am Mon-Fri.
Lundum's 117-119 Old Brompton Road, SW7 3RN (7373 7774). Breakfast served 9am-noon Mon-Sat. Map p278.
Providores & Tapa Room 109 Marylebone High Street, W1U 4RX (7935 6175). Breakfast served 9-11.30am Mon-Fri; 10am-3pm Sat, Sun. Map p277.
Yauatcha 15 Broadwick Street, W1F ODL (7494 8888). Meals served noon-11.45pm Mon-Sat; noon-10.45pm Sun. Map p268.
Zetter 86-88 Clerkenwell Road, EC1M 5RJ (7324 4455). Breakfast served 6.30-10.30am Mon-Fri; 7-11am Sat, Sun. Map p270.

Canteen

Yauatcha in Soho, though without a committed breakfast menu, serves excellent congees (savoury rice porridge, £4.80-£6), which are eaten as a breakfast dish in many Asian countries.

Brilliant bacon sarnies

With porridge in mind, you might fancy something humbler – less labour intensive – in the morning. For a simple bacon sandwich, there are few better places than at **Canteen** in Spitalfields (£4.50) and the **Rivington Bar & Grill** in Shoreditch (£4). The ground floor at **Smiths of Smithfields** do a cheaper bacon butty (£2.50) that's just as good. They also fry up five fab breakfast combos (£4.50-£6.50), which are a treat – even if they do insist on playing throbbing dance music before midday. Finally, Fergus Henderson's **St John Bread & Wine** in Spitalfields do a brisk trade with their own superlative bacon sarnies (£4.80), as well as some typically eccentric offerings. Try soft herring roes on toast (£5.40). 'If it's steadying you require in the morning,' Henderson advises, 'soft roes on toast is your man.'

Spend a little more than at your local greasy spoon, be a little more adventurous than a plasticky croissant, and discover a whole new side of breakfast. In a way, you're only doing what the doctor ordered.

Canteen *2 Crispin Place, off Brushfield Street, E1 6DW (0845 686 1122).* Breakfast served 8-11am Mon-Fri; 9-11am Sat, Sun. Map p271.
Rivington Bar & Grill *28-30 Rivington Street, EC2A 3DZ (7729 7053).* Breakfast served 8-11am Mon-Fri. Map p271.
St John Bread & Wine *94-96 Commercial Street, E1 6LZ (7251 0848).* Breakfast served 9-11am Mon-Fri; 10am-11am Sat, Sun. Map p271.
Smiths of Smithfield *67-77 Charterhouse Street, EC1M 6HJ (7251 7950).* Breakfast served 7am-4.30pm Mon-Fri; 10am-4.30pm Sat, Sun. Map p270.

CENTRAL

Barbican

Carnevale

*135 Whitecross Street, EC1Y 8JL
(7250 3452). Barbican tube/Old
Street tube/rail/55 bus.* **Lunch
served** noon-3.30pm Mon-Fri.
Dinner served 5.30-10.30pm
Mon-Sat. **Average £££. Minimum**
(noon-2.30pm Mon-Fri) £5.50. **Set
meal** (lunch Mon-Fri, 5.30-7pm
Mon-Sat) £13.50 3 courses.
Map p271. Vegetarian

Starters were the most promising
course at this tiny, vanilla-hued
Mediterranean restaurant, which
houses a deli and a conservatory.
They included roast Jerusalem
artichoke and pumpkin salad, and
intensely flavoured, soft-poached
egg atop a slab of toasted brioche. A
main course of roast pear caponata
(Italian sweet-sour aubergine
casserole) wasn't a successful
combination of flavours, and the
accompanying chilli polenta fritters
were lacking in chilli. Breaded
aubergine stuffed with smoked
mozzarella and ricotta was better –
the combination of the vegetable
and smoked cheese giving the dish
a meaty taste and texture. Our
desserts of white chocolate pudding
and chocolate rum pudding were
overly dense and disappointing.
Carnevale's menu is short and
repetitive in its use of ingredients,
and lacks the sunshine flavours of
the Mediterranean.

★ Fish Central

*149-155 Central Street, EC1V 8AP
(7253 4970). Old Street tube/rail/
55 bus.* **Lunch served** 11am-
2.30pm Mon-Sat. **Dinner served**
5-10.30pm Mon-Thur; 5-11pm Fri,
Sat. **Average ££. Map** p270.
Fish & Chips

The word is out: this once-popular
haunt of cabbies and tradesmen is
now heaving with suits, students
and pensioners. Oddly located in the
middle of a large council estate, Fish
Central certainly ain't posh, with
IKEA-style plastic tables and chairs,
but it is light and airy; on our visit,
the large front windows had been
opened out on to the street. The
yard-long menus list a generous
selection of shellfish and steak, as
well as various fish: deep-fried,
grilled or cooked in matzo meal. The
haddock was perfectly steamed,
with thick, chunky flakes encased in
a thin, crisp batter. Servings are
huge: one portion of chips or mushy
peas will easily stretch to two
people. Next door, the firm operates
a standard takeaway offering a
much-reduced menu.

Pham Sushi

*159 Whitecross Street, EC1Y 8JL
(7251 6336). Old Street tube/rail/
55 bus.* **Lunch served** noon-2.30pm
Mon-Fri. **Dinner served** 5-10pm
Mon-Sat. **Average £££. Map** p270.
Japanese

An unlikely find in the middle of
busy, grimy Whitecross Street,
Pham Sushi is something of a
Japanese oasis: calm, smart and
quiet, at odds with the market bustle
outside. Staff wear crisp uniforms;
conversation levels never exceed a
low hum; and, while there is a small
communal counter at the back, most
diners sit at sleek square tables.
More a restaurant than a quick-stop
canteen, then, but our sushi arrived
swiftly. Two mixed platters of sushi
and sashimi included the classics
(thickly sliced, vibrantly coloured
salmon sashimi, meaty sea bass
nigiri) as well as some interesting
'chef specials': we particularly liked
maki with soft-shelled crab.
Elsewhere on the menu, bento boxes
featuring tempura and stir-fried beef
tempted. Prices reflect the above-
average quality of the sushi (our
platters were around £15 each); care
should be taken not to swell the bill
beyond budget.

Bloomsbury

Bi-Won

24 Coptic Street, WC1A 1NT (7580 2660). Tottenham Court Road tube. **Meals served** noon-11pm daily. **Average** ££. Korean

Tucked away in a backstreet near the British Museum, this neat, cosy café, with cream walls and wooden floor, was packed with Korean students during our lunchtime visit. The restaurant is poorly ventilated, so it was rather smoky, but the food more than made up for that. Tasty kimch'i was brought over as soon as we'd ordered our meal. Mandu kuk was a generous bowlful of dumpling soup. Vegetable tolsot bibimbap was packed with shredded carrots, spring onions, mushrooms and peppers, and topped with raw egg; mixed with fiery koch'ujang (hot red bean paste), the dish was a delight. Porich'a (barley tea) was free, but we had to ask for it. The lunchtime set meals are exceptionally good value, particularly for a central London location; an à la carte menu is served only in the evenings.

Ultimate Burger NEW

34 New Oxford Street, WC1A 1AP (7436 6641/www.ultimate burger.co.uk). Tottenham Court Road or Holborn tube. **Meals served** noon-11.30pm daily. **Average** ££. Map p267. Burgers

Handy for the British Museum, this small chain (with two other branches in London) gives you no starters, but four variations on burgers of beef, chicken, lamb or vegetables (mushroom, aubergine and others). The toppings and treatments tend towards the classic rather than the outlandish – barbecue sauce, crispy bacon, satay sauce. The beef comes cooked medium as standard, and we couldn't complain about the big sesame seed bun or the quality of the

extras (the cheese was real cheese). Chips? Medium-cut, nicely fried until light golden, not too heavily salted. To drink: four flavours of milkshake, two choices each of red or white wine, two bottled lagers. Ultimate may not be the ultimate, but it does everything well, and leaves little room for complaint.

Wagamama

4A Streatham Street, WC1A 1JB (7323 9223). Tottenham Court Road or Holborn tube. **Meals served** noon-11pm daily. **Average** ££. **Map** p267. Oriental

Wagamama has stood the test of time well, with minimalist interiors (hardly changed since being designed in 1992) that still look contemporary, and menus that have stayed close to the original ethos of wholesome, basic fast food at a fair price. By Japanese standards, basic means basic: yaki soba (stir-fried ramen with titbits) wasn't massively interesting – a heap of egg noodles with bits of pork, chicken, and red ginger – but it pleased. Gyoza had a curiously dry filling – chicken is substituted for the more usual and much moister pork mixture. But Wagamama does a lot right: big steaming bowls of ramen are ever-popular, service demonstrates a Henry Fordesque efficiency, and bills are always reasonable. Such factors will no doubt ensure this chain continues to expand even beyond its current reach to cities such as Dubai and Auckland.

Yo! Sushi

Myhotel, 11-13 Bayley Street, Bedford Square, WC1B 3HD (7636 0076/www.yosushi.com). Tottenham Court Road tube. **Meals served** noon-11pm Mon-Sat; noon-10.30pm Sun. **Average** £££. **Map** p266. Japanese

This Bloomsbury branch – nestled on the ground floor of the rather nice Myhotel complex – is one of dozens

Busaba Eathai

Wardour Street
Phone 020-7255-8686
106-110 Wardour Street
London W1T 0TR

Store Street
Phone 020-7299-7900
22 Store Street
London WC1E 7DF
Pre-booking available
for groups of 12+
Take away available

Bird Street
Phone 020-7518-808
8–13 Bird Street
London W1U 1BU
Take away available

of branches of the Yo! chain which stretches across London and beyond. As in most outlets, tables are provided, but most diners choose to sit at stools in front of the long and winding conveyor-belt. Not the cheapest kaiten joint (plates £1.60-£4) and dishes can be a little bland, but the menu is always an interesting read, with plenty of hot options and seasonally changing specials. Kids in particular love the conveyor-belts and the colourful food; Yo!'s chirpy atmosphere and equally chirpy staff cater for them well. Every so often, almost at random it seems, Yo! run a great two-for-one sushi promotion; value for money that makes it worth the occasional check of their website.

Meal deals

Cigala *54 Lamb's Conduit Street, WC1N 3LW (7405 1717/www. cigala.co.uk).* Set meal (Sun) £10.50 1 course. **Map** p267. Spanish

In the area

Abeno *47 Museum Street, WC1A 1LY (7405 3211).* Branch of Abeno Too. **Map** p267.
Apostrophe *216 Tottenham Court Road, entrance in 20/20 Optical Store or 9 Alfred Place, W1T 7PT (7436 6688).* **Map** p266.
ASK *48 Grafton Way, W1T 5DZ (7388 8108).* **Map** p266.
ASK *74 Southampton Row, WC1B 4AR (7405 2876).* **Map** p267.
Busaba Eathai *22 Store Street, WC1E 7DS (7299 7900).* **Map** p266.
Giraffe *19-21 Brunswick Centre, WC1N 3AG (8457 2776).* **Map** p267.
Pizza Express *30 Coptic Street, WC1A 1NS (7636 3232).* **Map** p267.
Planet Organic *22 Torrington Place, WC1E 7HJ (7436 1929).* **Map** p266.
Ristorante Paradiso *35 Store Street, WC1E 7BS (7255 2554).* Branch of Pizza Paradiso. **Map** p266.

Tas *22 Bloomsbury Street, WC1B 3QJ (7637 4555).* Branch of EV Restaurant, Bar & Delicatessen. **Map** p267.
Wagamama *4A Streatham Street, WC1A 1JB (7323 9223).* **Map** p267.

Chinatown

Café de HK

47-49 Charing Cross Road, WC2H 0AN (7534 9898). Leicester Square or Piccadilly Circus tube. **Meals served** 11.30am-11pm daily. **Average** ££. **Map** p268. Chinese
Baseball hat-wearing Chinese teenagers favour this bright funky venue, as they hungrily tuck into meal-in-one plates of rice or noodles while watching the latest Hong Kong pop videos. There's a ground-floor canteen plus two further floors for dining, though lingering is discouraged by hard blond-wood benches and the abrupt staff. Avoid the 'Russian borsht soup' (which is like packet tomato) and plump for a hawker soup noodle meal (a development of noodle soup with a choice of ingredients like beef or curry stock). Ice pearl bubble tea is a popular thirst-quencher.

Café TPT

21 Wardour Street, W1D 6PN (7734 7980). Leicester Square or Piccadilly Circus tube. **Meals served** noon-1am daily. **Average** ££. **Set meal** £9.50-£11 per person 2 courses (minimum 2). **Map** p269. Chinese
New and old marry well at the bustling little TPT. Clued-up staff sport orange sweatshirts and keep the pace cranked up, while the chef chops succulent roast meats in his kiosk by the window. Roast duck (on the bone) is juicy indeed – and tender. Good too are the Malaysian-style cold drinks; black tea with milk and pearl tapioca is fun to try, full of ice and chewy balls to be sucked up

Osatsuma

MODERN JAPANESE DINING

56 Wardour Street, London, W1 020 7437 8338
www.osatsuma.com
⊖ PICCADILLY CIRCUS LEICESTER SQUARE
Open M-T 12-11 W-T 12-11.30 F-S 12-12 Sun 12-10.30

with a straw. The large menu has such delicacies as turbot in curry sauce, but this breezy spot is not the ideal place for a banquet.

Feng Shui Inn

4-6 Gerrard Street, W1D 5PG (7734 6778). Leicester Square or Piccadilly Circus tube. **Meals served** noon-11.30pm daily. **Average £££.** **Set lunch** (noon-4.30pm) £3.90 1 course incl tea, £5.90-£10.90 2 courses incl tea. **Set meal** £12.80-£26.80 per person (minimum 2). **Map** p268. Chinese

The brightly lit dining room at this Chinatown eaterie is broken into a warren of intimate spaces that is stuffed full with Chinese goodwill tokens, including imitation firecrackers and Chinese lanterns. Most of the menu consists of Anglo-friendly dishes, but there are also some less common choices including the restaurant's signature dish, 'kam sha' chicken. At first, this seems nothing special – deep-fried chicken covered with freshly deep-fried flakes of garlic – but the combination of moist flesh and crisp skin won us over. Stir-fried Chinese mushrooms with pak choi was decent, but both Cantonese-style pork chop and sweet and sour king prawn were doused in wishy-washy sauces that tasted similar and lacked flavour. Our waitresses, dressed in red sweatshirts, were friendly and attentive throughout.

Fook Sing

25-26 Newport Court, WC2H 7JS (7287 0188). Leicester Square or Piccadilly Circus tube. **Meals served** 11am-10.30pm daily. **Average ££.** **Unlicensed** no alcohol allowed. **No credit cards.** **Map** p268. Chinese

Head for the Fujianese specials at Fook Sing, a rudimentary tiled caff featuring easy-wipe tables and cheerful, kind staff. There's plenty here for the adventurous to get their teeth into. Chewy fried snails arrived spiced up with chilli and bulked up with mushrooms and carrots; hotchpotch soup contained nigh-on all the edibles that are known to humankind (from tripe to mussels, from ham to yam); and pork and cabbage stew was a warming broth featuring tender meat and a stock to savour. The portions are immense while the prices remain modest; three dishes plus rice for £14.50 is the best deal. Otherwise, come early for lunch before the delectable oyster cakes run out.

Golden Dragon

28-29 Gerrard Street, W1D 6JW (7734 2763). Leicester Square or Piccadilly Circus tube. **Meals served** noon-11.30pm Mon-Thur; noon-midnight Fri, Sat; 11am-11pm Sun. **Dim sum served** noon-5pm Mon-Sat; 11am-5pm Sun. **Average ££.** **Set meal** £12.50-£35 per person (minimum 2). **Map** p268. Chinese

Occasionally slapdash service and the slightly worn decor don't match the lustre of the wall mount at this prime site on Gerrard Street: an elaborate carving of a golden dragon, which dominates the main dining area. But the cooking is fine: a dish of braised belly pork was meltingly tender, served on preserved vegetables; and an interesting dish of pallid Chinese leaves, with threads of fragmented, orange-coloured dried scallops in the sauce, was excellent. The classic hot-and-sour soup had lots of flavour and colourful titbits to savour. However, the high noise levels and brusque feel of Golden Dragon don't make it a relaxing place for a meal.

Harbour City

46 Gerrard Street, W1D 5QH (7287 1526/7439 7859). Leicester Square or Piccadilly Circus tube. **Meals served** noon-11.30pm Mon-Thur; noon-midnight Fri, Sat; 11am-10.30pm Sun. **Dim sum served**

noon-5pm Mon-Sat; 11am-5pm Sun.
Average ££. **Set meal** £13.50-
£15.50 per person (minimum 2).
Map p268. Chinese

Despite a menu and furnishings that
have changed very little over the
years, the standards at Harbour City
remain reliably high. Try to get a
table on the airy first floor, rather
than the cramped ground level,
which has little natural light. We
did, and were comfy enough in a
room sporting wood-laminate or
pastel-yellow walls, white linen on
the tables and windows looking out
over Gerrard Street's Chinatown
arch. Best of the snacks on offer
were the crisp taro croquettes
enclosing juicy minced pork, though
we also relished the delectably
gelatinous meat in the five-spice beef
tendon, and the juxtaposition of
sponginess and springiness in the
fish maw with minced prawn paste.
Throw in some steamed whelks in
curry sauce, and the odd glutinous
rice roll (doughy exterior with a
chewy filling) and we left happy.

Hing Loon

*25 Lisle Street, WC2H 7BA (7437
3602/7287 0419). Leicester Square
or Piccadilly Circus tube.* **Meals
served** noon-11.30pm Mon-Thur;
noon-midnight Fri, Sat; noon-11pm
Sun. **Average** £. **Set lunch** £4.50
2 courses. **Set dinner** £5.80-£9.50
per person (minimum 2). **Map** p268.
Chinese

Hardly an introduction to the finer
points of Chinese cuisine, the £4.50
two-course 'economy' lunch (cash
only) features the likes of
mummified spring rolls, gelatinous
sweet-and-sour pork, vegetable fried
noodles (comprising mostly sliced
carrot and beansprouts) and,
bizarrely, chicken curry. The low
prices and substantial portions
prove enough of a draw for transient
tourists and wallet-watchers. We
say head for the specials list, which
rewards with higher quality and

more authentic fare: braised spare
ribs with bitter melon, or stir-fried
scallops with asparagus are two
good examples of what leaving
behind the 'economy' lunch will find.
Minced prawn and beancurd-stuffed
grilled green peppers, a typical
Cantonese dish, proved satisfyingly
savoury and succulent. A mix of
post-work locals and oriental
students sharing crispy roast pork
and Tsing Tao beer crowds the tiny
space tight in the evenings. The
atmosphere is lively at such times
and service is always gracious.

Imperial China

*White Bear Yard, 25A Lisle Street,
WC2H 7BA (7734 3388). Leicester
Square or Piccadilly Circus tube.*
Meals served noon-11.30pm
Mon-Sat; 11.30am-10.30pm Sun.
Dim sum served noon-5pm daily.
Average ££. **Set meal** £14.95-£30
per person (minimum 2). **Minimum**
£10. **Map** p268.

Imperial China has fully translated
its menus in the past year, revealing
some interesting dishes hitherto
hidden from diners unversed in
Chinese. These include steamed
scallop with rice vermicelli and dong
choi (preserved Chinese leaves); and
baked lobster with salted duck egg
yolk. Several items on the dim sum
menu are marked as 'not
recommended', but be wary of such
advice: these are simply dishes
considered popular only with
Chinese diners. Congee with sliced
fish, for example, wasn't too
challenging – just comforting rice
porridge studded with tender pieces
of fish fillet. Most of our other dim
sum choices were equally good, and
Hong Kong-style beancurd pudding
(also 'not recommended') proved a
cold and refreshing finale. Smarter
than most of the other Chinatown
eateries, Imperial China attracts
business people on weekdays and
Chinese diners at weekends.

Joy King Lau

*3 Leicester Street, WC2H 7BL
(7437 1132/1133). Leicester Square
or Piccadilly Circus tube.* **Meals
served** noon-11.30pm Mon-Sat;
11am-10.30pm Sun. **Dim sum
served** noon-4.45pm Mon-Sat;
11am-4.45pm Sun. **Average ££.**
Set meal £9.80-£35 per person
(minimum 2). **Map** p269. Chinese
In true Chinatown style, you might
find yourself seated on the second
floor next to a huge pile of dirty
dishes awaiting the dumb waiter, as
we invariably seem to at Joy King
Lau. But this shouldn't distract you
too much from the excellent dim
sum, which makes the clatter of
plates perfectly tolerable: prawn fun
gwor were very proper and correct,
like tiny cornish pasties with the
minced filling visible through the
translucent wheat-starch casing; har
gau had been made with an equally
delicate touch; 'deep-fried squids'
were an unexpected treat, like white
marshmallows inside but with
golden skin; and traffic cone-orange
chickens' feet had an interesting
texture, if a slight lack of flavour.
Ever reliable, a dim sum lunch here
is great value.

New World

*1 Gerrard Place, W1D 5PA (7734
0396). Leicester Square or Piccadilly
Circus tube.* **Meals served** 11am-
11.45pm Mon-Sat; 11am-11pm Sun.
Dim sum served 11am-6pm daily.
Average ££. Set meal £12-£50
per person (minimum 2). **Minimum**
£5 evening. **Map** p268. Chinese
Dining successfully at this huge,
well-worn restaurant, noted for
serving dim sum from trolleys,
requires forethought and patience.
First, time your visit well. Turning
up when the doors first open works
best as you're then guaranteed the
freshest dim sum: it won't have been
on the trolleys for long. Second, be
patient while you eat: you'll be
interrupted constantly by trolley

dollies hawking their dim sum
wares. Among the highlights of
these were tender slices of Cantonese
roast duck and soft cheung fun filled
with firm prawn. We also enjoyed
har gau, filled with minced prawn
and a little bamboo shoot for crunch.
Not the best dim sum in the (new)
world, but certainly worth trying.

Royal Dragon

*30 Gerrard Street, W1D 6JS (7734
1388). Leicester Square or Piccadilly
Circus tube.* **Meals served** noon-
3am daily. **Dim sum served** noon-
5pm Mon-Fri. **Average ££. Set
meal** £12.50-£25 per person
(minimum 2). **Map** p268. Chinese
In 2005 Royal Dragon re-emerged
from a lengthy refurbishment
completely transformed. The
previously tired and unassuming
interior is now almost trendy, with
comfortable seating, exposed air-
conditioning tubes and plentiful
dark wood. Dropping by for a
lunchtime bite we found the place –
like last year, pre-refit – empty.
Tasting the food, it wasn't obvious
why. Pan-fried pork chop with
salted fish also featured squid and
was generously portioned (salted
fish aplenty). 'Egg tofu with minced
pork served in pot' bubbled away
on arrival, rich with oyster sauce
and Chinese wine. Dim sum was
reasonably well executed too.
Staff are no longer resplendent in
sparkly green waistcoats and ties;
service is now cool, efficient and
dressed in black.

Tokyo Diner

*2 Newport Place, WC2H 7JJ (7287
8777). Leicester Square or Piccadilly
Circus tube.* **Open** noon-midnight
daily. **Average ££. Set meal**
(noon-6.30pm) £4.40-£8.80 incl
green tea, miso soup & rice.
Map p268. Japanese
The food can be erratic at this tight
cosy den on the borders of
Chinatown, but we've had some

good meals here in the past. The quality of sushi is decent – in particular the nigiri – and we had and a great piece of chicken katsu on our last visit. Another dish of note was a rice bowl topped with thin strips of salmon sashimi: the salmon cooked slowly throughout the meal, creating an interesting variable texture, depending which part of the dish is nibbled first. Green tea arrives unbidden and is continually topped up; other little touches, such as the forbiddance of tips in accordance with Japanese tradition, and the fact that the restaurant is open for an incredible 365 days a year, adds to the charm. The stools really are titchy, though.

Wong Kei

41-43 Wardour Street, W1D 6PY (7437 8408). Leicester Square or Piccadilly Circus tube. **Meals served** noon-11.30pm Mon-Sat; noon-10.30pm Sun. **Average ££.** **Set meal** £7-£12 per person (minimum 2). **No credit cards.** **Map** p268. Chinese
Once popular for being rude, Wong Kei now thrives on serving huge portions from a directory-length menu, cheaply, swiftly and efficiently. Even the staff wear Wong Kei T-shirts (£10; red or black). Communal to the point of canteen-like – everyone shares benches and little pots of Chinese tea – Wong Kei is huge, with scores of diners tucking into duck, pork and seafood. Among the ten vegetarian, 25 seafood and countless meat options are some unusual finds: baked crab in its shell with ginger and spring onion; steamed eel with roast pork; and fried intestine with salted veg. Specialities include cold barbecued meat (crispy pork belly, barbecued pork) on hot rice, and rice porridge congees (prawns and assorted meats). Among the drinks are Tsing Tao beer and, rather incongruously, Smirnoff Ice.

Zipangu

8 Little Newport Street, WC2H 7JJ (7437 5042). Leicester Square or Piccadilly tube. **Meals served** noon-11pm Mon-Sat; noon-10.30pm Sun. **Average ££.** **Set lunch** (noon-5.30pm) £6.50-£12.50. **Set dinner** £9.50-£14. **Map** p268. Japanese
The business card may bear the legend 'Japanese Restaurant', but this is really a caff – and a school locker-sized one at that. It turns out standard sushis, tempuras and teriyakis cheaply and quickly. True, it has waitress service (the same waitress who turns people away if the basement is also full). She plonks neat plates of sushi (£4.80 for three, £8.80 for six) and sashimi (£6.80 for five, £11 for nine) on to the tiny tabletops. It's nothing award-winning; just a step up from a takeaway to devour at your desk. Lunch deals involve chicken or salmon teriyaki preceded by bowls of miso soup (90p à la carte!) and accompanied by sushi. There's booze too: Asahi Super Dry, sake and plum wine – or a choice of average wines in the £12 a bottle range. Green tea and mint are among the varieties of ice-cream available.

Meal deals

Hong Kong *6-7 Lisle Street, WC2H 7BG (7287 0352/www. london-hk.co.uk).* Dim sum £2-£3.50. **Map** p269. Chinese
New China *48 Gerrard Street, W1D 5QL (7287 9889).* Set meal £10.50-£20.50 per person (minimum 2). **Map** p268. Chinese

City

★ Arkansas Café

Unit 12, Old Spitalfields Market, E1 6AA (7377 6999). Liverpool Street tube/rail. **Lunch served** noon-2.30pm Mon-Fri; noon-4pm Sun. **Average £££.** **Map** p271.
North American

This is not a stylish place: seating is whatever the gregarious Arkansan owner has put out that week (anything from folding chairs to church pews) and service can be very abrupt. But this is all part of the Arkansas' personality. Frankly, the barbecued food here is so good we would walk through fire to eat it, so bring on the bad vibes. We come for steaming plates of well-sourced, freshly grilled meats like huge platters of pork ribs and tender steaks of Irish beef. All platters are served on plastic plates with potatoes, coleslaw (fresh and light), purple cabbage salad, and beans (cooked from scratch). If you want more frills with your food, this ain't the place for you.

Market Coffee House `NEW`

50-52 Brushfield Street, E1 6AG (7247 4110). Liverpool Street tube/rail. **Open** 8am-6pm Mon-Fri; 10am-6.30pm Sat; 9am-6.30pm Sun. **Average** ££. **No credit cards**. **Map** p271. Café

Down a commuter estuary flowing from Liverpool Street's Bishopsgate exit, newly widened walkways house a host of breakfast and lunchtime options. Standing proudly among newer, trendier outfits is the pub-like Market Coffee House, with its stripped floorboards and heavy wood interior. On the walls, a *Times* from 1797 and an invoice from its fruit shop days in 1947. *Brief Encounter*-era morning and tea-time sticky treats include Tiptree strawberry jam with English muffins (marmalade or Marmite 30p extra) and Kentish apple among the juices. No grilled breakfasts here. Lunch features Gloucester Old Spot pork pie and salad, stilton ploughman's and some properly hearty sandwiches, roast ham and cheddar cheese or roast beef with horseradish sauce. There's a choice

of two hot soups available as well. Finish with a cake from the display on the bar: carrot and hazelnut looked the tastiest.

The Place Below

St Mary-le-Bow, Cheapside, EC2V 6AU (7329 0789). St Paul's tube/Bank tube/DLR. **Breakfast served** 7.30-11am, **lunch served** 11.30am-2.30pm, **snacks served** 2.30-3.30pm Mon-Fri. **Average** ££. **Unlicensed. Corkage** no charge. **Map** p271. Vegetarian

Vegetarian cookery writer Bill Sewell's smart canteen inside the Norman crypt of St Mary-le-Bow church continues to offer tasty breakfasts, salads, bakes and quiches, along with fresh juices and coffee. The Place is certainly worth a visit: maybe it's the redemptive power of the impressive location, or maybe it's the hearty, wholesome vegetarian menu. At £6.20, the daily-changing 'main course salad' may seem a little pricey but is generally worth the splash. Quiche (perhaps leek, dijon mustard and parmesan, or roast fennel with butternut squash and goat's cheese), served with rosemary roast potatoes is £5.70, as are hot dishes of the day such as spinach and ricotta lasagne. Sandwiches come in inventive flavour combinations: cream cheese with tomato, lemon, tarragon and watercress, or roast sweet potato with olive tapenade and rocket.

Meal deals

Barcelona Tapas Bar y Restaurante *13 Well Court, off Bow Lane, EC4M 9DN (7329 5111).* Tapas £3.25-£11.95. **Map** p271. Spanish

Barcelona Tapas Bar y Restaurante *15 St Botolph Street, entrance at 1 Middlesex Street, EC3A 7DT (7377 5222).* Tapas £3.25-£11.95. **Map** p271. Spanish

Barcelona Tapas Bar y Restaurante *24 Lime Street, EC3M 7HS (7929 2389).* Tapas £3.25-£11.95. **Map** p271. Spanish

Haz *9 Cutler Street, E1 7DJ (7929 7923/www.hazrestaurant.com).* Set meal £8.45 2 courses; set meze £12.95. **Map** p271. Turkish

Missouri Grill *76 Aldgate High Street, EC3N 1BD (7481 4010/ www.missourigrill.com).* Set dinner £12 2 courses. **Map** p271. North American

In the area

Apostrophe *3-5 St Bride Street, EC4A 4AS (7353 3704).* **Map** p270.

Apostrophe *10 St Paul's Churchyard, EC4M 8AL (7248 9100).* **Map** p270.

Giraffe *Unit 1, Crispin Place, E1 6DW (3116 2000).* **Map** p271.

Lahore Original Kebab House *2 Umberston Street, E1 1PY (7488 2551).* **Map** p294.

Leon *3 Crispin Place, E1 6DW (7247 4369).* **Map** p271.

Leon *12 Ludgate Circus, EC4M 7LQ (7489 1580).* **Map** p270.

Maison Blanc Vite *135 Fenchurch Street, EC3M 5DJ (7929 6996).* Branch of Maison Blanc. **Map** p271.

Paul *6 Bow Lane, EC4M 9EB (7489 7925).* **Map** p271.

Paul *147 Fleet Street, EC4A 2BU (7353 5874).* **Map** p270.

Paul *Kiosk, Tower of London, EC3N 4AB (7709 7300).* **Map** p271.

Paul *Paternoster Square, EC4M 7DX (7329 4705).* **Map** p270.

Pizza Express *1 Byward Street, EC3R 7QN (7626 5025).* **Map** p271.

Market Coffee House. See p29.

Pizza Express *1 New Fetter Lane, EC4A 1AN (7583 8880).* Map p270.

Pizza Express *2 Salisbury House, London Wall, EC2Y 5HN (7588 7262).* Map p271.

Pizza Express *7-9 St Bride Street, EC4A 4AS (7583 5126).* Map p270.

Pizza Express *20-22 Leadenhall Market, EC3V 1LR (7283 5113).* Map p271.

Pizza Express *125 Alban Gate, London Wall, EC2Y 5AS (7600 8880).* Map p270.

Pizza Express *232-238 Bishopsgate, EC2M 4QD (7247 2838).* Map p270.

Rocket *6 Adams Court, Old Broad Street, EC2N 1DX (7628 1DX).* Map p271.

S&M Café *48 Brushfield Street, E1 6AG (7247 2252).* Map p271.

Square Pie Company *16 Horner Square, Old Spitalfields Market, E1 6AA (7377 1114).* Map p271.

Strada *4 St Paul's Churchyard, EC4M 8AY (7248 7178).* Map p270.

Strada *88-89 Commercial Street, E1 6LY (7247 4117).* Map p271.

Thai Square *1-7 Great St Thomas Apostle, EC4V 2BH (7329 0001).* Map p271.

Thai Square *136-138 Minories, EC3N 1NU (7680 1111).* Map p271.

Wagamama *1A Ropemaker Street, EC2Y 9AW (7588 2688).* Map p271.

Wagamama *4 Great St Thomas Apostle, off Queen Street, EC4V 2BH (7248 5766).* Map p271.

Wagamama *22 Old Broad Street, EC3N 1HQ (7256 9992).* Map p271.

Wagamama *109 Fleet Street, EC4A 2AB (7583 7889).* **Map** p270.
Wagamama *Tower Place, off Lower Thames Street, EC3R 4EB (7283 5897).* **Map** p271.
Yard *140 Tabernacle Street, EC2A 4SD (7336 7758).* Branch of Café Pasta. **Map** p271.
Yo! Sushi *Condor House, 5-14 St Paul's Churchyard, EC4M 8AY (7248 8726).* **Map** p270.

Clerkenwell & Farringdon

Anexo
61 Turnmill Street, EC1M 5PT (7250 3401). Farringdon tube/rail. **Lunch served** 11.30am-2.30pm Mon-Fri. **Dinner served** 6-11pm Mon-Sat. **Tapas served** 11am-11pm Mon-Sat. **Average** ££. **Set lunch** £7.50 2 courses, £9 3 courses. **Set dinner** £10 2 courses, £12 3 courses. **Map** p270. Spanish
Wedged into the Turnmills building, Anexo offers a dark space heaving with office workers celebrating the home-time buzz; in summer the open frontage adds traffic noise to an already loud soundtrack. The ideal night here is a chat over jugs of cocktails with some food thrown in; the Gaudiesque decor captures well the feel of a Spanish bar. In general, the tapas is above par. Patatas bravas was creditable, along with meaty albóndigas, odd-looking but tasty spinach fritters, and a rich, spicy chorizo dish. The weakest links were tired sardines, and gambas a la plancha (shrimp with garlic), which were poor value at £10.50. Staff get full marks.

Le Comptoir Gascon [NEW]
61-63 Charterhouse Street, EC1M 6HJ (7608 0851). Farringdon tube/rail. **Lunch served** noon-2pm, **dinner served** 7-11pm Tue-Sat. **Average** £££. **Map** p270. French

The little, laid-back sister to pricier Club Gascon makes clever use of a sliver of a site in Smithfield. The tiny interior is all industrial chic, with lots of exposed brick and steel and there's a cut-down deli/bistro menu to go with the casual surroundings. The food, however, is mercifully simple, unpretentious and generally pretty good. We tried some textbook-perfect duck confit with lovely, fat french fries and a salad of curly leaves on the side. Smoky grilled squid came with a sweet tomato confit and creamy pearl barley. A worthwhile, reasonably priced bet in a busy area.

De Santis
11-13 Old Street, EC1V 9HL (7689 5577). Barbican tube/Old Street tube/rail. **Open** 8.30am-11pm Mon-Fri. **Average** ££. **Map** p270. Café
A little piece of Milan (home of the original De Santis) in Clerkenwell. This paninoteca is a sleek-looking joint with a smooth concrete floor and a quiet terrace at the back. As in Italy, not much is made of breakfast (coffee and a croissant about covers it); the action starts at lunch. Paninis are the backbone of the menu, and come with a wide variety of fillings: meats (speck, mortadella, bresaola, prosciutto), vegetables, cheese or fish. The bread is baked on the premises, and is light and delicious. Piattini (cold platters) and tartine (open sandwiches) also make a showing, as do hot dishes. These included lentil stew with garlic bruschetta and penne arrabiata, perhaps followed by pear and yogurt cake or tiramisu. A popular local restaurant with a quite justified sense of confidence.

Kipferl [NEW]
70 Long Lane, EC1A 9EJ (7796 2229). Barbican tube. **Open** 8am-7pm Mon-Fri; 9am-5pm Sat. **Average** ££. **No credit cards**. **Map** p270. Café

A handful of tables are squeezed into the small room of this Austrian café, alongside shelves holding a limited selection of Austrian wines and a range of deli items. Highlights include that great Styrian treasure, pumpkin seed oil, plus Zotter chocolate bars, Staud's pickles and jams, and a small choice of breads. A packed cold cabinet holds savoury filled rolls and open sandwiches, cheeses, meats, and cakes such as sachertorte, linzertorte and apple cake. More substantial lunchtime options include sausages and sauerkraut, salads, goulash soup and a hot dish of the day. Coffee is good – it comes with a chocolate or a cookie – and we're big fans of the melange (coffee with milk), though in summer you may be tempted by the Viennese iced coffee. Service comes with a smile from a bunch of young and enthusiastic Austrians.

Kurz & Lang NEW

1 St John Street, EC1M 4AA (7253 6623). Farringdon tube/rail. **Meals served** 11am-11pm Mon-Thur; 11am Fri-7am Sun; noon-8pm Sun. **Average** £. **Set dinner** (5-7pm) £5.50 1 course incl beer. **No credit cards**. **Map** p270. Austrian
Not, as you might imagine, the names of the founders, Kurz & Lang means 'short and long' in German, a reference to the top-notch speciality sausage sold at this cheerful stop just off St John Street. Just £3.60 gets you a hearty portion of best 'wurst' with bread, German mustard and ketchup; another 60p adds sauerkraut (really an essential accompaniment to cut through the fat of the meat) and grilled potato cubes. Choose from sausages such as bratwurst, currywurst, little nurnburgers or the pork-free rindswurst. The prominent corner site near Smithfield has proved a winner – not only for its traditional associations with meat and City

lunches, but because it's close to the clubs; at weekends, Kurz & Lang is open until 7am serving fortifying franks to the footsore and freaky.

Little Bay

171 Farringdon Road, EC1R 3AL (7278 1234). Farringdon tube/rail. **Meals served** noon-midnight Mon-Sat; 10am-11pm Sun. **Average** ££. **Map** p270. International
The eccentric surroundings and the menu where all starters, mains and desserts are grouped in equal price brackets – first and last courses £2.95, mains £7.95 (a little cheaper at lunch) – go toward marking Little Bay out as a relative of Le Mercury (*see p220*) and LMNT (*see p196*), which also offer quality dishes at knockdown prices. To start, duck terrine with figs and cranberries was rich and feast-like, while a plate-sized mushroom topped with blue cheese and spinach was meaty and earthily juicy. A special of sea bream on crushed potatoes made a satisfying main, but vegetarian options are a little uninspired (you're in trouble if you don't like goat's cheese). Our order was delivered speedily and the house white was an excellent bottle for the price.

Old China Hand NEW

8 Tysoe Street, EC1R 4RQ (7278 7678). Angel tube/Farringdon tube/rail. **Lunch served** noon-3pm Mon-Fri. **Dinner served** 6-10pm Mon-Sat. **Average** ££. **Map** p270. Oriental
Once of the Dorchester's Oriental restaurant, dim sum chef Ngan Tung Cheung, who was part of the Michelin star-winning team there, has resurfaced in this unassuming and atypical corner pub, producing a monthly changing menu. It's clear from the moment the dumplings arrive that this is no ordinary pub food. Gum sook jein gai beng (chicken and corn cakes) were perfectly fried, soft and sweet; gum

yue kau (steamed prawn 'goldfish' dumplings) were beautiful and contained firm, fresh prawn and diced water chestnut for crunch. Prices are slightly higher than elsewhere, but most dumplings arrive in fours, not threes. Staff, led by a jolly Belgian manageress are ultra-friendly. A wide selection of beers includes Kirin on tap.

Pho NEW

86 St John Street, EC1M 4EH (7253 7624). Barbican tube/Farringdon tube/rail. **Lunch served** noon-3pm, **dinner served** 6-10pm Mon-Fri. **Average** ££. **Map** p270.
Vietnamese

The English owners of this appealing and modern little café have taken a few Vietnamese street snacks, and turned them into a 'concept'. Pho, the beef broth and noodle soup, is the mainstay of the menu, coming in more than a dozen variations. The stock of ours was sublime: aromatic and richly flavoured yet clear, such that the accompanying seasonings (a little plate of fresh herbs, red chillies, beansprouts, squeeze of lime) were barely needed. The flat rice noodles also had a perfectly elastic texture, and both the meatballs and slices of steak were top quality. Much less impressive was a starter of summer rolls; most of the filling was bland rice noodles with hardly any prawn or herbs, so that not even the accompanying nuoc cham dipping sauce could pep it up.

La Porchetta

84-86 Rosebery Avenue, EC1R 4QY (7837 6060). Angel tube/Farringdon tube/rail. **Lunch served** noon-3pm Mon-Fri. **Dinner served** 5.30-11pm Mon-Fri; 5-11pm Sat. **Meals served** noon-11pm Sun. **Average** ££. **Map** p270. Pizza & Pasta

This north London stalwart started in Stroud Green and now has four branches, the most central being in

Holborn and the best known in Upper Street. But the nicest of the bunch is this charming Farringdon branch, occupying a roomy corner building on Rosebery Avenue. Food is fresh and filling, and pizzas are especially good. A simple margherita was crisp, tasty and enormous – too big for the plate. Staff are always chummy, although sometimes overly so – quite a few characters are employed here. But it all adds to the jovial atmosphere, which peaks when there's a birthday in the house and staff come out singing and clattering cutlery.

Meal deals

Ambassador *55 Exmouth Market, EC1R 4QL (7837 0009/ www.theambassadorcafe.co.uk).* Set lunch (Mon-Fri) £12.50 2 courses, £16 3 courses. **Map** p270.
Modern European

Cicada *132-136 St John Street, EC1V 4JT (7608 1550/www. cicada.nu).* Dim sum £3-£6. **Map** p270. Oriental

Potemkin *144 Clerkenwell Road, EC1R 5DP (7278 6661/ www.potemkin.co.uk).* Set lunch (Mon-Fri) £10 2 courses. **Map** p270. Polish

Quality Chop House *92-94 Farringdon Road, EC1R 3EA (7837 5093).* Set meal (lunch Mon-Fri, 6-7.30pm Mon-Sat) £9.95 2 courses. **Map** p270. British

Tinseltown *44-46 St John Street, EC1M 4DT (7689 2424).* Set lunch (noon-5pm Mon-Fri) £5 2 courses incl soft drink. **Map** p270. Café

Xich Lô *103 St John Street, EC1M 4AS (7253 0323/www.xichlo restaurant.com).* Set lunch £6 1 course. **Map** p270. Vietnamese

In the area

Carluccio's Caffè *12 West Smithfield, EC1A 9JR (7329 5904).* **Map** p270.

Konditor & Cook *46 Gray's Inn Road, WC1X 8LR (7404 6300).* **Map** p270.

wagamama

delicious noodles I **rice dishes**
freshly squeezed juices
wine I **sake** I **japanese beers**

bloomsbury I borough I brent cross I camden I canary wharf I
covent garden I croydon I earls court I fleet street I haymarket I islington I
kensington I knightsbridge I leicester square I mansion house I moorgate I
I tower 42 I putney I richmond I soho I southbank I tower hill I victoria I
west end I wimbledon I for other locations visit **wagamama.com**

Pizza Express *1 Clerkenwell Road, EC1M 5PA (7253 7770).* **Map** p270.

Pizza Express *26 Cowcross Street, EC1M 6DQ (7490 8025).* **Map** p270.

The Real Greek Souvlaki & Bar *140-142 St John Street, EC1V 4UA (7253 7234).* **Map** p270.

Strada *8-10 Exmouth Market, EC1R 4QA (7278 0800).* **Map** p270.

Tas *37 Farringdon Road, EC1M 3JB (7430 9721/9722).* Branch of EV Restaurant, Bar & Delicatessen. **Map** p270.

Yo! Sushi *95 Farringdon Road, EC1R 3BT (7841 0785).* **Map** p270.

Covent Garden

Abeno Too

17-18 Great Newport Street, WC2H 7JE (7379 1160). Leicester Square tube. **Meals served** noon-11pm Mon-Sat; noon-10.30pm Sun. **Average £££. Set lunch** £7.80-£12.80. **Map** p272. Japanese

Abeno Too is a neat little provider of okonomiyaki, a homely Japanese dish that's like a cross between Spanish omelette and savoury pancake. These are cooked on hot-plates set into the window tables and the main counter. A batter and cabbage base is flavoured with spring onions and ginger, then various hearty ingredients are added in combination ('okonomi' means 'your choice'). It may be as simple as prawn and squid, or as exotic as the kiso mix flavoured with lotus root, mushroom, cheese, bonito fish flakes and mayonnaise. Abeno's 'London mix' (pork, bacon, cheese and salmon) is surprisingly delicious. Salads, teppanyaki, rice and noodle dishes are also available. The original Bloomsbury branch, Abeno, is slightly more formal.

Assa

53 St Giles High Street, WC2H 8LH (7240 8256). Tottenham Court Road tube. **Lunch served** noon-3pm Mon-Sat. **Dinner served** 5pm-midnight daily. **Average ££. Set lunch** £4.50-£5.50 1 course. **Map** p267. Korean

Considering it charges the same – less, in fact – than those dreadful eat-all-you-dare buffets that plague the West End, Assa is really rather good. This cosy cabin of Koreana, decorated with authentic advertisements and cartoons, hums happily during its bargain-basement lunchtimes. It's close enough to Denmark Street to attract musicians, who mix in with the indigenous diners, attracted by the low prices between noon and 3pm, when £4.50 buys a plate of rice and stir-fried meats, prawns or spicy squid, flavoured with zingy red chilli. Plus unexpected side dishes of spinach and kimch'i of equal zing. *Plus* a cup of modest miso. Bargain. As an alternative, hot pots of tuna, marinated beef, spicy cod or mixed seafood sizzle on tabletop cookers. There's Korean beer to drink, plus herb or plum wine. Our only brickbats are the crass dish pictures in the front window.

Bistro 1

33 Southampton Street, WC2E 7HE (7379 7585). Covent Garden tube. **Open** noon-11.30pm Mon-Sat; noon-10.30pm Sun. **Average ££. Set lunch** £6.50 2 courses, £7.50 3 courses. **Set dinner** £8.90 2 courses, £9.90 3 courses. **Map** p273. Mediterranean

This is the type of no-frills eaterie beloved of backpackers; offering a hearty, budget-conscious feed for those more concerned with portion size than quality ingredients and presentation. However, on our visit a group of sedate pensioners lunching before a matinee were our fellow diners; a younger, livelier crowd packs out the tables in the evening. The menu's full of comforting Med staples (meze, boeuf bourguignon, calamares) of mixed

quality: lamb kebab was fatty and its accompanying salad (little more than some lettuce leaves) limp, but a vegetarian moussaka featured fresh-tasting veg and was served with a generous mound of rice. The decor's dated but inoffensive and, while they made no effort to be friendly, the eastern European staff were prompt enough.

Café Pasta

184 Shaftesbury Avenue, WC2H 8JB (7379 0198). Covent Garden or Tottenham Court Road tube. **Meals served** noon-11.30pm Mon-Sat; noon-11pm Sun. **Average ££.** **Map** p272. Pizza & Pasta

This is the Pizza Express chain's pasta-specialising offshoot, and every inch the imitator of its bigger sibling. No bad thing. Inoffensive, Italian-ish art adorns bright walls, customers eat from shiny marble table tops, and service – if not smiling – is swift. The food is Pizza Express-reliable, too. A vast portion of penne with a creamy mushroom sauce was very good: the pasta well cooked, the mushrooms plentiful. It almost finished us off. With a prime Covent Garden location, this branch is very much a tourist magnet, and often busy, but good use is made of the site: windows looking out on to

Pho. See p35.

Shaftesbury Avenue on one side and Monmouth Street on the other allow for plenty of light, and makes the restaurant perfect for a spot of people-watching over a meal.

Calabash

The Africa Centre, 38 King Street, WC2E 8JR (7836 1976). Covent Garden or Leicester Square tube. **Lunch served** 12.30-2.30pm Mon-Fri. **Dinner served** 6-10.30pm Mon-Sat. **Average** ££. **Map** p273.
African

Hidden away in the basement of the Africa Centre, this long-established restaurant still serves a wonderful range of African dishes from around the continent. The large room has cream walls decorated with pictures, a somewhat faded red carpet and colourful fabric tablecloths. Starters showed the style of the place: not spectacular, perhaps, but interesting and endearing. Alaco was slices of plantain in a rich sauce. A deep-fried meat sambusa was a lightly spiced and crisp parcel, not unlike a samosa. A main course of Calabash chicken was filling and robust. West African groundnut stew had a lovely thick nutty sauce and contained a tasty but bony fish; it came with a dish of doughy sticky yam. Service was knowledgeable and quietly efficient. Calabash is remarkably cheap and deserves its popularity with lovers of African food.

★ Canela

33 Earlham Street, WC2H 9LS (7240 6926). Covent Garden tube. **Meals served** 9.30am-10pm Mon-Thur; 9.30am-11pm Fri, Sat; 10am-8pm Sun. **Average ££. Map** p272.
Café

Covent Garden doesn't have enough in the way of unusual and appealing cafés, which makes this one particularly worth seeking out. It's a hole in the wall of the Thomas Neal Building, a high-ceilinged room that makes an attractive showcase for the interesting mix of Portuguese and Brazilian snacks and dishes. There are excellent baked dishes, such as bacalhau à bràs, made with salt cod, potatoes, eggs, onion and parsley, or there's the classic Brazilian black bean and pork stew, feijoada. Lighter is the flavoured Brazilian cheese bread, made with chorizo, basil, olives or just plain. The cakes are a distinct high point: the quindim is a little cake rich in yellow egg yolk, upturned to show the grated coconut base. Drinks range from galão (Portuguese cappuccino) through various Portuguese wines to Caipirinha cocktails. Never before has popping into town for a Brazilian been such an attractive prospect.

Food for Thought

31 Neal Street, WC2H 9PR (7836 9072). Covent Garden tube. **Meals served** noon-8.30pm Mon-Sat; noon-5pm Sun. **Average £. Minimum** (noon-3pm, 6-7.30pm) £2.50. **Unlicensed. Corkage** no charge. **No credit cards. Map** p272.
Vegetarian

This Covent Garden institution continues to dish up old-school vegetarian food but with a properly 21st-century zest and verve. A compact subterranean café, it is furnished with chunky wooden furniture and a small service counter crammed with friendly staff. Daily specials like hotpots, stir-fries and vegetable gumbos keep Food for Thought devotees happy. The quiches here are also well-loved: on our visit, the custard was filled with fresh leeks and the pastry was substantial without being stodgy. Salads are made from seasonal ingredients like new potatoes, broad beans and mint.

Gili Gulu

50-52 Monmouth Street, WC2H 9DG (7379 6888). Covent Garden or Leicester Square tube. **Open** noon-3pm, 5.30-11pm Mon-Thur; noon-11pm Fri, Sat; noon-10.30pm Sun. **Average £££. Set buffet** £13.95. **Set meal** £7.50 2 courses. **Map** p272. Japanese

Not quite the equal of local conveyor-belt sushi rival Kulu Kulu (*see p41*), Gili Guli nevertheless brings an important gimmick in to play: you can pluck as many dishes as you like from the two moving belts that weave around the sparsely decorated restaraunt, and yet you still only pay a set fee. At £13.95, this all-you-can-eat extravaganza ain't particularly cheap, but it surely should leave you well satisfied. Salmon nigiri was fresh-tasting and fine, but it was eel maki that we kept reaching for: wonderfully succulent meat, tinged with a moreish soy sauce. Forays into non-Japanese food were less successful: spring rolls tasted like they were from a packet, and stir-fried noodles were cold and greasy. Those not wanting to splash out can opt for a cheaper six-dish menu, or can pay by the plate. Select carefully, and you can eat pretty well here.

★ Just Falafs NEW

27A Covent Garden Piazza, WC2E 8RD (7240 3838). Covent Garden tube. **Meals served** 8am-9pm Mon-

Wed; 8am-11pm Thur, Fri; 10am-11pm Sat; 10am-8pm Sun. **Average £. No credit cards. Map** p273. Middle Eastern

Despite the sort of punning name that would make even Victor Lewis-Smith blanch, Just Falafs is an enlightened fast food eaterie – is there any other kind these days? – that ticks all the right boxes. The ingredients are mostly organic and seasonal, and the hot beverages are Fairtrade. Inside the tiny takeaway there are a few high chairs for eating in, and a small seating area outside, complete with parasol heaters. Falafels, flavoured with dill, fresh coriander and whole coriander seeds came with mild, creamy tahini, spiky green chilli sauce, and strident aubergine sauce inside khobez flatbreads, along with beetroot, carrot and nut, mixed sprouts, and other sprightly salads of choice. There's also an imaginative range of soft drinks on offer, plus porridge, soup and lentil dahl.

★ Kastner & Ovens

52 Floral Street, WC2E 9DA (7836 2700). Covent Garden tube. **Open** 8am-5pm Mon-Fri. **Average £££. No credit cards. Map** p272. Café

Located in central Covent Garden (at the Opera House end of Floral Street), K&O remains surprisingly unknown to the tourist hordes and consequently feels like a locals' takeaway lunch joint. Food quality is evident and prices keen. Cooks emerge via a spiral staircase from the basement kitchen with freshly prepared, daily changing dishes, displayed buffet-style on huge tables (savouries on the left, sweets on the right). Staff serve the uncomplicated, comfort fare with a welcome smile. Sandwiches, soup (butternut squash and ginger, for example) and salads (tabouleh, cabbage and apple) appear alongside pastries (spinach and feta filo, smoked chicken and

thyme pie), quiche (aubergine, spring onion and goat's cheese) and heartier specials. Make space for desserts – the apple pie and carrot cake shouldn't be missed. Drinks are largely bottled organic juices.

Kulu Kulu

51-53 Shelton Street, WC2H 9HE (7240 5687). Covent Garden tube. **Lunch served** noon-2.30pm Mon-Fri; noon-3.30pm Sat. **Dinner served** 5-10pm Mon-Sat. **Average £££. Map** p272. Japanese

The newest of the Kulu Kulu mini chain (there are three so far), this branch offers the same simple formula: a conveyor-belt carrying sushi, sashimi and Japanese cakes, plus a few hot dishes. The quality is fine considering they offer the cheapest kaiten plate tarriff we've yet seen in London (good salmon nigiri is £1.20 for two). Spinach roll was vibrantly coloured and fresh-tasting, dressed in a thick and sweet peanut sauce. 'Avocado salad' – in fact seaweed parcels filled with avocado and chopped seafood stick – was so popular dishes disappeared from the belt as soon as they were laid down. Better, though, were excellent hand rolls: soft-shell crab (a special), and prawn tempura with avocado and salmon sashimi: both delicious. The branch on Brewer Street is smaller and staff can get sniffy if you take up a seat for too long; this Covent Garden offshoot is more spacious and staff less uptight.

Photographers' Gallery Café NEW

The Photographers' Gallery, 5 Great Newport Street, WC2H 7HY (7831 1772). Leicester Square tube. **Meals served** 11am-5.30pm Mon-Sat; noon-5.30pm Sun. **Average £. No credit cards. Map** p272. Café

This tiny café inside one of the Photographers' Gallery buildings – just moments from the buzz of Leicester Square – remains a well-

Central

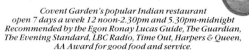

kept London secret, and when the surrounding streets and lunch spots are overflowing with people you can still be sure of getting a peaceful sandwich or cup of coffee at this hideaway. The seating consists of stools arranged around one spacious table; there are newspapers on hand for you to read, or alternatively you can study the gallery's photographs – the café is right in the middle of an exhibition space. Eating options are relatively limited, but they are all prepared to a high standard: savoury snacks on offer include tuna rolls, sundried tomato and mozzarella ciabatta or Greek salad, while sweets available include some truly sublime cakes (lemon, chocolate, carrot).

The Real Greek Souvlaki & Bar

60-62 Long Acre, WC2E 9JE (7240 2292). Covent Garden tube. **Meals served** 11.30am-11pm daily. **Average** ££. **Map** p272. Greek

This hip younger sister to the upmarket Hoxton original occupies the shell of an old Victorian pub. There's a healthy selection of mezédes here: gigandes (butter bean stew) was chilled and creamy; tender bite-sized dolmádes were equally lovely. But even these fine dishes were bettered by a quite faultless souvláki: the centrepiece of the simple menu. Chunks of chicken (lamb, pork, haddock and vegetarian alternatives are available) were perfectly char-grilled, wrapped in flatbread with a herby sauce (a modern twist on the traditional tzatzíki) and served in greaseproof paper. Desserts (baklavá, yoghurt and honey) are basic, but the choice of Greek wines (available by the carafe) and beers is vast and includes the underrated Mythos lager. There's a boisterous feel to this place, though service is professional, if a little slow.

Rock & Sole Plaice

47 Endell Street, WC2H 9AJ (7836 3785). Covent Garden tube. **Meals served** 11.30am-11pm Mon-Sat; noon-10pm Sun. **Average** £££. **Map** p272. Fish & Chips

Rows of sturdy wooden tables, fairy lights on trees, and a maître d' dressed in Bavarian garb give Rock & Sole Plaice the feel of a beer garden rather than a chippie. Nevertheless, tourists and suit-wearers beat a path here, ready to wait for pricey but super-sized fish suppers. The chips are hand cut and wide, lightly fried and potatoey in flavour. The same balance of moisture and crispness was exhibited in the fried fish, while the own-made mushy peas were of a perfect consistency – thick enough to stand your spoon in. For an alternative British experience, order one of the chunky own-made meat pies. Finish off with spotted dick, sticky toffee pudding or syrup sponge, all 'cheap as chips' at £2.50.

★ Silva's

220 Shaftesbury Avenue, WC2H 8EB (7240 0028). Tottenham Court Road tube. **Meals served** 7am-7pm Mon-Fri; 8am-4pm Sat. **Average** £. **Set breakfast** (all day) £4.30. **No credit cards**. **Map** p272. Café

More Italian diner than bog-standard caff, Silva's dispenses superior toasted ciabattas (basil with mozzarella, crayfish, parma ham), grilled meals (sirloin steak, plaice, scampi), pastas, salads and breakfasts to a warmly welcomed cast of dispatch riders, builders and theatre types. Many are greeted on first-name terms by the sweet, seen-it-all cockney-Italian lady of a certain age who polices the six rows of brown benches, swiftly interacting with the smiling grey-haired chef busying away in one corner. With this well-oiled machine in smooth operation from early hours, why bother with the

Just Falafs. See p40.

sandwich chains next door? Fresh juices feature orange, carrot and apple, one with a hint of ginger, and the creamy, potent Lavazza cappuccino puts to shame those army-sized tins of instant at your local greasy spoon. Piffolous prices are unaffected by Silva's prime position in Theatreland.

Woo Jung

59 St Giles High Street, WC2H 8LH (7836 3103). Tottenham Court Road tube. **Meals served** noon-1am Mon-Sat; 5pm-midnight Sun. **Average** ££. **Set lunch** £6.50-£10 1 course incl soup. **Set meal** £17-£30 2 courses incl soup. **Map** p267. Korean

This tiny no-frills eaterie does a brisk lunchtime trade. Yuk hwe was refreshing and came in large portions. Vegetable bindaedok, cooked with carrots and spring onions, had a lovely crisp texture yet was made with an egg and flour batter rather than the traditional mung beans. Vegetable tolsot bibimbap didn't come with koch'ujang (hot red bean paste) as it should, so we asked for it and mixed it in ourselves; in fact, service as a whole could be more attentive. Woo Jung keeps its prices down by using cheaper ingredients (the dipping sauce and soy sauce were of inferior quality, for instance), but at least the barley tea is free.

World Food Café

First floor, 14 Neal's Yard, WC2H 9DP (7379 0298). Covent Garden tube. **Meals served** 11.30am-4.30pm Mon-Fri; 11.30am-5pm Sat. **Average** ££. **Minimum** (noon-2pm Mon-Fri; 11.30am-5pm Sat) £6. **Map** p272. Vegetarian

Chris and Carolyn Caldicott have been running this charming, daytime diner for 16 years now, interrupting their daily routine as restaurateurs to travel and produce glossy global gastronomic guides. Their first floor space, decorated with exotic photographs, is filled with half-a-dozen sturdy tables, centrepieced by a four-square bar.

Behind it, a busy tabletop covered with vegetables is as colourful as the view of Neal's Yard façades that can be seen immediately below the picture windows. A chalked-up menu, familiar to the many regulars, features five main courses (£7.95), including Turkish, Indian and Mexican staples, plus lighter dishes such as oat pancake (£6.50) with melted cheese and fresh spinach. All the food is hearty and wholesome. Of note was the West African sweet potato cooked in a sauce of fresh ginger and cayenne. One soup and salad change daily. Among the teas are nettle and fennel; among the yoghurts, frozen elderflower.

Meal deals

Bank Aldwych *1 Kingsway,
WC2B 6XF (7379 9797/www.bank
restaurants.com).* Set meal (5.30-7pm,
10-11pm Mon-Sat) £13.50 2 courses.
Map p272. Modern European

Le Deuxième *65A Long Acre,
WC2E 9JH (7379 0033/www.
ledeuxieme.com).* Set meal (noon-
3pm, 5-7pm, 10pm-midnight Mon-
Fri; noon-11pm Sun) £11.95
2 courses, £15.50 3 courses.
Map p272. International

Mela *152-156 Shaftesbury
Avenue, WC2H 8HL (7836 8635/
www.melarestaurant.co.uk).* Set
lunch £2.95-£5.95 1 course; set meal
(5.30-7pm, 10-11pm) £10.95
3 courses. **Map** p272. Pan-Indian

Mon Plaisir *19-21 Monmouth
Street, WC2H 9DD (7836 7243/
www.monplaisir.co.uk).* Set meal
(5.45-7pm Mon-Sat; after 10pm
Mon-Thur) £12.50 2 courses.
Map p272. French

In the area

Café Pasta *2-4 Garrick Street,
WC2E 9BH (7497 2779).* **Map** p273.
Café Valerie *8 Russell Street,
WC2 5HZ (7240 0064).* Branch of
Pâtisserie Valerie. **Map** p272.
Hamburger Union *4-6 Garrick
Street, WC2E 9BH (7379 0412).*
Map p273.
Loch Fyne *2-4 Catherine Street,
WC2B 5JS (7240 4999).* **Map** p272.
Paul *29 Bedford Street, WC2E 9ED
(7836 3304).* **Map** p273.
La Perla *28 Maiden Lane, WC2E
7JS (7240 7400).* **Map** p273.
Pizza Express *9-12 Bow Street,
WC2E 7AH (7240 3443).*
Map p272.
Pizza Paradiso *31 Catherine
Street, WC2B 5JS (7836 3609).*
Map p272.
Strada *6 Great Queen Street,
WC2B 5DH (7405 6293).*
Map p272.
Wagamama *1 Tavistock Street,
WC2E 7PG (7836 3330).* **Map** p273.
Zizzi *20 Bow Street, WC2E 7AW
(7836 6101).* **Map** p272.

Edgware Road

Abu Ali

*136-138 George Street, W1H 5LD
(7724 6338). Edgware Road or
Marble Arch tube.* **Meals served**
9am-11pm daily. **Average ££. No
credit cards. Map** p276. Lebanese
Aesthetically, this is the Lebanese
equivalent of a greasy spoon, with
Formica tables, yellowing pictures
of Lebanese tourist spots and Arab
TV blaring in the corner. But we
wager you won't be disappointed by
the authentic, superb-value food.
Abundant starters and snacks (50p-
£3) come in the form of mini-
Lebanese pizzas, and hot and cold
meze, served with mounds of pitta;
on a recent visit, our crop yielded
impeccably fresh houmous and
zesty tabouleh; five falafel, each with
a perfect bite; and wonderfully
smooth baba ganoush. Succulent
meaty mains – chicken or lamb –
can be prepared in a bewildering
number of ways, all served with rice
or freshly cut chips. For lunch on the
go, Abu Ali's shawarma sandwiches
are unbeatable value at £2.75. Finish
with a freshly squeezed mango juice
or fresh mint tea.

Al-Dar

*61-63 Edgware Road, W2 2HZ
(7402 2541). Marble Arch tube.*
Meals served 8am-1am daily.
Average £££. Set meze £9.50-
£10.50. **Map** p276. Lebanese
At this fairly standard Lebanese
restaurant – turning out plates of
kebabs and rather bland vegetable
dishes – the large menus are
festooned with vintage photographs
of happier eras ('Lebanon in past
time'). This is about as exotic as
things get. A list of 25 vegetarian
starters and 15 carnivorous mains
smacks of meals for families in
shopping malls. Except the prices –
£9.50 for a dish of unmemorable
green beans. To be fair, breakfasts

of eggs with minced lamb or Lebanese pizzas of minced meat, peppers and pine kernels are not so meanly priced (£3.50-£5.25) and would rewardingly entice a West End nighthawk or early bird to this awful stretch of the Edgware Road.

Kandoo

458 Edgware Road, W2 1EJ (7724 2428). Edgware Road tube. **Meals served** noon-midnight daily. **Average ££. Corkage** no charge. **Map** p276. Iranian

The heart seems to have gone out of Kandoo. Once it even managed to transcend the sombre surrounds of Edgware Road and offer warmth and welcome to its customers. No more. On a recent visit the place was bare, harshly lit and not at all comfortable. The cooking, though, remains solid: a standard mix of starters and kebabs. The meat in the kebabs had been nicely marinated (in, so we were told, a concoction of lime juice, olive oil, vegetable oil and yoghurt). The masto musir was nicely thick and creamy and the kashk-e bademjan, a purée of aubergine in yoghurt, came with a swirl of runny goat's cheese and a sprinkling of fried onions. Bread was delivered hot from the tiled oven in the corner of the room.

★ Mandalay

444 Edgware Road, W2 1EG (7258 3696). Edgware Road tube. **Lunch served** noon-2.30pm, **dinner served** 6-10.30pm Mon-Sat. **Average ££. Set lunch** £3.90 1 course, £5.90 3 courses. **Map** p276. Burmese

Edgware Road isn't exactly known for its exotic pavilions and lush, tropical landscape, but it does contain a gem of a Burmese restaurant – London's one and only. Mandalay is a small, family-run set-up, the menu influenced by Thai, Indian and Chinese cooking, as well as Burmese cuisine. Expect plenty of

fish and seafood, fragrant bowls of rice and noodles, and light aromatic curries. If you enjoy healthy broths, opt for bottle gourd soup: scented with toasted garlic slivers and containing shrimps, rice noodles and strips of the gourd, it makes a superb palate cleanser. Staff are passionate about their craft and happy to take curious customers on a guided tour of the menu.

Mawar

175A Edgware Road, W2 2HR (7262 1663). Edgware Road tube. *Buffet* **Meals served** noon-10.30pm Mon-Sat; noon-10pm Sun. **Set meal** £4-£5 1 course. *Restaurant* **Lunch served** noon-3pm daily. **Dinner served** 6-10.30pm Mon-Sat; 6-10pm Sun. **Average ££. Corkage** no charge. **Map** p276. Malaysian

An anonymous, unpromising stairway leads down to this subterranean halal cafeteria, where you'll find easy-wipe tables, plain green walls and a steamy bain-marie counter. But who needs all those designer fripperies when you can queue at the counter and get rice and vegetables with three dishes of your choice for a mere £5? For a little more refinement, there's a separate restaurant area with clothed tables, fanned serviettes and long-stemmed (fabric) roses. Here you get waiter service, an à la carte menu, and your bottle of wine expertly opened – if you brought one along with you (Mawar is unlicensed). Even in the restaurant you'd be hard pressed to spend more than £25 for two. The food is sustaining enough for the price, but it's a shame so much of it looks like indeterminate chunks in a thick brown sauce.

Meya Meya NEW

13 Bell Street, NW1 5BY (7723 8983). Edgware Road tube. **Meals served** 9am-11pm daily. **Average ££. Corkage** £5. **No credit cards.** **Map** p276. Egyptian

The ground floor room, with nothing but a pizza furnace, counter and one table visible, might appear to be a takeaway. But look a little more closely and you'll see that freshly made rounds of hot fiteer (like an Egyptian pizza) are being whisked downstairs to a busy room with several tables. There is an extensive menu at Meya Meya, but the fiteer is the draw: envelopes of filo pastry filled with all manner of ingredients. The Cairo fiteer, with slices of basturma, tomato, pepper and olives, contained a generous portion of smoked beef with fresh vegetables. The menu also includes Egyptian staples such as fuul and taamaya (aka falafel). These were cooked well nigh perfectly: fuul was well seasoned and the taamaya were properly crunchy on the outside, while grease-free and an authentic green on the inside.

Patogh

8 Crawford Place, W1H 5NE (7262 4015). Edgware Road tube. **Meals served** 1pm-midnight daily. **Average** ££. **Corkage** no charge. **No credit cards. Map** p276.
Middle Eastern

The all-over rag-rolled shade of nicotine brown is somewhat overwhelming in what is a little space, but while Patogh is not going to win any prizes in the style stakes, it's an effortless winner when it comes to the food. This is in authentic Persian kebab restaurant vein: a few yoghurty starters plus sabzi – enormous discs of warm, house-baked flatbread – and great platters of meat served with Iranian-style rice. We have to confess that when we come here we usually stick to our favourite: a boneless chicken kebab, grilled without charring and tender. Saffron-hinted rice was light and fluffy, and – as per Iranian tradition – served with a knob of butter in the middle. Add some

lemony red sumac spice (on hand on the table), and you have all the ingredients necessary for a classic Persian eating experience.

Ranoush Juice Bar

43 Edgware Road, W2 2JR (7723 5929). Marble Arch tube. **Meals served** 8am-3am daily. **Average** ££. **No credit cards. Map** p276.
Middle Eastern

This is the fast-food part of the many-tentacled Maroush culinary empire. Bains-marie behind a long glass counter that runs the length of the room contain a variety of warm meze, including stuffed vine leaves and falafel. But a likely eight-out-of-ten customers are here for the shawarma (döner), possibly the best that can be found anywhere in town. Whether lamb or chicken, both come with sliced pickle, sliced tomatoes, chopped lettuce and onion, and a garlic sauce. Ranoush also does good squeezed-to-order fruit juices – choose your favourite combination from the array of fruit piled up behind the counter. As much a social centre as it is an eaterie, the place is busy throughout the day with local, expat and visiting Middle Easterners, and it remains buzzing right through to the early hours of the morning.

Meal deals

Arturo *23 Connaught Street, W2 2AY (7706 3388/www.arturo restaurant.co.uk).* Set meal £12.95 2 courses. **Map** p276. Italian

In the area

ASK *17-20 Kendal Street, W2 2AE (7724 4637).* **Map** p276.

Euston

African Kitchen Gallery

102 Drummond Street, NW1 2HN (7383 0918). Euston Square or Warren Street tube/Euston tube/rail.

Lunch served noon-3.30pm Tue-Sun. **Dinner served** 6-11pm Mon; 5.30-11pm Tue-Sun. **Average** ££. **Map** p266. African

Offering a fusion of African and Caribbean food, this tiny restaurant decked out with crafts, artefacts and jewellery (much of which is for sale) is a little African-Caribbean enclave among Drummond Street's mainly Indian restaurants. The benevolent owner takes pleasure in discussing the menu and offering his recommendations. A starter of diced and fried peppered plantain with chilled pepper sauce was a gorgeously spicy dish. Jerk chicken tasted great too. Unfortunately, we made a slight mistake in choosing spicy jollof to accompany it, instead of (as recommended) rice and peas, a drier option that would have better absorbed the pepper and hot sauce from the chicken. The place is tiny, but African Kitchen Gallery is usually quiet enough for you to bag one of the few tables.

Diwana Bhel Poori House

121 Drummond Street, NW1 2HL (7387 5556). Euston Square or Warren Street tube/Euston tube/rail. **Meals served** noon-11pm daily. **Average** ££. **Set buffet lunch** (noon-2.30pm) £6.50 (under-3s free; 3-7s half-price). **Set thalis** £5.95-£7.75. **Unlicensed**. **Corkage** no charge; no spirits allowed. **Map** p266. South Indian

Despite strong competition along a street thick with ethnic eateries beside Euston station, Diwana's adjoining twin rooms are almost permanently busy. The reason? Well turned out south Indian vegetarian cuisine at rock-bottom prices, swiftly delivered to your table by a neat, smiling staff. Dosas seem the way to go: the 'famous dosas of the coral coast', according to the dog-eared laminated menu, c.1980. These

are rich and hearty offerings, with smatterings of coconut sauce, nine in all. Traditional chaat starters, £3 each, combinations of yoghurt, pooris and chick peas, can be followed by a chef's daily special, such as Sunday's nourishing saag aloo. Alternatively, order an all-in-one thali, with rice, dahl, a vegetable curry and pooris. All standard stuff but it's the prices that bring people back. Desserts are superior, though: try malai of frozen milk and nuts.

Pasta Plus

62 Eversholt Street, NW1 1DA (7383 4943). Euston tube/rail. **Lunch served** noon-3pm Mon-Fri. **Dinner served** 5.30-10.30pm Mon-Sat. **Average** ££. **Map** p266. Pizza & Pasta

The grim and grimy surroundings of Euston station are not likely to whet anyone's appetite, but if you find yourself in the area, and hungry, this happy, air-conditioned restaurant offers a welcome refuge. Staffed by Italians and populated by regulars, it has a friendly family feel to it. A complimentary bowl of fat green and black olives was supplied while we scanned a menu big on Italian classics and, of course, pasta. A main dish of tagliatelli and huge prawns looked rather better than it tasted (the prawns were on the tough side), but another dish of tagliatelle with saffron, cream, bacon and mushrooms was deliciously fragrant, and left only just enough room for us to squeeze in a generous dollop of rich tiramisu.

In the area

Paul *Colonnade, Euston Station, NW1 2RT (7388 9382).* **Map** p266.
Pizza Express *Clifton House, 93-99 Euston Road, NW1 2RA (7383 7102).* **Map** p267.
Prezzo *161 Euston Road, NW1 2BD (7387 5587).* **Map** p266.
Rasa Express *327 Euston Road, NW1 3AD (7387 8974).* **Map** p266.

Fitzrovia

Adonis

56 Goodge Street, W1T 4NB (7637 7687). Goodge Street tube. **Meals served** noon-11pm Mon-Sat; noon-10.30pm Sun. **Average** ££. **Set meal** £12.50 2 courses. **Map** p266. Lebanese

A recent visit suggests that Adonis isn't quite as handsome and well-oiled as when it first opened, but it's still the best Lebanese in Fitzrovia. The prices are satisfyingly low and the Levantine meze dishes are still lip-smacking. The pickled baby aubergines stuffed with walnuts and garlic were a revelation, as was the kibbeh shamieh – lamb ground to a paste then mixed with cracked wheat to make Scotch egg-style cases. Vegetarian dishes are clearly marked. Don't miss the moutabal – grilled aubergine transformed into a delicious thick dip.

Carluccio's Caffé

8 Market Place, W1W 8AG (7636 2228). Oxford Circus tube. **Meals served** 7.30am-11pm Mon-Fri; 9am-11pm Sat; 10am-10pm Sun. **Average** ££. **Map** p266. Italian

Carluccio's is not well suited to people with hearing aids. The New York-style Italian deli chain has poor acoustics; clattering cutlery and cacophonous conversation ricochet off plain white walls and stripped wooden floors. Otherwise, the place is testimony to the fact that you can't keep a good brand down. Food is of a high quality and service equally so. Snacking or picnicking is half the deal here, with soups, antipasti, salads and pasta dishes leading the way by deploying classic combinations. Penne alla luganica (spicy sausage ragu) and gnocchi al gorgonzola are typically solid dishes. Daily specials supplement the fixed menu; coffee is of a standard you'd find in Italy.

dim T café

32 Charlotte Street, W1T 2NQ (7637 1122). Goodge Street tube. **Meals served** noon-midnight daily. **Average** ££. **Map** p266. Oriental

Baskets of fresh and flavoursome dim sum at affordable prices are the main event here. The steamed soupçons won't necessarily win any prizes for authenticity when pitted against Chinatown's best, but the parcels are prepared with care and – in a canny twist, that was once unconventional but is now more common – are served all day. The create-your-own-dish noodle menu lets you customise your meal; otherwise play safe with one of the handful of reliable Asian mains like Indonesian satay, Singaporean fried noodles, pad Thai, or Japanese teriyaki. The decor is gently modish, with its lilac banquettes and eastern design touches, and the service consistently friendly. Dim T scores well for affordable glamour: if you're careful (tap water, no puds), you can eat here for a tenner.

Eagle Bar Diner

3-5 Rathbone Place, W1T 1HJ (7637 1418). Tottenham Court Road tube. **Meals served** noon-11pm Mon-Wed; noon-midnight Thur, Fri; 10am-midnight Sat; 10am-6pm Sun. **Average** ££. **Map** p266. North American

This funky hamburger joint is increasingly attractive to the club crowd. These days it has a DJ spinning loud jammin' tunes at dinner time. Um, yay? Lunches, thankfully, are safe from this aural assault – for now. Food remains reliably good. The main attraction is the burgers. There are fish burgers, steak burgers, chicken burgers, ostrich burgers – they'll grill almost anything and serve it with fries. You get to choose your meat, your sauces and whether you want your fries fat or skinny. Along with burgers there are big, hearty sandwiches (the salt beef is excellent) and fresh salads, as well as US-style breakfasts served all day. For drinks there are cocktails, milkshakes and cokes served in old-fashioned bottles with straws. Service can be slow.

Fish Bone NEW

82 Cleveland Street, W1T 6NF (7580 2672). Great Portland Street or Warren Street tube. **Meals served** 11am-11pm Mon-Fri; 5-11pm Sat. **Average ££. Map** p266. Fish & Chips
Our visit to Fish Bone found the restaurant full of men sitting alone, heads down, furiously tucking into colossal steaming portions of Friday lunch magic. The male staff were over the moon to see some women enter this haunt of cabbies and lone-ranger office workers. The shoebox-sized restaurant is a bit of a squeeze on the inside, but the premises are clean and well decorated in dark red and brown. Fish comes grilled or fried in peanut oil, and is served with enough hand-cut chunky chips to make a family feast. If you feel like something a little stronger to drink, choose from the wide selection of bottled lagers or one of the few standard bottles of wine.

Fopp NEW

220-224 Tottenham Court Road, W1T 7PZ (7299 1640). Goodge Street tube. **Meals served** 10am-10pm Mon-Fri; 10.30am-8pm Sat; noon-6pm Sun. **Average £. Map** p266. Café
The downstairs cafeteria of this new flagship branch of Fopp, the record and DVD chain, produces superior toasties (£2-£3) with vibrant fillings such as Stilton with fruit and ale chutney, and meatballs with tomato and basil sauce; they come with a decent pile of salad on the side. Alternatively, go for one of the jacket potatoes (£3) offered with beans or coleslaw. Sweets include

crumbles, jam and coconut rings and a suitably gooey chocolate fudge-cake that comes drizzled with extra chocolate sauce. A good, simple stop while you shop for CDs.

Ikkyu

67A Tottenham Court Road, W1T 2EY (7636 9280). Goodge Street tube. **Lunch served** noon-2.30pm Mon-Fri. **Dinner served** 6-10.30pm Mon-Fri, Sun. **Average ££. Set lunch** £6.20-£9.60. **Set dinner** £6.10-£13.50. **Map** p266. Japanese
A long-standing Japanese all-rounder in an easy-to-miss basement, Ikkyu has much against it: decor is shabby, service brisk and unforgiving (especially if you linger at your table for too long), and a smell of fish pervades the small space. But food is genuine, as attested by the number of Japanese customers who pack in every lunchtime. A set sashimi platter was good value for less than a tenner: it included sea bream, sea bass, sardine and omelette slices, as well as the usual salmon and tuna, and came with rice and miso. The couple next to us at the counter were tucking in to an enormous blackened fish (we think it was sea bass) from the grill, and seemed to be enjoying every messy minute of it. Ikkyu is fast-paced and pushy, yes, but this bustle is at least authentically Japanese, and the quality of the food makes up for some rudeness.

Indian YMCA

41 Fitzroy Square, W1T 6AQ (7387 0411). Great Portland Street or Warren Street tube. **Lunch served** noon-2pm Mon-Fri; 12.30-1.30pm Sat, Sun. **Dinner served** 7-8.30pm daily. **Average £. Map** p266. Indian
There can be better places for culinary tourism in London. True, the surroundings are prosaic: the ground floor canteen of an office block. True also, the food is liable to be lukewarm if you arrive more than

ten minutes after kick-off. Long-simmered curries are the best bet. At lunch, simply take a tray, point to what you'd like, and pay at the till; then take your booty to a table, which you might share with office workers (Indians and others). At dinner, pay for your set meal in the entrance hall, then hand your chitty to the cooks. Communal bowls of rice and dahl are ready at the table. Most of the diners are Indian students and the set dinners change daily.

Istanbul Meze

100 Cleveland Street, W1P 5DP (7387 0785). Great Portland Street or Warren Street tube. **Meals served** noon-11pm Mon-Thur; noon-midnight Fri, Sat. **Dinner served** 5-11pm Sun. **Average ££. Set lunch** £7.90 2 courses. **Set dinner** £10.90 2 courses. **Set meze** £20. **Map** p266. Turkish

Turkish musicians play in the basement wine bar here at the weekend. So as we ate, their complex but unobtrusive rhythms could be heard through the floor. To start, our houmous was well presented, while börek was slightly overcooked but still enjoyable, and plenty of warm pitta bread accompanied both dishes. For mains, karni yarik (a large aubergine stuffed with diced lamb) produced a delicate fusion of flavours. Lokma kebab was fresh and tender: first rate. Istanbul Meze has much of the charm of a local restaurant, but is just around the corner from Great Portland Street. Well worth a visit.

Italiano Coffee Company

46 Goodge Street, W1T 4LU (7580 9688). Goodge Street tube. **Meals served** 7am-11pm Mon-Fri; 8.30am-11pm Sat, Sun. **Average £. Map** p266. Pizza & Pasta

The attraction at this pizza joint – commonly known as Icco – is the large, cheap pizzas. It's certainly not

the service: you queue at the counter, pay your money to the unsmiling staff, and – if they haven't lost your chit, which can happen – your name will be called out ten minutes later when the order's ready. Or at least, something will be called out; whether your name is Tom, Cath or Ali, the caller, a small woman with a nasal voice and suspect English, invariably sounds as if she's saying 'Plub'. The pizzas are big and thin-crusted, maybe a bit soggy, but then what do you expect for £3.50? The coffee's pretty good, and if you don't mind the noise (traffic noise through open doors, and ambient clatter), it's a fine place to fill up for a fiver.

La Perla

11 Charlotte Street, W1T 1RQ (7436 1744). Goodge Street or Tottenham Court Road tube. **Bar Open** 5-11pm Mon-Sat. *Restaurant* **Meals served** noon-10pm Mon-Sat; 5-9pm Sun. **Average ££. Map** p266. Tex-Mex

Tex-Mex food with a touch of sophistication is what this compact little place aims to offer – along with a strong emphasis on Margaritas. Best to avoid these if you want to stay within budget: a half-jug costs a whopping £17.95. Instead, order house wine and try the 'street tacos': big platters of half a dozen tacos, each with a different filling ranging from smoky prawn to spicy chicken to rich shredded pork, served with a large bowl of refried beans. Another option, the tostadas, resemble flat tacos: crispy corn tortillas piled high with beans, grilled chicken or beef, salad and sour cream. There are also sizzling fajitas (always reliable) which, for many people, will be big enough to share.

Ragam

57 Cleveland Street, W1T 4JN (7636 9098). Goodge Street tube. **Lunch served** noon-3pm daily. **Dinner served** 6-11.15pm Mon-

Thur; 6-11.30pm Fri, Sat; 6-10.30pm Sun. **Average £. Set lunch** (Mon-Thur) £5 3 dishes. **Map** p266.

South Indian

The stock in (roaring) trade at this small, sparsely decorated Fitzrovia restaurant is authentically fresh and spicy southern Indian cuisine. The unadventurous might be content sticking with the handful of curry-house staples on the menu – chicken korma, butter chicken et al – but that would be missing the point. Ragam's real strength lies in its long list of well-executed, fairly priced Keralite specialities. Chief among these delicacies are dosas (£3-£4.95) – crispy, crêpe-like pancakes made with lentil flour and stuffed with all manner of gorgeous fillings. Try the traditional masala dosa, filled with potato masala and served with coconut chutney, or branch out with utthappam, a south Indian 'pizza' made of rice and lentil flour. Service is professional and friendly, but expect a high turnover of diners – even on weekdays.

★ **Rasa Express**

5 Rathbone Street, W1T 1NX (7637 0222). Goodge Street or Tottenham Court Road tube. **Lunch served** noon-3pm Mon-Fri. **Average £.** **Map** p266. South Indian

Run from the back door of Rasa Samudra restaurant and part of the Rasa chain that originated in Stoke Newington (*see p201*), this lunch-only offshoot is worth a review in its own right. The lunch trays are quite simply fantastic, and almost embarrassingly cheap to go with it. The vegetarian box (£2.95) contains two vegetable curries, a side dish, rice, bread, and dessert; the non-vegetarian version (£3.50) is similar, except that one vegetable curry is substituted with chicken curry or biriani. Daily changing curries come in varieties such as beetroot with spinach or tomato with black-eye beans. The side dishes might include green plantain stir-fry or savoy cabbage thoran. The desserts may be rice, vermicelli, or mango and semolina puddings. It's really quite staggeringly good value and, though primarily a takeaway venture, you can eat inside at no extra charge. First class cheap eats.

RIBA Café

66 Portland Place, W1B 1AD (7631 0467). Great Portland Street tube. **Meals served** 8am-6pm Mon-Fri; 10am-4pm Sat. **Average ££. Set meal** (Mon-Fri) £12.95 1 course. **Map** p266. Brasserie

Not your average office canteen, this – unless your office happens to be the Royal Institute of British Architects. The café shares the first floor with exhibitions, pillars and a lot of space and light. With unobtrusive but stylish design (we love those semi-circular couches), smart and respectful service and generous spacing between tables, this is a serene and rather special place: particularly good for long catch-ups or business lunches. Set against such flawless background, our food was a tad disappointing on a recent visit, although still pretty reasonable for the price bracket. The menu eschews red meat, proffering seared, smoked and roasted fish, along with poultry and veg dishes in simple modern presentations. Roasted sea bream with a bean and tomato salad was punchy and satisfying, but baby plaice was overwhelmed by char-grilling.

Squat & Gobble NEW

69 Charlotte Street, W1T 4RJ (7580 5338). Goodge Street tube. **Open** 7am-5pm Mon-Fri; 9am-5pm Sat. **Average £. No credit cards.** **Map** p266. Café

This no-frills café sits at the unfashionable northern end of Charlotte Street. Its tightly packed tables – chunky wood inside the

café, metal outside – overflow at lunchtimes, so time your visit if you don't want to queue (but there's also a roaring takeaway trade for those who need their midday feast). The unfeasibly long menu covers almost every conceivable option from breakfast items (porridge, steak and eggs) through to soup, salads, jacket potatoes, daily specials and sandwiches (the 'posh' fish fingers, served on thick white bread with own-made tartare sauce, have achieved classic status). Prices are a steal – you'll be hard-pressed to spend more than a fiver – and plates come piled high. A real treasure.

Zizzi NEW

33-41 Charlotte Street, W1T 1RR (7436 9440). Goode Street tube. **Meals served** noon-11.30pm daily. **Average ££. Set meal** £15.95 2 courses. **Map** p266. Pizza & Pasta

In what is clearly a clever bid to corner the A and Z of the telephone directory, Zizzi is owned by the same people who run the ASK pizza chain. It is a slightly downmarket version of its sister chain, featuring restaurants that tend to be large and homogenous, though the logs surrounding the wood-fired pizza oven offer a pretence of authenticity. Zizzi can be hit and miss; we've had passable meals here, but also some that were pretty poor (a chicken caesar salad, for example, with limp leaves and miserly nubs of meat). The size of the Charlotte Street branch makes it ideal for group outings, although don't come if you're in a hurry as the service can be a little slack. Best for groups with time on their hands.

Meal deals

Archipelago *110 Whitfield Street, W1T 5ED (7383 3346).* Set lunch £12.50 per person (minimum 2) tasting menu. **Map** p266. International

Cleveland Kitchen *145 Cleveland Street, W1T 6QH (7387 5966).* Set lunch £6 1 course incl drink, £11 2 courses. **Map** p266. Pizza & Pasta

Crazy Bear *26-28 Whitfield Street, W1T 2RG (7631 0088/ www.crazybeargroup.co.uk).* Dim sum £2.50-£3.50. **Map** p266. Oriental

Ozer *5 Langham Place, W1B 3DG (7323 0505/www.sofra.co.uk).* Set lunch (noon-6pm) £8.95-£12.95 2 courses; set dinner (6-11pm) £11.95-£15.95 2 courses. **Map** p266.Turkish

In the area

Apostrophe *40-41 Great Castle Street, W1W 8LU (7637 5700).* **Map** p266.
Harry Morgan's *6 Market Place, W1N 7AH (7580 4849).* **Map** p266.
Nando's *57-59 Goode Street, W1T 1TH (7637 0708).* **Map** p266.
Pizza Express *7 Charlotte Street, W1T 1RB (7580 1110).* **Map** p266.
Pizza Express *4-5 Langham Place, W1B 3DG (7580 3700).* **Map** p266.
Pizza Paradiso *3 Great Titchfield Street, W1W 8AX (7436 0111).* **Map** p266.
Pure California *47 Goode Street, W1T 1TD (www.purecalifornia.co.uk).* **Map** p266.
Strada *9-10 Market Place, W1W 8AQ (7580 4644).* **Map** p266.
Ultimate Burger *98 Tottenham Court Road, W1T 4TR (7436 5355).* **Map** p266.

Gloucester Road

Meal deals

Pasha *1 Gloucester Road, SW7 4PP (7589 7969/www.pasha-restaurant.co.uk).* Set lunch £6 4 dishes, £8-£15 6 dishes. **Map** p278. North African

In the area

ASK *23-24 Gloucester Arcade, SW7 4SF (7835 0840).* **Map** p278.
Paul *73 Gloucester Road, SW7 4SS (7373 1232).* **Map** p278.

Holborn

Aki NEW

*182 Gray's Inn Road, WC1X 8EW
(7837 9281). Chancery Lane tube.*
Lunch served noon-2.30pm Mon-
Fri. **Dinner served** 6-11pm Mon-
Fri; 6-10.30pm Sat. **Average £££.**
Set lunch £7.80-£14.70. **Map** p267.
Japanese

An izakaya is a bar/restaurant
where Japanese salarymen go to eat
and drink away the frustrations of
the day, and Aki epitomises shabby
izakaya homeliness: staff wear
faded happi coats and sweet smiles;
furnishings include a glowing red
lantern and indigo noren curtains;
and the cooking features choice
ingredients and thoroughbred
techniques. Dinner courses are fairly
standard, but of a decent quality.
Our tempura set started with a
generous platter of sashimi, followed
by good yakitori (skewered chicken),
miso soup, rice, and tempura
(prawn, fish and vegetable). It was
rounded off with that classic set-
meal fresh-fruit ensemble of
strawberries and orange segments.
There's a remarkably long list of
specials too, where you can get a fix
of natto (fermented soybeans), raw
quails' eggs, mountain yam,
yellowtail jaw and other less
mainstream fare. So much to choose
from, so little time to eat… repeat
visits are recommended.

Bar Polski NEW

*11 Little Turnstile, WC1V 7DX
(7831 9679). Holborn tube.* **Meals
served** 4-10pm Mon; 12.30-10pm
Tue-Fri; 6-10pm Sat. **Average ££.**
Map p267. Polish

We love the new look at this popular
bar, formerly called Na Zdrowie.
Cool, blond-wood is decorated with
the hippest folk motifs this side of
the Vistula: colourful cockerels,
storks and delicate black filigree
work, traditionally paper-cut. Bar

Polski is best enjoyed early in the
week when it's quieter. Then, you're
more likely to get a seat to sample
the tasty food, cooked as it would be
back in Poland, the impressive
choice of Polish bottled beers and the
huge selection of vodkas. Tender
herring, served alone or as part of a
beetroot and mixed salad; potato
pancakes with mushroom sauce;
garlicky Polish sausage with
mustard and mash; and pleasingly
light pierogi stuffed with meat,
cabbage or cheese – all these dishes
marry perfectly with the drinks.

Fryer's Delight

*19 Theobald's Road, WC1X 8SL
(7405 4114). Holborn tube.* **Meals
served** noon-10pm Mon-Sat.
Average £. Minimum £2.10.
Unlicensed. Corkage no charge.
No credit cards. Map p267.
Fish & Chips

You'll probably smell Fryer's
Delight before you see it, and the
greasy smell will linger in your
clothes, hair and skin afterwards.
But this café, decked out in 1950s
diner decor, is exactly what a chippie
should be: no-frills. The fried plaice
was the best we've tasted this side
of Scarborough, which must have
something to do with being double-
fried in beef dripping. The chips, too,
were equally good: chunky, moist,
and loads of them. Team your fish
and chips with a big mug of sweet
tea, two paving-stone thick slices of
bread and butter, and a pot of thick,
sweet mushy peas, and you're set for
the night. It's sad to see Fryer's so
empty these days, so enjoy its
proper fish suppers while you can.

Meal deals

The Terrace *Lincoln's Inn Fields,
WC2A 3LJ (7430 1234/www.the
terrace.info).* Set meal (noon-3pm,
5.30-7pm) £10.50 2 courses, £12.75
3 courses. **Map** p267.
Modern European

In the area

Café Pasta *95-97 High Holborn, WC1V 6LF (7242 4580).* **Map** p267.
Paul *296-298 High Holborn, WC1V 7JH (7430 0639).* **Map** p267.
Pizza Express *99 High Holborn, WC1V 6LF (7831 5305).* **Map** p267.
Pizza Express *114-117 Southampton Row, WC1B 5AA (7430 1011).* **Map** p267.
La Porchetta *33 Boswell Street, WC1N 3BP (7242 2434).* **Map** p267.

King's Cross

Addis

42 Caledonian Road, N1 9DT (7278 0679). King's Cross tube/rail. **Meals served** noon-midnight Mon-Fri; 1pm-midnight Sat, Sun. **Average** ££. **Map** p267. Ethiopian

Addis is a usually buzzing restaurant that serves a wide range of – the name rather gives it away – Ethiopian food. The walls are decorated with words in the exotic-looking Amharic alphabet, and the restaurant has a choice of western-style tables and traditional low seating. A starter of selata aswad – delicious fried aubergine with tahini – showed the eaterie's potential. Main courses are served in the traditional manner, on a tray covered in a large pancake of tangy injera bread – a roll of injera is supplied for every diner. The taste is light, but the bread is filling. We tried doro wot – chicken and boiled egg served in a very hot sauce – and derek tibs; delightfully crispy, diced lamb fried with onion. The friendly atmosphere and wide range of dishes available make this a good place to come for novices of Ethiopian cooking.

Konstam

109 King's Cross Road, WC1X 9LR (7833 2615). King's Cross tube/rail. **Meals served** 8am-4pm Mon-Fri; 8.30am-4.30pm Sat, Sun. **Average** ££. **Map** p267. Café

An itsy-bitsy-teeny-weeny café that offers a smart, daily changing lunch menu of light meals and heartier options. Around six salads (£1.20 each or for £5.70 you can have all of them plus bread) are available from the dedicated counter: maybe chickpeas with red onion and dill; chargrilled veg with sesame, carrot and lentil; and roast new potatoes with mayo and chives. These are also available as sides to the tortilla and tart of the day. Soup might be French onion, or spinach and potato, served with toast. There'll be pasta, as well as hot dishes (char-grilled chicken with bearnaise sauce, baked haddock with peas and pancetta), and a range of sweeties such as date and walnut loaf.

Merkato Restaurant

196 Caledonian Road, N1 0SL (7713 8952). King's Cross tube/rail. **Meals served** noon-midnight daily. **Average** ££. African

This light and welcoming high-ceilinged café is a popular hangout for local Ethiopians. Brightly coloured cloths cover the walls and ceiling and there is a fenced-off area of tables on the wide pavement outside. On to a traditional bed of tangy injera bread was added yebeg wot, a very spicy lamb stew; the house special, kitfo (traditionally made with marinated raw minced beef); and ystsome beye-aynetu, a kind of vegetable 'mixed meze'. The latter dish was poured out in neat stripes. We particularly enjoyed the lentils and a mix of carrot and green beans. Portions were, if anything, too large; we had to leave food. Staff were exceptionally helpful, giving advice and tips on what was available and what was recommended.

In the area

Rasa Maricham *Holiday Inn, 1 King's Cross Road, WC1X 9HX (0871 075 7217).* **Map** p267.

Knightsbridge

In the area

Leon *136 Brompton Road, SW3 1HY (7589 7330).* **Map** p274.

Pâtisserie Valerie *17 Motcomb Street, SW1X 8LB (7245 6161).* **Map** p274.

Pâtisserie Valerie *32-44 Hans Crescent, SW1X 0LZ (7590 0905).* **Map** p274.

Pâtisserie Valerie *215 Brompton Road, SW3 2EJ (7823 9971).* **Map** p274.

Pizza Express *7 Beauchamp Place, SW3 1NQ (7589 2355).* **Map** p274.

Ranoush Juice Bar *22 Brompton Road, SW1X 7QN (7584 6999).* **Map** p274.

Wagamama *Lower ground floor, Harvey Nichols, 109-124 Knightsbridge, SW1X 7RJ (7201 8000).* **Map** p274.

Yo! Sushi *Fifth floor, Harvey Nichols Food Hall, 109-125 Knightsbridge, SW1X 7RJ (7201 8641).* **Map** p274.

Leicester Square

Corean Chilli `NEW`

51 Charing Cross Road, WC2H 0NE (7734 6737). Leicester Square tube. **Meals served** 11am-11pm daily. **Average** ££. **Map** p268. Korean
An unassuming Korean rice and noodle bar, this small venue, set over two floors, is pleasantly decorated with colourful murals, clipped plants, and grooves in the grey cement wall tiles. The menu is more adventurous than other Korean eateries in the area. We liked the crispy fried pork dumplings, and slender pancakes of candyfloss-light silken tofu, prettily studded with green chillies and mild, musky, bright red Korean chilli threads. Also satisfying was vegetable bibimbap: choi sum (oriental greens), bamboo shoot slivers, cucumber slices and beansprouts arranged like wheel spokes on plain rice, topped with a fried egg and nori seaweed strips, all mixed at the table with red chilli sauce. Not a destination restaurant by any means, but for a no-frills, inexpensive place to eat, it's much better than most.

Gaby's

30 Charing Cross Road, WC2H 0DB (7836 4233). Leicester Square tube. **Meals served** 11am midnight Mon Sat; noon-10pm Sun. **Average** ££. **No credit cards**. **Map** p273.
Jewish
This clean little Jewish café is non-kosher, so you can mix cheesecake with salt beef, or cappuccino with chopped liver sandwich. Some dishes are better bets than others: the salt beef special has a generous filling that's almost as fat as a dictionary. But the latkes were soggy and disappointing; better stick to the wide range of salads, or the bowls of straightforward soups (lentil, bean and barley). Gaby's isn't just for aficionados of Jewish food (though this undoubtedly helps): there's a laminated menu showing colour photographs of the main dishes, in case you're not sure what falafel with pitta or couscous royale might be.

Saharaween

3 Panton Street, SW1Y 4DL (7930 2777). Piccadilly Circus tube. **Meals served** noon-11.30pm daily. **Average** £££. **Unlicensed**. **Corkage** no charge. **Map** p269.
North African
First impressions aren't great here. The main entrance is framed by two columns that look as though they're made of painted cardboard, and the ground floor and basement both feel like Portobello market knick-knack emporiums. It is only when it comes to the kitchen that Saharaween displays some serious good taste(s). The menu is short, but among its handful of standard tagines are a couple of unusual items, including a

tagine safira of slow-cooked chicken with 'cheesey bread balls' and a tagine mhama of lamb with glazed apple, plum, pine nuts and 'lamb juice'. The latter dish was terrific, with the fruit reduced to a soft gooiness that beautifully complimented the generous hunk of tender, almost flaky meat.

Meal deals

Café Fish *36-40 Rupert Street, W1D 6DW (7287 8989/www.sante online.co.uk/cafefish).* Set meal £12.50 2 courses, £14.95 3 courses. **Map** p269. Fish

In the area

Burger Shack *17 Irving Street, WC2H 7AU (7839 3737).* **Map** p269.
Pizza Express *80-81 St Martin's Lane, WC2N 4AA (7836 8001).* **Map** p273.
Strada *39 Panton Street, SW1Y 4EA (7930 8535).* **Map** p269.
Wagamama *14A Irving Street, WC2H 7AB (7839 2323).* **Map** p269.
Yo! Sushi *St Albans House, 57 Haymarket, SW1Y 4QX (7930 7557).* **Map** p269.

Marylebone

★ Ali Baba

32 Ivor Place, NW1 6DA (7723 7474/5805). Baker Street tube/ Marylebone tube/rail. **Meals served** noon-midnight daily. **Average ££. Unlicensed. Corkage** no charge. **No credit cards. Map** p277. Middle Eastern
Minutes away from the hubbub of Marylebone Road is this one-of-a-kind restaurant offering nothing but fresh Egyptian food. Vine leaves stuffed with fluffy, flavoursome rice are a must, and a far cry from the gloopy degraded specimens found in tins. Houmous with warm pitta was equally good, and we could have

ordered another bowl easily. Mains were even more impressive. Shish kebab delivered succulent char-grilled chunks of lamb cooked to absolute perfection. Moussaka, made with tender pieces of aubergine, oozed béchamel and gently spiced meaty juices. A scorchingly hot om ali – a creamy filo pastry version, crammed with sultanas – is plenty for two. Service is attentive, the prices are reasonable and you get baklava on the house after your meal.

Apostrophe

23 Barrett Street, W1U 1BF (7355 1001). Bond Street tube. **Open** 7.30am-8pm Mon-Fri; 9am-8pm Sat, Sun. **Average ££. Map** p277. Café
Sandwiches here, made with their own-baked breads, have evocative French names and ingredients that place them a cut above many outlets. 'Marseille' (£2.80), a smoked salmon sandwich, comes with lemon-tasting sorrel, capers and mayonnaise. Crayfish (or 'Sète') isn't paired with traditional rocket but with celeriac remoulade, capers and baby gem. 'Lyon' is a tasty combination of chicken, crème fraîche and chilli jam (though what it's got to do with Lyon we cannot fathom). Three options are available toasted, including 'Alsace' with pastrami, emmental cheese, sauerkraut and mustard. Pastries include organic cheesecake, pear tart, profiteroles and coconut macaroons. Diners sit at long communal benches in eight (soon to be nine) London branches.

Bang! Sausage Bar & Grill NEW

4 Bryanston Street, W1H 7BY (7224 2475). Marble Arch tube. **Meals served** noon-10.30pm daily. **Average ££. Map** p277. Café
Continuing the trend of upgrading old-fashioned prole food for the well-salaried masses, Bang! tackles

Lunch box

Like chains the world over, one day **Pret a Manger** will seem the most unadventurous lunch option possible, the next a godsend if you're stuck in an area devoid of decent cafés. The truth is, there's little chance of getting a bad sandwich here – just as there's small hope of an exceptional one. Constants like chicken caesar salad, brie and tomato baguette, and the Pret 'super club' (chicken and bacon with a tangy mayonnaise) take up most of the shelf space, joined by weekly-changing specials such as prawns with yoghurt or avocado and cheese (all £1.25-£2.90). Salads (£2.85-£3.90) come in big plastic bowls, but are often a little bland and lettuce-heavy; soups (£2.29-£2.59) like carrot and cumin, green thai spinach and sausage hotpot are better.

EAT stands as the only real competitor to Pret's dominance of the gourmet sandwich market. Their produce is marginally superior: soups such as chicken hotpot, tomato with mozzarella balls, and beef stew (£2.40-£3) are heartier and more vibrant, often topped with cutesy extras like pie crusts, sprinkled herbs or cheese. Sandwiches (£1.20-£3.20) such as turkey and cranberry and prawn cocktail come with heftier fillings; many, like smoked chicken and basil, can be toasted (Pret has only recently added three hot wraps to their menu). Salads (£2.50-£2.70) are slightly smaller than at Pret; we're fans of the filling moroccan chicken couscous. EAT also seem to put more effort into their morning menu than Pret's on-the-counter breakfast baguettes: particularly popular here are filled toasted muffins (£1.70-£2.50) and excellent birchermuesli (muesli soaked in fruit juice then mixed with yoghurt, £1.70).

American franchise **Subway** has grown slowly but surely in the UK over the last few years, offering tailor-made 'subs', or long, soft rolls. Standard subs (£2.20-£4.30) like the Subway club (turkey, ham and beef), italian BMT (ham, salami and pepperoni), and meatballs in tomato sauce come in six-inch or foot-long sizes, and are made to order; not quite the treat it sounds when you see a slice of ham or turkey peeled from its pile. Still, the daily-changing 'sub of the day' is good value: a six-incher for £1.99. At the bottom end of the market, **Benjy's** is a world away from Pret and Eat in terms of sandwich quality, but price is what matters here. Meal deals are the order of the day: basic sandwiches (99p-£2.59 on their own) with crisps, fruit and a drink for an extra £1. Many branches also run a happy hour (3-5pm), offering any sandwich left after the lunch rush for a quid. Now *that's* a cheap eat.

Benjy's *www.benjys-sandwiches.com*
EAT *www.eat.co.uk*
Pret a Manger *www.pret.com*
Subway *www.subway.co.uk*

sausages – funking them up a bit and slapping on a 'gourmet' tag. The operation works well. In a tough-to-find basement space below a hotel, diners sit at tables over-looked by LCD screens or in cosy boothed alcoves. The menu lists around 30 sausage varieties, divided up by country of origin or inspiration: we tried a weisswurst (boiled veal sausage) from Germany, a chorizo number from Latin America, and a vegetarian cheese variety from Wales. The bangers – each mounted with a little name flag – are then served with mash and salad; piquant sauerkraut is optional. Service was leisurely but amiable on our visit, the waitress happy to talk through the enormous selection once she eventually got to us.

Busaba Eathai

8-13 Bird Street, W1U 1BU (7518 8080). Bond Street tube. **Meals served** noon-11pm Mon-Thur; noon-11.30pm Fri, Sat; noon-10pm Sun. **Average £££. Map** p277. Thai

Comfort isn't paramount at this mini-chain (three outlets in central London), where people share the chunky wooden tables, food arrives in a trice, it is consumed quickly, then everyone moves on, making space for new diners. Lanterns create pools of light over each table and theatrical waiters buzz around like black-clad hoverflies. With the fast food concept, there's always a risk of rushed cooking, and that's what happened with stir-fry of cod fillet and krachai (a mildly spicy root vegetable): it was a dry combination of ingredients, lacking in flavour. Khanom jin noodles were a big improvement, drenched in a subtle and savoury green curry sauce. Probably the biggest hits were pad kewtio (an upmarket version of pad Thai with smoked chicken and holy basil) and an inspired fruit smoothie with jasmine, passion fruit and yoghurt.

Café T at Asia House NEW

63 New Cavendish Street, W1G 7LP (7307 5454). Oxford Circus tube. **Meals served** 11am-5pm Mon-Sat. **Average ££.** Oriental

This airy, high-ceilinged café, with slate-grey walls and an ornate fireplace, is located inside Asia House, which promotes the art and literature of different Asian cultures. It's operated by Cyrus Todiwala, the chef-proprietor of Café Spice Namaste. The food is cooked in Café Spice's kitchen and finished here. The pan-Asian menu encompasses sandwiches, snacks, salads, Vietnamese and Burmese noodles, Chinese dishes, and Indian, Thai and Malaysian curries. We enjoyed beetroot and coconut samosa, and parsee dhansak. There's an excellent selection of teas, including the fragrant jasmine flower, and rarely-seen varieties like 'kashmir ruby leaf'. A bespoke bento box, which includes a starter, main course, vegetable, rice and salad, costs only £13.95.

Eat & Two Veg

50 Marylebone High Street, W1U 5HN (7258 8595). Baker Street tube. **Meals served** 9am-11pm Mon-Sat; 10am-10pm Sun. **Average ££. Map** p277. Vegetarian

This hip venue, furnished with red leather banquettes and pale turquoise Formica-topped tables, looks like an American-style diner. Tiles, bricks, wooden panels, industrial pipes, painted surfaces and suspended lamps give plenty of character to floors and walls. So how's the food? Fine, as long as you like meat substitutes like TVP, quorn and tofu. It's the dishes cooked without these that work the best. We started with smoky lemony roasted almonds. Grilled halloumi salad was made with top-quality cheese, and fresh, zestily dressed leaves. Beetroot and goat's cheese

Bang! Sausage Bar & Grill. See p61.

croquettes were bland, as was the schnitzel, though this did have a good crisp texture. Thai green curry, made with sweet potatoes, had a lively, assertive flavour and was accompanied by vegetable rice.

Garden Café NEW
Inner Circle, Regents Park, NW1 4NU (7935 5729). Baker Street or Regent's Park tube. **Open** 9am-dusk daily. **Average** ££. Café
Part full-restaurant, part service-counter offering sandwiches and salads, the Garden Café has a smashing location, its 300 seats split between its recently rejuvenated 1964 building and the lawns and patios outside. So far, so delightful, but service in the restaurant can be muddled – you may be forgotten

about if you sit at the outside tables on the raised area slightly removed from the restaurant. Pity: the food is pretty impressive. Cauliflower and cumin soup had an appealing tang, while a fullish plate of nicely sourced asparagus polonaise (with a breadcrumb-based topping) was excellent value at £5.50. A plump portion of baked haddock came soaked in a creamily moreish parsley sauce; linguine with herbs and parmesan, although on the cold side of lukewarm, had the makings of a smashing summer dish.

Golden Hind
73 Marylebone Lane, W1U 2PN (7486 3644). Baker Street or Bond Street tube. **Lunch served** noon-3pm Mon-Fri. **Dinner served**

6-10pm Mon-Sat. **Average** ££.
Minimum (lunch) £4, (dinner) £5.
Unlicensed. Corkage no charge.
Map p277. Fish & Chips
Run by a set of tough-looking Greek
men, the Golden Hind oozes
character. Portion sizes are fairly
variable, as are the opening hours,
but don't let this put you off – the
food is top notch. Fish, fresh as a
daisy, comes coated in a batter
second to none. Chips have a
tendency to be slightly undercooked,
but you'll soon forgive this once you
try the creamy own-made tartare
sauce. The Hind is packed most
evenings, so arrive early. Its BYO
alcohol option is also worth taking
advantage of. The atmosphere is
fun, young and friendly, offset by a
soundtrack of light American jazz.
Fish and chip junkies might be
interested in the decommissioned art
deco fryer by F Ford of Halifax, now
displayed in the dining room.

Grand Bazaar
*42 James Street, W1N 5HS (7224
1544). Bond Street tube.* **Meals
served** noon-11pm Mon-Thur, Sun;
noon-midnight Fri, Sat. **Average**
££. **Set lunch** £6.50 2 courses. **Set
meze** £9.45. **Map** p277. Turkish
Popular with groups of young
people, the interior is shadowy and
cluttered with twinkling lamps and
incense burners – aiming to recreate
the feel of the Grand Bazaar in
Istanbul, we presume. For starters,
houmous kavurma combined very
smooth houmous with olive oil and

Palms of Goa

SWAGATHAM (Welcome)

South indian cuisine in the heart of London
A new benchmark in Indian dining has been reached

Eugine Dias teamed up with Shabdin Gharuk and opened the firs[t]
Goan restaurant in central London, 1994. With their vast experien[ce]
in cooking together they offered authentic and unheard of dishes th[at]
were not seen in other restaurant menus.

"The tarka dal and the breads we tried were carefully prepared. Service
by Mr Dias is courteous and responsive to an interest in the food."
- Evening Standard

"be prepared for the appeal of lamb xacutti, 'a very famous Goan dish
prepared with coconuts, vinegar and hot spices' that's all the more welco[me]
because it's not actually famous enough to have found its way onto the me[nu]
of most curry houses." - Time Out

"(apart from Palms of Goa) most Indian restaurants have failed to reali[se]
that taste should go hand in hand with more healthy and reduced-fat dish[es]
- Tandoori Magazine

PALMS OF GOA. FITZROVIA

160 New Cavendish Street, London W1W 6YR
T: 020 7580 6125

Underground: Gt Portland St (Bakerloo, Circle Hammersmith
& City) Warren Street (Northern & Victoria) Goodge Street (Northern)

Palms of Goa Opening Times: Monday-Saturday
12pm-3pm & 6pm 11pm   Sunday - Closed

---

www.palmsofgoa.com

bite-size chunks of lamb. Sucuk izgara, grilled spicy sausage on lettuce, was also up to standard, though it lacked the subtle taste gradations of some of the starters. Accompanying pide was puffy, inflated like a balloon. Imam bayıldı was offered as a main course: it was a satisfying dish, though the vegetable stuffing was surprisingly heavy on the peas. As a meaty alternative, köfte in sauce with yoghurt was very good.

Le Pain Quotidien NEW

72-75 Marylebone High Street, W1U 5JW (7486 6154). Baker Street or Bond Street tube. **Open** 7am-7pm Mon-Fri; 8am-6pm Sat; 9am-6pm Sun. **Average** ££. **Map** p277. Café
A popular chain in Belgium and France, LPQ's ethos of good, daily handmade bread is accented in its menu; delicious slabs of chewy organic sourdough accompany soups, salads and platters, or star as the base for tartines. These tartines, or open sandwiches, feature largely Mediterranean ingredients (Milano salami, prosciutto with artichoke paste, Gruyère with cornichons; soup of the day might be pea and mint. Huge salads (Fourme d'Ambert cheese, pear, rocket and walnuts, for example) and platters (smoked salmon with prawns and guacamole, houmous, baba ganoush and tabouleh) are appealing lunchtime dishes. With rustically-exposed brick, a large focal communal table (surrounded by numerous smaller ones) and floor-to-ceiling windows, the spacious interior exudes light and warmth – an ambience that is only enhanced by the smell of fresh baked goods from the oven.

Paul

115 Marylebone High Street, W1U 4SB (7224 5615). Baker Street or Bond Street tube. **Open** 7.30am-8pm Mon-Fri; 8am-8pm Sat, Sun. **Average** ££. **Map** p277. Café

Founded in Lille in 1889, this stylish chain – at last count there were 13 branches in London – focuses on high-quality, attractive pâtisserie, sweet and savoury tarts and artisan breads. The café's smart, black decor may seem exclusive, but the French staff are welcoming and the menu uncomplicated. Light lunches include quiche (lorraine, trois fromages), salads (chicken, smoked salmon, cured ham) and paillasson – grated potato pancakes. Ours, topped with mushrooms and a fried egg, was delicious; an omelette complet (ham, Emmental, bacon and mushrooms) was equally good, although – puzzlingly – it arrived sitting in water. Great service, relaxed surroundings and good food: Paul is deservedly popular, so visit in quieter times to enjoy a lingering latte and macaroon.

★ Paul Rothe & Son

35 Marylebone Lane, W1U 2NN (7935 6783). Bond Street tube. **Meals served** 8am-6pm Mon-Fri; 11.30am-5.30pm Sat. **Average** £. **No credit cards**. **Map** p277. Café
This store dates back to around 1900 and wears it well, making Marylebone Lane's charming caff-grocer an architectural as well as a foodie curiosity. Two soups – one meat, one vegetarian – are offered daily and these are made fresh by Paul Rothe himself. Lamb broth, chicken and ham broth, tomato, stilton and celery are all hugely popular, especially in winter, and cost £1.40-£2.30. Sandwich fillings are also made on site, and include Austrian liptauer, made with cream cheese, herbs, anchovy paste, paprika and capers; and kummelkase, a blend of Stilton, caraway and cream cheese. These can be used to fill bagels, ciabattas, baps, baguettes, bloomer bread or Ukrainian rye bread. What would the Earl of Sandwich have thought?

Prince Ali

*108 Seymour Place, W1H 1NH
(7258 3651), Edgware Road tube.*
Open 11.30am-11.30pm daily.
**Average ££. Unlicensed.
Corkage** no charge. **Map** p276.
Middle Eastern

A satellite to Edgware Road's high
concentration of Arabic restaurants
and bars, this tiny establishment, set
in the much quieter confines of
western Marylebone, similarly
caters to a mostly Arabic and
Middle Eastern clientele – largely, it
seemed to us, the good friends of the
proprietors. Squeeze in alongside
them to sample freshly cooked
standards like falafel, houmous and
baba ganoush along with tasty
flatbreads made on the premises.
There are also stews and kebab
dishes for something more
substantial. It's all very low-key and
unassuming, and there's nothing on
the menu fans of Middle Eastern
food won't have seen before (except
the entries in Arabic, perhaps), but
the chirpy, welcoming management
help to make this a pitstop worth
contemplating if you're nearby.

Quiet Revolution

*28-29 Marylebone High Street, W1V
4PL (7487 5683). Baker Street or
Bond Street tube.* **Open** 9am-6pm
Mon-Sat; 11am-5pm Sun. **Average**
££. Map p277. Café

Locating an organic café within eco-
chic Aveda is inspired; slate-tiled
and calm, Quiet Revolution's
healthy, largely vegetarian menu
appeals to its green-leaning clientele.
Well-groomed model types sip
wheatgrass shots and shuffle
shopping bags at communal tables
to make space for yummy mummies
wise to the fact that, while the prices
reflect its Marylebone address, the
portions – especially from the
children's menu – are huge, and go
far. Market availability dictates the
freshly prepared daily menu:

chunky soups (pea and mint,
beetroot and horseradish), salads
(lentil with feta, roast salmon), stews
served with brown rice (Thai-style
pumpkin curry, lamb with parsnips)
and specials (chilli con carne, pasta,
frittata). Fantastic freshly made
juice combos and smoothies are a
bonus, as is the pleasant service.

Square Pie Company

*Selfridges Food Hall, 400 Oxford
Street, W1A 1AB (7318 2460/
www.squarepie.com). Bond Street
tube.* **Meals served** 10am-8pm
Mon-Fri; 9.30am-8pm Sat; noon-6pm
Sun. **Average £. Set meal** £4.95
1 person. **Map** p277. Café

A Square Pie fits the hole in a round
belly perfectly. From laid-back
market stall origins at Spitalfields,
the company has expanded to office-
friendly destinations including
Canary Wharf and this Selfridges
branch, in a bustling corner of the
food hall. You'll find a cavalcade of
beefy options plus varieties like
chicken, leek and ham, lamb and
rosemary, and 'Friday Fish Pie'.
Vegetarians will be satisfied with
mushroom and asparagus pie with
a vegetarian onion gravy. Our
favourite detail is that Maris Piper
potatoes are mashed skin-on. To
drink, there's scrummy Chegworth
Valley apple juices.

Strada

*31 Marylebone High Street, W1U
4PP (7935 1004). Baker Street or
Bond Street tube.* **Meals served**
noon-11pm Mon-Sat; noon-10.30pm
Sun. **Average ££. Set meal** (3-
6.30pm Mon-Fri) £5.95 1 pizza.
Service 12.5%. **Map** p277.
Pizza & Pasta

Strada has managed to kid
everybody into thinking it's a
superior sort of pizza chain by the
simple method of associating itself
with a superior sort of London locale
– Blackheath, Islington, Exmouth
Market as well as this Marylebone

branch – and banging on about wood-burning ovens. In reality, our experiences here have been mixed. We've had some fine pizzas (a simple bufala, with sweet cherry tomatoes complementing creamy buffalo mozarella), but also a couple so bad that they couldn't be finished (a Fiorentina that was overcooked, rendering the spinach damp and tasteless). Perhaps it's not quite the middle-class pizza-topia that its cheerleaders proclaim, but that didn't stop the company getting a spot in the lucrative new Royal Festival Hall franchise. One thing we really like: the way they put free bottles of water on every table, without anyone having to ask.

Meal deals

Eat-Thai.net 22 St Christopher's Place, W1U 1NP (7486 0777/ www.eatthai.net). Set lunch £8.95 2 courses. **Map** p277. Thai

Garbo's 42 Crawford Street, W1H 1JW (7262 6582). Set lunch (Mon-Fri) £10.95 2 courses, £11.95 3 courses; £12.95 smörgåsbord. **Map** p276. Scandinavian

Ishtar 10-12 Crawford Street, W1U 6AZ (7224 2446/www.ishtar restaurant.com). Set lunch (noon-6pm) £6.95 2 courses; 3 courses £9.95. **Map** p277. Turkish

Levant Jason Court, 76 Wigmore Street, W1U 2SJ (7224 1111/www. levant.co.uk). Set lunch (Mon-Fri) £8-£15 2 courses. **Map** p277. Lebanese

Original Tagines 7A Dorset Street, W1U 6QN (7935 1545/ www.originaltagines.com). Set lunch £9.50 2 courses. **Map** p277. North African

Phoenix Palace 5 Glentworth Street, NW1 5PG (7486 3515). Dim sum £2-£3.80. **Map** p277. Chinese

Royal China 24-26 Baker Street, W1U 3BZ (7487 4688/www.royal chinagroup.co.uk). Dim sum (noon-4.45pm) £2.30-£4.60. **Map** p277. Chinese

Royal China Club 40-42 Baker Street, W1U 7AJ (7486 3898/www. royalchinaclub.co.uk). Dim sum £2.60-£6.80. **Map** p277. Chinese

In the area

Apostrophe 23 Barrett Street, W1U 1BF (7355 1001). **Map** p277.

ASK 56-60 Wigmore Street, W1U 2RZ (7224 3484). **Map** p277.

ASK 197 Baker Street, NW1 6UY (7486 6027). **Map** p277.

Carluccio's Caffè St Christopher's Place, W1U 1AY (7935 5927). **Map** p277.

Fine Burger Company 50 James Street, W1U 1HB (7224 1890). **Map** p277.

Fresco 31 Paddington Street, W1U 4HD (7486 6112). **Map** p277.

Fresco 34 Margaret Street, W1G 0JE (7493 3838).

Giraffe 6-8 Blandford Street, W1H 3HA (7935 2333). **Map** p277.

Pâtisserie Valerie at Sagne 105 Marylebone High Street, W1U 4RS (7935 6240). **Map** p277.

Paul 277-278 Regent Street, W1D 2HD (7491 8957).

Pizza Express 13-14 Thayer Street, W1U 3JS (7935 2167). **Map** p277.

Pizza Express 21-22 Barrett Street, St Christophers Place, W1U 1BF (7629 1001). **Map** p277.

Pizza Express 133 Baker Street, W1U 6SF (7486 0888). **Map** p277.

Pizza Paradiso 9 St Christopher's Place, W1U 1NE (7486 3196). **Map** p277.

The Real Greek Souvlaki & Bar 56 Paddington Street, W1U 4HY (7486 0466). **Map** p277.

Tootsies Grill 35 James Street, W1U 1EA (7486 1611). **Map** p277.

Wagamama 101A Wigmore Street, W1U 1QR (7409 0111). **Map** p277.

Woodlands 77 Marylebone Lane, W1U 2PS (7486 3862). **Map** p277.

Yo! Sushi 15 Woodstock Street, W1C 2AQ (7629 0051). **Map** p277.

Zizzi 35-38 Paddington Street, W1U 4HQ (7224 1450). **Map** p277.

Zizzi 110-116 Wigmore Street, W1U 3RS (7935 2336). **Map** p277.

Central

Mayfair

Chisou

4 Princes Street, W1B 2LE (7629 3931). Oxford Circus tube. **Lunch served** noon-2.30pm, **dinner served** 6-10.15pm Mon-Sat. **Average £££. Set lunch** £9-£17. **Map** p268. Japanese

By day, Chisou – with its Japanese screens, rice-paper lamps and cushioned banquettes – is fast, efficient and businesslike. At night, groups linger over a bottle, picking and pecking at degustation-style dishes from the daily list of out-there specials, including pan-fried spicy burdock, and monkfish liver with ponzu. More familiar is the black cod with miso, which tasted fine but felt squidgy. All was forgiven with the arrival of the nigiri sushi – beautifully buttery salmon and bright, fresh tuna which literally melted in the mouth. Also good were four plump, mouth-filling Irish rock oysters topped with spicy radish, spring onion and ponzu. Dish of the night was a plate of mixed sashimi and avocado served with a beachcomber salad of mizuna, rocket and seaweed: bliss.

El Pirata

5-6 Down Street, W1J 7AQ (7491 3810). Green Park or Hyde Park Corner tube. **Meals served** noon-11.30pm Mon-Fri; 6-11.30pm Sat. **Average £££. Set lunch** (noon-3pm) £9 2 dishes incl glass of wine. **Set meal** £13.95-£17.75 per person (minimum 2) 8 dishes. **Map** p274. Spanish

As one of the few affordable dining options in this plush neighbourhood of hotels, private clubs and expense accounts, El Pirata enjoys immense popularity with local business folk. It provides a reliable lunch or after-work spot in which to knock back a few reasonably priced tapas dishes. It's spread over two floors; the ground floor bar is nicer than the basement, offering walls cheerfully decorated with Picasso and Miró reproductions, close-packed tables and unflaggingly amiable waiters adding to the buzzy atmosphere. We eschewed the specials for tapas; standouts were gambas al pil pil (chilli prawns); a rich, cheesy dish of aubergines; and montaditos (slices of bread) topped with first-class serrano ham, but we also enjoyed a tasty fabada (bean stew), meatballs, plus fair renditions of arroz negro (rice cooked with squid ink) and patatas bravas.

Prezzo

17 Hertford Street, W1J 7RS (7499 4690). Green Park or Hyde Park Corner tube. **Meals served** noon-11.30pm Mon-Sat; noon-11pm Sun. **Average ££. Map** p274. Pizza & Pasta

Prezzo has only three outlets in London and presents itself as a slightly better class of pizza chain, something epitomised by the grandeur of the Mayfair branch – all dark-wooden panelling and English country house art (offset on our visit by what appeared to be an inflatable nun in one corner). Similarly, the nosh is a cut above, flirting with a standard that could be termed 'gourmet'. In our experience, the pizzas and pastas are uniformly excellent, while mains also stretch into more imaginative territory – such as a fine mozzarella and red pesto burger, and various (free-range) chicken dishes. The pizzas are very decent; we particularly like the lip on the crust, which provides a smidgen more crunch than most.

Rocket

4-6 Lancashire Court, off New Bond Street, W1Y 9AD (7629 2889). Bond Street or Oxford Circus tube. Bar **Open** noon-11pm, **meals served** noon-10pm Mon-Sat. **Average £££. Restaurant**

Rocket

Lunch served noon-3pm, dinner served 6-11pm Mon-Sat. Average £££. Pizza & Pasta

Hidden in a cobbled alley behind Bond Street, Rocket is evidently popular with local office workers, who spill out of the ground-level bar on fine evenings. In contrast to the intimate den below, the first floor restaurant is an airy space whose soaring proportions are enhanced by a massive skylight. Pizzas are somewhat eclipsed by inventive (and enormous) salads. A salad of succulent marinated Thai bourgois fish (similar to red snapper), with bok choi (Chinese cabbage), roasted pineapple and cucumber ribbons bettered an unremarkable aubergine pizza. While starters such as deep-fried baby squid with a sweet chilli, plum and lemon dip looked inviting, we found our choice – roquefort on a 'carpaccio' of beetroot and chewy kohlrabi cabbage – rather hard work. Wine choice spans the globe, bottles divided into helpful categories. Despite being rushed off their feet, the fresh-faced waiting staff were charming.

Meal deals

Momo 25 Heddon Street, W1B 4BH (7434 4040/www.momoresto.com). Set lunch £11 1 course, £13 2 courses, £16 3 courses. Map p269. North African

Princess Garden 8-10 North Audley Street, W1K 6ZD (7493 3223/www.princessgardenofmayfair. com). Dim sum £2.50-£3.80; set lunch £12 per person (minimum 2). Map p277. Chinese

Sofra 18 Shepherd Street, W1Y 7HU (7493 3320/www.sofra.co.uk). Set lunch £8.95 2 courses. Set dinner £11.95 2 courses. Set meze £12.95-£15.95 per person (minimum 2). Turkish

Sotheby's Café Sotheby's, 34-35 New Bond Street, W1A 2AA (7293 5077). Set tea (3-4.45pm Mon-Fri) £5.25. Café

In the area

ASK 121-125 Park Street, W1K 7JA (7495 7760). Map p277.
Carluccio's Caffé Fenwick of Bond Street, W1S 3BS (7629 0699).
Itsu 1 Hanover Square, W1S 1HA (7491 9799).
Pizza Express 23 Bruton Place, W1J 6ND (7495 1411).
Rasa W1 6 Dering Street, W1S 1AD (7629 1346).
Strada 15-16 New Burlington Street, W1S 3BJ (7287 5967). Map p269.
Thai Square 5 Princes Street, W1B 2LF (7499 3333). Map p268.

Paddington

★ Satay House

13 Sale Place, W2 1PX (7723 6763). Edgware Road tube/Paddington tube/rail. Lunch served noon-3pm, dinner served 6-11pm daily. Average £££. Set meal £13.50 per person (minimum 2). Map p276. Malaysian

Occupying a neat, tidy, cottage-like space, Satay House is populated by regulars who make themselves at home with newspapers and favourite dishes. Satays are the real thing: sizzling, scorchy and hot off the grill, served with a killer peanut sauce. With every dish, our meal got better. Begedil (spicy meat and vegetable balls) were soft and squidgy inside, crisp outside; a whole grilled mackerel with a tamarind sauce was firm, fat and flavour-packed; and kangkong belacan (water spinach with shrimp paste) was a crunchy green pleasure to eat. Then came the best nasi lemak we've had in London – a bowl-shaped mound of perfect coconut rice with crunchy little ikan bilis, roasted peanuts, hard-boiled egg, and an extremely good, dark chilli-laden sambol filled to capacity with fresh, bouncy prawns. What a treat.

In the area

Fresco *93 Praed Street, W2 1NT (7402 0006).* **Map** *p276.*

Yo! Sushi *The Lawn, Paddington Station, W2 1HB (7706 9550).*

Zizzi *17 Sheldon Square, W2 6EP (7286 4770).*

Piccadilly

Miso

66 Haymarket, SW1Y 4RF (7930 4800). Piccadilly Circus tube. **Open** 11.30am-11pm Mon-Thur; 11.30am-11.30pm Fri, Sat; 11.30am-10pm Sun. **Average** ££. **Map** p269. Oriental

With eight branches currently open around London (and more planned), Miso is a reliable option if there isn't a Wagamama nearby and you don't fancy a non-chain noodle joint. Following the usual format (low-priced, freshly-prepared Oriental fare served canteen-style in minimalist surroundings), Miso is less crowded than most noodle bars and the staff seem more relaxed about turnover; postprandial lingering over green tea refills is no problem. Good thing too, since the enormous portions command a longer chow time. Noodles (wok-fried, soup- or sauce-based) are the mainstay; along with rice dishes (Malaysian curry, Sichuan chicken, hot-and-sour mixed seafood), bento boxes, and dim sum. Drinks include seasonal fruit juices, freshly-pressed; best of the lot is the gorgeously summery watermelon.

New Piccadilly

8 Denman Street, W1D 7HQ (7437 8530). Piccadilly Circus tube. **Meals served** noon-8.30pm daily. **Average** ££. **Unlicensed**. **Corkage** no charge. **No credit cards. Map** p269. Café

Hardly altered since it opened in the 1950s, NP is filled with white-tunicked staff, ceiling fans, plastic flowers, Formica tables and glass cups and saucers evocative of post-war Soho. The menu also transports you straight back to Arthur Askey's Britain, with dated Brit-Ital dishes like steak with risotto, chicken casserole, or semolina pudding. While our mixed salad was fine, the ravioli was overcooked, the filling a mystery sludge, and the only flavour came from added hot tomato sauce and a tablespoon of pesto. We have a soft spot for the peach melba, though, made from condensed milk and tinned peaches. Come here for retro decor (check out the old-fashioned till), atmosphere (complete with soothing classical music on the radio), and a chat with owner and local hero Lorenzo – not for the food and drink.

Nouveauté NEW

Habitat, 121-123 Regent Street, W1B 4HX (7287 6525). Oxford Circus or Piccadilly Circus tube. **Open** 8.30am-6.30pm Mon-Wed, Fri; 8.30am-7.30pm Thur; 10am-6.30pm Sat; 11.30am-5.30pm Sun. **Average** ££. **Map** p269. Café

The new Regent Street Habitat store is inside a grade II-listed building that has seen £4.5 million invested in its restoration. Beautiful original features sit well around Tom Dixon's dark wood and metal stairway and mezzanine on the building's first floor. Customers serve themselves from a neat display of salads, plump rolls and cakes. Respectable tortilla was offered with a choice of six or so salads for £7.50. We liked the Mediterranean mix of aubergine, yellow pepper, red onion and tomatoes, the herby new potato salad, and bowl of sprightly undressed leaves. The filled rolls looked excellent and were generously portioned. The bright Australian service and classy vibe make this a tempting retreat from the thoroughfare outside.

In the area

Apostrophe *16 Regent Street SW1Y 4BT (7930 9922).* **Map** p269.
ASK *14-16 Quadrant Arcade, 15A Air Street, W1B 5HL (7734 4267).* **Map** p269.
C&R Café *3-4 Rupert Court, W1D 6DY (7434 1128).* **Map** p268.
Ed's Easy Diner *The Trocadero, 19 Rupert Street, W1V 7HN (7287 1951).* **Map** p269.
Maison Blanc Vite *193 Piccadilly, W1J 9EU (7287 6311).* Branch of Maison Blanc. **Map** p269.
Pâtisserie Valerie *162 Piccadilly, W1J 9EF (7491 1717).* **Map** p269.
Pizza Express *26 Panton House, SW1Y 4EN (7930 8044).* **Map** p269.
Prezzo *8 Haymarket, SW1Y 4BP (7839 1129).* **Map** p269.
Wagamama *8 Norris Street, SW1Y 4RJ (7321 2755).* **Map** p269.
Woodlands *37 Panton Street, SW1Y 4EA (7839 7258).* **Map** p269.
Yo! Sushi *The Trocadero, 19 Rupert Street, W1D 7DH (7434 2724).* **Map** p269.

Pimlico

Jenny Lo's Tea House

14 Eccleston Street, SW1W 9LT (7259 0399). Victoria tube/rail. **Lunch served** noon-3pm Mon-Fri. **Dinner served** 6-10pm Mon-Sat. **Average** ££. **Minimum** £5. **No credit cards. Map** p275. Chinese

Local workers flock to this miniscule Chinese 'tea house' at lunchtime for fast and fragrant noodle and rice dishes, prepared with plenty of fresh ingredients, and without MSG or excess oil. Apply yourself to the serious business of putting away an enormous bowl of chilli beef soup noodles, featuring abundant fresh coriander and plenty of kick, or choose from a variety of wok-fried noodle dishes, Thai curries or homely rice dishes. Favourite sides include the crispy seaweed, veggie spring rolls and super-crunchy stir-fried French beans with garlic. Wind up with the gorgeous ginger and honey ice-cream and a 'therapeutic' tea. Jenny Lo's is attractively clean-cut, but the communal refectory tables and bench-style seating make it more suited to a fuel stop than a romantic rendezvous.

Mekong

46 Churton Street, SW1V 2LP (7630 9568). Pimlico tube/ Victoria tube/rail. **Lunch served** noon-2.30pm, **dinner served** 6-11.30pm daily. **Average** ££. **Set meal** £13-£17 per person (minimum 2) 3 courses. **Map** p275. Vietnamese

It doesn't take many diners to fill this teeny local Vietnamese, so come expecting cosy conditions, complemented by a spot of inter-table joviality. In an area lacking in cheap restaurants, Mekong does a sterling job on providing the fuel of Pimlico with freshly prepared Vietnamese food at very fair prices. The comprehensive menu is divided into meats, poultry, fish and vegetarian, plus there's a Thai section. But we recommend plumping for one of the good-value set menus to share, taking in a variety of dishes, such as delicious crispy aromatic duck pancakes, sizzling chicken with lemongrass (though the zesty aroma seemed curiously absent on our last visit) and sesame prawn fingers, followed by tea or coffee. Service is friendly but not indulgent.

Meal deals

Kazan *93-94 Wilton Road, SW1V 1DW (7233 7100/ www.kazan-restaurant.com).* Set lunch (noon-6pm) £9.95 per person (minimum 2). **Map** p275. Turkish

In the area

Pizza Express *25 Millbank, SW1P 4QP (7976 6214).*
Pizza Express *46 Moreton Street, SW1V 2PB (7592 9488).* **Map** p275.

Soho

Amato

*14 Old Compton Street, W1D 4TH
(7734 5733). Leicester Square or
Tottenham Court Road tube.* **Open**
8am-10pm Mon-Sat; 10am-8pm Sun.
Average ££. Map p268. Café
Step back in time at this delightful
Italian brasserie – everything about
it has a charmingly old-fashioned
vibe, from the art deco posters to the
dark wood-panelled walls. But it's
the lavish display of pâtisserie that
is the lure to shoppers and Soho
bohos. Cakes topped with ruffled
chocolate fans; whipped whirls of
cream, rising like beehive hairdos
from pastry tartlets; and individual
mousses: they all tempt lovers of
naughty-but-nice. Before diving
straight into chocolate profiteroles,
take the edge off your appetite with
a simple, homely pasta dish – we're
always satisfied with the pasta
sauces. Service, like the cooking, is
friendly and informal.

Beatroot

*92 Berwick Street, W1F 0QD
(7437 8591). Oxford Circus or
Piccadilly Circus tube.* **Meals
served** 9.15am-9pm Mon-Sat.
**Average £. No credit cards.
Map** p268. Vegetarian
Tucked in between the record shops
and fruit stalls, the praiseworthy
Beatroot serves up a wealth of
vegetable dishes, piping hot, to pot-
bellied ex-longhairs and life-long
Sohoites. There are ten of these daily
changing staple dishes, amply
portioned; plus salads in almost
equal measure (staff insist on
cramming as much into a tub as
possible). You can ask for mixtures
squeezed therein, such as bean
hotpot with dollops of vegetable
lasagne. Beatroot also excels in
fresh juices and smoothies; a
jingly indie aural backdrop might
be interrupted by the whirr of
smoothie-destined mangos in the
masher. Carrots, ginger, beetroot,
spinach and apples in various
combinations comprise the small
(£2.20) and large (£2.90) juices. The
communal feel is accentuated by the
half-dozen circular bench-tables
inside and out, designed for sharing.

Brasil by Kilo

*17 Oxford Street, W1D 2DJ (no
phone). Tottenham Court Road tube.*
Open 11am-9pm daily. **Average
££. No credit cards. Map** p268.
Brazilian
The Brazilian 'pay for food by kilo'
system seems to suit this manic,
style-devoid corner of London.
Fortunately, the food on show here
is fresh, tasty and filling. It's homely
fare forged by a mixing of African
and Portuguese palates. Highlights
include the frango ensopado
(chicken sautéed with spices), deep-
fried banana and roast pork,
alongside staple accompaniments of
rice, beans, cheesy bread and salad.
Brazil's 'national dish', feijoada is
often available and is not to be
missed. If all this seems heavy and
you need some vitamins and fibre,
try some stimulating guaraná or one
of the fruit juices, made from
cupuaça, cashew, and passion fruit,
imported as purées from Brazil.

Breakfast Club NEW

*33 D'Arblay Street, W1F 8EU
(7434 2571). Oxford Circus or
Tottenham Court Road tube.*
Meals served 8am-6pm Mon-
Fri; 9.30am-5pm Sat. **Average £.
Map** p268. Café
As the name suggests, this caff does
a decent line in breakfast dishes that
aren't the usual fry-ups: you could
have Special K with toast and
Marmite or jam, plus tea/coffee and
fresh orange juice. Or get in touch
with your inner sybarite and have
the peanut butter and banana
toasties, or even the Nutella version.
It's a nice place for lunch too:

Breakfast Club. See p75.

the split-level room is quiet, and attractively decorated in a decidedly uncorporate, renovated-warehouse kind of way. The young staff are friendly, and the range of food includes toasted sandwiches such as tuna melts, prettily presented on a plate with lots of salad garnish. The espresso-based coffees are decent, and there are iMacs on a counter that allow customers free internet access.

Burger Shack NEW

14-16 Foubert's Place, W1F 7BH
(7287 6983). Oxford Circus tube.
Meals served 11am-midnight
Mon-Sat; 11am-10.30pm Sun.
Average ££. **Map** p268. Burgers

Burger Shack, just off Carnaby Street, produces perfectly good food that differs little from the other gourmet burger chains: decent fries, burgers, good buns – with nothing too outré on the menu that might scare off the tourists. The differences to the competition are largely cosmetic: walls adorned with photographs of the gods of rock music, plus a few rock dinosaurs and some fossils. It seems well targeted at its customers, who include one-visit shoppers, tourists and slackers passing through west Soho. At the end of 2005 this outlet was taken over by Smollensky's, which has now added two more branches in the West End – by transforming what had been Smollensky's Metro sites into Burger Shacks.

Café Boheme

13 Old Compton Street, W1D 5JQ
(7734 0623). Leicester Square tube.
Open 8am-3am Mon-Sat; 8am-10.30pm Sun. **Meals served** 8am-2.30am Mon-Sat; 8am-10pm Sun.
Average ££. **Set meal** (noon-7pm)
£11.50 2 courses, £13.50 3 courses.
Map p268. Brasserie

Café Bohème may not be the kind of place you make a special trip to, but if you're looking for somewhere to eat in the West End, it passes muster. Leaving aside the fact that steak frites with béarnaise sauce had to go back because it was stone cold, the flavour and texture of the replacement – as well as that of a huge fillet steak with creamy roquefort sauce – couldn't be faulted. The chips and (mixed green) salad panachée served in pretty aluminium pots were crisp and fresh. A pot of moules marinière was equally delicious, as was the bourbon vanilla crème brûlée. A strength of Café Bohème is its wide menu; lots of petit plats and salads mean you don't need to linger.

Café Emm

17 Frith Street, W1D 4RG
(7437 0723). Leicester Square
or Tottenham Court Road tube.
Lunch served noon-2.30pm
Mon-Sat. **Dinner served** 5.30-10.30pm Mon-Thur; 5-11.30pm Fri, Sat. **Meals served** 1-10.30pm Sun.
Average ££. **Set lunch** (Mon-Thur) £6.85 2 courses. **Set meal** (5.30-6.30pm Mon-Fri) £8.95 2 courses. **Map** p268. International

This small, ever-popular, family-run restaurant serves traditional British dishes (steak and ale pie and the like) as well as more modern concoctions (melon and ginger soup). Though certainly atmospheric, with its pseudo-Parisian façade and unobtrusive, sophisticated interior, our meals were mediocre at best. After arriving disquietingly fast, blackened Cajun salmon lacked flavour and finesse; vegetarian lasagne was fine, served with a simple salad, but hardly lit up our world. Maybe we should have gone for one of the interesting burgers (minted lamb, lentil and bean). Still, Emm thrives, its fair prices attracting a large crowd come the evening – the queue sometimes snakes out the door.

Café at Foyles

Foyles, 113-119 Charing Cross Road, WC2H 0EB (7440 3207). Tottenham Court Road tube.
Meals served 8am-9pm Mon-Sat; 10am-6pm Sun. **Average** ££. **Map** p268. Café

The easy-going Café at Foyles shares floor space with one of London's most cultivated jazz collections – modern, avant-garde, soul, world and blues are all covered – so it figures that it serves up some correspondingly tasteful fodder. All the café standards are chalked up (salads, toasted sarnies, paninis, flapjacks, muffins, lattes), but it's the use of premium ingredients in enlightened combinations – as well as the first-rate soundtrack, of course – that make this a worthy West End pit stop. Think tangy comté cheese, tomatoes and salad on nutty bread; freshly-whizzed apple and fresh ginger juice; and seriously fruity banana cake. Bench seating along the windows is perfect for solo snacking, while scanning your inbox (the café is wi-fi-enabled) or watching – maybe a little smugly – punters come and go at the blander Borders opposite.

Café Libre NEW

22 Great Marlborough Street, W1F 7HU (7437 4106). Oxford Circus tube. **Meals served** 8am-10pm Mon-Thur; 8am-11pm Fri, Sat; 10am-9pm Sun. **Average** ££. **Map** p268. Café

This prime location opposite the north end of Carnaby Street, with its panoramic view over the mock-Tudor splendour of the Liberty store, is a good place to rest your bags during a daytime shopping trip. Café Libre frees you for a short while to tuck into appealing sandwiches (until 6pm only), morsel-packed salads, or more substantial main courses. The tuna of our niçoise salad was grilled well, and

there were plenty of other titbits to raise it above the norm: boiled quails' eggs and a handful of soybeans, for example. The cream tea's not bad either, with lashings of clotted cream on raisin scones. As in most cafés in West Soho, prices are on the high side, but that comes with the territory.

Chowki

2-3 Denman Street, W1D 7HA (7439 1330). Piccadilly Circus tube. **Meals served** noon-11.30pm Mon-Sat; noon-10.30pm Sun. **Average** ££. **Set meal** £12.95 3 courses. **Map** p269. Indian

Among the throng of low-budget curry houses just off Piccadilly Circus, Chowki stands out not for its perfunctory looks but for its interesting dishes. The menu changes every few weeks, always highlighting three regional cuisines of India, with excellent-value set meals that allow you to try a selection of small dishes. Highlights might include a subtly-spiced Bengali fish curry simmered in coconut milk, or a Parsi prawn curry rich with the sweetness of jaggery but also sour with the tang of tamarind and lime juice. On our visit the details were excellent: two unusually flavoured rotis, and a perfect khichadi (rice dish). Be warned that the jal jeera, often drunk as a digestif in India, has a strong sulphurous smell from 'black salt'; it can be a shock if you're not expecting it.

Crepeaffaire NEW

173 Wardour Street, W1F 8WT (7479 7722). Oxford Circus or Tottenham Court Road tube. **Meals served** 9am-11pm Mon-Fri; 10am-11pm Sat; 10am-9pm Sun. **Average** £. **Map** p268. Café

From one kiosk in Hammersmith Broadway Shopping Centre, this company has now expanded to include a snazzy and more spacious

Café at Foyles

Hummus Bros. See p82.

crêperie in Soho. Despite the French origins of the crêpe, this affair is all cosmopolitan London. Savoury varieties include Thai and tikka chicken, a Brazilian (ham, cheese and pineapple), three vegetarian options and a Londoner (scrambled egg, crispy bacon and cheese). For afters there are various ways with banana, chocolate, Nutella and lemon. A tidy little Soho lunch spot.

Ed's Easy Diner

12 Moor Street, W1V 5LH (7434 4439). Leicester Square or Tottenham Court Road tube. **Meals served** 11.30am-11.30pm daily. **Average ££. Minimum** (6pm-midnight Fri-Sun) £4.55. **Map** p268. North American

This chain of 1950s-style diners – all shiny chrome and determinedly cheerful red and white colour schemes – is where to find fast food done well. Each branch is more or less the same: bar stools at the counter around the open kitchen, a scattering of booths and tables, rock hits of the past on loop, and a menu devoted almost exclusively to burgers and 'dogs. Most of the time, we have good experiences at Ed's: burgers are reliably fresh and piled high with onions, pickles and lettuce; the fries and onion rings are crisp, and portions are generous. The milkshakes and malts are dangerously delectable and arrive in copious amounts. Waiters are almost relentlessly perky, despite listening to that music all day long.

The Garden Café

4 Newburgh Street, W1V 1LH (7494 0044). Oxford Circus tube. **Open** *Summer* 8am-7pm Mon-Fri; 9am-7pm Sat; 11am-6pm Sun. *Winter* 8am-7pm Mon-Fri; 9am-7pm Sat. **Average ££. Minimum** (12.30-2.30pm) £5. **Map** p268. Café

Serving modest but appetising fare such as burgers, pizzas and sandwiches, the Garden Café is that rare thing, a Soho eaterie without airs. Simple food, friendly staff and mismatched cutlery create the impression of eating in a friend's kitchen, making for a pleasant escape from the noise of nearby Carnaby Street and Oxford Circus. Food here is unassuming and all the better for it; a range of sweet and savoury pancakes are the house speciality, and dishes such as spaghetti bolognese may be basic but are satisfying nonetheless. The airy interior and few tables out front make it perfect for a laidback summer lunch, particularly as an alternative to the more haughty nearby restaurants.

Hamburger Union

23-35 Dean Street, W1D 3RY (7437 6004www.hamburger union.com). Leicester Square or Tottenham Court Road tube. **Meals served** 11.30am-9.30pm Mon; 11.30am-10.30pm Tue-Fri; 12.30-10.30pm Sat; 1-8pm Sun. **Average ££. Map** p268. Burgers

The Soho location ensures that this diner gets more than its share of people tapping into BlackBerries, arranging the slope of their jeans and wearing hats indoors. Self-regard apart, the Soho bohos know a good thing when they see it. Chips are properly chunky and the hamburgers are made from happy cows, we don't doubt. Homage is paid to the chorizo burger pioneered by the Brindisa stall at Borough Market with the chorizo sausage with olive oil, piquillo pepper and rocket in a bap, but otherwise there's little funny stuff, just well-textured beef patties cooked medium and served in a good-looking bun. Only a few details disappoint, such as the plasticky-textured cheese. But after one of their malts (vanilla, chocolate, strawberry or banana) you'll probably forgive them.

★ Hummus Bros NEW

88 Wardour Street, W1F 0TJ (7734 1311). Leicester Square or Tottenham Court Road tube. **Meals served** 11am-10pm Mon-Wed; 11am-11pm Thur, Fri; noon-11pm Sat. **Average** £. **Map** p268. Café

At this small, stylish fast-food café and takeaway in busy Soho, houmous – that ever-present dip, that perennial garnish – is upgraded and given main event status. It works. The eponymous chickpea and tahini purée is served in shallow bowls with a hollow in the middle that is filled with Levantine-inspired extras, such as chicken in tomato sauce, chunks of stewed beef, fava beans, guacamole or a mushroom mix, plus one or two daily changing specials. The resultant combo is then scooped up with warm white or brown pitta bread. No forks, no fuss, no cucumber sticks. Excellent side dishes such as tabouleh, roasted aubergine and vegetable salads complete an ultra-compact menu. Diners pack in to sit at the long shared tables and benches, but many also takeaway in tubs.

Imli NEW

167-169 Wardour Street, W1F 8WR (7287 4243). Oxford Circus or Tottenham Court Road tube. **Meals served** noon-11pm daily. **Average** £££. **Set lunch** £7 3 dishes. **Map** p268. Indian

Popular with young office types, Soho newcomer Imli focuses on tapas-style light bites for sharing, rather than weighty Indian stalwarts. A spacious venue, it blends contemporary fittings with Indian antiques and vibrant splashes of orange colour across the walls. Punjabi-style samosas made a promising start to our meal, with richer, more crumbly pastry than the usual filo, and a filling of potatoes spiced with toasted coriander seeds.

Makhani dahl was a dream dish; made with black lentils, it was as creamy and indulgent as that of pricier sister restaurant Tamarind – at a fraction of the cost. On the whole, Imli's curries are adequate, but need bolder, more confident spicing to deliver the goods. This spot has great potential.

★ Italian Graffiti

163-165 Wardour Street, W1F 8WN (7439 4668). Oxford Circus or Tottenham Court Road tube. **Lunch served** noon-3pm, **dinner served** 5.30-11.30pm Mon-Fri. **Meals served** noon-11.30pm Sat. **Average** £££. **Map** p268. Pizza & Pasta

Run by the same family for two decades, this cosy trattoria is a Soho gem: unpretentious and reasonably priced, with roaring fires or air-con for comfortable year-round ambience. Simple is sometimes best; the kitchen produces good basic Italian cooking in vast amounts, but the wood-fired oven-baked pizzas are what most people come for. Tasty vegetarian and seafood toppings balance out meaty favourites such as americana and speck; the bases are authentically thin and crispy. Just-right fettuccine with a rich, tomatoey sauce, was good. For seafood fans, swordfish is recommended: two large slabs, grilled with olive oil, herbs and garlic, and served with potatoes and beans – simple and delicious. Book at peak times; this place has many fans.

Itsu

103 Wardour Street, W1F 0UQ (7479 4790). Leicester Square or Tottenham Court Road tube. **Meals served** noon-11pm Mon-Thur; noon-midnight Fri, Sat; 1-10pm Sun. **Average** £££. **Map** p268. Japanese

The long line of Soho regulars queuing up outside these premises

With breezier decor than most of the competition, the dining room at Myung Ga feels bright and airy, and the atmosphere is more cosy and friendly than at most of the competition. Fried, wun tun-style goonmandu (meat dumplings) arrived on a flat basket with carved vegetable garnishes. Of the mains, yukkaejang was sublime – a complex, spicy soup with layers of chilli heat and tender strips of shredded sirloin beef. Spicy daeji bulgogi (barbecued pork) was prepared behind the scenes, but arrived on a sizzling platter in a brilliant spicy sauce. For our money, this is the best Korean in Soho for a post-work dinner: prices are fair, food is excellent and there are numerous pubs along Kingly Street for a drink before or after.

★ Nara

9 D'Arblay Street, W1F 8DR (7287 2224). Oxford Circus or Tottenham Court Road tube. **Lunch served** noon-3.30pm Mon-Sat. **Dinner served** 6-11pm daily. **Average** ££. **Set lunch** £6.50 1 course. **Set dinner** £7.50 1 course. **Map** p268.
Korean

Good value lunches are the big draw here. The menu features dozens of Japanese and Korean meals, available as cheap lunches or slightly more expensive dinners. Inside, Nara looks like every other Korean restaurant in Soho (black tables and chairs, potted palms), but we defy anyone to find a cheaper Korean barbecue. When we visited, people were still trying to gain entrance after the kitchen had closed at 3pm. We decided against the Japanese menu and went for a Korean set lunch of dol bibimbap, a crucible-like hot-pot filled with rice, vegetables and seasoned beef, topped with an egg and folded together at the table with hot chilli sauce. This is probably the most filling dish on the menu, so we were quite happy with the small size of the side dishes.

Pâtisserie Valerie

44 Old Compton Street, W1D 4TY (7437 3466). Leicester Square tube. **Open** 7.30am-8.30pm Mon, Tue; 7.30am-9pm Wed-Fri; 8am-9pm Sat; 9.30am-7pm Sun. **Average** ££. **Map** p268. Café

We keep returning to this branch of Pâtisserie Valerie, but more for its quirky atmosphere and first-floor views on to Old Compton Street life than for its pâtisserie. If appearances mean anything, it delivers the goods with an impressive glass counter crammed with sumptuous gateaux, flans, tartlets, mousse cakes and cute little marzipan figurines. If you're a late riser, this spot serves breakfast until 4pm, and the lunch menu – although hardly outstanding – offers salads, quiches, omelettes and light bites. On our last visit, afternoon tea was a combination of hits and misses: a wedge of tiramisu gateau delivered the goods, but an accompanying strawberry cheesecake was let down by cream that was anything but fresh. Good service made up for shortfalls on the table.

Ping Pong NEW

45 Great Marlborough Street, W1F 7JL (7851 6969). Oxford Circus tube. **Dim sum served** noon-midnight Mon-Sat; noon-10.30pm Sun. **Average** £££. **Set dim sum** (noon-6pm) £9.90-£11.90. **Map** p268. Oriental

There's no booking at this 'designer dim sum' joint and queues can stretch almost to Liberty's down the road. Inside, the dramatic decor is very 21st century, with stools ranged around curving counters and a huge glass wall looking on to a Japanese-style garden. Service is friendly, but can slow as things get busy. Chilli squid cakes were good

in a mildly bouncy sort of way. But the squidgy paste in the delicately crested har gau (shrimp dumpling) wasn't very prawn-like; the shanghai siew long bun (pork and crab parcel) fell apart on first touch; and the crispy duck fried rolls left a lingering flavour of cloying hoi sin sauce. The only tea is jasmine, served in a theatrical long glass, complete with budding flower inside. Prices are reasonable, but go for the vibe rather than the food.

Pizza Express
29 Wardour Street, W1D 6PS (7437 7215). Leicester Square tube. **Meals served** 11.30am-midnight daily. **Average ££. Map** p269.
Pizza & Pasta

With a staggering 96 branches in the capital, Pizza Express has arguably superceded American chain Pizza Hut as the most recognisable pizza brand in the capital. Like Starbucks and free newspaper vendors, you are always within walking distance of one in central London. The company started with this restaurant in Wardour Street, then spread to Coptic Street and from there has all but taken over the country. Restaurants tend to be uniformly styled in a tasteful, Habitat way, and the food is similarly enjoyable – always good but never outstanding. In summer 2006, the company added a 'sicillian passion' element to the menu, with starters, pizzas and salads inspired by the Mediterranean island. While there are pasta and salad dishes on the menu, you'd be well advised to stick to the pizzas – the clue is in the name.

Pure California NEW
39 Beak Street, W1F 9SA (0845 601 9141/www.purecalifornia.co.uk). Oxford Circus tube. **Meals served** 8am-7pm Mon-Fri; 10am-6pm Sat; 11am-5pm Sun. **Average £. Map** p268. Café

After failing to squeeze into west Soho's slender fashions, you might feel the need for nourishment that doesn't fill your love handles. Head for Pure California, a juice bar that also offers some delicious and health-conscious salads and wraps. We liked the Greek salad, simple but satisfying with frilly lettuce, cherry tomatoes and dollop of houmous. There are also low GI or high protein salads, and even one called 'celebrity skin salad' (celebrities beware). To drink there's 'anti-oxidising' juices and 'functional smoothies'. To go in these, peculiar Brazilian superfruit açaí appears alongside wheatgrass: a police line-up of odd flavours beloved of health food geeks. The long narrow room doesn't have a lot of space to linger; most of the trade is takeaway.

Red Veg
95 Dean Street, W1V 5RB \ (7437 3109). Leicester Square or Tottenham Court Road tube. **Meals served** noon-9.30pm Mon-Sat; noon-6.30pm Sun. **Average ££. No credit cards. Map** p268.
Vegetarian

Formed by two travellers who met by chance in Vietnam, Red Veg is a mini-chain of ethically-led establishments offering vegetarian fast food. Burgers, wraps, wurst and falafels are cooked to order and presented in packaging emblazoned with pseudo-Cyrillic script and five-pointed red stars. Burgers come in six varieties, spicy or non-spicy, the stand-out being the hickory-smoked option with Monterey jack cheese, wholesome and hangover-curing. Falafels are similarly varied and side dishes include stuffed jalapeno peppers and breaded mushrooms. Although the fridge is filled with Whole Earth brand organic ginger and such worthy beverages, you can also pick up a Dr Pepper or an Orangina. The only snag, at this

Pure California. See p89.

Wardour Street branch in any case, is the space. Should you want to eat in, there are only four cramped tables.

Ryo

84 Brewer Street, W1F 9UB (7287 1318). Piccadilly Circus tube.
Meals served 11.30am-midnight Mon-Wed, Sun; 11.30am-1am Thur-Sat. **Average ££. Set meal** £5.50-£10. **No credit cards. Map** p269. Japanese

No nonsense about this Japanese caff. Walk in and immediately to your left is a busy counter with a menu (categorised under 'rice', 'noodles', 'sushi', side menus and set menus of rice plus miso soup) sellotaped on to it. Here, somewhat inconveniently, given the hubbub and enticing selections, you must choose and order before finding a table in the neat black-and-white room embellished with two flat-screen TVs. When it comes, swiftly, the food is almost universally good. Sushi (standard set £10.50) is varied, with nigiri and gunkan; noodles (meat options only) come in humungous bowls with mixed pork, seafood and vegetables. Many plump for a rice dish: combinations of pork or eel, complemented by egg and onion are in the £8-£12 range. Pork gyoza stands out among the side dishes.

Sabzi

3 Princes Street, W1B 2LD (7493 8729). Oxford Circus tube.
Meals served 7am-7.30pm Mon-Fri; 10.30am-6pm Sat; 10.30am-5.30pm Sun. **Average ££. Unlicensed** no alcohol allowed. **No credit cards. Map** p268. Café

The temptation to take the easy option and opt for a Pret lunch is always great, but those in the vicinity of Oxford Circus at midday should give Sabzi a try. Here, sandwiches, soups and salads are superior, and no more expensive. We were able to nab a window seat on our visit – lucky, as the bright but compact space gets very busy at lunch and most people takeaway. We started with a rich and warming mexican chicken soup; to follow, a good quality ham and cheese baguette. After polishing things off with banana and honey in greek yoghurt, we left well satisfied. Doing the three courses might seem pricey for a stop-and-go lunch (about £15 for two) but, like we said, 'tis no more expensive than Pret.

Stockpot

18 Old Compton Street, W1D 4TN (7287 1066). Leicester Square or Tottenham Court Road tube.
Meals served 11.30am-11.30pm Mon, Tue; 11.30am-midnight Wed-Sat; noon-11.30pm Sun. **Average £. Set meal** (Mon-Sat) £4.95-£6.50 2 courses; (Sun) £6.50 2 courses. **No credit cards. Map** p268. Café

It serves popular British and continental dishes at rock-bottom prices, yet it's sited in a prime central London location that the big chains usually gobble up. Just how does the Stockpot do it? Not by cutting corners with the food, in our experience; the dishes always pass muster. Penne pasta was perfectly al dente, with generous amounts of ham and spinach for £3.95. We love the retro feel of the Stockpot's menu: maybe egg mayonnaise as a starter, vegetarian moussaka to follow, jelly and cream for pudding. It might remind some of school dinners, but then school didn't sell bottles of wine at £7.60. For reliably good, affordable food right in the heart of Soho, the Stockpot has no peers.

Ten Ten Tei

56 Brewer Street, W1R 3PJ (7287 1738). Piccadilly Circus tube. **Lunch served** noon-2.30pm Mon-Fri; noon-4pm Sat. **Dinner served** 5-10pm Mon-Sat. **Average ££. Set lunch** £6.50-£12. **Map** p268. Japanese

It ain't pretty, but for generously proportioned well-made sushi at a streetwise price, Ten Ten Tei is hard to beat. This Soho stalwart has the look of a back-lane noodle bar and the bustle of a British caff, with its plain wooden tables ready-loaded with napkins, chopsticks, toothpicks, pepper pots, chilli pepper sprinkles, soy and tonkatsu sauce. Some dishes may lack finesse, but they're great value. Crisp-skinned grilled mackerel (packed with omega-3) was a treat; salt-grilled squid legs were chewy but clean-tasting. But the best order here is the sushi – of tuna, salmon, red snapper, scallop and mirin-sweetened omelette.

Yming

35-36 Greek Street, W1D 5DL (7734 2721). Leicester Square tube. **Meals served** noon-11.45pm Mon-Sat. **Average ££. Set lunch** (noon-6pm) £10 3 courses. **Map** p268. Chinese
Yming has built up a loyal following of western regulars over the years. Located just outside Chinatown, the restaurant has a bustling atmosphere yet retains the feel of a 'best-kept secret'. On a previous visit, we were bowled over by a sublime double-braised pork hotpot comprising slices of unctuous melt-in-the-mouth meat, cloaked in a rich savoury sauce. This time we opted for 'village duck': it was full of tender meat, with a hint of the earthy flavour of fermented beancurd. Not everything was up to scratch – chicken in hot sesame sauce was dry and bland – but Yming definitely executes some of its repertoire extremely well.

Meal deals

Arbutus *63-64 Frith Street, W1D 3JW (7734 4545).* Set meal (lunch daily, 5-7pm Mon-Sat) £13.50 2 courses. **Map** p268.
Modern European

Dong San *47 Poland Street, W1F 7NB (7287 0997).* Set lunch £7-£7.50 2 courses. **Map** p268. Korean

Jin *16 Bateman Street, W1D 3AH (7734 0908).* Set lunch £7.50 2 courses. **Map** p268. Korean

Patara *15 Greek Street, W1D 4DP (7437 1071).* Set lunch £11.95-£14.95 2 courses. **Map** p268. Thai

Pierre Victoire *5 Dean Street, W1V 5RN (7287 4582).* Set lunch £6.90 2 courses. Set dinner (4.30-7pm) £8.90 2 courses. **Map** p268. Brasserie

Red Fort *77 Dean Street, W1D 3SH (7437 2115).* Set lunch £12 2 courses. **Map** p268. North Indian

In the area

Burger Shack *147-149 Charing Cross Road, WC2H 0EE (7287 8728).* **Map** p268.

Busaba Eathai *106-110 Wardour Street, W1F 0TR (7255 8686).* **Map** p268.

Fresh & Wild *69-75 Brewer Street, W1F 9US (7434 3179).* **Map** p269.

Gourmet Burger Kitchen *15 Frith Street, W1D 4RE (7494 9533).* **Map** p268.

Konditor & Cook *Curzon Soho, 99 Shaftesbury Avenue, W1D 5DY (7292 1684).* **Map** p268.

Kulu Kulu *76 Brewer Street, W1F 9TX (7734 7316).* **Map** p269.

Maoz Vegetarian *4 Brewer Street, W1F 0SB (7734 9414).* **Map** p268.

Masala Zone *9 Marshall Street, W1F 7ER (7287 9966).* **Map** p268.

Nando's *10 Frith Street, W1D 3JF (7494 0932).* **Map** p268.

Paul *49 Old Compton Street, W1D 6HL (7287 6261).* **Map** p268.

Pizza Express *6 Upper James Street, Golden Square, W1F 9DG (7437 4550).* **Map** p268.

Pizza Express *20 Greek Street, W1D 4DU (7734 7430).* **Map** p268.

Pizza Express Jazz Club *10 Dean Street, W1D 3RW (7439 8722).* **Map** p268.

Wagamama *10A Lexington Street, W1F 0LD (7292 0990).* **Map** p268.

Yo! Sushi *52 Poland Street, W1V 3DF (7287 0443).* **Map** p268.

South Kensington

Daquise

*20 Thurloe Street, SW7 2LT (7589
6117). South Kensington tube.*
Meals served noon-11pm daily.
Average ££. **Set lunch** (noon-3pm
Mon-Fri) £7.50 2 courses incl glass of
wine, coffee. **Map** p278. Polish
Need an antidote to over-hyped
dining? Then repair to Daquise.
With over 50 years' experience, this
venerable South Ken institution
certainly knows what it's doing.
Everything is highly retro: from
the plastic tablecloths and the
worn leatherette banquettes to the
motherly, unreconstructed waiting
staff. Robust, beetrooty barszcz;
herrings with apple, smothered in
sour cream; and fluffy blini with
smoked salmon – all are here, just
like babcia used to make. We're big
fans of the mixed Polish platters:
ideal if you can't make up your mind
between all the calorific delights.
Both meat and vegetarian versions
offer a great combination of pierogi,
golabki (stuffed cabbage) and
bigos – and potato pancakes to
die for. We also love the zrazy and
nutty kasza gryczana (roasted
buckwheat). For home-style Polish
food, nobody does it better.

Jakob's

*20 Gloucester Road, SW7 4RB
(7581 9292). Gloucester Road tube.*
Meals served 8am-10pm daily.
Average ££. **Map** p278. Polish
It can get frenetic here on a busy
lunchtime as well-heeled locals
popping in for takeaway tabouleh
and olives get entangled with the
eat-in crowd. The system of staking
claim to a table, ordering drinks
from the staff, then rejoining the
throngs to order food at the counter
can be challenging. Once this is
negotiated, however, the superior
quality of the café shines through.
Choose from half a dozen hot dishes

such as grilled halibut, Armenian-
style dolma (the owner's Armenian
roots are shown also by the old
photos of goatherds in mountainous
landscapes) or chicken and pepper
stew served with two veg. We
particularly rate the wide choice of
salads; intense blistered grilled red
peppers, houmous, delectable grated
carrots with cumin and cinnamon,
and chewy brown rice with lentils
are among our favourites.

The Oratory

*234 Brompton Road, SW3 2BB
(7584 3493). South Kensington tube.*
Lunch served noon-4pm daily.
Dinner served 6-11pm Mon-Sat;
6-10.30pm Sun. **Average** £££.
Map p278. International
Few wine bars get it as right as the
Oratory, a delightful place for a
drink where the chef also turns out
restaurant-standard food. Far
enough from Harrods to miss the
tourist hordes, it's close to expensive
Georgian family villas that provide
a pleasant backdrop amid rustling
trees. The interior is just the right
side of camp with gold paint
swirling on blue walls around fish-
eye mirrors and multicoloured
chandeliers. Staff are well trained,
bringing plates of beautifully
char-grilled lamb, plus fast-fried
spinach and long-cooked puy lentils
promptly and without fuss. While
the Ralph Lauren-shirted clientele
may not be to everyone's taste,
everything else about this bar comes
highly recommended.

Spago

*6 Glendower Place, SW7 3DP
(7225 2407). South Kensington tube.*
Meals served noon-11.30pm daily.
Average ££. **Map** p278. Italian
With a mixture of homeland heroes
on the wall (note Marlon Brando as
the Godfather next to a Da Vinci
reproduction) and all the usual
suspects on the menu (pizza, pasta
and salads), the only thing that

broke the Italian illusion on our visit to this quirky trattoria was Stevie Wonder playing in the background. Light crispy pizzas, mostly fish-filled salads, and generously sized pastas: these are the reasons Spago draws a crowd, even in the week. Check out the daily changing specials board for own made dishes like vegetarian lasagne with aubergine and courgettes. Otherwise, do as most of the crowd: stick to the excellent pizzas.

Tootsie's Grill

107 Old Brompton Road, SW7 3LE (7581 8942/www.tootsies restaurants.co.uk). South Kensington tube. **Meals served** noon-11pm Mon-Thur; noon-11.30pm Fri; 10am-11.30pm Sat; 10am-11pm Sun. **Average** ££. **Map** p278. Burgers
Most branches of Tootsie's have elements of their decor in common: round wooden tables, bistro-style chairs, lots of windows and light. The menu promises the 'best burger you've ever eaten'. While that might not be the case (the gourmet burger market is fiercely competitive), the burgers aren't bad, and the selection is massive, ranging from the usual beef and vegetarian versions to Thai chicken burgers, pork and apple burgers, and lamb and rosemary variations. Further options include baby-back ribs (tender and juicy), steaks and other grills, salads and a wide choice of sandwiches. Shakes and malts vie with wine and beer on the drinks list. Great for families.

Meal deals

Awana *85 Sloane Avenue, SW3 3DX (7584 8880/www.awana.co.uk).* Set lunch £12.50 2 courses. **Map** p278. Malaysian
Ognisko Polskie *55 Exhibition Road, Prince's Gate, SW7 2PN (7589 4635/www.ognisko.com).* Set meal £11 3 courses. **Map** p278. Polish

In the area

Carluccio's Caffè *1 Old Brompton Road, SW7 3HZ (7581 8101).* **Map** p278.
Paul *17 Thurloe Place, SW7 2LQ (7581 6034).* **Map** p278.
Thai Square *19 Exhibition Road, SW7 2HE (7584 8359).* **Map** p278.

St James's

Meal deals

Quilon *41 Buckingham Gate, SW1E 6AF (7821 1899/www.the quilonrestaurant.com).* Set lunch £12.95 2 courses, £15.95 3 courses. **Map** p274. South Indian

Strand

Exotika

7 Villiers Street, WC2N 6NA (7930 6133). Embankment tube/Charing Cross tube/rail. **Meals served** 8am-11pm Mon-Wed; 8am-midnight Thur, Fri; noon-midnight Sat. **Average** ££. **Set meal** (5.30-8.30pm Fri, Sat) £5.50 1 course. **Map** p273. Café
This hole in the wall beside Charing Cross station shouts 'fast food'; with its high stools and bright lighting, it's not somewhere to linger. Despite this, the menu is much more diverse than the usual kebab or sandwich joints, with dishes ranging from Moroccan lamb tagine to chicken fajitas. In the past we've enjoyed the salads, such as 'italian parma' and 'spanish tuna', and the curries, especially rogan josh; but on our most recent visit, some chunks of haddock over packet egg noodles, supposedly rendered 'Japanese-style' by the addition of ginger, was soggy and disappointing. Tiramisu is served in an individual plastic tub, supermarket aisle-style. Unusually for a fast-food place, it's licensed, and sells a selection of potable wines as well as bottled lagers.

India Club

Second floor, Strand Continental Hotel, 143 Strand, WC2R 1JA (7836 0650). Covent Garden, Embankment or Temple tube/Charing Cross tube/ rail. **Lunch served** noon-2.30pm, **dinner served** 6-10.50pm daily. **Average ££. Set meal** £12-£15 per person (minimum 2) 4 courses. **Unlicensed. Corkage** no charge. **No credit cards. Map** p273. Indian
The location of India Club is unpromising: up two flights of dingy stairs. And though the restaurant's walls received a lick of lemon paint a few years back, its cracked red lino flooring, wobbly tables and mismatched seating look as if they haven't had a makeover for decades. Nevertheless, the Club exudes faded charm. Our top marks went to fried minced lamb, cooked with heaps of ginger and garlic, and studded with garden peas. Less impressive was the tandoori chicken, which tasted like an Indian-inspired rendition of deep-fried battered chicken. Lamb pilau, although hardly authentic, made a tasty dish with its robust masala base of fried onions, ginger, garlic and chillies working well with tender meat morsels and fluffy rice grains. Portions aren't huge, but the prices are rock bottom, and service is sweetness itself.

Meal deals

Smollensky's on the Strand

105 Strand, WC2R 0AA (7497 2101/www.smollenskys.co.uk). Set meal (noon-6.30pm, after 10pm Mon-Fri) £10.95 2 courses, £12.95 3 courses. **Map** p273. North American

In the area

Pizza Express *147 Strand, WC2R 1JA (7836 7716).* **Map** p273.

Exotica. See p95.

Pizza Express *450 Strand, WC2R 0RG (7930 8205).* **Map** *p273.*
Thai Square *21-24 Cockspur Street, SW1Y 5BN (7839 4000).* **Map** *p273.*
Thai Square on the Strand *148 Strand, WC2R 1JA (7497 0904).* Branch of Thai Square. **Map** *p273.*
Zizzi *73-75 Strand, WC2R 0DE (7240 1717).* **Map** *p273.*

Victoria

ASK

160-162 Victoria Street, SW1E 5LB (7630 8228/www.askcentral.co.uk). Victoria tube/rail. **Meals served** noon-11pm Mon-Sat; noon-10.30pm Sun. **Average** ££. **Map** p274.
Pizza & Pasta
Second in line after Pizza Express when it comes to dominating the capital's cheese-on-flat-bread scene, this Italianate chain might seem to be cut from the same cloth as its main rival – but it does have its own style. Namely, a slightly breezier atmosphere and a willingness to offer pizza combinations at which others might balk, such as huz-a-rie (spicy sausage, roast pepper, roast onions) or tropicale (ham and pineapple), the latter rarely being seen outside of Domino's these days. The vibe in this Victoria branch, as in most, is friendly and the quality of pizza usually good. We prefer Pizza Express's daintier options (just), but ASK seems to be pitched a notch above the other main pizza presence, its sister chain Zizzi. Service can be slow when things get busy, but ASK is a safe bet in the unlikely event of there being no 'Express in the vicinity.

Seafresh Fish Restaurant

80-81 Wilton Road, SW1V 1DL (7828 0747). Victoria tube/rail. **Lunch served** noon-3pm, **dinner served** 5-10.30pm Mon-Fri. **Meals served** noon-10.30pm Sat. **Average** ££. **Map** p275. Fish & Chips
Five minutes' walk from Victoria station, this central chippie attracts a mishmash of customers, from noisy suits to lost-looking tourists. The recently refurbished dining room is bright and airy, with light wooden tables and picture windows. All the fish is fried or grilled, and the portions are generous. One serving of chips does for two, especially as they can be a bit dry. Worthwhile alternatives are the own-made fish pie, and the fisherman's platter that comes with haddock, cod, lemon sole, skate wing, king prawns and calamares. The only downside is it's a little expensive for a chippie. Then again, you can order much of the menu at the significantly cheaper takeaway next door. Steer well clear of the spam fritters.

Sekara

*3 Lower Grosvenor Place, SW1W
0EJ (7834 0722). Victoria tube/rail.*
Lunch served noon-3pm, **dinner
served** 6-10pm daily. **Average**
£££. **Set lunch** (Mon-Sat) £4.40-
£6.95 1 course. **Set buffet** (Sun)
£9. **Map** p274. Sri Lankan
This intimate, primrose-coloured
eaterie is incredibly comfortable,
with softly spoken, exceedingly
polite service and the sort of thick
patterned carpet you'll want to sink
your feet into. To start, vegetable
pancake rolls and mutton rolls
looked similar, and were both
spikily spiced and flavoursome.
Next, meaty, robustly flavoured
seerfish curry came with a tangle of
expertly created string hoppers
made from roasted Sri Lankan red
rice. Vegetable kothu roti – stir-fried
with shredded leeks, red and green
chillies, peppers, carrots, fennel
seeds and curry leaves – was
substantially flavoured and light in
texture. Aubergine curry was
aromatic and gorgeously spiced
with cinnamon, cardamom, cloves
and star anise. An ideal place for a
relaxed, unhurried meal.

Tiles

*36 Buckingham Palace Road,
SW1W 0RE (7834 7761/www.tiles
restaurant.co.uk). Victoria tube/rail.*
Lunch served noon-2.30pm,
dinner served 5.30-10pm Mon-
Fri. **Average** £££. **Map** p274.
International
It may look more like a tea room
than a wine bar, but the paucity of
choice around Victoria makes Tiles
seem heaven-sent. The name comes
from the attractive stone flooring,
which you can view from tables
spread out in the narrow main room.
Strangely, most people seem to
opt for the basement bar, with its
IKEA-like tall paper lamps, dark
colours and average food. The food
disappointed a spot: fish cakes were

stodgy and lacking in flavour,
though they came with decent chips
and a tasty salad. Don't come here
expecting the best, but that said, you
could do a great deal worse.

In the area

Baker & Spice *54-56 Elizabeth
Street, SW1W 9PB (7730 3033).*
Map p275.
Nando's *107-108 Wilton Road,
SW1V 1DZ (7976 5719).* **Map** p275.
Wagamama *Roof garden level,
Cardinal Place, off Victoria Street,
SW1E 5JE (7828 0561).* **Map** p274.
Yo! Sushi *Main Concourse,
Victoria Station, SW1V 1JT.*
Map p274.
Zizzi *Unit 15, Cardinal Walk,
SW1E 5JE (7821 0402).* **Map** p274.

Westminster

★ The Vincent Rooms

*Westminster Kingsway College,
Vincent Square, SW1P 2PD (7802
8391/www.westking.ac.uk). St
James's Park tube/Victoria tube/rail.*
Lunch served noon-1.15pm Mon-
Fri. **Dinner served** 6-7.15pm Tue-
Thur. **Closed** 2 wks Apr, July-Sept,
2wks Dec-Jan. **Average** ££.
Map p275. International
It's a great idea: this restaurant
serves the day's lesson from the
college that trained chefs like Jamie
Oliver and Ainsley Harriott. Food
can veer from the likes of paupiettes
of sole stuffed with a salmon mousse
with chilled Cointreau grapes, to
braised belly of pork on black
pudding mash with cider jus. There
aren't many establishments offering
dishes like that for under a tenner.
Spinach and gorgonzola ravioli was
moreishly fresh, while Moroccan
lamb was fabulous, accompanied by
subtly spiced apricot and almond
couscous. The high ceiling, bay
windows overlooking a leafy square
and widely spaced tables all serve to
create a calm, elegant atmosphere.

WEST

Acton

The Coyote

100-102 Churchfield Road, W3 6DH (8992 6299). Acton Town tube/ Acton Central rail. **Dinner served** 5-11pm Mon-Fri. **Meals served** 11am-11pm Sat; 11am-10.30pm Sun. **Average £££.** North American

As at the Chiswick-based original, the Coyote's well-priced food speaks with a Southwestern US twang. Starters includes gooey nachos and tangy chicken wings alongside more novel options such as cool tuna ceviche marinated in lime juice, or spice-crusted baby-back ribs. Most are big enough to share. The mains list ranges from the exotic (peppered ostrich steak) to the mundane (burgers), but stick to dishes that use smoky Southwestern flavours: the lamb marinated in dried Central American spices and crusted in pecans is a prime example. Service is sharp and the mood relaxed – the Coyote is a fine choice way out west.

Home Cooking

17 High Street, W3 6NG (8992 9139). Acton Town tube/Acton Central rail. **Lunch served** 11am-3pm, **dinner served** 6-10pm Mon-Sat. **Meals served** noon-10pm Sun. **Average ££.** **Set lunch** £6 1 course incl beer or glass of wine. **Set dinner** £7.95 2 courses, £9.95 3 courses. International

Large portions and comforting fare are the hallmarks of a home-cooked meal and, happily, the menu at Home Cooking does not disappoint in either respect. Several of the starters were off the menu on the evening we visited, but Parma ham with mozzarella and rocket was certainly a decent fall-back. Feta parcels with yoghurt were slightly less successful – the yoghurt was not quite tart enough to cut through the oiliness of the pastry. Mains were excellent: pan-fried sea bream,

perfectly cooked and served with a moreish spring onion mash, along with a tender lamb steak that came with Lyonnaise potatoes and spinach. As my dining partner remarked, a restaurant that does exactly what it says on the, erm, tin.

★ North China

305 Uxbridge Road, W3 9QU (8992 9183). Acton Town tube. **Lunch served** noon-2.30pm, **dinner served** 6-11pm daily. **Average £££. Set meal** £14-£21 per person (minimum 2). Chinese

This smart, intimate restaurant in Acton Town is a 30-year-old treasure. It is evidently appreciated by the locals, so we were glad we'd reserved a table. When booking we'd ordered our Peking duck. This was duly presented to us in its golden-glazed glory, then whisked away to be carved, ready for us to wrap in handmade, wafer-thin pancakes. Rather than over-indulging on the two final stages of the duck ritual (stir-fry and soup), we turned our attention to other regional delights. Highlights (from the owner's home province of Shandong) included green beans in a deliciously sticky garlic sauce, gungbao prawns and various own-made dumplings and noodles. Service was as charming as the old Peking Opera photos lining the apricot-coloured walls.

Bayswater

Fresco

25 Westbourne Grove, W2 4UA (7221 2355). Bayswater or Royal Oak tube. **Meals served** 8am-11pm daily. **Average ££. Set meze** £9.95. **Map** p280. Lebanese

The juicer's constantly on the go at Fresco, squeezing all manner of produce for the single juices, combos, vegetable juices and fruity milkshakes that are at the heart of the café's winning formula. The cheery yellow decor and buzz of activity only adds to the sense of health and vitality. Portions are generous: £2.95 bought a huge sundae-style glass of tropical-tasting banana, strawberry and orange juice. Serious juice fans might enjoy the 'energisers', such as a carrot, broccoli and beets combination. At lunchtime, queues form at the counter for takeaways: on display are Lebanese vegetarian meze dishes (many of which can be served in pitta bread as a sandwich). Grilled chicken kebab and western-style sandwiches are also on the menu. There's also a table-service café if you want to eat in.

Hafez

5 Hereford Road, W2 4AB (7221 3167/7229 9398). Bayswater tube.
Meals served noon-midnight daily.
Average ££. No credit cards.
Map p280. Iranian
Outdoor tables on a quiet street off Westbourne Grove make this Persian restaurant a particularly apt choice for dinner on a balmy summer night. To start, kashk-e bademjan – baked aubergine purée, here mixed with yoghurt, walnuts and olive oil – was a richly flavoured accompaniment to the warm Iranian bread. Then came the kebabs. A twinning of lamb and minced lamb comprised beautiful juicy meat, cooked to perfection, served with the traditional buttery rice. Poussin wasn't so special: the perky notes we had been expecting from the saffron-tinged bird marinated in lime juice were hard to detect. Overall, though, Hafez provided us with a pleasant taste of Persian cooking.

Mr Fish   NEW

9 Porchester Road, W2 5DP (7229 4161). Royal Oak tube. **Meals served** 11am-11pm daily. **Average ££. Set lunch** (11am-3pm) £4.99 cod & chips incl soft drink, tea or coffee. **Map** p280. Fish & Chips

Walk through the takeaway area at Mr Fish and you'll find a restaurant that looks like a 1950s ice-cream parlour, with a black and white tiled floor, pink and lime coloured chairs, and wooden walls painted aquamarine. There's much more on the menu than the restaurant's name would suggest, with chicken (southern-fried or barbecue-roasted), hamburgers, beanburgers and wraps, as well as various fish options. To drink, you can choose from 18 wines, beers, spirits and liqueur coffees. The starters are fabulously cheap: seafood chowder cost only £2.20, and was thick and flavoursome. The haddock was a little skinny, but came in a delicious golden crispy batter. The mushy peas are a must: rich in flavour and thick and gloopy in texture.

Planet Organic   NEW

42 Westbourne Grove, W2 5SH (7727 2227). Bayswater tube.
Meals served 8.30am-8.30pm Mon-Sat; noon-6pm Sun.
Average ££. Map p280. Café
You don't need to be vegetarian to eat here, but it helps. Established in 1995, Planet Organic has branches in Fulham, W1's Torrington Place and this Bayswater outlet on Westbourne Grove, where diners queue for hot dishes such as vegan tofu stir-fry and vegetable lasagne, vegetarian shepherd's pie, and side dishes including roast tatties. Food is sensibly priced by tub size rather than weight; even the small £2.80 container (the largest is £5.80) holds plenty of tucker. In the chiller cabinets are sushi, wraps and salads from outside companies. If you're feeling flush treat yourself to some of the range of fun American snacks made from sesame seeds, almonds and the like. Clive's gluten-free cakes (made with proper ingredients like almond flour rather than ersatz flours) are utterly delicious too.

Meal deals

L'Accento 16 Garway Road,
W2 4NH (7243 2201). Set meal
£14.50 2 courses. **Map** p280. Italian
Royal China 13 Queensway,
W2 4QJ (7221 2535/www.royal
chinagroup.co.uk). Dim sum
(noon-5pm Mon-Sat; 11am-5pm Sun)
£2.20-£4.50. **Map** p281. Chinese

In the area

Alounak Kebab 44 Westbourne
Grove, W2 5SH (7229 0416).
Map p280.
ASK 41-43 Spring Street, W2 1JA
(7706 0707).
ASK Whiteley's Shopping Centre,
Queensway, W2 4SB (7792 1977).
Map p280.
Broadwalk Café Kensington
Gardens, W2 4RU (7034 0722).
Map p281.
Fresco Second floor, Whiteleys
Shopping Centre, Queensway,
W2 4YN (7243 4084). **Map** p280.
Mr Jerk 19 Westbourne Grove,
W2 4UA (7221 4678). **Map** p280.
Nando's 63 Westbourne Grove,
W2 4UA (7313 9506). **Map** p280.
Pizza Express 26 Porchester Road,
W2 6ES (7229 7784). **Map** p280.
Yo! Sushi Whiteley's Shopping
Centre, Queensway, W2 4YN
(7727 9392). **Map** p281.

Chiswick

Meal deals

Fish Hook 6-8 Elliott Road,
W4 1PE (8742 0766/). Set meal
(noon-2.30pm, 6-7pm Mon-Fri;
noon-3.30pm, 6-7pm Sat, Sun)
£12.50 1 course, £16.50 2 courses,
£18.50 3 courses. Fish
Sam's Brasserie & Bar
11 Barley Mow Passage, W4 4PH
(8987 0555/www.samsbrasserie.
co.uk). Set lunch (Mon-Fri) £11.50
2 courses, £15 3 courses; set dinner
(6.30-7.30pm daily) £13.50 2 courses.
Modern European

In the area

Carluccio's Caffè 344 Chiswick
High Road, W4 5TA (8995 8073).
The Coyote 2 Fauconberg Road,
W4 3JY (8742 8545).
Giraffe 270 Chiswick High Road,
W4 1PD (8995 2100).
Gourmet Burger Kitchen
131 Chiswick High Road, W4 2ED
(8995 4548).
Maison Blanc 303 Fulham Road,
SW10 9QH (7795 2663).
Nando's 187-189 Chiswick High
Road, W4 2DR (8995 7533).
Pizza Express 252 Chiswick High
Road, W4 1PD (8747 0193).
Strada 156 Chiswick High Road,
W4 1PR (8995 0004).
Tootsies Grill 148 Chiswick High
Road, W4 1PS (8747 1869).
Woodlands 12-14 Chiswick High
Road, W4 1TH (8994 9333).
Zizzi 231 Chiswick High Road,
W4 2DL (8747 9400).

Ealing

★ Café Grove

65 The Grove, W5 5LL (8810
0364). Ealing Broadway tube/rail.
Meals served 10.30am-11pm
Mon-Sat; 10.30am-10.30pm Sun.
Average ££. Polish
In an effort to rein in the hyperbole,
we will say that we can think of one
downside to an evening spent dining
at Café Grove – a meal there does
serve to encourage gluttony of the
highest order. A steaming bowl of
borscht made for the perfect starter.
We followed that with pierogi that
were little parcels of discovery –
some filled with potato, some
sauerkraut, some meat or cheese –
and each of the discoveries was a
happy one. Ordering from an ample
specials board provided the greatest
treat of all: golonka (stewed pork
knuckle) was exceptionally tender
and tasty, served with an enormous
pile of chips and veggies, all for less
than £7. Our advice: come with an
empty stomach, then try to fill it.

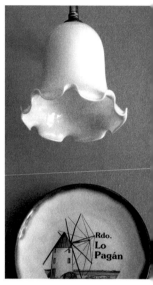

Los Molinos.
See p106.

Rdo.
Lo
Pagán

★ Sushi-Hiro

*1 Station Parade, Uxbridge Road,
W5 3LD (8896 3175). Ealing
Common tube.* **Lunch served**
11am-1.30pm, **dinner served**
4.30-9pm Tue-Sun. **Average ££.**
**Set meal £5-£14. No credit
cards.** Japanese

Sushi-Hiro, run by a friendly
husband-and-wife team, occupies a
prime position on the route from the
tube to the Japanese expat enclaves
of Ealing. Eating at the well-lit
counter or the half-dozen scrubbed
tables, you get no gimmicks or frills
but straight-forward sushi made
with fine ingredients and faultless
technique. The £12 ten-piece tokujo
set includes startlingly fresh scallop
and sweet prawn, plus melting chu-
toro (the belly area of the tuna) and
sea eel. The kampyo (pickled gourd)
maki and the inari (sushi rice
wrapped in deep-fried tofu) were

delicious too. This restaurant can be
busy even on weekday lunchtimes,
and note the early hours, which suit
its primarily Japanese clientele.

In the area

Carluccio's Caffé *5-6 The Green,
W5 5DA (8566 4458).*
Nando's *1-2 Station Buildings,
Uxbridge Road, W5 3NU
(8992 2290).*
Pizza Express *23 Bond Street,
W5 5AS (8567 7690).*
La Siesta *11 Bond Street, W5 5AP
(8810 0505).* Branch of Jamón Jamón.
Tootsies Grill *35 Haven Green,
W5 2NX (8566 8200).*

Hammersmith

Fez

*58 Fulham Palace Road, W6 9PH
(8563 8687). Hammersmith tube.*
Meals served noon-11.30pm daily.
Average ££. Set lunch £7.95-

£8.95 2 courses. **Set dinner**
£12.95 2 courses. **Map** p282.
North African

Changes at Fez since our last visit
mean that the upstairs room now
has a slightly barn-like feel with
heavy wooden tables in serried
ranks against the walls, rather than
the previous intimate arrangement
with decorative ironwork furniture.
Is the restaurant becoming more of
a fuelling stop for the small disco bar
downstairs? The menu has been
watered down to include many more
international dishes, but there's still
a reasonable range of Moroccan fare,
though fewer choices than before.
Zaalouk (served warm here) was
garlicky and packed quite a punch
with rich chilli undertones; light
crispy briouat (pastry) came stuffed
with goat's cheese; couscous was
served as a one-plate dish with no
extra broth or harissa to add, and

was consequently a touch too dry.
That said, tender well-cooked lamb
and vibrantly spiced merguez
sitting atop juicy squash, courgettes,
carrots and chickpeas was a very
tasty dish indeed. Finishing with
fragrant mint tea, we were left
satisfied by the all-round experience.

Lowiczanka Polish Cultural Centre

*First floor, 238-246 King Street, W6
0RF (8741 3225). Ravenscourt Park
tube. Café* **Open** 9.30am-9pm daily.
Restaurant **Lunch served** 12.30-
3pm daily. **Dinner served** 6.30-
11pm Mon-Thur, Sun; 7pm-midnight
Fri, Sat. **Average** ££. **Set lunch**
(Mon-Sat) £8.50 3 courses; (Sun)
£9.90 3 courses. **Map** p282. Polish

Functioning like a portal into a
different country and another time,
Lowiczanka is housed in a concrete
cultural centre that seems to have
been airlifted-in from a pre-

Time Out **Cheap Eats** 105

Solidarity version of Warsaw. Indeed, the Soviet-style welcome (dour security guards instruct you to check-in your bag, whether you want to or not) begins immediately. The restaurant, tucked away on the second floor, resembles a Travelodge breakfast room. However, Barszcz (borscht) with mushroom dumplings, and a rich wild boar pâté were both great starters. To follow, the shared Polish 'meze' for two showcased some of the best of the menu: delicious smoked sausage, potato balls with minced meat, golabki, meaty hunter's stew and a superb carrot salad. Our advice: come for the food, not the decor.

Los Molinos

127 Shepherd's Bush Road, W6 7LP (7603 2229). Hammersmith tube. **Lunch served** noon-3pm Mon-Fri. **Dinner served** 6-10.45pm Mon-Sat. **Average** ££. **Map** p282. Spanish

Los Molinos is a perennial favourite with local diners on account of its welcoming atmosphere, cheerful and attentive service, and accomplished kitchen. The small main dining room is done out sweetly – peach walls, blond wood, a little garden visible out back – and despite its size it manages not to feel overcrowded even when the place is packed, as it was on the weeknight of our visit. Highlights of our tapas were squid cooked in its own ink, and veal in a cream and brandy sauce; grilled sardines were also good. Two textbook tapas choices – albóndigas and patatas bravas – were not successful: both came in very thin, almost watery sauces. Originality is laudable, but we're not sure it's a good idea in this case; these dishes are old favourites. But they hardly detracted from a very pleasant meal, accompanied by some bottles of the Spanish lager, Estrella.

Polanka

258 King Street, W6 0SP (8741 8268). Ravenscourt Park tube. **Meals served** noon-10pm Mon-Sat; noon-8pm Sun. **Average** ££. **Corkage** £3 wine; £5 spirits. **Map** p282. Polish

You'll find Polanka tucked away at the back of a Polish delicatessen. Jars of gherkins and packets of dumpling mix give way to a small informal room sporting blond wood, paper tablecloths and bright lighting. Straw dolls and bric-a-brac festoon the walls. Service was slow and a little haphazard on our visit, despite the small number of diners. Our soup and wine orders were mixed up, but all was taken in good humour – why grumble when the house red is only £8? Cooking is a homely affair: comfort food rather than anything more ambitious. We started with wonderfully savoury cabbage soup and a tangy bowl of red borscht. To follow, Hussar's roast beef with potatoes was hearty and filling, while the golabki was pure comfort. For dessert, choose from a shelf of Polish cakes.

★ Sagar

157 King Street, W6 9JT (8741 8563). Hammersmith tube/266 bus. **Lunch served** noon-2.45pm Mon-Fri. **Dinner served** 5.30-10.45pm Mon-Thur; 5.30-11.30pm Fri. **Meals served** noon-11.30pm Sat; noon-10.45pm Sun. **Average** ££. **Set thali** £8.95-£11.45. **Map** p282. Indian

Since our first visit to this soothing, minimally decorated restaurant when it opened in 2002, we've had consistently fabulous meals. Our most recent trip didn't disappoint. Crisp, fluffy masala dosa came with a beautifully spiced filling of roughly mashed potatoes. Delicate lemon rice was so delicious we could have eaten a large bowlful on its own. Sagar specialises in Udupi cuisine – the natural, additive-free, vegetarian, temple-style cooking from Karnataka, a coastal region in southern India. Udupi curries are often based on pumpkins and marrows, and Sagar's vegetable kootu (yoghurt- and coconut-based curry) and sukee bhaji (pan-fried vegetables) are made from daily changing veg. On our visit, kootu was made from chow-chow (a type of gourd): it was exquisite. Service was friendly and professional.

Meal deals

The Brackenbury *129-131 Brackenbury Road, W6 0BQ (8748 0107).* Set lunch (12.30-2.45pm Mon-Fri) £12.50 2 courses. **Map** p282. Modern European

In the area

Pizza Express *158 Fulham Palace Road, W6 9ER (8563 2064).* **Map** p282.

Holland Park

In the area

Maison Blanc *102 Holland Park Avenue, W11 4UA (7221 2494).* **Map** p281.
Tootsies Grill *120 Holland Park Avenue, W11 4UA (7229 8567).* **Map** p281.

Kensington

Papaya Tree

209 Kensington High Street, W8 6BD (7937 2260). High Street Kensington tube. **Lunch served** noon-3.30pm, **dinner served** 6-11pm daily. **Average £££. Set lunch** £5-£7 1 course. **Map** p278. Thai
With its understated all-white decor, Papaya Tree exudes a Zen-like calm and feels pleasantly spacious and airy, in spite of its basement setting. The usual Thai favourites are interspersed with a few more interesting departures, such as crab claws in yellow curry or fisherman's hot pot. Service is obliging and attentive; even on a busy evening, our waitress brought over glasses of tap water unprompted. A satisfying dish of stir-fried duck with chilli and holy basil had a subtle, spicy kick, while king prawns with peanut and red curry was well-executed and full of flavour. Prices are generally slightly on the high side, so you may struggle to stay within budget.

Stick & Bowl

31 Kensington High Street, W8 5NP (7937 2778). High Street Kensington tube. **Meals served** 11.30am-11pm daily. **Average £. No credit cards. Map** p278. Oriental
This bustling Chinese canteen is an anomaly in Kensington High Street, where smart, chi-chi establishments are more the done thing. Portions are workmanlike and prices are low; plates of noodles are immense, while half a crispy duck, one of the more expensive dishes, is a meal for two in itself. It does a roaring trade, with a steady stream of office workers, students and shoppers popping in for takeaways or perching on the bar stools to eat at the narrow Formica counters. Sometimes you have to wait, but staff are quick to point out available seats. Quality can be slightly hit and miss and investing in the slightly more expensive dishes does pay dividends: a portion of prawns with black bean sauce (£6) was packed with plump and juicy crustaceans, whereas beef with ginger and spring onion (£4.60) was let down by some cheap and thoroughly tasteless meat.

Meal deals

11 Abingdon Road *11 Abingdon Road, W8 6AH (7937 0120/ www.abingdonroad.co.uk).* Set lunch (noon-2.30pm Mon-Sat) £13.50 2 courses. **Map** p278. Modern European

Gastro goners

You might wonder why there are no gastropubs listed elsewhere in this guide. It's simple: over the last couple of years gastropub prices have crept up, in many cases exceeding the cost of an equivalent meal in a restaurant. There are now so few good gastropubs offering a decent cheap eat that we list all nine of them below.

So what went wrong with the democratically-priced gastropub? When the Eagle pub in Clerkenwell installed an open kitchen, a blackboard menu and Mediterranean cuisine back in 1991, the aim of founders Michael Belben and (chef) David Eyre was that a pub should also be an affordable, casual, fun place to eat; somewhere you can seamlessly make the transition from pint to polenta, and back again. A spate of other chefs saw what the Eagle had done, and took advantage of the numerous pubs being sold off by the brewery-pub conglomerates as a result of anti-monopoly legislation at the time. The rents were cheap, the sites had planning permission to serve food and drink – and a whole generation of chefs wanting their own place became pub landlords. Now, there's barely a neighbourhood of London without its own gastropub – or several.

In recent years the gastropub has gone upmarket, with much investment in smart interiors, menus boasting increasingly complex dishes, and – the coup de grâce for the gastropub concept – dining areas segregated from the bar. But, as Michael Belben once said, 'A gastropub should be a pub. Keep it real.' Here are a few that keep it real.

Anchor & Hope *36 The Cut, SE1 8LP (7928 9898). Map p288.*
Castle *65 Camberwell Church Street, SE5 8TR (7277 2601).*
Charles Lamb *16 Elia Street, N1 8DE (7837 5040). Map p299.*
Coach & Horses *26-28 Ray Street, EC1R 3DJ (7278 8990). Map p270.*
Cumberland Arms *29 North End Road, W14 8SZ (7371 6806).*
Eagle *159 Farringon Road, EC1R 3AL (7837 1353). Map p270.*
Earl Spencer *260-262 Merton Road, SW18 5JL (8870 9244).*
Freemasons *2 Wandsworth Common Northside, SW18 2SS (7326 8580). Map p284.*
Royal Oak *73 Columbia Road, E2 7RG (7729 2220). Map p294.*

Randa *23 Kensington Church Street, W8 4LF (7937 5363).* Set lunch (noon-5pm Mon-Fri) £12 2 courses. **Map** p278. Lebanese

Whits *21 Abingdon Road, W8 6AH (7938 1122/www.whits.co.uk).* Set lunch (12.30-2.30pm Tue-Fri) (express menu) £12.95 2 courses incl wine. **Map** p278. Modern European

In the area

Al-Dar *221 Kensington High Street, W8 6FG (7938 1547).* **Map** p278.

ASK *222 Kensington High Street, W8 7RG (7937 5540).* **Map** p278.

Café Pasta *229-231 High Street Kensington, W8 6SA (7937 6314).* **Map** p278.

Feng Sushi *24 Kensington Church Street, W8 4EP (7937 7927).* **Map** p278.

Giraffe *7 Kensington High Street, W8 5NP (7938 1221).* **Map** p278.

Maison Blanc *7A Kensington Church Street, W8 4LF (7937 4767).* **Map** p278.

Ottolenghi *1 Holland Street, W8 4NA (7937 0003).* **Map** p278.

Pâtisserie Valerie *27 Kensington Church Street, W8 4LL (7937 9574).* **Map** p278.

Pizza Express *35 Earl's Court Road, W8 6ED (7937 0761).* **Map** p278.

Prezzo *35A Kensington High Street, W8 5BA (7937 2800).* **Map** p278.

Ranoush Juice Bar *86 Kensington High Street, W8 4SG (7938 2234).* **Map** p278.

Strada *29 Kensington High Street, W8 5NP (7938 4648).* **Map** p278.

Wagamama *26-28 Kensington High Street, W8 4PF (7376 1717).* **Map** p278.

Ladbroke Grove

Armadillo Café NEW

11 Bramley Road, W10 6SZ (7727 9799). Latimer Road tube. **Open** 8am-4.30pm Mon-Fri; 10am-3pm Sat. **Average** ££. **Unlicensed.**

Corkage no charge. **No credit cards**. **Map** p282. Café

This small café caters mainly to people working at the Chrysalis offices next door, and there are lots of pavement tables in summer where you can sit and spot Heart FM's presenters on their way to work. High-class coffee is a speciality, and food comes from the attached Armadeli, which has links to Wiltshire farms and organic suppliers. A selection of tasty ready-made sandwiches with good bread includes classics such as Wiltshire ham and farmhouse cheddar; ingredients are of a high quality. A Mexican tuna baguette was disappointingly low on the Mexican, with just a bit of sorry sweetcorn to justify the name. Still, own-made brownies were delicious and sold out by early afternoon.

Babes 'n' Burgers NEW

275 Portobello Road, W11 1LR (7229 2704). Ladbroke Grove tube. **Meals served** 10am-11pm daily. **Average** ££. **Map** p280. Burgers

The transformation of the dedicated kiddy room into an eating area dominated by a large screen shows that B&B has grown up a little. Not too much – there are still toys, children's meals and high chairs – but the children aren't the only pebbles on this beach. The front area of the café is presided over by a perspiring chef and sidekicks, flipping organic hamburgers, constructing salads, whizzing smoothies and shouting at the waiting staff. As 'healthy' fast food is the selling point, we opted for the 'halloumicado' burger, a toasted bun filled with seared halloumi cheese, avocado and plenty of sliced salad items, washed down with a smoothie (the orange and strawberry was very refreshing). We passed on side orders of lecithin granules in favour of marinated olives and guacamole.

Books for Cooks `NEW`

*4 Blenheim Crescent, W11 1NN
(7221 1992). Ladbroke Grove tube.*
Open 10am-6pm Tue-Sat. **Set
lunch** £4 1 course, £5 2 courses,
£7 3 courses. **Unlicensed. Corkage**
no charge. **Map** p280. Café

This iconic bookshop is a treasure-
trove for cookery book collectors,
but the café at the back of the shop
is much more hit-or-miss. The cooks
are amateurs, and every day prepare
a handful of dishes from the shop's
thousands of books. There are only
six small tables, yet even by 1.30pm
the café can often run out of dishes;
on our most recent visit they could
only offer an (excellent) bruschetta
starter and a choice of cakes for
afters. Had we arrived earlier we
might have been able to enjoy
chicken pasta with green beans
and goat's cheese from Peter
Gordon's *Salads* book. Despite its
shortcomings – you can't even book
a table – the Books for Cooks café is
an institution we can recommend for
a proper lunch – just make sure that
you get there early enough.

★ Café Garcia

*248-250 Portobello Road, W11 1LL
(7221 6119). Ladbroke Grove tube.*
Tapas served 9am-5pm Mon-Thur,
Sun; 8am-11pm Fri, Sat. **Average**
££. **Map** p280. Spanish

Annexed to the veteran Spanish
supermarket/importers R Garcia
and Son, this place is just what its
name suggests: a café. There is no
table service. You point out your
tapas choices from under the glass
counters at the front and then take a
seat; your selections are dished out,
warmed (if necessary) and brought
over. It's a straightforward, no-frills
set-up – and a tremendous success.
We picked a faultless tortilla with
chorizo, some albóndigas in a nice,
rich ragú, a fine salt-cod empanada
(stuffed pastry) and some asparagus
wrapped in serrano ham. A vast

Armadillo Café.
See p109.

paella was hauled out just as we
finished eating; it looked fantastic.
Garcia's classy and bright interior
wasn't that busy even though it was
market day on Portobello Road. The
other remarkable thing was our bill:
£21 covered all the food, plus a
fantastic dessert (chestnut-cream
cake), two espressos and two beers.
Top marks.

Galicia

*323 Portobello Road, W10 5SY
(8969 3539). Ladbroke Grove tube.*
Lunch served noon-3pm Tue-Sun.
Dinner served 7-11.30pm Tue-Sat;
7-10.30pm Sun. **Average** £££. **Set
lunch** £7.50 3 courses; (Sun) £8.50
3 courses. **Map** p280. Spanish

Most Spanish restaurants in London
try – with varying degrees of
success – to emulate a Spanish tapas
bar or taberna; Galicia is the real
thing. The staff are Spanish, the
neighbourhood is Spanish (the
restaurant forming the social hub of
upper Portobello's little Hispanic
enclave), the clientele is largely
Spanish, and the cooking is
convincingly, authentically Spanish.
You might also say that the
occasionally slow service and the
odd substandard plate show a
stereotypically Spanish laxness of

approach. Our misgivings are minimal, however. Every element of our most recent meal was in order: excellent tapas, such as fried whitebait (fresh fish, crispy batter), chorizo al vino (rich, succulent chunks) and garlic prawns (enormous and perfectly cooked) were followed by substantial, hearty mains. Both hake with clams, prawns and asparagus, and veal escalope with mushrooms boasted large, tender cuts of fish and meat dressed in first-rate sauces.

George's Portobello Fish Bar

329 Portobello Road, W10 5SA (8969 7895). Ladbroke Grove tube.
Meals served 11am-11.45pm Mon-Fri; 11am-9pm Sat; noon-9.30pm Sun.
Average £. Corkage no charge.
No credit cards. Map p280.
Fish & Chips

Open since 1961 and boasting Julien Macdonald and Jamie Oliver among its famous advocates, this small, family run business is clearly doing something right. Join the queue behind suited businessmen, dusty workmen and mums and children in this cramped American-style diner for baked spuds, shish kebabs, BBQ chicken, veggie burgers or the

obvious fish and chips. Fresh cod (£5) is battered to perfection while you wait and thrown into a bag with a week's worth of thick cut, non-greasy chips (from £1.20), all wrapped up with a quaint slice of lemon. Sink your teeth into this good stuff and you'll see why George's is more than just a traditional British hangover haunt.

★ Hummingbird NEW

133 Portobello Road, W11 2DY (7229 6446). Ladbroke Grove or Notting Hill Gate tube.
Meals served 10am-5.30pm Tue-Sat; 11am-5pm Sun.
Average £. Map p280. Café
A grotto for cup cakes, frostings and icings, Hummingbird celebrates the Stateside version of sweet extravagance with aplomb, self-assurance and bling. Forget delicate new-wave flavours – this spot delivers a mean wedge of devil's food cake, the best blueberry cake in town, and lemon pie crowned with a mile-high duvet of meringue. It's a homely set-up, just a couple of stools and a few tables outside the café, but it's the cake and cup cake display that really impresses. On our visit, two staff members, armed with palette knives, a tray of cup cakes

and a cavernous bowl of icing, were slathering on the frosting, then selling them on within minutes. We struck gold with our choice: a dreamy match of chocolate sponge and caramel frosting – at less than £2 each, they're a bargain.

★ Moroccan Tagine

95 Golborne Road, W10 5NL (8968 8055). Ladbroke Grove or Westbourne Park tube. **Meals served** 11am-11pm daily. **Average £L. Unlicensed** no alcohol allowed. **Map** p280. North African

Despite being a no-frills street café in a relatively insalubrious area of west London, the cooking at Moroccan Tagine puts to shame almost every other North African restaurant in town. It's the work of the genial, bearded Hassan, a Berber from the Rif Mountains; his extensive menu boasts no less than six kinds of lamb tagine alone, including with artichokes, with prawns and boiled egg, and with okra and tomatoes. Also, with one of London's best fishmongers up the street, it's not surprising that there's also a good showing of seafood: sardines stuffed or grilled, calamares, fish tagine and a fish platter with salad. Our only complaint is that it's really messy trying to debone sardines when they sit on top of a mound of unnecessary salad. There's no alcohol, but there are fruit cocktails, such as a 'Berber cooler' of raspberries, strawberries and blackberries shaken with lemon, apple and fresh orange juice.

Oporto Pâtisserie

62A Golborne Road, W10 5PS (8968 8839). Ladbroke Grove or Westbourne Park tube. **Meals served** 8am-7pm daily. **Average £. No credit cards. Map** p280. Portuguese

Like Lisboa Pâtisserie (57 Golborne Road, W10 5NR, 8968 5242) next door, this similarly busy, similarly intentioned Portuguese outfit does what it sets out to do, providing a range of generic and nation-specific snacks and drinks – but the quality is very variable, and it's not the case that the Portuguese pastries and fritters are the best choice. A chicken fritter was especially disappointing, its taste unclear. Pastéis de nata always work – but it would be time to pack up and head for the port if you were of Portuguese persuasion and couldn't deliver a good custard tart. On one level, it doesn't matter; prices are low and nobody's expecting Michelin stars, but choose carefully. Stick to what looks good on the outside, because the interior is sometimes unknown, even unappealing, territory.

Uli

16 All Saints Road, W11 1HH (7727 7511). Ladbroke Grove or Westbourne Park tube. **Dinner served** 6.45-11.15pm daily. **Average £L. Map** p280. Oriental

This sweetly decorated eaterie boasts an outdoor patio where Salman Rushdie was dining on the night of our visit. Little touches such as cushioned seats and an abundance of potted plants convey a feeling of comfort and attention to detail. The menu offers standard pan-Asian staples interspersed with several intriguing choices for those who feel adventurous. We opted for more unusual dishes: both fried oysters and salt-and-pepper frogs' legs were juicy and tender, but their flavour was overwhelmed by overly thick batter. A plate of mildly hot chillies stuffed with prawns and served with black bean sauce went down a treat, but our final dish of squid with sweet chillies took an unreasonably long time to arrive and even when it did come we found it was undercooked. We'd advise ordering carefully and sticking to the tried-and-tested favourites.

Uncles

*305 Portobello Road, W10 5TD
(8962 0090). Ladbroke Grove tube.*
Meals served 9am-6pm Mon-Sun.
Average ££. **Map** p280. Café
Snuggled between antique clothing
stores and arty boutiques just north
of Portobello Market, this
kaleidoscopic café is frequented by
Notting Hill's arty set. Choose from
all day breakfasts, hefty sandwiches
and burgers, or from the daily
changing blackboard menu with its
choice of meat and vegetarian dishes
(we saw moussaka, salmon steak and
spaghetti bolognese). There's also a
choice of paninis, and pint-sized fresh
juices. We went for the grilled
chicken sandwich with chorizo,
avocado and salad, which was huge;
similarly, a standard burger alone
was big enough for two without its
chips or salad accompaniment. Staff
were too cool to smile, but faultlessly
efficient. Watch out for Saturdays if
you like your food fast: the menu
says that's when Uncles gets busy.

Meal deals

Essenza *210 Kensington Park
Road, W11 1NR (7792 1066/
www.essenza.co.uk).* Set lunch
(12.30-6.30pm Mon-Fri) £10
2 courses. **Map** p280. Italian
Food@The Muse *269 Portobello
Road, W11 1LR (7792 1111/
www.foodatthemuse.co.uk).* Set
lunch (noon-4pm) £6 1 course.
Map p280. International
Mediterraneo *37 Kensington Park
Road, W11 2EU (7792 3131/www.
mediterraneo-restaurant.co.uk.* Set
lunch (12.30-3pm Mon-Fri) £12.50
2 courses incl coffee. **Map** p280.
Italian
Mika *78 Tavistock Road, W11 1AN
(7243 8518/www.mikalondon.com).*
Set lunch £5.50-£8.50. **Map** p280.
Japanese

In the area
S&M Café *268 Portobello Road,
W10 5TY (8968 8898).* **Map** p280.

Maida Vale

★ Red Pepper

*8 Formosa Street, W9 1EE (7266
2708). Warwick Avenue tube.*
Dinner served 6.30-11pm Mon-Fri.
Meals served noon-11pm Sat;
noon-10.30pm Sun. **Average** ££.
Map p283. Pizza & Pasta
Red Pepper is packed every night of
the week (so do book), but diners
definitely come for the food, not the
atmosphere. The place is tiny, the
tables are cramped, the acoustics are
lousy, and service can be scatty (five
waiters tried to give us a bottle of
wine when we'd asked for a glass).
The food, however, makes up for all
shortcomings. A starter of deep-fried
baby squid tempura, surrounding a
pile of thin threads of deep-fried
courgette, fresh, crisp and cloud-
light, received a rapturous response.
Likewise, spaghetti with crab,
tomatoes and rocket couldn't be
faulted. Best was the basilico pizza:
a thin, elastic crust topped with
tomato sauce, fresh tomato,
gorgeously textured mozzarella and
basil oil. For those with healthy
appetites, desserts such as tiramisu
or pears poached in red wine keep to
the Italian theme, as does the short,
all-Italian wine list.

Notting Hill

Costas Fish Restaurant

*18 Hillgate Street, W8 7SR (7727
4310). Notting Hill Gate tube.*
Lunch served noon-2.30pm,
dinner served 5.30-10.30pm
Tue-Sat. **Average** £. **No credit
cards**. **Map** p281. Fish & Chips
Some of the best fish and chip shops
in London are run by Greek-
Cypriots, and Costas is a textbook
example. It is tucked away off the
noisy main road, and at first sight
looks like a simple takeaway. But a
half-hidden restaurant right of the

Café Garcia. See p110.

counter offers a private, quiet sanctuary. Costas has Greek-Cypriot starters of pitta bread with houmous or taramasalata, and avocado in a number of styles. The main course choices are somewhat more limited, with the standard fish you'd expect as well as chicken goujons. On our last visit the haddock tasted a little sour, but this was not in keeping with the usual high standards. The chips were as good as ever: hand-cut and moist. To finish, there's baklava, banana fritters and super-strength Greek coffee.

Feng Sushi

101 Notting Hill Gate, W11 3JZ (7727 1123). Notting Hill Gate tube. **Meals served** 11.30am-10pm Mon-Wed; 11.30am-11pm Thur-Sat; noon-10pm Sun. **Average** ££. **Set meal** £8 bento box. **Map** p281. Japanese
Branches of this expanding chain stick to what seems a successful formula, offering eat-in dining alongside a busy takeaway business. Feng Sushi is notable for a couple of reasons: it takes sourcing seriously (the salmon is sustainably farmed in Loch Duart, for instance); and its menu has enough dishes to satisfy vegetarians – even vegans won't go hungry. We tried dishes with a 'new' symbol next to them, including 'new-style' sea bass sashimi, which came dressed with chilli oil, sesame oil and fresh coriander: it was both pretty and flavourful. Sushi of line-caught Cornish mackerel tasted super-fresh, and a salad of cold soba noodles topped with pine nuts was enlivened by peppery rocket leaves and yuzu (a citrus fruit). We've found staff at this branch more attentive than at the other Feng Sushis. A drawback, though, is seating that verges on the downright Lilliputian (on tiny rattan stools) in the upstairs dining room.

Greek Affair NEW

1 Hillgate Street, W8 7SP (7792 5226). Notting Hill Gate tube. **Lunch served** noon-3pm, **dinner served** 5.30-11pm Tue-Sun (Oct-Apr). **Meals served** noon-11pm daily (May-Sept). **Average** £££. **Unlicensed**. **Corkage** £1.80. **Map** p281. Greek
This charming, laid-back restaurant is a welcoming spot: bright and airy on the first floor, where diners share a huge wooden table, and intimate downstairs. The emphasis is on mezédes and the selection, both hot and cold, is extensive. A simple dish of revithósalata mé spanáki (warm salad of chickpeas and spinach) had been excellently prepared. However, in contrast, kalámari cooked in a soupy tomato sauce tasted somewhat flat. Of the mains, a huge slab of hearty moussaka was gorgeously satisfying. But a plate of garides mesogíon (prawns in a tomato and pepper sauce, served over a mound of rice) proved rather dull; the underwhelming sauce and the slippery, painstaking-to-peel prawns proved to be something of an appetite suppressant. Never mind: decadent honey-soaked kataïfi (syrup-soaked 'shredded-wheat' rolls), which arrived with the bill, was a lovely sweetener.

Nyonya

2A Kensington Park Road, W11 3BU (7243 1800). Notting Hill Gate tube. **Lunch served** 11.30am-2.45pm, **dinner served** 6-10.30pm Mon-Fri. **Meals served** 11.30am-10.30pm Sat, Sun. **Average** ££. **Set lunch** (Mon-Fri) £8 2 courses. **Map** p281. Malaysian
This is as close as Malaysian dining gets to groovy: a bright, light dining room with moulded stools, and young, good-natured staff. The menu offers a variety of dishes based on the uniquely fused cooking style of Straits-born Chinese-Malay

(Peranakan) families. Some servings are quite small, and dishes tend to come in a rush, but the food is well put together, and flavours are bright, snappy and not overly sweet. Star of the night was nasi lemak, an uncharacteristically large serving of steamed coconut rice, moist curried chicken, crisply fried mackerel and chilli-laden sambol sauce. We also liked the soft crunch of beansprouts with salted fish, and the scorchy, earthy flavour of the Penang char kway teow noodles with lup cheong (sausage) and prawns, served with rice sticks instead of noodles.

In the area

Apostrophe *138 Notting Hill Gate, W11 3QG (7243 1683).* **Map** p281.
ASK *145 Notting Hill Gate, W11 3LB (7792 9942).* **Map** p281.
Pizza Express *137 Notting Hill Gate, W11 3GQ (7229 6000).* **Map** p281.
Zizzi *2-6 Notting Hill Gate, W11 3JE (7243 2888).* **Map** p281.

Olympia

★ Alounak NEW

10 Russell Gardens, W14 8EZ (7603 7645). Kensington (Olympia) tube/rail. **Meals served** noon-midnight daily. **Average** ££. **Corkage** no charge. Iranian
Alounak impresses with its consistency. We've been eating here since at least the early 1990s, when the restaurant was a prefab cabin beside the railway tracks, and we've yet to come away less than 100% satisfied. Except perhaps for the marinated grilled sea bass (served with head and tail intact), the menu has little to differentiate it from London's other Iranian restaurants. Starters include the usuals, such as mirza ghasemi (crushed baked aubergines, tomatoes, garlic and herbs, mixed with egg), halim

bademjan (mashed char-grilled aubergine with onions, herbs and walnuts) and salad olivieh, while the mains are kebabs. But when the food arrives the rice is always light and fluffy, and the meat always tender and flavourful. In addition, Alounak scores highly with us for its bright, cheerful and family-friendly atmosphere, although the cosy front area with its rusticated brickwork and hanging bauble lights is far preferable to the rear part of the restaurant, which is slightly gloomy and often filled with large parties.

Chez Marcelle

34 Blythe Road, W14 0HA (7603 3241). Kensington (Olympia) tube/rail. **Meals served** 5-10pm Tue-Thur; noon-10pm Fri-Sun. **Average** ££. **No credit cards**. **Map** p282. Lebanese
Marcelle has been running her restaurant for 13 years now. It is still very much a one-woman show, with this formidable Lebanese lady doing all the cooking herself in the large kitchen that occupies the rear of the one modest room. The menu is a laminated card of 36 meze, plus standard grilled meat mains. Portions are generous: the falafel are the size of tennis balls, and chicken livers come in a mountainous heap, swimming in a rich gravy far too good to leave (the dish comes with a heap of bread for mopping up said gravy). Three or four meze make more than a meal for two, so order sparingly. Mains include a highly recommended 'stuffed lamb', which isn't stuffed but baked, cut thinly, layered on cinnamon rice and topped with sliced pistachios and almonds. Note that the restaurant is cash or cheque only, with the nearest ATM a 20-minute walk away on Kensington High Street.

Yas

*7 Hammersmith Road, W14 8XJ
(7603 9148). Kensington (Olympia)
tube/rail.* **Meals served** noon-
4.30am daily. **Average** ££. Iranian

Yas is an unassuming Iranian
neighbourhood eatery with sunny
yellow walls and a blue-tiled clay
oven fulfilling the promise of
delicious, puffy, fresh-baked Iranian
bread. The modest menu offers the
usual Iranian staples: kashk-e
bademjan (aubergine purée with
mint and goats cheese), good salad
olivieh, and, our favourite, sabzi-e
paneer – a pile of mouth-tingling
fresh herbs (in which tarragon is the
predominant flavour) with salty feta.
A lamb, aubergine and split pea
stew with dried limes is a revelation
for tastebuds unaccustomed to
Iranian flavours – a deliciously
robust sauce with the sharp hook of
the limes tempered by a certain
mustiness. The lamb itself, though,
was rather meagre and tired-tasting.
Mains all come with huge mounds of
the fluffiest, lightest chello rice with
a characteristic crunchy crust. It's
worth a visit just for this.

In the area

Pizza Express *The Addison
Rooms, Olympia Exhibition Centre,
Hammersmith Road, W14 8UX
(7602 6677).*

Shepherd's Bush

Abu Zaad

*29 Uxbridge Road, W12 8LH (8749
5107). Shepherd's Bush tube.* **Meals
served** 11am-11pm daily. **Average**
££. **Map** p282. Syrian

A rather forbidding corner site
complete with barred windows
gives way to a far cheerier interior
at Abu Zaad, with artefacts and
giant-sized photographs of
Damascus on the walls, a central
juicing and coffee-making area, and

a grill station at the back. Some of
the dishes in our meze lunch may
have lacked the precision and vivid
colours of an Edgware Road version,
but nearly everything was full of
taste. Batata hara (potatoes fried
with peppers and chilli) had plenty
of bite, fattoush (vegetable salad)
was crunchy and spicy. Fatayer bi
lahm were little canoes of soft pastry
filled with delicately spiced minced
lamb. Only foul makala (broad
beans with coriander and lemon,
cooked in olive oil) proved to be
something of a disappointment,
featuring flavourless beans with
chewy skins. A glass of sweet own-
made lemonade proved to be a good
accompaniment to a happy meal.

Adam's Café

*77 Askew Road, W12 9AH (8743
0572). Hammersmith tube then
266 bus.* **Dinner served** 7-11pm
Mon-Sat. **Average** ££. **Set dinner**
£10.50 1 course, £13.50 2 courses.
Unlicensed. Corkage £3.
Map p282. North African

Local restaurants don't get much
better than this: friendly service, a
cheerful buzz of diners of all ages,
and well-prepared fresh food. The
owner hails from the island of
Djerba, so fish is a speciality, and
you'll get the rare chance to try a few
Tunisian dishes from the North
African menu. Complimentary
rustic bread, fiery harissa with olive
oil, pickled veg and tiny herby
meatballs appeared as soon as we
sat down. Do try a Tunisian brik au
thon to start: a fragile shell of crisp,
deep-fried ouarka pastry that breaks
to reveal a yummy egg, potato and
tuna filling. Couscous royale filled
nicely: a delicious mix of grilled and
stewed meats served with a
whopping great vat of pungent
spiced broth, tender veg and harissa
on the side. Our neighbours tucked
into a baked whole mullet, four-year-
old and 74-year-old alike.

West

Bush Garden Café `NEW`

59 Goldhawk Road, W12 8EG (8743 6372). Goldhawk Road tube. **Meals served** 7.30am-7pm Mon-Fri; 8am-5pm Sat. **Average ££**. **Map** p282. Café

Situated right next to Goldhawk tube, this organic, veggie haven is a chilled café frequented by all types, from suits in need of a vitamin booster to mothers and children in search of a bit of a treat (there is a children's menu and a play area in the garden). Standard café fare sits next to more exotic options, such as the refreshing acerola (a Brazilian fruit rich in vitamin C) smoothie or the Heidi pie, made with sweet potato, spinach and goat's cheese. The bohemian atmosphere is welcoming, as are the groaning shelves of organic produce available for you to purchase, take home and try for yourselves.

★ Esarn Kheaw

314 Uxbridge Road, W12 7LJ (8743 8930). Shepherd's Bush tube. **Lunch served** noon-3pm Mon-Fri. **Dinner served** 6-11pm daily. **Average ££**. **Map** p282. Thai

Pastel green is the dominant colour at small, completely authentic Esarn Kheaw: the walls are green, the ceiling is green, so are the napkins and plates. We could tell from the first bite that everything was own-made. Esarn-style sausage was delicious, with a subtle sour flavour that really grew on us. Likewise, the sweet, crisp spring rolls were some of the best we've tried. With the mains, we could have been more adventurous (there's Esarn-style catfish, for instance). 'Tiger Cry' (Thai-style steak) had a fine marinade and a fiery sauce, but at the end of the day, it was just a steak. In contrast, the house pad Thai was spectacular: sweet, flavoursome and full of peanuts, egg and fresh spring onion.

Patio

5 Goldhawk Road, W12 8QQ (8743 5194). Goldhawk Road tube. **Lunch served** noon-3pm Mon-Fri. **Dinner served** 6-11.30pm daily. **Average ££**. **Set meal** £14.90 4 courses incl vodka shot. **Map** p282. Polish

Patio is a cosy, reassuring place: a home-from-home that locals use regularly, sure of a welcome from the charming Polish owner. They are also attracted by one of London's best bargain set meals. Heavy velvet drapes, an eclectic mix of artworks and a piano topped with cut-glass vases of flowers conjure up the feel of an elderly Polish relative's apartment. The quality of the home-style cooking can be variable, but it's a steal at £14.90 for three courses (four really, as pre-dessert chewy coconut cake and fruit are always proffered), with a shot of vodka to boot. Herrings, bigos (hunter's stew) and peppery barszcz (borscht, here topped with sour cream and dill) are dependable starters, but if you've a delicate or small appetite, beware ordering the heavy, torpedo-like blini with smoked salmon. It's the main courses that sometimes disappoint. Our hunter's-style lamb was bony and fatty; and the duck arrived overcooked and dry. Desserts – the usual calorie-fest of cheesecake, sweet-cheese pancakes and so on – are pretty good.

Som Tam House

131 Askew Road, W12 9AU (8749 9030). Ravenscourt Park or Shepherd's Bush tube. **Lunch served** noon-3pm, **dinner served** 6-11pm Mon-Sat. **Average ££**. **Set lunch** £4.95 1 course. **Map** p282. Thai

Som Tam House is a little jewel box of a restaurant, serving well above average Thai food to a Ravenscourt Park and Acton crowd. The dining room is cosy – lined with wooden panels and adorned with papier

West

Mosob. See p122.

West

mâché masks and other bits of Thai bric-a-brac – and the menu features a full range of Thai curries, stir-fries and noodles, plus some good choices for vegetarians. To start, Thai spare ribs were some of the best that we've eaten anywhere in London, steeped in a sweet, chilli-hot marinade and cooked as a rack to keep the meat moist and tender. Penang curry with beef was slightly less earth-moving but still competent, prepared with sliced bell peppers and subtly spiced. Best of all, food comes in generous portions and everything arrives in double quick time.

★ **Vine Leaves**

71 Uxbridge Road, W12 8NR (8749 0325). Shepherd's Bush tube. **Lunch served** noon-3pm, **dinner served** 5pm-midnight Mon-Thur. **Meals served** noon-1am Fri, Sat; noon-11.30pm Sun. **Average** ££. **Set meal** (Mon-Thur, Sun) £9.95 3 courses incl coffee. **Set mezédes** £9.95 mini, £13.95 mixed. **Set lunch** (Mon-Fri) £5.75 2 courses. **Map** p282. Greek

Like the bustling multicultural street on which it stands, what this small neighbourhood taverna might lack in intimacy it more than makes up for with a buzzy, down-to-earth vibe. As perfect accompaniments to the atmosphere, we found that the service is friendly and the food is satisfying. The extensive menu covers all the proper Greek culinary bases – from soutzoukákia (spicy meatballs in tomato sauce) and moussaká to grilled fish and lamb chops. From the large list of hot and cold meze, both the tzatziki (creamy with a hint of mint) and the houmous (rich and granular) were faultless. Fat fingers of hot dolmádes, served in a tomato sauce, were herby and hearty. Only the tiropitákia (small filo triangles filled with feta) let down the high standard: too much filo, not enough feta, but the addition of chillies with the crumbly cheese was inspired. To follow all this up a main course of inch-thick grilled king prawns cooked in chilli and coriander, though succulent, in the end defeated us.

In the area

Nando's 284-286 Uxbridge Road, W12 7JA (8746 1112). **Map** p282.

West Kensington

Best Mangal II

66 North End Road, W14 9EP (7602 0212). West Kensington tube. **Meals served** noon-1am daily. **Average** ££. Turkish
This second branch of the renowned Mangal mini-chain of Turkish restaurants is ever so slightly more upmarket than the original further along the road and tends to be less crowded. It remains a good source of ockbaşı cooking. A starter of muska böreği (cheese-filled filo pastry parcels) came in a sizeable portion, with a tangy cheese. To follow, karisik (mixed) kebab offered a selection of grilled meat dishes; all had a hearty smoked flavour, though the pirzola lamb chop and

kaburga (spare ribs) we found particularly impressive. The dish was served with a mix of thin saç and fat pide bread, as well as a fresh salad – but no rice. All portions were enormous and in danger of spilling from the plate. To finish we had a thoroughly satisfying baklava. Staff were friendly and attentive.

★ 222 Veggie Vegan NEW

222 North End Road, W14 9NU (7381 2322). West Kensington tube/28, 391 bus. **Lunch served** noon-3.30pm, **dinner served** 5.30-10.30pm daily. **Average** ££. **Set buffet** (lunch) £4.95 takeaway, £5.95 eat in. **Map** p279. Vegetarian
Since our visit last year, this vegan eaterie – with cream walls, wooden furniture, potted plants and funky pictures of seashells – has been spruced up. Even better, the standard of the cooking has also risen by several notches. Every dish that we sampled was carefully and competently cooked by Ghanaian-born head chef Ben Asamani, beautifully presented, and packed with flavour, texture and colour. The restaurant's signature dish, '222 Gardens', combines African-Caribbean-style plantain and okra with Middle Eastern falafel, oriental-style soy-marinated aubergines and courgettes, and Mediterranean-style tomato sauce. It is deeply delicious. Rich, creamy stroganoff made from mushrooms and seitan (wheat gluten) also got our enthusiastic thumbs-up. A customer at the next table, cheered on by fellow diners, lifted up her plate and licked it clean. We didn't go quite that far, but we know why she did it.

In the area

Best Mangal 104 North End Road W14 9EX (7610 1050). **Map** p279.

Westbourne Grove

C&R Café

*52 Westbourne Grove, W2 5SH
(7221 7979).* **Meals served** noon-11pm daily. **Average** ££. **Map** p280. Oriental

We're trying to work out what C&R stands for. Clean & Respectable? Curry & Roti? The unprepossessing exterior of this plain, shopfronted Westbourne Grove newcomer belies the interior with its moody lighting, clothed tables, tall blond chairs and folded napkins. Best of our orders was a generous serving of Singaporean-style spicy chilli crab, which was gloriously gloopy, sticky, spicy and sweet. Other dishes paled in comparison: flat roti bread served with a good curry sauce was excessively oily and lamb satays had flavour aplenty but were tough. Still, we'll be back for that crab, with plenty of C&R's impressively fluffy coconut rice on the side. Ah, that's what it means: Crab & Rice.

Fresh & Wild

*210 Westbourne Grove, W11 2RH
(7229 1063). Notting Hill Gate tube.*
Meals served 8am-9pm Mon-Fri;
8am-8pm Sat; 10am-7pm Sun.
Average ££. **Map** p280. Café

The largest organic food retailer in the UK, Fresh & Wild is now part of America's Whole Foods, the largest organic retailer in the world. Don't be overawed: unlike their US counterparts, most branches have a higgledy-piggledy layout and at the Camden store in particular the opportunity to sit down is limited. This Westbourne Grove branch has a lovely self-service eaterie with a great salad bar offering quiches, salads, couscous and pilau, individually weighed and priced. Adjacent is the hot food counter, where the dishes of the day could be anything from chilli con carne to Thai chicken curry or Sicilian meatballs. There's also a juice bar where you can knock back a shot of wheatgrass to get your afternoon going on a natural high.

Taqueria `NEW`

*139-143 Westbourne Grove, W11
2RS (7229 4734). Notting Hill Gate
tube.* **Meals served** noon-11pm
Mon-Thur; noon-11.30pm Fri, Sat;
noon-10.30pm Sun. **Average** ££.
Set lunch (noon-4.30pm daily)
£5.50-£7.50 1 course. **Map** p280.
Mexican

Taqueria is a small, casual eaterie with white walls, polished dark wood and cool light fixtures that manages, somehow, to look very Latin American. It's loosely based on the corner taco shops that pack in lunchtime crowds in Florida, California and Texas. Yes, the service can be amateurish, and yes, sometimes the tacos arrive colder than we might hope, but in general Taqueria provides good, cheap food. Tacos are the house special – as the name implies – and most use soft corn tortillas made fresh in-house (a rarity in London), topped with what seems like everything in the kitchen: marinated tuna, spicy chicken, black beans, roast peppers, potatoes and cheese… you name it. Regular specials, to have with or instead of the tacos, include the likes of huevos rancheros (fried eggs with beans and salsa) and enchiladas (corn tortillas, filled, rolled up and baked). There are also side salads, rice and beans, and (relatively) cold Mexican beers.

Tom's Delicatessen

*226 Westbourne Grove, W11 2RH
(7221 8818). Notting Hill Gate tube.*
Open 8am-6.30pm Mon-Sat; 9am-6.30pm Sun. **Average** ££. **Map**
p280. Café

This Westbourne Grove favourite has had a bit of a refurb, but its quirky, stylish feel hasn't changed. Display cases show 1950s products for a bit of tongue-in-cheek nostalgia and new booths are made from old public transport seats. The menu still offers all the old American-style favourites. A posh toasted muffin with scrambled eggs and smoked salmon came with a dollop of caviar, while eggs benedict featured perfect poached eggs and hollandaise. There are club sandwiches, salads and smoothies, as well as cup cakes, beautifully packaged sweets and classy sandwiches to take away. With tables in the garden, clever clip-on high chairs and very tasty coffee, Tom's is still getting it right in its second decade.

Meal deals

Al Waha *75 Westbourne Grove, W2 4UL (7229 0806/www.waha-uk.com).* Set lunch £12.50 5 dishes. **Map** p280. Lebanese

In the area

Carluccio's Caffé *Westbourne Corner, 108 Westbourne Grove, W2 5RU (7243 8164).* **Map** p280.
Gourmet Burger Kitchen *50 Westbourne Grove, W2 5SH (7243 4344).* **Map** p280.
Ottolenghi *63 Ledbury Road, W11 2AD (7727 1121).* **Map** p281.

Westbourne Park

Lucky 7

127 Westbourne Park Road, W2 5QL (7727 6771). Royal Oak or Westbourne Park tube. **Meals served** 10am-11pm Mon-Thur; 9am-11pm Fri, Sat; 9am-10.30pm Sun. **Average** ££. **Map** p280.
North American
Tom Conran's take on the American diner theme, Lucky 7, is a small, low-key joint. Within you'll find big booths (which must be shared with others when the place gets crowded), lots of mirrors, and a short but solid menu of burgers, sandwiches, salads and shakes. The tantalising smell of sizzling burgers and steaming fries

will lure you to the unhealthiest items on the menu. The burgers are big and heavy, with all the fixings. The fries are skinny, and served hot and crisp. But it's the milkshakes that separate the men from the boys. They're served in three levels of thickness, starting at £4 for a regular, with prices climbing rapidly the thicker they get. The thinnest version is thick enough for most. Breakfasts are big and fresh, with eggs and pancakes leading the way.

★ Mosob NEW

339 Harrow Road, W9 3RB (7266 2012). Westbourne Park tube. **Meals served** 1pm-midnight Mon-Sat; 1-11.30pm Sun. **Average** ££. **Map** p280. Eritrean
Mosob is enchanting, and as accessible to non-Eritreans as it is authentic. The atmosphere is warm and welcoming, the dining room and small lounge unselfconsciously chic. Mum is in the kitchen, her three charming boys serve, soft loungey sounds fill the air, and food comes beautifully presented on mosobs (woven patterned stands). Sambusas (samosas) were a perfect combo of taste and texture – crisp, fresh, with a chilli bite. Main-course qulwa was a mound of juicy, flavourful scraps of lamb, rich and bright with spice. We also tried ajibo mes hamli, spinach flecked with cottage cheese, tomato and spiced butter; and shiro, a comforting paste of pounded chickpeas. All were served with fresh salad on wonderful injera, with more provided. As Eritrean ladies drift in and out clutching takeaway and the boys flash their smiles, you'll realise that Mosob has woven its spell on you.

Meal deals

Angie's African Cuisine *381 Harrow Road, W9 3NA (8962 8761/www.angies-restaurant.co.uk).* Set buffet (1.30-9pm Sun) £10. African

West

SOUTH WEST

Barnes

Meal deals

The Depot *Tideway Yard, 125 Mortlake High Street, SW14 8SN (8878 9462/www.depotbrasserie. co.uk).* Set lunch (noon-3pm, Mon-Fri) £13.50 2 courses. Brasserie

In the area

ASK *Old Sorting Office, Station Road, SW13 0LJ (8878 9300).*
Pizza Express *14-15 Barnes High Street, SW13 9LW (8878 1184).*
Strada *375 Lonsdale Road, SW13 9PY (8392 9216).*

Chelsea

Chelsea Bun Diner

9A Lamont Road, SW10 0HP (7352 3635). Earl's Court tube then 328 bus. **Meals served** 7am-midnight Mon-Sat; 9am-7pm Sun. **Average** ££. **Map** p279. Burgers
Could the Chelsea Bun Diner be the nearest thing that London has to an American-style truck-stop café? There's even a bus depot directly out front to give you that pitstop-on-an-American-highway feel. The menu is huge, as are the portions, especially if you opt for one of the enormous, eponymous burgers. We had gripes: our salad was drowned in dressing and almost inedible, the fries looked cheap and machine-cut, and the burger buns fell apart too easily. But what the CBD lacks on the plate, it makes up for in atmosphere: staff and customers, all smiles, created a jovial buzz. Choosing beyond the house wine might take you out of budget, but those keen for even more Americana might want to try one of the delicious coke floats.

Chelsea Kitchen

98 King's Road, SW3 4TZ (7589 1330). Sloane Square tube. **Meals served** 8am-11.45pm daily.

Mirch Masala.
See p131.

Average £. **Set lunch** £5.20-£5.50 2 courses. **Set dinner** £8-£9 3 courses. **Map** p275. International
A rare, affordable find for the bargain hungry of the King's Road, Chelsea Kitchen may look a little bit out of date, but this is part of its odd allure. Set amid designer cafés and trendy coffee shops, it's one of the area's only ungentrified eateries. You can get a decent niçoise salad for a fiver or a tasty home made curry for £4.10; otherwise, choose an all-day breakfast, hearty omelette or spaghetti bolognese before turning back the years for dessert with an old school favourite like jelly and ice-cream. Whether you sit upstairs in a booth or venture downstairs for the

pew-like seating and some secluded alcoves, staff are friendly and quick to serve. The Kitchen is a welcome time-warp in modern-day Chelsea.

The Market Place NEW

Chelsea Farmers' Market, 125 Sydney Street, SW3 6NR (7352 5600). South Kensington tube/11, 19, 22, 49 bus. **Meals served** *Apr-Sept* 9.30am-5pm Mon-Fri; 9.30am-6pm Sat, Sun. *Oct-Mar* 9.30am-5pm daily. **Average** **£££. Map** p279. Brasserie
Somewhat at odds with its posh address, this largely outdoor eaterie, in the boho shopping enclave that is the Chelsea Farmers' Market, has a beach-café feel due to its umbrella-shaded picnic tables and Virgin radio blasting from the speakers. The vaguely shambolic air of the place is reinforced by friendly but rather dippy staff. A browse through the menu yields Mediterranean-influenced salads, burgers and pasta, plus ciabatta sandwiches. We were pleasantly surprised by the quality: a seared asparagus salad with rocket, parmesan and sun-dried tomato relish was attractively presented, the vegetables fresh and firm. Grilled tuna niçoise, while cooked right through, remained tender and there wasn't a wilted salad leaf anywhere in sight. Salmon fish cakes featured reassuring chunks of fish and a tangy chilli dip. A convenient shopping pit stop.

Vingt-Quatre

*325 Fulham Road, SW10 9QL
(7376 7224). South Kensington tube.*
Open/meals served 24hrs daily.
Average ££. **No credit cards.**
Map p279. Café

Slide into a seat next to the loose
loafer-wearing males and Burberry-
clad blondes of Chelsea for some
nosh twenty-four hours (or vingt-
quatre heures) a day. Licensed until
midnight, V-Q's smart staff serve
classy versions of comfort food to a
mixed south-west London crowd in
search of sustenance. Clubbers, in
particular, love it here. A full
English breakfast starts at £6.95;
the menu also features fish and
chips, steak, pasta varieties, club
sandwiches, and such Asian-inspired
options as crayfish spring rolls. To
drink, pick from an interesting array
of herbal infusions that offer help
with anything from slimming to
sexual health to something called
'Yoga Balance' – priced at a Harley
Street-shaming £3 each.

Meal deal

Big Easy *332-334 King's Road,
SW3 5UR (7352 4071/www.bigeasy.
uk.com).* Set lunch (noon-5pm Mon-
Fri) £7.95 2 courses. **Map** p279.
North American
Bluebird *350 King's Road, SW3
5UU (7559 1000/www.conran.com).*
Set lunch £12.95 2 courses.
Map p279. Modern European
Sophie's Steakhouse & Bar
*311-313 Fulham Road, SW10 9QH
(7352 0088/www.sophiessteakhouse.
com).* Set meal (noon-6pm Mon-Fri)
£10.95 2 courses. North American

In the area

Al-Dar II *74 King's Road, SW3
4TZ (7584 1873).* **Map** p279.
ASK *300 King's Road, SW3 5UH
(7349 9123).* **Map** p279.
Baker & Spice *47 Denyer Street,
SW3 2LX (7589 4734).* **Map** p275.
Ed's Easy Diner *362 King's Road,
SW3 5UZ (7352 1956).* **Map** p279.

Itsu *118 Draycott Avenue, SW3
3AE (7590 2400).* **Map** p275.
Maison Blanc *11 Elystan Street,
SW3 3NT (7584 6913).* **Map** p275.
Pâtisserie Valerie *81 Duke of
York Square, SW3 4LY (7730
7094).* **Map** p279.
Pizza Express *The Pheasantry,
152-154 King's Road, SW3 4UT
(7351 5031).* **Map** p279.
Ranoush Juice Bar *338 King's
Road, SW3 5UR (7352 0044).*
Map p279.

Earl's Court

As Greek As It Gets NEW

*233 Earl's Court Road, SW5 9AH
(7244 7777). Earl's Court tube.*
Lunch served noon-3pm, **dinner
served** 6-11pm Mon-Fri. **Meals
served** noon-11pm Sat, Sun.
Average ££. **Map** p279. Greek

As the tables full of eagerly eating
young Greeks suggest, this brightly
lit souvlaki joint is thoroughly
authentic. It specialises in an array
of meaty treats served with genuine
souvlaki flatbread. The fun, modern
outlook of the place is typified by the
novel mix-and-match approach of its
souvlaki menu, whereby you can
combine any of five meats with a
variety of fillings and sauces. Staff
are friendly and efficient. A square
slice of spinach pie was a great
improvement on our last visit to As
Greek As It Gets and struck a good
balance between feta creaminess
and spinachy richness. We also
sampled the 'mixed greek': a giant's
feast of a grill that included a rich,
succulent country sausage of
particular note. And at the end we
were presented with a modest bill.

Meal deals

Lou Pescadou *241 Old Brompton
Road, SW5 9HP (7370 1057).* Set
lunch (noon-3pm Tue-Sat) £10.90
3 courses; set dinner (Sat) £14.50
3 courses. **Map** p279. Fish

In the area

Masala Zone *147 Earl's Court Road, SW5 9RQ (7373 0220).* **Map** p278.
Nando's *204 Earl's Court Road, SW5 OAA (7259 2544).* **Map** p278.
Pizza Express *246 Old Brompton Road, SW5 0DE (7373 4712).*
Pizza Express *Ground Floor, Earl's Court Exhibition Centre, SW5 9TA (7386 5494).* **Map** p279.
Strada *237 Earl's Court Road, SW5 9AH (7835 1180).* **Map** p279.
Wagamama *180-182 Earl's Court Road, SW5 9QG.* **Map** p278.
Zizzi *194-196 Earl's Court Road, SW5 9QF (7370 1999).* **Map** p278.

Earlsfield

Amaranth

346-348 Garratt Lane, SW18 4ES (8874 9036). Tooting Broadway tube/Earlsfield rail. **Dinner served** 6.30-11.30pm Mon-Sat. **Average** ££. **Set dinner** £15 2 courses. **Unlicensed. Corkage** £2.50 (wine). Thai
Amaranth is the busiest restaurant in Earlsfield, and booking is essential. The cacophony doesn't make it the place for a quiet tête-a-tête; people come for the low prices and a BYO policy that allows you to eat very decently, within budget. The menu kicks off with a series of set menus which offer a surfeit of food. Not the finest royal Thai cuisine, but the basic curries and stir-fries – from squid with peppercorns to pad Thai – are competently prepared. Service is brisk, though not brusque.

Kazans

607-609 Garratt Lane, SW18 4SU (8739 0055). Earlsfield rail/44, 77, 270 bus. **Dinner served** 6-11pm Mon-Fri. **Meals served** 11am-11pm Sat, Sun. **Average** ££. Turkish
The big double frontage at Kazans opens on to a restaurant and a bar. When it began trading a couple of years ago, this family-run enterprise

seemed very cagey about its Turkish heritage. However, as Earlsfield has come to love the place, the reticence has disappeared. Dishes now have their Turkish names on the menu, and a wider range of Turkish cooking is available. The interior is decorated with stylish enlargements of family photos from Turkey in the 1960s. Mixed cold meze came with the usual dips of houmous, tarama and cacik, but also some more adventurous choices that included enginar (artichokes) and fava bean purée. Grilled snapper fillet (a special) was a pleasing and large portion. Couples like Kazans, and the restaurant is usually busy.

Fulham

Megan's Deli NEW

571 King's Road, SW6 2EB (7371 7837). Fulham Broadway tube. **Meals served** 8am-5.30pm Mon-Fri; 9am-6pm Sat; 10am-4pm Sun. **Average** ££. **Map** p279. Café
This pretty deli has cosy niches and a 'secret garden' at the back. Dishes prepared on site using additive-free, traceable ingredients include soups, cheese or antipasti platters, savoury tarts, and sandwiches using a variety of breads such as rye, sourdough and ciabatta. Hot dishes are the likes of salmon coconut curry with spinach and potatoes. Megan's salads often have an Asian spin (think Japanese cucumber with ginger and coriander, and oriental vegetable coleslaw). Cakes and desserts range from Anzac chocolate chip cookies to wheat-free brownies.

★ Rossopomodoro NEW

214 Fulham Road, SW10 9NB (7352 7677). South Kensington tube then 14 bus. **Meals served** 11.30am-midnight Mon-Sat; 11.30am-11.30pm Sun. **Average** ££. **Set lunch** £10 2 courses. **Map** p279. Pizza & Pasta

Kazans

Colourful pop-art canvases and woven cane chairs lend a retro flourish to this branch of the growing London chain (it's already big in Italy), but it's the gleaming open kitchen that grabs and holds the attention of diners. Yes, it's noisy and sometimes chaotic, but the marketplace vibe seems appropriate (if you want somewhere quieter to eat ask to sit on the first floor). Our pizza looked pretty much like a regular margherita, but on cutting, its crisp, golden-edged base yielded to a deliciously creamy ricotta cheese filling, flecked with garlicky salami shreds. Richly indulgent, this was the star dish. Paccheri pasta tubes, scattered with peas and beefy meatballs, worked well with a moat of herby tomato sauce, but was marred by a shortfall of meat. Still, this place brims with energy, boasts a great laid-back atmosphere and the pizzas are a real treat.

Zimzun
Fulham Broadway Retail Centre, Fulham Road, SW6 1BW (7385 4555). Fulham Broadway tube. **Meals served** noon-10pm Mon, Sun; noon-10.30pm Tue-Thur; noon-11pm Fri, Sat. **Average** ££. **Set lunch** £5.95 1 course. **Map** p279. Oriental

A prime location in the shopping centre above Fulham Broadway tube station ensures that this sleekly decorated den is often full of young locals tucking into generous portions served by friendly staff. Clear beaded curtains hang down over large, square communal tables. We began with battered squid with ginger, garlic, coriander and young peppercorns; it was tasty but arrived cold. Lamb red curry was an even bigger disappointment, consisting of chewy, overcooked meat coated in a sauce that was too creamy. Things improved with a crunchy, spicy and sour som tam salad, and a grilled

duck noodle salad that combined soft slices of duck with cherry tomatoes, lettuce and mung bean noodles, plus a dressing of chilli, lime and garlic. Large one-plate dishes seem the best value here; come for the noodle salads.

Meal deals

Sukho *855 Fulham Road, SW6 5HJ (7371 7600).* Set lunch (noon-3pm daily) £7.95 1 course, £10.95 2 courses. Thai

In the area

ASK *345 Fulham Palace Road, SW6 6TD (7371 0392).*
Brinkley's *47 Hollywood Road, SW10 9HX (7351 1683).* Branch of The Oratory. **Map** p279.
Carluccio's Caffè *236 Fulham Road, SW10 9NB (7376 5960).* **Map** p279.
Feng Sushi *218 Fulham Road, SW10 9NB (7795 1900).* **Map** p279.
Gourmet Burger Kitchen *49 Fulham Broadway, SW6 1AE (7381 4242).* **Map** p279.
Joe's Brasserie *130 Wandsworth Bridge Road, SW6 2UL (7731 7835).* Branch of The Oratory.
Little Bay *140 Wandsworth Bridge Road, SW6 2UL (7751 3133).*
Ma Goa *194 Wandsworth Bridge Road, SW6 2UF (7384 2122).*
Nando's *Unit 20, Fulham Broadway Retail Centre, Fulham Road, SW6 1BY (7386 8035).* **Map** p279.
La Perla *803 Fulham Road, SW6 5HE (7471 4895).*
Pizza Express *363 Fulham Road, SW10 9TN (7352 5300).* **Map** p279.
Pizza Express *895-896 Fulham Road, SW6 5HU (7731 3117).*
Pizza Express *Unit 4, Fulham Broadway Development, SW6 1BW (7381 1700).* **Map** p279.
Planet Organic *25 Effie Road, SW6 1EL (7731 7222).* **Map** p279.
Yo! Sushi *Fulham Broadway Centre, Fulham Road, SW6 1BW (7385 6077).* **Map** p279.

Norbury

Mirch Masala

*1416-1418 London Road, SW16 4BZ
(8679 1828/8765 1070). Norbury rail.*
Meals served noon-midnight daily.
Average ££. **Set buffet** (noon-4pm
Mon-Sat) £6.99. **Unlicensed**.
Corkage no charge. Indian

Mirch Masala (meaning 'chilli and
spice') has had a refurb. But fans of
this no-frills canteen needn't worry:
the tables are still wipe-clean, the
stainless-steel kitchen is still visible
through the back, and the service is
still brusque. Popadoms arrive
unbidden on your table, but they're
complimentary, so don't worry. The
secret to a successful meal here is to
order carefully. There's no need for
rice when the nan breads are so
sublime. People come here for the
karahis and the 'deigi' (which just
means cooked in a big pan) dishes,
both of which can be spiced to taste,
mild or hot. The deigi karela dahl
birji had a pleasant tartness because
of the slow-cooked karela. The best
dish was a starter of Mirch Masala
fish: boneless, even chunks from a
large fillet of coley, rubbed with
spices then fried.

Parsons Green

Wizzy NEW

*616 Fulham Road, SW6 5PR
(7736 9171/www.wizzyrestaurant.
co.uk). Parsons Green tube.* **Lunch
served** noon-3pm, **dinner served**
6-11.30pm daily. **Average** £££.
Korean

This small restaurant opened in a
blaze of publicity in 2005, not least
because it has a Korean woman chef,
and serves Korean food with a
modern contemporary twist. Some
dishes work, but others miss the
mark. Naju pear (one of the fragrant
varieties of pears from South Korea)
and mango salad arrived looking

like a window box; there were so
many mixed salad leaves that we
had to play 'spot the pear and
mango' (four or five pieces were
eventually uncovered). Spring onion
pancake resembled a thick, deep-
fried quiche, yet was packed with
fresh vegetables and so tasted better
than it looked. Beef stew was
scrumptious; the meat had been
slow-cooked and was exceptionally
tender, and the gravy, flavoured
with bone marrow, was rich and
caramel-like. Despite our caveats, we
would rate Wizzy as a wonderful
local eaterie – as opposed to a
wonderful Korean restaurant.

In the area
Strada *175 New Kings Road, SW6
4SW (7731 6404).*

Putney

Hudson's

*113 Lower Richmond Road, SW15
1EX (8785 4522). Putney Bridge
tube/Putney rail.* **Meals served**
10am-10.30pm Mon-Sat; 10am-10pm
Sun. **Average** ££. **Map** p293.
International

With its ceiling fans and green
wooden furniture, Hudson's smacks
of continental cool. The menu lists
international cuisine, leading to
some difficult decisions: do you
plump for the gooey pleasures of
deep-fried Camembert, or the tangy
spice of Moroccan potato cakes? The
menu is revised on a regular basis,
although certain dishes are always
on offer. The presentation of meals
is excellent – mixed fish platter
arrived on a bed of artichoke spears
with a rich orange dollop of sweet
potato mash – while a decent
selection of wines and quality lagers
are an apt primer for a night out on
Putney High Street. In sum you can
expect well-cooked food in a friendly,
unpretentious environment.

Ma Goa

Ma Goa NEW

*242-244 Upper Richmond Road,
SW15 6TG (8780 1767). East
Putney tube/Putney rail/74, 337 bus.*
Lunch served noon-2.30pm Tue-
Fri; 1-4pm Sun. **Dinner served**
6.30-11pm Tue-Sat; 6-10pm Sun.
Average ££. **Set dinner** (6.30-
8pm) £10 2 courses. **Set buffet**
(Sun lunch) £10. **Map** p293. Indian

This, London's leading Goan
restaurant, does the classics well:
flavourful pork vindaloo with its
sour-spice contrasts; the pleasing
spice after-rush of a prawn balchao
(pickled prawn); and fish caldine, a
peppery, vinegary preparation made
with expertly deboned, chunky
white fish. Dish presentation is also
exquisite, from the tiny white bowls
of low-fat curries and side dishes on
geometric serving plates, to the
extraordinary east-west fusion
desserts made exclusively for Ma
Goa by a pâtissier (try the traditional
bebique or bibenca – a layered
confection of coconut milk, egg and
jaggery (unrefined sugar) – or the lime
cheesecake topped with rosewater
jelly). The service at this stylishly
modern restaurant also takes some
beating: polite, attentive, and cheery.

Olé

*240 Upper Richmond Road, SW15
6TG (8788 8009). East Putney
tube/Putney rail. Bar* **Tapas served**
noon-midnight Mon-Sat; noon-11pm
Sun. **Average** ££. *Restaurant*
Meals served noon-11pm Mon-Sat;
noon-10.30pm Sun. **Average** £££.
Set lunch (noon-6pm Sun) £9.95 2
tapas and glass of wine. **Set meal**
(Sun) £12.50 2 courses. **Map** p293.
Spanish

The name might be a cliché, but
that's as far as it goes; Olé's menu
makes considerable departures from
the usual conventions of a Spanish
restaurant in London. Recently
moved to Putney, it features white
walls, floor-to-ceiling windows,
blond wood furniture and floors,

with no likeness to tacky pseudo-
tabernas. Cooking is Spanish with
some interesting Modern European
twists: octopus with paprika was
astonishingly tender; prawns in
garlic were nice and juicy, as was the
pork fillet in a rich, stocky
mushroom sauce. Mains, too, were
good – fillet steak being particularly
notable. On a weekday night the
spacious dining room was empty
and hushed. But with food of this
standard it should begin to gain a
new and loyal following.

Il Peperone

*26 Putney High Street, SW15
1SL (8788 3303). Putney Bridge
tube/Putney rail.* **Lunch served**
11am-3.30pm, **dinner served**
6-11.30pm Tue-Sun. **Average**
££. **Set lunch** £5.95 1 course.
Set dinner £10.95 3 courses.
Map p293. Pizza & Pasta

Il Peperone, a family-run pizzeria
that occupies a prime site on bustling
Putney High Street, is a stone's
throw from the river and many bars.
However, the food on our visit was a
bit of a let down. Bruschetta starter
arrived on untoasted bread, with a
less-than-generous topping of
tomatoes and sliced olives. Pizza
mains were likewise unreliable. A
prosciutto and rucola version was
mediocre; disappointingly, the rocket
had been cooked beneath the ham.
Formaggio di capra (goat's cheese,
roast aubergine and mozzarella) was
more successful, with a generous
serving of cheese. The menu also
offer a choice of pasta, fish and meat
dishes. On the plus side, the service
was some of the most genuinely
friendly we've experienced in
London, and the house wine, at
£9.95, was very drinkable.

Rasa Penang

*315 Putney Bridge Road, SW15
2PP (8789 3165). East Putney or
Putney Bridge tube.* **Open** noon-
2.30pm, 6-11pm daily. **Average** ££.

Set lunch £7.90 2 courses incl coffee. **Set dinner** £14.50 2 courses incl coffee. Map p259. Malaysian

The stellar chef of the pretty Rasa Penang deserves a better audience for his creations. As it was, Bill Withers' 'Just The Two Of Us' aptly echoed around a space occupied by 20 empty tables, one waitress and this diner. Culinary advice from the helpful waitress led us through an encyclopaedic list of Thai, Malay and Chinese dishes. Malay is the speciality cuisine, with sambol sauces and shrimp pastes informing the varied fish, beef and goreng noodle dishes. A Malaysian king prawn curry proved rich and moreish, a mix of subtle flavours. Couples should beat a path to this criminally underused facility beside a row of almshouses to take advantage of the romantic intimacy and perhaps the two-person set meals. A house Jacques Veritier at £10.50 a bottle makes a decent sip.

Thai Square

Embankment, 2 Lower Richmond Road, SW15 1LB (8780 1811). Putney Bridge tube. Bar **Open/ snacks served** noon-midnight Mon-Thur; noon-2am Fri, Sat; noon-10.30pm Sun. **Average** ££. *Restaurant* **Lunch served** noon-2pm daily. **Dinner served** 5.30-11pm Mon-Sat; 5.30-10.30pm Sun. **Average** ££. Map p293. Thai

It's no surprise Thai Square is the flagship branch of this chain, since it features some postcard-perfect views of Putney Bridge. Inside, a wave-like white wall of moulded plaster sweeps upstairs from the ground-floor bar to a sophisticated split-level dining room with floor-to-ceiling windows. The menu is extensive, yet still holds few surprises (though rambutan- and lychee-flavoured cocktails sounded interesting). We started with a convincing portion of tod mun pla (fish cakes) that came, rather

disappointingly, with a side salad topped with french dressing. Koh Samui-style fish salad was better: crisp deep-fried fish, cashew nuts and fresh pineapple in a tart, spicy dressing. We were also lucky with the mains: drunken duck was a stimulating, peppery stir-fry of duck, bamboo shoots, chilli and peppercorns. The Thames view, though, is the real star here.

Meal deals

L'Auberge *22 Upper Richmond Road, SW15 2RX (8874 3593/ www.ardillys.com).* Set dinner (Tue-Thur) £12.95 2 courses. French

Enoteca Turi *28 Putney High Street, SW15 1SQ (8785 4449/ www.enotecaturi.com).* Set lunch £13.50 2 courses. Map p293. Italian

Marco Polo *6-7 Riverside Quarter, Eastfields Avenue, SW18 1LP (8874 6800).* Set lunch £9.95 2 courses. Italian

Phoenix Bar & Grill *162-164 Lower Richmond Road, SW15 1LY (8780 3131/www.sonnys.co.uk).* Set lunch (Mon-Sat) £15.50 2 courses. Map p293. Modern European

Royal China *3 Chelverton Road, SW15 1RN (8788 0907).* Dim sum (noon-3.30pm daily) £2-£5. Map p293. Chinese

In the area

Carluccio's Caffé *Putney Wharf, SW15 2JQ (8789 0591).* Map p293.

Gourmet Burger Kitchen *333 Putney Bridge Road, SW15 2PG (8789 1199).* Map p293.

Maison Blanc *125 Putney High Street, SW15 1SU (8789 6064).* Map p293.

Nando's *148 Upper Richmond Road, SW15 2SW (8780 3651).* Map p293.

Pizza Express *144 Upper Richmond Road, SW15 2SW (8789 1948).* Map p293.

The Real Greek Souvlaki & Bar *31-33 Putney High Street, SW15 1SP (8788 3270).* Map p293.

South West

Rocket Riverside Brewhouse Lane, ICL Tower, SW15 2NS (8789 7875). Branch of Rocket. **Map** p293.

Strada 147 Upper Richmond Road, SW15 2TX (8789 6996). **Map** p293.

Tootsies Grill Unit 3B, 30 Brewhouse Street, SW15 2TG (8788 8488). **Map** p293.

Wagamama 50-54 Putney High Street, SW15 1SQ (8785 3636). **Map** p293.

Raynes Park

★ Cah Chi

34 Durham Road, SW20 0TW (8947 1081). Raynes Park rail/57, 131 bus. **Lunch served** noon-3pm, **dinner served** 5-11pm Tue-Fri. **Meals served** noon-11pm Sat; noon-10.30pm Sun. **Average** ££. **Unlicensed. Corkage** 10% of bill. **No credit cards.** Korean

This is easily the most accessible Korean restaurant in south-west London, particularly for newcomers to the cuisine. Staff are happy to explain the ins and outs of Korean cooking and the waitresses cut seamlessly from speaking Korean to Home Counties English. Inside, children's drawings adorn the walls and a liberal use of varnished pine adds to the kindergarten feel. Soups are a big hit: maeun jang (spicy fish broth) had plenty of chilli heat but was refreshingly clean on the palate. Marbled medallions of beef tenderloin were lightly grilled at the table, dipped in seasoned sesame oil, then popped hot on to the plate, ready to wrap in lettuce leaves with koch'ujang (hot red pepper sauce) and tangy shreds of marinated spring onion. All meals come with a selection of Korean nibbles.

★ Cocum

9 Approach Road, SW20 8BA (8540 3250/8542 3843). Morden tube then 163 bus/Raynes Park rail.

Lunch served noon-2.30pm Mon-Thur, Sat, Sun. **Dinner served** 5.30-11pm Mon-Thur; 5.30-11.30pm Fri, Sat; 5.30-10.30pm Sun. **Average** £. **Set lunch** £5.50-£6.50 2 courses. South Indian

Against the incongruous backdrop of the commuter trains rattling to nearby Raynes Park station, Cocum is a London outcrop of idyllic Kerala, the culinary paradise of south-western India that is washed by the Arabian Sea and sealed off from the rest of India by the Western Ghats. Three things make it a delight: humble, helpful staff; the decorative touches of a Keralite ceremonial boat and line drawings from the region; and, most importantly, authentic Keralite cuisine, effectively imported to SW20. Thick coconut milk was the base for a deliciously dense, varied seafood soup. A paste of garlic, ginger, turmeric and chilli sparkled in a wonderful spinachy chemmeen cheera kootu (prawn curry). To accompany, a zing of lemon infuses the rice dish naranga choru. There are dosas, too, plus standard stews and curries, but we recommend exploration of the excellent Keralite fish dishes.

Wandsworth

Brady's

513 Old York Road, SW18 1TF (8877 9599). Wandsworth Town rail/28, 44 bus. **Lunch served** 12.30-3pm Tue-Fri; 12.30-4pm Sat, Sun. **Dinner served** 6.30-10pm daily. **Average** ££. **Map** p284. Fish & Chips

Now something of a local landmark, Brady's continues to serve up reasonably priced fish and chips to the contented and well-fed burghers of Wandsworth. The slightly faded lime green decor is reminiscent of a mid-1980s wine bar, but there's nothing old or run-down about the food – excellently sourced fresh fish with beautifully cut golden chips. It's simple fare with none of the pretension you might expect to find in a posh sit-down chippie. The haddock arrived tenderly cooked in a batter light enough to sleep a baby in. Tuna was juicy and well done. Alongside the standard ketchup and tartar sauces are some more unusual dips for your chips: dill, tarragon, and tomato and basil mayonnaises.

Dexter's Grill & Bar

20 Bellevue Road, SW17 7EB (8767 1858). Wandsworth Common rail/ 319 bus. **Meals served** noon-11pm Mon-Fri; 11am-11pm Sat; 11am-10.30pm Sun. **Average £££.** North American

This small branch of the Tootsies chain on the edge of Wandsworth Common is a good choice for families – and many local families certainly take advantage of the fact. During the day, the spacious dining room, with its exposed brick walls, wood beams and polished wooden floors, is just about given over to mothers, pushchairs and toddlers. So child friendly is Dexter's that there's a kind of kiddie heaven in the back devoted to sweets and ice-cream. However, in the evening, the lights dim and the venue takes on a more grown-up air. But both day and night the menu is the same: basic Americana that veers from the healthy (big mix-and-match salads, where you can add the meat and dressing of your choice from a wide selection), to the unhealthy (burgers and divine ice-cream desserts), via somewhere in between (steaks). The atmosphere is casual and relaxing, and the staff are eager to help.

In the area

Nando's *Unit 12, Southside Shopping Centre, SW18 4TF (8874 1363).*
Pizza Express *539-541 Old York Road, SW18 1TG (8877 9812).*
Map p284.

Wimbledon

Jo Shmo's NEW

33 High Street, SW19 5BY (8879 3845). Wimbledon tube/rail then 93 bus. **Meals served** noon-11pm Mon-Thur, Sun; noon-11.30pm Fri, Sat. **Average ££.** North American

Proving that family restaurants can be slick and attractive too, Jo Shmo's smoothly offers the best of both worlds – families with children eating by day, while couples and groups of friends fill it at night. The restaurant is large enough for waiting staff to seat people with children away from the mainstream clientele of troughing couples, and everyone is happy. The menu helps make Jo Shmo's versatile, with nearly as many milkshakes as cocktails among the options. The food is good value and substantial. For starters, crayfish popcorn arrived hot, if less crisp than the name implied, while rib fingers were tender and smoky. Mains include burgers (thick and juicy), steaks, grilled chicken dishes and plenty of good salad options. Children can order from a menu of scaled-down treats.

Meal deals

Makiyaki *149 Merton Road, SW19 1ED (8540 3113).* Set lunch £7.50-£11.50. Japanese

In the area

Giraffe *21 High Street, SW19 5DX (8946 0544).*
Gourmet Burger Kitchen *88 The Broadway, SW19 1RH (8540 3300).*
Nando's *1 Russell Road, SW19 1QN (8545 0909).*
Pizza Express *84 High Street, SW19 5EG (8946 6027).*
Strada *91 High Street, SW19 5EG (8946 4363).*
Tootsies Grill *48 High Street, SW19 5AX (8946 4135).*
Wagamama *46-48 Wimbledon Hill Road, SW19 7PA (8879 7280).*

South West

SOUTH

Balham

Ciullo's NEW

31 Balham High Road, SW12 9AL (8675 3072). Clapham South tube/Balham tube/rail. **Dinner served** 6-11pm Mon-Thur; 6-11.30pm Fri, Sat. **Meals served** 1-10.30pm Sun. **Average** ££. **Map** p285. Pizza & Pasta

This pizzeria and ristorante is done up in a resolutely old style, despite it having been open for only a few years; to be honest, it looks a bit like something out of the 1970s. The starters are fine, and the meat and fish dishes mostly live up to expectations, but it's the pizza and pasta dishes at which the Ciullo family excel. Pastas are always al dente, pizzas thin and crisp. Penne all'arrabiata was agreeably spicy, and, at only £4, no dearer than many budget caffs. If you can handle the naffness of the dodgy art on the walls and the twinkling fairy lights at the entrance, Ciullo's won't disappoint on the plate.

Fine Burger Company

37 Bedford Hill, SW12 9EY (8772 0266). Balham tube/rail. **Meals served** noon-10pm Mon-Sat; noon-9.30pm Sun. **Average** ££. **Set meal** (noon-7pm Mon-Fri) £5.95 burger and drink. **Map** p285. Burgers

A new menu introduced in 2006 includes unusual variations on the beefburger theme, such as teriyaki sauce and stilton cheese. We wondered if FBC had lost its way on the path to hamburger heaven? Not in our experience, as the medium-cooked patty is still just right, the bun's firm, and details such as the cheese and lettuce leaves are top quality. The chips are made from real potatoes (you can see the skins) and are cooked just-so. We're less certain about some of the side orders, though: the onion rings are

the size and colour of doughnuts, while the 'sweet chilli and sour cream' dip is no more than a dollop of sour cream with a squirt of sweet chilli sauce on top.

The Nightingale NEW

97 Nightingale Lane, SW12 8NX (8673 1637). Clapham South tube/Wandsworth Common rail. **Open** 11am-midnight Mon-Sat; noon-11pm Sun. **Meals served** noon-10pm daily. **Average** ££. Brasserie

This brasserie is as child-friendly as it gets, with plenty of room for pushchairs and a children's menu that includes fish fingers and chips, and organic beefburger. Adults aren't second-class citizens, though, with soups, sandwiches, snacks, salads and main courses such as grilled tuna steak with green beans, sun-dried tomatoes and artichokes to choose from. Our weekend fry-up was excellent, with perfectly poached eggs and organic beef sausages. Note the beef: despite this being a former butcher's shop, there is no pork or bacon on the menu.

Polish White Eagle Club

211 Balham High Road, SW17 7BQ (8672 1723). Tooting Bec tube/Balham tube/rail/49, 155, 181, 319 bus. **Lunch served** 11.30am-3pm, **dinner served** 6-10pm Mon-Sat. **Meals served** 11.30am-10pm Sun. **Average** ££. **Set lunch** £7 2 courses incl coffee. **Set dinner** £9.90 2 courses incl coffee. **Map** p285. Polish

The recent influx of young Polish émigrés to SW17 has improved the fortunes of this long-established social club. The dining room has had a *Changing Rooms*-style makeover, moving it on from Soviet-era to Solidarity-era decor. The menu includes all the Polish classics, such as brine-pickled herrings and light, fluffy blinis topped with lashings of

South

Ciullo's

sour cream and smoked salmon.
Portions are so large that the platter
of mixed Polish specialities, which
we ordered for one person, could
easily have served two. It included a
flavoursome bigos, breaded pork
chop, stuffed cabbage, Polish
sausage and more besides. It's small
wonder that the Club is so popular
with Polish family groups.

Tagine NEW

*1-3 Fernlea Road, SW12 9RT
(8675 7604). Balham tube/rail.*
Dinner served 5-11pm Mon-Fri.
Meals served noon-11pm Sat,
Sun. **Average £££. Unlicensed**.
Corkage no charge. **Map** p285.
North African

Tagine's interior is more enticing
than the noisy pavement tables,

what with its Moroccan-style chandeliers, low brass tables and heaps of other kasbah tat to give it a louche, just-back-from-Marrakech look. The empty wine glasses on the tables stay that way, though, as Tagine doesn't serve alcohol; the Moroccan tea is a good substitute. Most of the dishes are pleasingly fresh, such as zaalouk salad with an appealing tang of cumin. Among all the usual starters, couscous dishes, grills and tagines, are a few dishes that stand out. Couscous zizou gives you the full Moroccan monty: a herb-rubbed brochette of lamb, a little merguez sausage, some well-cooked chickpeas and mushy vegetables, all capped with a dome of turmeric-stained cabbage leaf.

Meal deals

Balham Kitchen & Bar *15-19 Bedford Hill, SW12 9EX (8675 6900/www.balhamkitchen.com).* Set lunch (noon-4pm Mon-Fri) £10 2 courses, £13 3 courses. **Map** p285. Brasserie

Bar Viva *238 Balham High Road, SW17 7AW (8673 6705).* Set dinner £9.95 2 courses. **Map** p285. International

In the area
Nando's *116-118 Balham High Road, SW12 9AA (8675 6415).* **Map** p285.
Pizza Express *47 Bedford Hill, SW12 9EY (8772 3232).* **Map** p285.

Battersea

★ L'Antipasto
511 Battersea Park Road, SW11 3BW (7223 9765). Clapham Junction rail. **Lunch served** noon-2.30pm, **dinner served** 6.30-11.30pm Mon-Fri; noon-11.30pm Sat; noon-11pm Sun. **Average** ££. **Set meal** (Mon, Thur, Sat, Sun) half-price meals, not incl drinks or dessert. **Map** p284. Italian
On Mondays, Thursdays, Saturdays and Sundays, this sweet, homely neighbourhood tratt slashes its

L'Antipasto

Boiled Egg & Soldiers

already reasonable food prices by half. But what astonishes more – at these prices, at any rate – is that L'Antipasto's Italian staples are authentic, fresh and served with easy charm by a team of experienced waiters. Among our tried and trusted faves are the beautifully creamy fusilli a la gorgonzola, the polenta with wild mushroom starter, and the simple but hugely effective spaghetti al pesto. The specials board is also worthy of attention, with passing pleasures such as grilled flat mushrooms with garlic and fresh chilli, and two roast baby chickens with potatoes and green beans. Battersea locals are fully aware of their good fortune – L'Antipasto is permanently busy.

Banana Leaf Canteen

75-79 Battersea Rise, SW11 1HN (7228 2828). Clapham Junction rail. **Lunch served** noon-3pm, **dinner served** 6-11pm Mon-Fri. **Meals served** noon-11pm Sat, Sun. **Average** ££. **Map** p284. Oriental Basic canteen-style decor coupled with a colourful Battersea clientele creates the vibe of an urban traveller's café here. This is in

keeping with a menu that leans towards Malaysian food, but also includes dishes from other regions of south-east Asia. A starter of stuffed beancurd 'filo' pastry with whole tiger prawns was not quite crisp enough to be called filo, but contained a fresh and bouncy filling, and the portion was generous for its price. Char-grilled chicken bakar jawa, described as being marinated in Javanese aromatic spices, was tender and full of big flavours when drizzled with the wedge of sour lime and sweet chilli salsa that accompanied it. Fast service, hearty portions and low prices keep the customers coming back.

Boiled Egg & Soldiers

63 Northcote Road, SW11 1NP (7223 4894). Clapham Junction rail. **Meals served** 9am-6pm Mon-Sat; 9am-4pm Sun. **Average** ££. **No credit cards. Map** p284. Café Northcote Road's well-heeled twentysomethings come here for the hangover breakfasts and comfort food that takes them back to their childhoods. But those who aren't suffering will also enjoy the slap-up all-day brekkies, which include the usual combos as well as less common options such as smoked haddock and poached egg. Of course, the eponymous boiled egg and soldiers make an appearance, served in comedy chicken eggcups. There's also a 'posh breakfast' that comes with a glass of fizz. The nursery nostalgia theme continues with Marmite on toast, baked potatoes filled with baked beans and grated cheeese, and various salads. It's a small, squashed space with laid-back (borderline haphazard) service and bright, child's bedroom-style decor. Battersea's young crowd (and their kids) love it.

Crumpet
66 Northcote Road, SW11 6QL (7924 1117). Clapham Junction rail. **Meals served** 9am-5.30pm Mon-Sat; 10am-5.30pm Sun. **Set tea** £4.95 (2-4pm). **Average** ££. **Map** p284. Café

This place is all about children. Bright, airy and uncluttered, it has ample space for buggies, plenty of high chairs, a special play den at the back and a serious focus on simple, healthy fare. A tempting assortment of old-fashioned cakes is on display, and the menu offers a good range of sandwiches, salads, snacks and smoothies. We didn't doubt that a tasty goat's cheese and sweet onion marmalade sandwich was 'hand-cut' – its doorstep proportions gave it away. A long tea list is accompanied by cutesy descriptions: decaff is 'the pregnant one' and Darjeeling 'the posh one'. Slightly austere classroom furniture adds to the sensible nature of the place, which is fantastic for families. Those without small children may want to think twice.

★ Fish Club
189 St John's Hill, SW11 1TH (7978 7115). Clapham Junction rail. **Meals served** noon-10pm Tue-Sat; noon-9pm Sun. **Average** ££. **Map** p284. Fish & Chips

The guys at Fish Club have put in the effort and it has paid off handsomely. The stylish modern furnishings (curvy mirrors, running water under a Perspex floor) attract a young, trendy crowd – not the sort of folk often seen in your average chippie. There's a broad range of high-quality fish, which changes seasonally: fresh mackerel, red mullet and razor clams have all made appearances, displayed in a wet counter so you can specify how you'd like them cooked. There are many other interesting options too: prepare yourself for prawn and chorizo kebabs, trays of sushi, and chips made from sweet potato. Potatoes also come boiled, mashed or chipped. Fish Club's dedication to own-made dishes stretches from its condiments to its seasonal English puds.

Fish in a Tie
105 Falcon Road, SW11 2PF (7924 1913). Clapham Junction rail. **Lunch served** noon-3pm, **dinner served** 6pm-midnight Mon-Sat. **Meals served** noon-11pm Sun. **Average** ££. **Set meal** (noon-3pm, 6pm-midnight Mon-Thur, Sun; noon-3pm Fri, Sat) £6.50 3 courses. **Map** p284. International

At this endearingly named bistro, prices are so darned low that it is regularly crammed to the rafters. The homely interior, with candles precariously stuck into bottles, adds to the atmosphere. From an expansive menu, we had the very shareable pasta of the day starter for a wallet-friendly £3.95, then moved on to main courses that were equally good: rack of lamb, and chicken with stilton and pears were simple plates of fab grub for less than a tenner. FT's not going to win acclaim as a fine dining venue, but if it's a fantastic local or chilled night with friends you're after, pop along. They even give you a free slice of watermelon at the end. Bless 'em.

South

★ Gourmet Burger Kitchen

44 Northcote Road, SW11 1NZ (7228 3309). Clapham Junction rail/49, 77, 219, 345 bus. **Meals served** noon-11pm Mon-Fri; 11am-11pm Sat; 11am-10pm Sun. **Average ££. Map** p284. Burgers
GBK was the first gourmet burger chain and it remains our favourite to this day. Its purchase at the end of 2004 by Clapham House (an umbrella company that runs a few restaurant chains) and GBK's subsequent rapid expansion has seen no dip in standards – or, at least, none that we've noticed. The sesame-flecked buns still have a firm texture, the tasty fillings are prime quality, and you'll find no finer Aberdeen Angus beef patties. Portions are huge, the fat chips are golden and just right, and the extras have no corners cut. Among the many fabulous variations is the beetroot- and pineapple-layered kiwiburger – much better than it sounds, honest. And the service at this (the original) branch is as friendly and welcoming as ever.

Their secret? We think it's due in part to the strong Kiwi influence; the three founders and many of the upbeat staff are from New Zealand.

Niki Noodle NEW

60 Northcote Road, SW11 1PA (7585 1392). Clapham Junction rail. **Meals served** noon-10.30pm daily. **Average ££. Map** p284. Oriental
The diner-style interior of Niki Noodle makes a bow to the Far East with its shared tables, bench seating, Chinese lamps, Japanese collage on the walls and shelves decorated with rows of oriental sauce bottles. However, Niki's dishes are like a backpacker interpretation of Asian food, so don't come here expecting authenticity. Laksa, the soup noodle staple of Singapore and Malaysia, was more like a modern Australian interpretation of the dish with its abundance of toppings such as spinach leaves and seared beef. But, as long as you don't hanker after the taste of the real thing, the dishes are fine, and puddings such as passion fruit and coconut panna cotta make a welcome change from the usual run of oriental desserts.

Fish in a Tie. See p143.

Pizza Metro

64 Battersea Rise, SW11 1EQ
(7228 3812/www.pizzametro.com).
Clapham Junction rail. **Dinner**
served 6-11pm Tue-Fri. **Meals**
served noon-11pm Sat; noon-
10.30pm Sun. **Average** ££.
Set meal £6.50 (minimum 6)
2 courses. **Map** p284. Pizza & Pasta
Pizza Metro is a good argument for
never having to eat at one of the
high-street pizza chains again.
Service is cheerful, friendly and
Italian, while the checked tablecloths
conspire to make you feel like you're
really in Italy – or perhaps a slightly
Disneyfied version of the country.
Appealing starters, including
meatballs and refreshing cold
courgettes fried and marinated in
olive oil, lemon, balsamic vinegar
and mint, were a warm-up for the job
at hand: ploughing through a platter
of pizza. Metro bakes their pizzas in
an oblong shape, serving them on a
huge metal tray, which stretches
across the table. While this might be
a bad idea for allergy sufferers (there
is some cross-contamination of
toppings), it is rather fun and makes
it a popular place for parties. The
crusts of the pizzas are perfectly thin
and crisp, and the menu lists classic
fresh Italian toppings.

Swayam Ruchi NEW

2 Battersea Rise, SW11 1ED
(7738 0038). Clapham Junction rail.
Lunch served noon-3pm, **dinner**
served 6-11pm daily. **Average**
££. **Set lunch** £4.99 2 courses.
Map p284. Indian
This family-run Keralite restaurant
has replaced an earlier South Indian
venue on the same site; and but it
remains a cool and quiet place to eat.
Chef-proprietor Ajit Kumar used to
be the head chef at Rasa (see p201)
in the restaurant's early days –
something evident in the menu,
which recreates many of Rasa's
greatest hits. Many dishes were of a
high standard, such as a pert and
succulent cabbage thoran, and the
cheera parippu (a lentil curry made
with yellow dahl and spinach).
Snacks such as the banana boli (sliced
and fried with peanut sauce) were a
little heavy, but tasted just fine.
Although Swayam Ruchi would
benefit from a little more attention to
detail in the kitchen, it's a welcoming,
relaxing restaurant with a good menu
and fine, careful service.

Meal deals

Le Bouchon Bordelais *5-9*
Battersea Rise, SW11 1HG (7738
0307/www.lebouchon.co.uk). Set
lunch (noon-3pm Mon-Fri) £10
2 courses, £13 3 courses. Set menu
(noon-3pm, 6-7pm Mon-Fri) £15
3 courses. **Map** p284. French
Cinnamon Cay *87 Lavender Hill,*
SW11 5QL (7801 0932/www.
cinnamoncay.co.uk). Set dinner
(6-10.30pm Mon-Wed; 6-7pm Thur,
Fri) £13.95 2 courses. International
The Food Room *123 Queenstown*
Road, SW8 3RH (7622 0555/
www.thefoodroom.com). Set lunch
£13.50 2 courses. French
Osteria Antica Bologna *23*
Northcote Road, SW11 1NG (7978
4771/www.osteria.co.uk). Set lunch
(noon-3pm Mon-Fri; noon-5.30pm
Sat) £10.50 2 courses, £13 3 courses.
Map p284. Italian

In the area

Giraffe *27 Battersea Rise, SW11*
1HG (7223 0933). **Map** p284.
Little Bay *228 York Road, SW11*
3SJ (7223 4080). **Map** p284.
Nando's *1A Northcote Road, SW11*
1NG (7228 6221). **Map** p284.
Pizza Express *230-236 Lavender*
Hill, SW11 1LE (7223 5677).
Pizza Express *46-54 Battersea*
Bridge Road, SW11 3AG (7924
2774). **Map** p284.
Strada *11-13 Battersea Rise, SW11*
1HG (7801 0794). **Map** p284.
Tootsies Grill *1 Battersea Rise,*
SW11 1HG (7924 4935).
Map p284.

South

Brixton

Asmara

*386 Coldharbour Lane, SW9 8LF
(7737 4144). Brixton tube/rail.*
Dinner served 5.30pm-midnight
daily. **Average** ££. **Map** p286.
Eritrean
Asmara is an East African enclave
on Brixton's Coldharbour Lane. The
food is authentic Eritrean cuisine,
along with a few pasta dishes, a nod
to Italy's one-time colonial influence
on the country. But it's the spiced
beef, lamb or chicken stews that are
most popular, along with huge
platters of injera for mopping up.
Best of all is the Eritrean coffee:
the freshly roasted, still smoking
beans are presented for infusion at
each table and served with an
incongruous but endearing bowl of
warm salted popcorn. Asmara is
a budget restaurant, but with the
staff all in traditional dress, serene
and benevolent service, banks of
traditional seating, and the coffee
ceremony, it's a definite step up from
your average cut-price venue.

Baan Thai

*401 Coldharbour Lane, SW9 8LQ
(7737 5888). Brixton tube/rail.*
Lunch served noon-2.30pm Mon-
Sat, **dinner served** 6-11.30pm
Sun-Thur; 6pm-midnight Fri, Sat.
Average ££. **Map** p286. Thai
This eaterie seems to have lost some
slickness since opening a few years
ago. The menu is unchanged, with
generous sized portions of prawn
toast and pork dumplings with
dipping sauce making a very decent
starter for two. Mains were less
consistent: the special Baan Thai
noodles came in an unimpressive
and overly sweet, sticky sauce with
plenty of unshelled prawns. Kai
yang (charcoal grilled chicken in
honey) was perfectly moreish on its
own, and the rice with spring greens
provided a less ordinary side dish.

Bamboula

*12 Acre Lane, SW2 5SG (7737
6633). Brixton tube/rail.* **Meals
served** 11am-11pm Mon-Fri; noon-
11pm Sat; 1-9pm Sun. **Average**
£££. **Map** p286. Caribbean
A bijou restaurant that has a big
character to match, Bamboula's
bright interior, lush foliage and
regular playing of old-school reggae
makes it a real Brixton favourite,
drawing a wide range of customers.
One thing that attracts them is value
for money. The dish named
'satisfaction' (a quarter of jerk
chicken with rice and peas, plantain
and a soft drink) provides just that,
an all-in-one bumper-sized meal for
a mere £5.50. For an extra quid you
can have jerk lamb with the same
rice and plantain combination.
Lighter dishes include a gorgeous
red pea soup with pumpkin, yam
and potato; and Bamboula house
salad, with lettuce, tomato, mango,
avocado and soft cheese. In fact, the
menu is extensive and versatile,
with ample room to mix and match
– you can have curried chicken with
callaloo leaves, for example, instead
of the more usual rice.

Coma y Punto

*94-95 Granville Arcade, Coldharbour
Lane, SW9 8PS (7326 0276).
Brixton tube/rail.* **Meals served**
9am-6pm Mon, Tue, Thur-Sat; 9am-
3pm Wed. **Average** ££. **No credit
cards**. **Map** p286. Colombian
Little has changed at this friendly
Colombian café and local gathering
spot on the edge of Brixton market.
The bold, fake red brick fascia
still welcomes from afar and there
is plenty of seating both outside
and in, despite limited interior
space. Portions are hearty and
comforting with most main courses
accompanied by cassava, plantain
and mounds of rice topped with a
blob of tomato ketchup. Alongside
the breakfasts and snacks there are

also a few fish dishes including red mullet, which is served whole and comes with a satisfyingly crispy skin. Alternatively, flattened chicken steaks were nicely tender and came with a tangy, mild salsa. The hot home-made salsa adorning the condiment stand should however be used with caution.

Hive NEW

11-13 Brixton Station Road, SW9 8PA (7274 8383). Brixton tube/rail. **Lunch served** noon-4pm, **dinner served** 6-10pm Mon-Fri. **Meals served** 10am-10pm Sat, Sun. **Average** ££. **Map** p286.
International

A bar-cum-diner on the edge of Brixton Market that straddles these two functions and as a result defies easy categorisation. It serves breakfast, lunch, dinner and drinks, and has become a one-stop shop for lounging, live music and exhibitions. The Hive also manages to maintain a high standard on the food front. Decor is light and bright, with stencilled bees on sage green walls. Sit downstairs at large wooden tables, or upstairs, on the first floor, where soft sofas provide a more laid-back vibe. Daytime snacks include first-rate sandwiches with salad or own-made fries, roast organic beef ploughman's, and pasta dishes. The evening menu offers an enticing range of well-thought-out dishes. Prawn and pea risotto was excellent, with bumper-sized crustacea and smooth, creamy rice. Also enjoyable was vegetarian tagliatelle with red onions, sun-dried tomatoes and green olives. Service was efficient and friendly. To drink, there's a wide range of wine and plenty of champagne, plus some cocktails, both classic and contemporary.

New Fujiyama

7 Vining Street, SW9 8QA (7737 2369). Brixton tube/rail. **Meals served** noon-4pm, 5-11pm Mon, Tue; noon-4pm, 5pm-1am Wed, Thur; noon-1am Fri, Sat; noon-midnight Sun. **Average** ££.
Map p286. Japanese

Tucked into a backstreet off Atlantic Road, New Fujiyama provides decent music, long shared tables, and a lengthy menu of well-priced food served in generous portions. No wonder the locals appreciate it. The menu ranges widely (perhaps alarmingly for such a small place) across China, Japan and Thailand, with stops for noodle soup, rice plates, sushi and dumplings. We dined well. An order of regular sashimi included prawns and ark shell, yellowtail and bass, and salmon: all wonderful. Gyoza was a triumph of bright flavours. And a big helping of spinach ohitashi was good, though more Chinese than the traditional Japanese rolled greens as it arrived in a sea of sweet sauce, like a Cantonese stir-fry.

Phoenix Restaurant

441 Coldharbour Lane, SW9 8LN (7733 4430). Brixton tube/rail. **Meals served** 6.30am-5pm Mon-Sat. **Average** ££. **No credit cards. Map** p286. Café

This unpretentious back street café was quite subdued on our recent weekend visit although the custom seemed constant; the emphasis is definitely not on hanging around after you finish wiping the gravy from your plate. The food is cheap and cheerful, with most platefuls costing around a fiver and worth every penny. The thick cut ham, egg and crispy chips proved far from greasy spoon and even the huge breakfasts were well above average café fodder. There are healthier choices, such as freshly prepared chunky salmon salad with leaves and avocado. The small blackboard at the back lists the long-standing special of ownmade meat pie along with a list of traditional English desires. This is the ultimate venue for comfort food, well-brewed tea and a flick through the weekend paper.

In the area
Eco Brixton *4 Market Row, Brixton Market, Electric Lane, SW9 8LD (7738 3021).* **Map** p286.
Nando's *234-244 Stockwell Road, SW9 9SP (7737 6400).* **Map** p286.

Clapham

Abbevilles Restaurant
88 Clapham Park Road, SW4 7BX (7498 2185). Clapham Common tube/35, 37 bus. **Meals served** 11.30am-3.30pm Mon-Fri. **Average £. No credit cards. Map** p286. International

Not only is this a very reasonably priced bistro, it's also an enterprise run by the First Step Trust that gives people with mental disabilities the opportunity to participate in the running of a restaurant. The short menu takes in bistro classics – including a solid steak with chunky chips – but also trots the globe with freshly seasoned Thai fish cakes with chilli sauce and a decent rendition of crispy aromatic duck with pancakes. Portions are huge and carefully presented. The front might be vivid orange but inside the decor is the fustier side of old-fashioned – bag a table outside in fine weather.

Café Sol
56 Clapham High Street, SW4 7UL (7498 8558). Clapham Common or Clapham North tube. **Meals served** noon-midnight Mon-Thur, Sun; noon-1am Fri, Sat. **Average ££. Map** p286. Latin American

This Clapham stalwart is a classic Tex-Mex. The vast dining room has been decorated to look like a Mexican restaurant in Texas, with sunny paintings, arched doorways,

and wooden tables and chairs shoved close together. The menu may be basic by-the-book burritos 'n' tacos fare, but it's well done, and service is friendly. Join the throngs for big plates of cheesy nachos with beans, salsa, sour cream and plentiful jalapeño chillies. Then dive into the beef or chicken fajitas, or a good taco salad, which arrives in an edible bowl made of a fried flour tortilla, filled to the brim with crisp greens and fresh fajita chicken. This place gets packed later on, so arrive early to avoid the crowds.

Café Wanda
153 Clapham High Street, SW4 7SS (7738 8760). Clapham Common tube. **Meals served** noon-11pm Mon-Fri; 11am-11pm Sat; 11am-7pm Sun. **Average ££. Map** p286. Polish

An unexpected find amid the bland gastropubs and wine bars of Clapham High Street, Café Wanda can rustle up anything from a takeaway cake to a full meal of Polish home cooking. It's an informal spot, furnished with potted plants and eastern European art, and is populated by a steady stream of Polish diners, all of whom seem to know the staff by name. The small menu of Polish staples and mainstream European dishes allows diners to pick and mix; vegetarians are well looked after. Our waiter's comedic patter was relentless, but service overall was tip-top. Café Wanda makes a fine venue for a quiet supper during the week and is an even better choice for a raucous group dinner at the weekend.

Eco
162 Clapham High Street, SW4 7UG (7978 1108). Clapham Common tube. **Lunch served** noon-4pm, **dinner served** 6.30-11pm Mon-Fri. **Meals served** noon-11.30pm Sat; noon-11pm Sun. **Average ££. Map** p286. Pizza & Pasta

Larger, and a few years younger than its sibling in Brixton, Eco is popular enough to warrant booking, especially at weekends. Of the list of 30 pizzas, a fine choice is the vegetarian option with huge porcini mushrooms, fontina cheese and truffle oil. Spicy chicken pizza (with chilli sauce, courgette and onion) was equally bumper-sized, although a slightly crispier base would have been better. Among the non-pizza options, worth trying is penne with mushrooms, cream sauce and fresh basil. Or there are large fresh salads, with own-made dressings that feature, among others, gorgeous crab meat and smoked salmon with fresh herbs and capers; a Parma ham and bresaola platter with artichoke, avocado, dill and chervil; and chicken caesar salad with baked chicken breast, pancetta, fresh anchovies and salad leaves.

★ Macaron NEW

22 The Pavement, SW4 0HY (7498 2636). Clapham Common tube. **Meals served** 7.30am-8pm Mon-Fri; 9am-8pm Sat, Sun. **Average ££. No credit cards. Map** p286. Café

Picture-perfect and charmingly old-fashioned, Macaron looks as if it has been lifted from a 1930s French film set. It's a celebration of nostalgia – lovely china cake plates, flowery cups and saucers, and jars filled with loose leaf teas complement a fabulous array of pâtisserie and freshly baked bread. Our current raves include Le Lingot, a deliciously light apricot mousse with coconut cream and a buttery biscuit base. Other treats include the Paris-Brest (choux pastry rings, crammed with praline and custardy cream), tangy lemon tarts, and scrumptious mini macaroons. Customers sit around a big communal table and soak in the spectacle of chefs whipping icings and piping rosettes on to pastries, visible through the kitchen window. Sweet temptation doesn't get better than this.

★ The Pavement

21 The Pavement, SW4 0HY (7622 4944). Clapham Common tube. **Open** 7am-7pm Mon-Fri; 8am-7pm Sat, Sun. **Average £. No credit cards. Map** p286. Café

The people behind this small and easy-going café clearly understand the concept of a hangover hangout. With soul on the stereo, a full rack of newspapers and comfort food par excellence on the menu, the Pavement is the sort of place you come in for a (Fairtrade) coffee and end up staying in for the rest of the afternoon, chowing your way through a huge veggie fry-up (£5.75) before moving on to the contents of the bounteous cake counter. There's nothing radical about the decor – chunky wooden tables and chairs – or the menu, which has all the café classics covered, including all-day breakfasts, baked potatoes, freshly made sandwiches (check out the loaded triple-deck club sandwich, £5.75) and soup. If that last oat-sprinkled muffin was a snack too far, go horizontal on Clapham Common, just metres away.

Sea Cow

57 Clapham High Street, SW4 7TG (7622 1537). Clapham Common or Clapham North tube. **Meals served** noon-11pm Mon-Sat; noon-9pm Sun. **Average ££. Map** p286. Fish & Chips

Sea Cow is one of the few chippies that offers organic options (salmon, for instance). This Clapham branch remains somewhat in the shadow of the original restaurant in East Dulwich, but appears to be popular nonetheless (there's also a branch in Fulham). Its über-trendy minimal decor is a big hit with Clapham's sometimes almost painfully fashion-conscious twentysomethings, who banter with the fun, friendly staff. The menu is short but to the point – as it should be. Fish, fresh from Billingsgate Market, is displayed like pieces of art in the wet counter. Our fried cod came in slightly soggy batter, but the minted mushy peas were so flavourful we could have eaten them on their own. Variations include crab cakes, which are served with a sharp lime mayonnaise.

Meal deals

Gastro 67 Venn Street, SW4 0BD (7627 0222). Set lunch (noon-3pm Mon-Fri) £9.95 2 courses incl coffee. **Map** p286. French
Newtons 33-35 Abbeville Road, SW4 9LA (8673 0977/www.newtons restaurants.co.uk). Set lunch (noon-3pm Mon-Sat) £8 2 courses, £10.50 3 courses. **Map** p286. Brasserie
Verso 84 Clapham Park Road, SW4 7BX (7720 1515/www. versorestaurant.co.uk). Set meal (7-11.30pm Mon, Wed-Fri; noon-7pm Sat; 4-10.30pm Sun) £10 2 courses. **Map** p286. Pizza & Pasta

In the area

Fresh & Wild 305-311 Lavender Hill, SW11 1LN (7585 1488). **Nando's** 59-63 Clapham High Street, SW4 7TG (7622 1475). **Map** p286.
Pizza Express 43 Abbeville Road, SW4 9JX (8673 8878). **Map** p286.
Strada 102-104 Clapham High Street, SW4 7UL (7627 4847). **Map** p286.
Tootsies Grill 36-38 Abbeville Road, SW4 9NG (8772 6646). **Map** p286.

Kennington

Meal deals

The Lobster Pot 3 Kennington Lane, SE11 4RG (7582 5556/ www.lobsterpotrestaurant.co.uk). Set lunch £11.50 2 courses. **Map** p287. Fish

In the area

Pizza Express 316 Kennington Road, SE11 4LD (7820 3877). **Map** p287.

Stockwell

Bar Estrela

111-115 South Lambeth Road, SW8 1UZ (7793 1051). Stockwell tube/Vauxhall tube/rail. **Breakfast served** 8am-noon, **meals served** noon-11pm daily. **Average** ££. **Map** p287. Portuguese
This lively and easy-going bar/restaurant is all that you would expect from a proper breakfast-till-late venue, with a few regulars and assorted others dropping in for a cold drink or a cake, and all the staples in place. Given the heat on our visit during the summer's heatwave, we snacked on fish cakes and pasteis de nata, following them up with Portuguese bottled beers. It was all perfectly enjoyable, but not about to shake the world (and we weren't expecting it to). Mains of squid and bacalhau were going down a treat at the next table. If you're in the neighbourhood, do stop by.

O Moinho

355A Wandsworth Road, SW8 2JH (7498 6333). Stockwell tube/Vauxhall tube/rail/77, 77A bus. **Meals served** 10am-11pm daily. **Average** ££. **Map** p287. Portuguese
After entering this cool and airy café/restaurant on the steaming Wandsworth Road we headed for the intimate back area near the bar. Service was swift and friendly, and the cover elements, which were delivered unprompted, were extensive, with fish pâtés in addition to olives. We opened with grilled squid (slightly tough), then followed with an excellent mixed fish and grilled vegetable kebab. We ended up taking the latter away – no

problem at all – it was packed well and stayed hot. We would happily return, for both the food and service.

A Toca

343 Wandsworth Road, SW8 2JH (7627 2919). Stockwell tube/ Vauxhall tube/rail. **Meals served** 9am-midnight daily. **Average** ££. **Map** p287. Portuguese

A Toca is a busy hangout for the locals of 'Little Lisbon', and also for people who know a good thing when they eat it. The decor is modest but self-assured, a balance that reflects the quietly excellent cooking. The menu boasts an impressive array of grilled seafood: from grilled sardines to boiled octopus. Basically, if it lives underwater you can eat it here. For landlubbers there are plenty of tasty alternatives, like peppered steaks wrapped in Parma ham or marsala-laced chicken breasts stuffed with mushrooms. Whatever your choice, the generous servings should guarantee happy bellies all around. It's also worth saving room for dessert: the honey and almond ice-cream comes in a cute little pot and is a fine way to polish off dinner.

Streatham

Wholemeal Café NEW

1 Shrubbery Road, SW16 2AS (8769 2423). Streatham/Streatham Hill rail. **Meals served** noon-10pm daily. **Average** ££. Vegetarian

Popular with the locals, this small no-frills caff serves hefty old-fashioned vegetarian staples such as stews, casseroles, bakes, quiches, jacket potatoes and cakes. There's a blackboard of daily changing specials, but no written menu. Garlic mushrooms and pitta bread came with fresh mixed salad; a carrot, celery and aubergine stew was pleasantly flavoured with coriander and cumin. Homity pie, which was once a beloved dish at the now-defunct chain of Cranks restaurants, has all but disappeared from London's vegetarian dining scene. Here it makes a nostalgia-inducing appearance and is at least as good as the classic Cranks version (but with thinner pastry). We recommend the desserts; own-made carrot cake was beautifully moist and topped with a simple drizzle of sugar syrup, rather than the more ubiquitous icing.

In the area

Nando's *6-7 High Parade, Streatham High Road, SE16 1ES (8769 0951).*
Pizza Express *34 Streatham High Road, SW16 1DB (8769 0202).*

Tooting

Kastoori

188 Upper Tooting Road, SW17 7EJ (8767 7027). Tooting Bec or Tooting Broadway tube. **Lunch served** 12.30-2.30pm Wed-Sun. **Dinner served** 6-10.30pm daily. **Average** ££. **Set thalis** £8.50-£16.25. **Minimum** £7. **Map** p285. Indian

Vegetarians and, in particular, vegans come from miles around to eat at this sparklingly clean and long-established East Gujarati restaurant. The venue itself is striking, with a deep-blue carpet and matching padded chairs, bright yellow table linen, and cream walls hung with stone reliefs of a female dancer. Robustly flavoured masala kachori was served like a chaat: crumbled and topped with yoghurt and tamarind sauces and vivid red chilli powder. Fresh tomato curry was vibrantly flavoured, but the green pepper curry in peanut and sesame sauce was too oily. Together with chowri (aduki bean) curry, all the dishes tasted rather similar with their cinnamon-laced tomato sauce. Moreover, the onions used in the sauce base were undercooked. Still, the place is worth a visit.

Masaledar

121 Upper Tooting Road, SW17 7TJ (8767 7676). Tooting Bec or Tooting Broadway tube/155, 219, 355 bus. **Meals served** noon-midnight daily. **Average** £. **Set lunch** (noon-6pm Mon-Fri) £2.95 1 course incl salad and rice. **Unlicensed. Corkage** no charge. **Map** p285. East African Punjabi

The good news is that Masaledar is one of London's best-value Pakistani restaurants, with excellent East African Asian cooking and a BYO policy. The bad news is that it's Tooting's worst-kept secret, and is perenially packed with customers queuing to sit in or takeaway. If you don't mind the wait and the bustle, the food is a real treat. Masaledar's specials include achari gosht, lamb cooked in pickling spices that give it an appealing sour tang; and marage, a red kidney bean curry with an earthy heat that's nicely matched with doughnut-like mandazi bread. Masala aubergine is meltingly soft and unctuous, and the pilau rice is food-colouring-free, flavoured with cumin and browned onions. Make sure you try the fresh passion fruit juice, which is simply sublime.

Radha Krishna Bhavan

86 Tooting High Street, SW17 0RN (8682 0969). Tooting Broadway tube. **Lunch served** noon-3pm daily. **Dinner served** 6-11pm Mon-Thur, Sun; 6pm-midnight Fri, Sat. **Average** £. **Set thalis** (noon-3pm Sun) £5.95-£7.95. **Minimum** £5. **Map** p285. Indian

This Keralite venue dares to be different from the standard curry house. Its walls are covered with bold and brightly coloured photographic wallpaper of palm-fringed beaches and sunsets, and strewn with kathakali masks. There's also a life-size statue of a kathakali dancer. A long menu contains much that is standard curry-house fare, but stick to the Keralite dishes and you won't

go far wrong. Idli vadai sambar was a large bowl of mellow lentil broth crammed full to overflowing with vegetable drumsticks, a chunky idli and a hefty lentil fritter floating on top – tasty and substantial. Adai was a large, thin pancake made fiery and fragrant with cracked black pepper, hot chilli powder and curry leaves. On our visit, good-looking twenty- and thirtysomethings were having fun tackling the enormous 'ghee roast' masala dosas.

Rick's Café NEW

122 Mitcham Road, SW17 9NH (8767 5219). Tooting Broadway tube. **Lunch served** noon-3pm daily. **Dinner served** 6-11pm Mon-Sat; 6-10pm Sun. **Average** ££. **Map** p285. Modern European

The first time we visited Rick's, on a Wednesday (without booking, we must admit), the place was full to bursting. It was 'Spanish night', with a flamenco guitarist and all. The next time we went, on a Monday, the restaurant was busy again. Something good must be happening here. Our starter of haddock chowder bore this out, delivering a perfect balance of smoked fish and hot peppers. A dish of asparagus was, however, slightly overcooked, but it was flavoursome nonetheless. Both main courses were excellent. Pork fillet was presented in bite-size portions charred round the edges, with a fried egg on top that oozed into the tasty, chunky chips. Ribeye steak wasn't as thick as most, but had a heart of fat that spread flavour to all its edges. We'll be back, however busy Rick's is.

Sree Krishna

192-194 Tooting High Street, SW17 0SF (8672 4250). Tooting Broadway tube/57, 155, 219 bus. **Lunch served** noon-3pm daily. **Dinner served** 6-11pm Mon-Thur, Sun; 6pm-midnight Fri, Sat. **Average** ££. **Set lunch** (Mon-Sat) £4.95 3 courses.

Kastoori. See p151.

Set thalis (noon-3pm Sun) £5.95-
£7.95 3 courses. Minimum £7.50
(dinner). Map p285. South Indian
Sree Krishna has been going strong
since 1973, but has just had a bit of
a spruce-up: with its new marble
floor, mirrored pillars and Krishna
wall carvings, it now looks like a
South Indian palace. The menu
remains the same as ever, a mix of
South Indian snack dishes and
breakfast dishes (dosai, idli, vadai),
fish and vegetable dishes from
Kerala, plus a few formula curries
aimed at vindaloo fans. But eschew
the familiar and instead order the
impeccably thin and crisp dosai
pancakes, aromatic lemon rice,
wonderfully light thorans, and
seafood curries. The Alleppey fish
curry is typical of the Keralite dishes
they do so well: a small pomfret in a
rich, layered sauce redolent of
coconut milk with complex, layered
spicing. The service is old-school
Indian: sweet, and lots of it.

Suvai Aruvi

*96 High Street Colliers Wood,
SW19 2BT (8543 6266). Colliers
Wood tube.* **Open** 11am-midnight
daily. **Average** ££. **Unlicensed.**
Corkage No charge. **No credit
cards. Map** p285. Sri Lankan
This Tamil caff is inside a basic shop
unit with Tamil satellite TV blaring
over strip-lit tables. Takeaway,
therefore, is very popular – and
prices are absurdly low. The menu's
a comprehensive selection of Sri
Lankan veg and non-veg dishes,
covering all the classics from string
hoppers through richly-spiced
seafood dishes to sothi. We're fond of
the kuttu roti, strips of thin bread
fried up with mutton or vegetables to
make a spicy biriani-like dish. As an
alternative to ordinary rice, try the
pittu: rice flour and coconut steamed
in bamboo to make a starchy 'log'.
Snacks are fine too, and with a
mutton roll (a Sri Lankan version of
a spring roll) costing only 60p, you'll
be back for more.

In the area

Mirch Masala *213 Upper Tooting
Road, SW17 7TG (8672 7500).*
Map p285.
Nando's *224-226 Upper Tooting
Road, SW17 7EW (8682 2478).*
Map p285.

Sakonis *180-186 Upper Tooting Road, SW17 7EW (8772 4774).* **Map** p285.

Vauxhall

Bonnington Centre Café `NEW`

11 Vauxhall Grove, SW8 1TD (no phone/www.bonnington cafe.co.uk). Vauxhall tube/rail. **Lunch served** noon-2pm, **dinner served** 7-11pm daily. **Average** £. **Unlicensed. Corkage** no charge. **No credit cards. Map** p287.
Vegetarian

Located just off the suitably bohemian environs of Bonnington Square, this vegetarian restaurant – decked out with endearingly mismatched chairs and tables, and dripping candles in the evening – is community-run, and uncommonly friendly as a result. Local chefs take their turns at the helm each night, so the cuisine – and therefore rather inevitably the standard – varies wildly. The prices however are consistent, and low: £10 for three courses (and BYO). On our last visit, the food far exceeded this price tag: mains of just-so penne panna, packed with porcini mushrooms, and comforting tomato nut roast were both accompanied by a beautifully dressed bean salad. Help yourself to crockery and cutlery, and note that Thursday is vegan night. We've had so-so meals in the past, but caught on the right night (check the website for details of who's cooking), Bonnington Square Café offers one of the best dinner deals to be found in south London.

Café Madeira

46A-46B Albert Embankment, SE1 7TN (7820 1117). Vauxhall tube/rail. **Meals served** 6am-9pm daily. **Average** £. **Set buffet** (6am-11am) £4, (11am-4pm) £5. **Map** p287. Portuguese

Anyone who knows the Albert Embankment will appreciate that this major thoroughfare is not best suited to an intimate tête-à-tête over coffee and cake. More suited, as it is, to exhaust repair and bathroom wholesale, it does, however, contain a short stretch of converted arches where the pace chills dramatically. Several eateries are dominated by the Madeira operation, with bakery, deli and café, and an easy-going atmosphere. There's a mixture of Portuguese talent – fish pasties and fritters, pasteis and rice cakes – alongside all the usual suspects on the sandwich and sweet front. Hot mains, including paella and curry, also appear. Tasty, friendly, relaxed; these are important qualities.

★ Hot Stuff

19 Wilcox Road, SW8 2XA (7720 1480). Vauxhall tube/rail. **Meals served** noon-10pm Mon-Fri; 3-10pm Sat. **Average** ££. **Unlicensed. Corkage** no charge. **Map** p287.
East African Indian

This immensely popular BYO curry house (and takeaway), on a seldom-explored Vauxhall backstreet, is run with charm – and plenty of chat – by the Dawood family. The order of the day is homely Indian-West African dishes, prepared with care, plenty of fresh ingredients and none of the bland, formulaic sauces that afflict many a neighbourhood Indian. The masala fish (Wed-Sat only, £4.25), an East African curry, is the stuff of local legend: chunks of tilapia fish are marinated at length before being cooked in a rich, freshly seasoned sauce to gratifying effect. The specials board warrants your close attention: look out for (really very special) dahl makani, black lentils slow-cooked in butter, and the lighter green banana curry. Grab your beers at the off licence next door, and book at weekends – Hot Stuff has an army of local fans and only 25 seats.

Waterloo

★ EV Restaurant, Bar & Delicatessen

The Arches, 97-99 Isabella Street, SE1 8DA (7620 6191/www.tas restaurant.com). Southwark or Waterloo tube/rail.
Bar **Open/meze served** noon-11.30pm Mon-Sat; noon-10pm Sun.
Average ££. *Deli* **Open** 7am-10pm Mon-Sat; 9am-10pm Sun.
Restaurant **Meals served** noon-11.30pm Mon-Sat; noon-10.30pm Sun. **Average ££. Set meal** £8.25 2 courses, £18.25 3 courses person (minimum 2). **Set meze** £8.25-£10.25 per person (minimum 2).
Map p288. Turkish
The upmarket Tas chain of eateries has expanded from London Bridge to Waterloo, and up into the West End. The restaurants have many features in common, despite being called variously Tas, Tas Café, Tas Pide and EV (which means 'home' in Turkish). Set in three old railway arches, EV has a large bar located next to an equally capacious restaurant, plus a bakery/deli. For starters, balik böreği is gorgeous: filo pastry filled with mixed seafood, mushrooms and cashar cheese. Although not quite as exciting, çilbir (fried egg and sun-dried tomato, served with yoghurt and olive oil) was also good. Mains kept up the quality of the starters with a notably tasty balik köftesi (fish cakes in a fresh tomato and coriander sauce). In general, the inventiveness of EV's menu pays off handsomely.

Giraffe

Riverside, Royal Festival Hall, Belvedere Road, SE1 8XX (7928 2004). Embankment tube/Waterloo tube/rail. **Meals served** 8am-10.45pm Mon-Fri; 9am-10.45pm Sat; 9am-10.30pm Sun. **Average ££. Set meal** (5-7pm Mon-Fri) £6.95 2 courses; (7-11pm Mon-Fri) £8.95 2 courses. **Map** p288. Brasserie

Giraffe's successful formula of familiar global menu favourites and unobtrusive world music in relaxed surroundings has been embraced by Londoners; the South Bank makes a great location for this fast-expanding, family-friendly chain. The balance is just right – not too gimmicky or nappy-happy – mixing families during the day and, later, groups gathering for post-work, two-for-one drinks. Weekend queues are standard. Pancakes with banana and blueberries, fry-ups and french toast are popular for weekend brunch, and the Surf Skewer Bar offers the likes of fiery tiger prawns, barbeque chicken wings and teriyaki salmon. Mains include Vietnamese curries, Tex-Mex burritos, salads, steaks and burgers (the veggie falafel with grilled pepper, rocket, halloumi cheese and harissa is recommended). Staff are smiling, unflappable and efficient.

Inshoku

23-24 Lower Marsh, SE1 7RJ (7928 2311). Waterloo tube/rail.
Lunch served noon-3pm Mon-Fri.
Dinner served 5.30-10.30pm Mon-Sat. **Average ££.** **Set lunch** £4-£8.40. **Set meal** (noon-2pm Mon-Sat) £6 bento box. **Map** p288. Japanese
Not in Waterloo station itself, you'll find Inshoku among a parade of shops in the street market of Lower Marsh. Most of the lunchtime clientele seems to come in from the immediate locality, rather than heading over from the station. The interior, furnished with worn-looking parasols and ukiyo-e prints, needs redecorating, and both the lighting and the cleanliness of the dining area could be improved. We sampled some good gyoza, some acceptable miso soup, and enjoyed the comfort-food taste of oyako-don (chicken pieces on rice). Service was friendly too. However, our sushi,

though copious, was mostly left on the plate; it just didn't seem to have that zinging-fresh quality of the best fish. Prices are low but, sadly, so can be the standard of food.

Masters Super Fish

191 Waterloo Road, SE1 8UX (7928 6924). Waterloo tube/rail. **Lunch served** noon-3pm Tue-Sat. **Dinner served** 5.30-10.30pm Mon; 4.30-10.30pm Tue-Thur, Sat; 4.30-11pm Fri. **Average** ££. **Set lunch** (noon-3pm Tue-Sun) £6 1 course incl tea/coffee or soft drink. **Map** p288. Fish & Chips

With its brick walls painted green and brown, glaring lighting and plastic furnishings, Masters Super Fish resembles a motorway services café. A heavy smell of batter and vinegar permeates the room (why not open a window?). But what the place lacks for in sophistication, it more than makes up for in the food stakes. Three complimentary shell-on prawns and a basket of baguettes arrive at the table seconds after you do. The extensive menu also offers everything from Cromer crab to hamburgers. You can even have your fish grilled if you're willing to wait 30 minutes. Not one of our fellow diners – mainly cabbies and pensioners – could manage to eat all of the large portions. The fried plaice was vast, but tasted exceptionally light and came in a thin moist batter. The scampi was the biggest and juiciest we've tasted to date.

Pizza Paradiso NEW

61 The Cut, SE1 8LL (7261 1221). Southwark tube/Waterloo tube/rail. **Meals served** noon-midnight Mon-Sat; noon-11pm Sun. **Average** ££. **Map** p288. Pizza & Pasta

From its base in Store Street, where it set root as the Ristorante Olivelli in 1934, Pizza Paradiso has (very) slowly grown into a mini-chain of six branches, each of which still manages to retain the feel of a neighbourhood trattoria through strategic use of floral displays and signed photographs. Pizzas are consistently good, with fine, fresh toppings and solid bases. There are also a number of steak and fish dishes on the menu, which help to elevate it above the chain norm, while the pasta dishes are more than just an afterthought. We've never had a bad meal here. Still the most individually appealing of London's chain pizzerias.

Meal deals

Baltic *74 Blackfriars Road, SE1 8HA (7928 1111/www.baltic restaurant.co.uk).* Set meal (noon-3pm, 6-7pm Mon-Sat) £11.50 2 courses, £13.50 3 courses; (noon-10.30pm Sun) £13.50 2 courses incl drink, £15.50 3 courses incl drink. **Map** p288. Polish

Tamesa@oxo *Second floor, Oxo Tower Wharf, Barge House Street, SE1 9PH (7633 0088/www. coinstreet.org).* Set meal (noon-3.30pm, 5.30-7pm, 10-11.30pm Mon-Sat) £12.50 2 courses. **Map** p288. Brasserie

Troia *3F Belvedere Road, SE1 7GQ (7633 9309).* Set lunch (noon-4pm) £8.75 2 courses. Set meze £9.95 per person (minimum 2). **Map** p288. Turkish

In the area

Konditor & Cook *22 Cornwall Road, SE1 8TW (7261 0456).* **Map** p288.

Pizza Express *3 The White House, Belvedere Road, SE1 8YP (7928 4091).* **Map** p288.

Strada *Riverside, Royal Festival Hall, Belvedere Road, SE1 8XX (7401 9126).* **Map** p288.

Tas *33 The Cut, SE1 8LF (7928 2111).* **Map** p288.

Wagamama *Riverside Level 1, Royal Festival Hall, SE1 8XX (7021 0877).* **Map** p288.

Yo! Sushi *Unit 3B, County Hall, Belvedere Road, SE1 7GP (7928 8871).* **Map** p288.

SOUTH EAST

Bankside

Tate Modern Café: Level 2

Second floor, Tate Modern, Sumner Street, SE1 9TG (7401 5014/www.tate.org.uk). Southwark tube/London Bridge tube/rail. **Breakfast served** 10-11.30am, **lunch served** 11.30am-3pm, **afternoon tea served** 3-5.30pm daily. **Dinner served** 6.30-9.30pm Fri. **Average £££. Map** p289.
Brasserie

Tate Modern's contemporary feel continues in this light, spacious café, which has a long, sleek bar, well-spaced tables and wall-hung art. The café makes the most of its excellent location with floor-to-ceiling windows that overlook the Thames. The prices are rather high, but the view is great and the food is a cut above usual museum-café cooking. The menus (breakfast, lunch, afternoon tea, plus dinner on late-closing nights) have a Modern European/ Mediterranean leaning – try roast Loch Duart salmon with pesto, or white bean cassoulet and pancetta, for example. A tapas-style light lunch of spiced chickpeas, houmous and aubergine salad with grilled flatbread was bursting with rich Med flavours: simple and delicious. Desserts are tempting too; elderflower sorbet melting into warm poached rhubarb with shortbread was a glorious mix of flavours and textures.

In the area

Pizza Express *Benbow House, 24 New Globe Walk, SE1 9DS (7401 3977).* **Map** p289.
The Real Greek Souvlaki & Bar *Units 1&2, Riverside House, 2A Southwark Bridge Road, SE1 9HA (7620 0162).* **Map** p289.
Tas Pide *20-22 New Globe Walk, SE1 9DR (7633 9777).* **Map** p289.

Bermondsey

Arancia

52 Southwark Park Road, SE16 3RS (7394 1751). Bermondsey tube/Elephant & Castle tube/rail then 1, 53 bus. **Lunch served** 12.30-2.30pm, **dinner served** 7-11pm Tue-Sat. **Average £££. Set lunch** £7.50 2 courses, £10.50 3 courses. Italian

Incongruously nestled between housing estates, this quirky gem uses fresh ingredients to create intelligent flavour combinations after an Italian fashion. Our line-up of dishes included rosemary-stuffed sardines; delicate lasagne with own-made pasta and asparagus; belly pork with borlotti beans; and beautifully cooked lamb. Desserts are excellent, and at these prices you'd be silly not to order one. The semifreddo in particular is popular for good reason; it provided a rich end to a lovely meal. Baked ricotta cheesecake with lemon peel was also superb. The all-Italian wine list isn't fancy, but hits the right tone with the food. Orange walls, wooden floors, exposed brick and flickering candles create an aura of calm. Arancia is the ideal inexpensive neighbourhood stalwart. It serves food of a higher quality and greater finesse than many places charging twice the price.

Blackheath

Chu & Cho

52 Charlton Church Lane, SE7 7AB (7642 1014). Charlton rail. **Tapas served** noon-11pm Fri; 11am-11pm Sat; 11am-10.30pm Sun. **Average £££. No credit cards.** Spanish

It's a shame this tapas-serving café opens only three days a week, as its simple but well-chosen and very well-executed menu of Spanish classics deserves more of an audience than this limited outing allows. The short hours must have something to do with the oft-quiet location, on a normally sleepy hill in Charlton; but just round the corner is the foodball stadium, so it's a different scene on match days, when the compact eating space quickly gets filled up. Try standards such as calamares a la romana and gambas ajillo, or plump for more unusual regional dishes like papas mojó picón (potatoes dressed with a sauce of cumin and chilli) or a plate of idiazabal, a terrific smoked sheep's cheese from the Basque country. As well as draught San Miguel there are also great fresh coffee. With prices that come in at around £3 or less for most savoury dishes, you can stuff yourself here on quality food for next to nothing.

★ Laicram

1 Blackheath Grove, SE3 0DD (8852 4710). Blackheath rail.
Lunch served noon-2.30pm, **dinner served** 6-11pm Tue-Sun.
Average ££. **Map** p291. Thai

Blackheath residents would rather you didn't know about Laicram. There are barely enough tables to go around on week nights as it is. A certain chintziness prevails in the decor (wooden trellises covered in plastic flowers and bright pictures of Thai royalty on the walls), but the space is surprisingly intimate, and made more interesting by the intriguing dessert trolley near the door. We ordered everything together, from a familiar royal Thai menu, and were bowled over. Tom kha (hot and sour chicken soup) was full-flavoured and fabulously spicy, while the Thai fried rice was sweet and moreish – best with a sprinkling of prik nam (fish sauce with chillies). Best of all, red curry with beef was an unmitigated delight, full of bamboo shoots and moist aubergines that radiated chilli heat.

El Pirata

15-16 Royal Parade, SE3 0TL (8297 1880). Blackheath rail.
Meals served noon-11.45pm Sun-Thur; noon-12.30pm Fri, Sat.
Average £££. **Set Lunch** (noon-6pm daily) £7.95 2 courses.
Map p291. Spanish

This spacious Spanish themed restaurant's splendid view over the Blackheath common wins hands down before you've even sampled the sangria and tapas, especially on a warm summer night when you can sit out front. The choice covers everything you'd expect from a tapas menu and dishes are usually big enough for two people to share quite happily. Patatas bravas, garlicky mushrooms, spicy chorizo and pincho de pollo (chicken skewers) were all enjoyable although we left plates of overly chewy calamares and pungent whitebait barely touched. The staff are quietly friendly and despite the few dud seafood dishes, the food and surroundings were enjoyed equally.

In the area

Pizza Express *64-66 Tranquil Vale, SE3 0BN (8318 2595).* **Map** p291.
Strada *5 Lee Road, SE3 9RQ (8318 6644).* **Map** p291.
'Za London *17 Royal Parade, SE3 0TL (8318 5333).* Branch of Mar i Terra. **Map** p291.

Camberwell

Chumleigh Gardens Café

Chumleigh Gardens, Burgess Park, SE5 0RJ (7525 1070). Elephant & Castle tube/rail then P3, 12, 42, 63, 68, 171, 343 bus. **Meals served** 9am-5pm Mon-Fri; 10am-5pm Sat, Sun. **Average** £. Café

The quaint Chumleigh almshouses and magnificent gardens are a pleasant surprise in rather barren

Burgess Park. The café, situated between the compact Mediterranean and Islamic Gardens, is a cheerful and unpretentious place, with its incongruous mix of bright, plastic tablecloths, samba music and peaceful outdoor seating around a fountain and tiled pond. You'll find gorgeous, hearty salads, a huge array of sandwiches made to order, all-day breakfasts, omelettes, baked potatoes and individually wrapped cakes. The coffee is Fairtrade. Our only grumble was that meals were literally served one at a time, and a 20-minute wait for a sandwich on a quiet weekday lunchtime was a little frustrating. Parents beware – there are some (signposted) poisonous plants at toddler level.

La Luna

380 Walworth Road, SE17 2NG (7277 1991). Bus 12, 35, 40, 45, 68, 68A, 171, 176. **Lunch served** noon-3pm, **dinner served** 6-11pm Tue-Sat. **Meals served** noon-10.45pm Sun. **Average** ££. **Set lunch** £5.50 1 course incl coffee. **Map** p292. Pizza & Pasta

This real local draws equally real locals for a rustic Italian experience. The menu is chock full of pizzas and pastas (the main attraction for regulars), with a smattering of fish and meat dishes, and an interesting specials boards. To start we enjoyed a salmon salad and a flavourful parmigiana di melanzane with lashings of mozzarella. After this hearty and promising opening, our pizza was a little average (excellent base, let down by the quality of some toppings). A prawn pasta special was better: subtly zesty. Did La Luna shine? The decor is very Italian (we even forgot we were on Walworth Road), as was the service: after a charming welcome, we were rather forgotten about, waiting longer between courses than fellow diners who had arrived after us. Frustrating.

Meal deals

Mozzarella e Pomodoro

21-22 Camberwell Green, SE5 7AA (7277 2020). **Set lunch** (Mon-Fri) £7.50 2 courses. **Map** p292. Pizza & Pasta

In the area

Nando's *88 Denmark Hill, SE5 8RX (7738 3808).* **Map** p292.

Catford

Sapporo Ichiban

13 Catford Broadway, SE6 4SP (8690 8487). Catford Broadway rail. **Lunch served** noon-3pm Mon-Fri; noon-4pm Sat, Sun. **Dinner served** 6-11pm daily. **Average** £££. **Set meal** £8.50-£12 per person 2 courses (minimum 2). Japanese

Faced with a lurid cascade of oriental knick-knackery out front – there's even an ornamental fish pond – we were pleasantly surprised and soothed by the simple white decor we found inside. Sapporo Ichiban seems like a fish out of water, peddling sashimi, tempura, yakitori (grilled chicken on skewers) and soba on Catford Broadway. However, for a Monday night, business didn't look bad at all. Although our dishes didn't always look the part (agedashidofu cut into minuscule cubes and scattered over a plate, salmon and avocado sushi made to look like quaintly English, triangular crustless sandwiches), they did nevertheless taste properly Japanese. Everything came in generous portions but at skinflint prices. Service might be termed erratic: the waiter asked to take our order three times before we'd decided; once ready, we couldn't get eye contact for love nor money.

In the area

Nando's *74-76 Rushey Green, SE6 4HW (8314 0122).*

Sapporo Ichiban

Crystal Palace

★ Domali

38 Westow Street, SE19 3AH (8768 0096). Gipsy Hill rail. **Meals served** 9.30am-10.30pm daily. **Average** £. **Set lunch** (vegetarian) £4.50 1 course, (fish) £5.50 1 course. Vegetarian
Every home should have a Domali to hand. Wide-ranging (and, where possible, free range, fair trade and veggie) fare from breakfast to boozer closing time nourishes all-comers: giggling newly-mets in need of a morning-after fry-up; lunchbreakers laying into the great-value weekday fish or veggie specials; pram-pushing parents after a comforting mid-afternoon brie BLT; and post-work locals in for happy-hour cocktails in the rectangle of paved back garden. Olive oil is drizzled,

salad leaves are mixed, thick salmon and peppers are impeccably chargrilled – care and detail abound. An indie jangle at conversational volume spreads around the simple, wooden room brightened by Dave Bailey's nudes and muso portraits. Seriously recommended.

Spirited Palace NEW

105 Church Road, SE19 2PR (8771 5557). Crystal Palace or Gipsy Hill rail. **Meals served** 11am-9.30pm Tue-Fri; 2-9.30pm Sat, Sun. **Average £. Set meal** £5.80 1 course. **No credit cards**. Vegetarian

A vegan restaurant with a health food shop attached, the SP has a Caribbean chef cooking Ital food (meaning 'vital, healthy and natural' in Rastafarian patois). The Ital dietary laws forbid the use of meat, poultry, fish, alcohol, cow's milk, coffee and sometimes even added salt. Despite these restrictions, our food was delicious. Tofu is sliced in wafer-thin squares, fried in tempura-like batter and topped with herbs and spices. Kale in coconut milk was creamy, with mineral overtones. Even the brown rice was plump, shiny and well seasoned. Tangy barbecued strips of gluten were particularly tasty. We're told the owners are looking for larger premises: good news, as the dining area consists of two poky rooms in the basement, and this cooking deserves a wider audience.

In the area

Pizza Express *70 Westow Hill, SE19 1SB (8670 1786).*

Deptford

Noodle King

36 Deptford Broadway, SE8 4PQ (8692 9633). New Cross tube/rail. **Meals served** 11.30am-11pm daily. **Average £. Set lunch buffet** £5.50. **Map** p290. Chinese

Expect to see diners staggering out into the street clutching their swollen stomachs at Deptford's take on the ubiquitous Chinese greasy spoon equivalent. The food tends towards the oily, but it's more about quantity than quality at this canteen-style Chinese eaterie, with the massive portions on offer spilling so far over the sides of plates that customers waddle out leaving tables that look like a Birmingham motorway intersection. The all-you-can-eat buffet is a cut above Soho counterparts such as Mr Wu, with the unlimited supply of a pleasantly soft salt and pepper squid making it worth the money alone (£5.50-£6.95 depending on when you visit). Be warned though, they're often in no rush to top up the dishes, so don't order it if you're in a hurry.

Tandoori Xpress

111B Deptford High Street, SE8 4NS (8320 2555). Deptford rail. **Meals served** 11.30am-11pm Mon-Sat; noon-3pm, 6-10.30pm Sun. **Average £. Unlicensed. Corkage** no charge. **Map** p290. Indian

Re-heated home-made cooking is the order of the day at this mega-cheap Indian takeaway. A tower of lurid orange jalebis balances on top of the counter, teetering unsteadily like a sugary Jenga tower, as the chefs re-heat the curries and fry up glistening naan breads on the hotplate. The crackle of flies hitting the blue light bug zapper is a little disconcerting, and you can't help but wonder just why there's an abandoned fridge in the corner, but the super-friendly service and fantastically tender curry goat provide more than enough reason to pop in if you're in the area. You may want to take your own cutlery though. This being Deptford, the sharpest implement that they're prepared to offer to customers is a plastic spoon.

West Lake

207 Deptford High Street, SE8 3NT (8465 9408). Deptford rail. **Meals served** 11.30am-10pm daily. **Average** £. **Unlicensed**. **Corkage** no charge. **No credit cards**. **Map** p290. Vietnamese

Amid Asian supermarkets, African food shops and 99p stores, you'll find this small Vietnamese café. The dim lighting and wooden decoration exude an oriental ambience. Aside from the usual Vietnamese pork, beef, seafood and vegetarian dishes, there are less common ingredients on the menu such as squid tentacles, quail and jellyfish. We tried the frogs' legs with onions, seasoned with pepper and salt. Dunked in a sauce made of salt, lime and chillies, these lean, little legs were delightful. The beef in 'lot' leaves that followed was too greasy, however, with tough and unpleasant-tasting meat. Sour soup with tomatoes, spring onions, beansprouts, taro stem and fish cake was dominated by lime juice, though dill and the chewy fish cake produced added flavour. A decidedly mixed experience, then.

Yune

25 Dartmouth Road, SE23 3HN (8699 0887). Forest Hill rail. **Lunch served** noon-3pm Mon-Sat. **Dinner served** 5pm-11.30pm Mon-Thur; 5pm-midnight Fri, Sat. **Meals served** noon-11pm Sun. **Average** ££. **Set lunch** £5.95 bento box. **Set buffet** (Mon-Thur, Sun) £13.90 per person; (Sat) £15.90 per person. Oriental

By the time you realise you're in the former Fu Lee, you've got a napkin placed on your lap and a basket of prawn crackers under your nose. Once you choose from the 150-item Cantonese, Thai and Malay menu options, and 20-strong wine list, your drink will be poured and portions delicately served from dinky, lidded pots. The rather stylish Yune, opened in July 2006, offers five-star service at two-star prices – and four-star cuisine by a chef of 20 years' service in Chinatown. The starters feature deep-fried crab claw, crispy aromatic whole leg of lamb and generous platter combos, mains include stir-fried lobster in six choices of sauce, three types of Thai curry and, among 16 meat-free options, sea-spiced aubergine and vegetarian duck. Sauces zing, seafood gently sates, broccoli crunches and the rice satisfyingly separates.

Dulwich

Au Ciel

1A Carlton Avenue, SE21 7DE (8488 1111). North Dulwich rail/ 37 bus. **Meals served** 8.30am-5.30pm Mon-Sat; 10am-5.30pm Sun. **Average** £. **Map** p292. Café

The refinement of this classy little pâtisserie suits its genteel Dulwich Village location to a tee. While partaking of a silver pot of the unusual infusions (Golden Flowers, Royal Plum, White Tangerine or Dragon Eye Oolong) and gorging on a moist slab of Belgo cake (truffle base, whipped cream and thick chocolate icing), your eyes will feast on the vast array of be-ribboned bonbons, beautifully packaged teas and gilded biscuit boxes stacked on the shelves, or the handmade chocolates adorning the counter. Stick to the cakes, breads or divine Di Sotto's ice-creams, however. A leaden slab of quiche arrived microwaved and unadorned by even the teeniest salad garnish.

Pavilion Café

Dulwich Park, SE21 7BQ (8299 1383). West Dulwich rail/P4 bus. **Open** *Summer* 8.30am-6pm Mon-Fri; 9am-6pm Sat, Sun. *Winter* 8.30am-3.30pm Mon-Fri; 9am-3.30pm Sat, Sun. **Average** £. **No credit cards**. **Map** p292. Café

The child-free zone here is calm and cool, and feels nicely distanced from the rest of this otherwise bustling café in Dulwich Park. Little ones have toys to play with, and ice-creams and fairy cakes to guzzle. Watermelon and feta cheese salad, and asparagus and salmon quiche topped the bill, which also features sandwiches (that usually run out by 3pm), all-day breakfasts and own-made cakes. Militant red signage (multiplied since 2005, due to a regrettable increase in vandalism) makes the atmosphere slightly uncomfortable, but the staff are relaxed and the operation runs like clockwork. Large French windows keep the interior airy and the simple pale walls are perfect for displaying work by local artists.

Meal deals

Barcelona Tapas Bar y Restaurante *481 Lordship Lane, SE22 8JY (8693 5111)*. Set lunch £5.95 3 tapas incl glass of wine. Set tapas buffet (noon-5pm Sun) £13.99 eat all you like. **Map** p292. Spanish

In the area
Pizza Express *94 The Village, SE21 7AQ (8693 9333)*. **Map** p292.
Sea Cow *37 Lordship Lane, SE22 8EW (8693 3111)*. **Map** p292.

East Dulwich

Blue Mountain Café
18 North Cross Road, SE22 9EU (8299 6953). *East Dulwich rail*. **Meals served** 9am-5pm daily. **Average** ££. **Set breakfast** £6.95 includes tea or coffee. **Map** p292. Café
The Blue Mountain Café boasts a cool interior and a laid-back attitude to match. There is something deeply reassuring about the place – perhaps it's just the sense that everyone is happy to be here. Food is simple but satisfying: hefty steak sandwiches,

platters of olives with grilled halloumi (cheese) and ever-moreish strips of fried plantain with sweet chilli dip. Occasional specials also include wilder fare like pan-fried red snapper and butternut squash ravioli. In the evenings the tempo picks up and the wine flows, while Sunday mornings see the café become a popular retreat from the world for the hungover. It's little surprise: the cheerful staff are always on hand to dispense vast plates of bacon and eggs, and they serve a fine cup of coffee too.

Jerk Rock
153 Lordship Lane, SE22 8HX (8693 5544). *East Dulwich or Forest Hill rail*. **Meals served** noon-10.30pm Tue-Thur; noon-11.30pm Fri; 2-11.30pm Sat; 2-9pm Sun. **Average** ££. **Set meal** £5.95 1 course. **Map** p292. Caribbean
Don't be fooled by the simple appearance: this quiet little eaterie will knock you for six. Jerk Rock is the master of its art, serving up plate after plate of piping hot meat. The traditional Caribbean menu offers curried goat and brown fish stew, but the real stars of the show are the jerk dishes: melt-in-the-mouth chunks of pork and chicken, doused in some worryingly addictive spices. It would take a mighty appetite indeed to make light work of the enormous helpings, but they taste so good that you'll be sure to give it your best shot. Vegetarian options are available, but let's face facts: this is a carnivore's paradise.

Pistachio Club
44 Lordship Lane, SE22 8HJ (8693 7584). *East Dulwich rail*. **Lunch served** noon-2.30pm Mon-Thur. **Dinner served** 6pm-midnight daily. **Average** ££. **Set buffet** (Sun) £6.95. **Map** p292. Bangladeshi
A safe bet for a curry on ruby-heavy Lordship Lane. We kicked off with paneer shaslick (cheese marinated in

the chef's own recipe) which was flavoursome enough, if a tad overcooked. Much more successful were the mains: boro chingri bhuna, a tangy tomato based dish crammed with succulent, juicy king prawns, and murg kadai, which hit the spot with its moist chicken bathed in rich and smoky sauce. The wine list wouldn't look out of place in a high-end gastropub and service was all smiles and attention. Admittedly, we were the only diners, but it was a hot Monday evening.

Thai Corner Café

44 Northcross Road, SE22 9EU (8299 4041). East Dulwich rail/ 185, 176 bus. **Lunch served** noon-3pm, **dinner served** 6-10.30pm daily. **Average £E. Set dinner** £15 2 courses, £18 3 courses. **Unlicensed. Corkage** 35-50p (beer), £2 (wine). **No credit cards. Map** p292. Thai

Good things come in small packages. This snug restaurant only holds 30 people at a time, but those lucky 30 must be the happiest diners in Dulwich. Start with a few chicken skewers: they look innocent enough, but carry incredibly potent flavour. A high-standard all-round makes it difficult to set a foot wrong: the prawn and cashew nut stir fry was a worthy choice for mains, but better was a wonderful duck curry and its accompaniment of coconut, pineapple and baby tomatoes (they popped deliciously in our mouths). Authentic and well-cheffed, the Thai Corner Café is a genuine treat. One thing to note: no alcohol is served, so bring a bottle of your own.

Meal deals

Franklins *157 Lordship Lane, SE22 8HX (8299 9598/www. franklinsrestaurant.com).* Set lunch (Mon-Fri) £9 2 courses, £12 3 courses. **Map** p292. British

The Green *58-60 East Dulwich Road, SE22 9AX (7732 7575/ www.greenbar.co.uk).* Set lunch (noon-3.30pm Mon-Sat) £8.50 2 courses, £11.50 3 courses; (noon-5pm Sun) £13.95 2 courses, £16.95 3 courses. **Map** p292. Brasserie

Elephant & Castle

Pizzeria Castello

20 Walworth Road, SE1 6SP (7703 2556). Elephant & Castle tube/rail. **Meals served** noon-11pm Mon-Thur; noon-11.30pm Fri. **Dinner served** 5-11.30pm Sat. **Average £E. Map** p287. Pizza & Pasta

Despite a recent change in the management at Pizzeria Castello, the things that matter – the pizzas – remain tastily tomatoey, and the better toppings, such as rocket, four seasons, pepperoni, are as generous as they have always been. Anchovies and capers liven up the medium-grade mozzarella, and fresh leaf salads provide roughage. The upstairs, decorated in bright reds with local art photos on the wall, is very busy most nights, and the cosy basement gets a few drinkers and diners too. Steak, seafood and fish dishes are offered, but neither these nor the pastas are as good as the pizzas: the bolognese was simply too bland and seemed bereft of the wine reduction that usually gives the sauce its glory. Desserts (gelatos and pastries) are rather dull, but the coffee is excellent. Castello continues to be a bastion of good eating amid the Elephant's Latino snack bars and run-down malls.

In the area

Nando's *Unit 4, Metro Central, 119 Newington Causeway, SE1 6BA (7378 7810).* **Map** p287.

Buenos Aires
Café & Deli

Gipsy Hill

Mangosteen NEW

*246 Gipsy Road, SE27 9RB
(8670 0333). Gipsy Hill rail/322 bus.*
Lunch served 11am-3pm, **dinner
served** 6-11pm Mon-Sat. **Average**
£££. Oriental

Mangosteen has a clean, subdued
interior with neatly arranged
cushions lining the walls. The food,
like the decor, is nicely presented
and combines simple pan-oriental
flavours and textures. To start, juicy
pork won ton parcels and prawn
crackers came with the usual hot
chilli and soy dipping sauces. The
mains that we ordered were more
experimental, but sadly rather less
consistent in their execution. An
appetising mild coconut and lime
sea bream came topped with an
attractive nest of crispy leeks.
However, the caramelised ginger
chicken had a very watery and
lacklustre texture – despite being
strongly flavoured. Portions are
generous. Although Mangosteen
isn't in the most accessible of
locations, its impeccable service and
beautifully arranged food deserve to
attract a wider clientele than just
local devotees.

Meal deals

Numidie *48 Westow Hill, SE19
1RX (8766 6166/www.numidie.
co.uk).* Set dinner (Tue-Thur) £13.50
2 courses. Mediterranean

Greenwich

Buenos Aires
Café & Deli NEW

*86 Royal Hill, SE10 8RT (8488
6764). Greenwich rail/DLR.* **Meals
served** 8am-7pm Mon-Fri; 9am-6pm
Sat; 9am-5pm Sun. **Average** £.
Corkage £1 (beer), £2.50 (wine).
Map p290. Café

Step inside this homely Argentinian-inspired café-cum-deli and you might be forgiven for thinking that you'd stepped into the culinary equivalent of a junk shop. Battered leather sofas sprawl in the centre, surrounded by chests of drawers stuffed with multicoloured farfalle pasta, and sideboards cluttered with spices, preserves and Argentinian confectionaries. Chattering couples sip coffee, watched by a picture of Che Guevara, sipping on a gourd of Argentinian tea, mate. There are a range of different flavours of the beverage itself, with the Chai version adding a nice cinnamony tang to the natural woodiness. Food is more Mediterranean than South American, however, with a vast plate of thick slices of salami Milano and a goat's cheese salad slimy with unctuous preserved peppers being among the highlights.

Greenwich Park Bar & Grill NEW

1 King William Walk, SE10 9JY (8853 7860). Greenwich rail/Cutty Sark DLR/108, 177, 180, 472 bus. **Bar Open** 11am-11pm daily. **Lunch served** 11am-4pm, **dinner served** 6-9.30pm daily. **Average ££.** *Restaurant* **Lunch served** noon-4pm Mon-Fri; 11am-4pm Sat, Sun, **dinner served** 6.30-10pm daily. **Average £££. Map** p290. Modern European

The meal commenced with bread so deliciously fresh we had to wait for it to come out of the oven. A starter of thickly cut, almost meaty smoked salmon with asparagus spears followed, equally fresh and worth savouring. Sea bass (more appealing to us than the T-bone or lamb cutlets from the grill), baked with carrots and celery and served with green vegetables, was simple, substantial and cooked to perfection. The quality of ingredients was high (some rocket all but exploded on the tongue), but the cooking was not without some slips. A baked crème brûlée cheesecake was sickly, and not helped by the over-sweetness of its accompanying mango salsa. The portion sizes were also uneven (a measly two scallops comprised one main). Some attention to detail and a little work on the rough edges would do wonders.

Peninsula

Holiday Inn Express, Bugsby's Way, SE10 0GD (8858 2028). North Greenwich tube. **Meals served** noon-11pm Mon-Fri; 11am-11.30pm Sat; 11am-11pm Sun. **Dim sum served** noon-5pm Mon-Fri; 11am-5pm Sat, Sun. **Average ££. Set meal** £15-£19 per person (minimum 2) 3 courses. **Map** p291. Chinese
At the weekend crowds of Chinese families and friends flock to this large dining room, just a stone's throw from the Millennium Dome, to drink tea, feast on dim sum and catch up on the gossip. While the cooking is not up to the refined standards you'll find in London's premier Chinese establishments, it is competent and very reasonably priced. On our visit lunch was a mixture of both hits and misses. Successes included steamed half-moon dumplings filled with crunchy prawns and water chestnuts; and the 'three kinds of cheung fun'. Less tasty were some under-fried savoury meat croquettes, which contained a bland, nondescript filling; and Shanghai dumplings that had leaked the stock which should have been filling them. Never mind: some hot flaky egg-custard tarts provided a sweet finish to the meal.

Meal deals

Inside *19 Greenwich South Street, SE10 8NW (8265 5060/www.inside restaurant.co.uk).* Set lunch £11.95 2 courses. **Map** p290.
Modern European

In the area

Nando's *UCI Cinema Complex, Bugsy's Way, SE10 0QJ (8293 3025).*

Pizza Express *4-6 Church Street, SE10 9BG (8853 2770).* **Map** p291.

Herne Hill

3 Monkeys

136-140 Herne Hill, SE24 9QH (7738 5500). Herne Hill rail/3, 37, 68 bus. **Lunch served** noon-2.30pm, **dinner served** 5.30-10.30pm Mon-Sat. **Meals served** noon-10.30pm Sun. **Average £££. Set lunch** (Mon-Thur, Sun) £7.95 2 courses. **Set dinner** (Mon-Thur, Sun) £12.95 2 courses. **Map** p292. Indian

Our meal at this smart venue didn't start well. Despite having booked in advance and being the only customers on an early evening visit, we were shown to a tiny table behind a pillar (one of many; despite the slick cream and purple decor, the layout remains awkward). The manager insisted that all other tables had been reserved, yet the restaurant remained mostly empty right through until closing time. From an ambitious North Indian menu, fig-stuffed, fennel-flecked green banana kebabs were delicious; as was paneer and fresh fenugreek curry, flavoured, Kashmiri-style, with dried ginger. Disappointing dishes included bland batter-fried soft-shell crab with insipid crab meat, and pot-roasted lamb tikka that was tough and dry. The food here is good – but the management might be a little more friendly.

Lombok

17 Half Moon Lane, SE24 9JU (7733 7131). Herne Hill rail/37 bus. **Lunch served** noon-3pm Tue-Sun, **dinner served** 6-10.30pm Tue-Thur, Sun; 6-11pm Fri, Sat. **Average ££. Map** p292. Oriental

This compact eaterie has long-standing popularity among Herne Hill's residents, who are drawn to its high-quality and, in places, unusual Vietnamese and Thai cuisine. The service was polite and efficient on our visit, but seating is quite closely packed in – not so comfortable when the place is busy, although fine during weekend afternoons when it's virtually empty. For starters, we opted for a simple and enjoyable chicken satay alongside crispy chilli corn and okra fritters with a spicy dipping sauce. There are several seafood options for the main course, and the generous serving of stir-fried scallops with pak choi and wild mushrooms was perfect. Various curries, given names like 'Thai', 'Rangoon' and 'Bangkok' sit alongside simple, simple dishes such as a chilli-laced chicken, scattered with Thai basil leaves.

Meal deals

Brockwells *75-79 Norwood Road, SE24 9AA (8671 6868).* Set buffet (2.30-8pm Sun) £9.95. **Map** p292. Caribbean

Lewisham

Arru Suvai NEW

19 Lee High Road, SE13 5LD (8297 6452). Lewisham rail/DLR. **Meals served** 11am-11pm daily. **Average £. No credit cards. Map** p291. Indian

You'll always find Sri Lankan expats dining *en famille* at this large Lewisham eaterie. Decked out with hanging flowers, golden statues and flashing deities, the space looks grand. The menu is massive but few are here for the standard South Indian korma, biriani or madras curries. Perhaps first nibbling on a pattie, roti or vadai (have a look what's on display in the cabinet), they're here for the dosais, string

South East

Arru Suvai

hoppers and kothus, chunky, cheap and wonderfully flavoursome, or for something spicy, extra spicy in fact, devilled mutton or prawn. There are cool glasses of mango lassi available to soothe the tongue. Weekends witness the all-you-can-eat challenge of a £5 buffet – but you'll be hard pushed to spend anything near a tenner whatever day it is.

Everest Curry King

24 Loampit Hill, SE13 7SW (8691 2233). Lewisham rail/DLR. **Meals served** 11am-11pm daily. **Average** £. **Set meal** £4.95 3 courses. **Map** p290. Sri Lankan

Don't be put off by the plastic laminate signs on the windows bearing promises of takeaway pizzas, Everest Curry King is about as close as you're likely to get to a decent Sri Lankan meal this side of Tooting. Look beyond the two-tone lilac interior and black and white 1950s style tiling behind the counter, and you'll notice that the fridges are stocked with Sri Lanka's prime soft drinks brand, Elephant, and even the bottles of ketchup here are Sri

Lankan. Highlights included a thick aubergine curry, sticky with tamarind, and the coriander-seed pungency of a rich mutton curry. At £3.50 for a meat curry and £1.75 for a veg curry, it's no wonder that this is a home away from home for the area's Sri Lankan community.

★ Meze Mangal

245 Lewisham Way, SE4 1XF (8694 8099). St John's rail/Lewisham rail/ DLR. **Meals served** noon-2am Mon-Thur; noon-3am Fri-Sat; noon-1am Sun. **Average** £. **Set meze** £10 per person (minimum 2), £14.50 per person (minimum 4). **Map** p290. Turkish

The Gok brothers arrived at this culinary desert of breakfast caffs and launderettes from the Black Sea in 2000, establishing the discerning cheapskate's restaurant destination of choice. Now this long space, centrepieced by an open grill and wood-fire oven, augmented by a back room and a basement for hire, is booked every night, even on this rainy, pre-payday Tuesday. The reason? Traditional Turkish treats –

The Table

marinated grilled lamb cubes, oven-fired pide breads layered with spinach, peppers and Turkish sausages, herb-marinated swordfish – served with bonhomie and relaxed formality. All the food is prepared on site, on the day: 20 starters, 20 mains, four vegetarian ones and 15 pides, at £3 a starter, £8 a main and £6 a pide. A bottle of crisp Villa Doluca house white has been £10 since any of the regulars can remember. Book and splurge.

Something Fishy
117-119 Lewisham High Street, SE13 6AT (8852 7075). Lewisham rail/DLR. **Meals served** 9am-5.30pm Mon-Sat. **Average** £. **No credit cards**. **Map** p290.
Fish & Chips
You can get well fed for a fiver at this much-loved chip shop close to Lewisham market. Something Fishy's plastic seating and Formica tables might sport a greasy film on the odd occasion, but when it comes to that which matters – the food – there's absolutely nothing fishy

going on. Some of London's finest fish and chips are served here. Huge portions of flaky fish come in crispy light batter, complemented by tartar sauce (bought in, but of a high quality). The mushy peas were a little sweet, but the hand-cut chips are as big as fish fingers. Pie and mash and saveloys are further options. Staff are friendly enough, but don't expect them to waste time discussing the weather. The posher first-floor restaurant is now open only on Fridays and Saturdays.

In the area
Nando's *16 Lee High Road, SE13 5LQ (8463 0119).* **Map** p291.

London Bridge & Borough

Konditor & Cook
10 Stoney Street, SE1 9AD (7407 5100). London Bridge tube/rail. **Open** 7.30am-6pm Mon-Fri; 8.30am-5pm Sat. **Average** ££. **Map** p289.
Café

Plenty of locals flock here for a daily changing selection of appealing lunches: soups and salads supplemented with well-filled sandwiches, smoked salmon frittata, spinach and ricotta tartlets, plus hot meals and daily specials (gnocchi in fresh tomato and basil sauce with black olives, for example). But dieters beware: we've yet to witness the most nonchalant of browsers leave without some heavenly orange lavender slab cake, or a dark chocolate-chip brownie. K&C's commitment to high-quality ingredients is evident in their baked goods; even the humble flapjacks taste deliciously indulgent. Breakfast baking (buns, scones, croissants) includes deliciously savoury spinach parmesan muffins (so filling we had no room left for coffee). K&C's speciality cakes are justifiably legendary – the Curly Whirly double-layer chocolate cake with real vanilla bean frosting is eye-closingly good.

Southwark Cathedral Refectory

Southwark Cathedral, Montague Close, SE1 9DA (7407 5740). London Bridge tube/rail. **Meals served** 10am-5pm daily. **Average** ££. Map p289. Café
Southwark Cathedral's charming riverside courtyard is reason enough for a visit, and the dining space itself (airy and modern, yet retaining grander ecclesiastical elements like an arched ceiling and stone flagged floor) is alluring. Digby Trout-run, all food is cooked on site with no GM ingredients. Sandwiches, salads and soup (watercress, minted pea) combos are good value quick lunches at £4.95. Heartier hot dishes such as pork escalope (well-cooked and tender) with a tasty chilli, mango and corn salsa are served with herbed new potatoes, braised red cabbage with apple and thyme;

vegetarian options include stuffed field mushrooms on a polenta cake and stuffed aubergine calzone (£5.95). Huge slabs of tempting cakes, coffee and organic juices are also offered for quick stops.

★ The Table NEW

83 Southwark Street, SE1 0HX (7401 2760). Southwark tube/ London Bridge tube/rail. **Open** 8am-6pm Mon-Thur; 8am-11pm Fri. **Average** ££. **Corkage** £2.50. Map p289. Café
On an otherwise grim stretch of Southwark Street hides this gem of a café, on the ground floor of the offices of the architects Allies and Morrison – who designed the space. The winner of *Time Out* Best Cheap Eats 2006, the Table features a wonderful, Mediterranean-inspired salad bar and a long window display of sandwiches. Selections such as baby shrimp pasta salad or roasted pumpkin with spinach leaves are charged by weight and change weekly. Dishes like minute steak, chicken breast and tuna are ordered at a different counter, then supplemented with your choice of pre-prepared Italian 'garnishes', such as stewed aubergine with capers and pine nuts. At breakfast, this counter dishes out bowls of porridge and bacon sarnies. There are plans afoot to expand evening dining once the huge Bankside 1-2-3 development opens across the road in 2007. We can't wait.

Tapas Brindisa NEW

18-20 Southwark Street, SE1 1TJ (7357 8880). London Bridge tube/ rail. **Breakfast served** 9-11am Fri, Sat. **Lunch served** noon-3pm Mon-Thur; noon-4pm Fri, Sat. **Dinner served** 5.30-11pm Mon-Sat. **Average** £££. Map p289. Spanish
The interior is basic and hard-edged, and you can't book in advance, but this class act on the edge of Borough Market never fails to pack them in.

Tapas Brindisa. See p171.

It's not hard to see why. Our most recent meal was superb. Even when just opening tins, say for a selection of cured fish (sardines, tuna loin, smoked mackerel, anchovies), the result is fat, succulent and of the highest quality. Portions are small plates rather than tiny dishes and choosing three or four will provide an enjoyable mix of vibrant tastes. A nicely done classic Catalan dish of spinach with pine nuts and raisins teamed well with first-class chorizo cooked in cider, while pan-fried asparagus with fried duck egg and serrano ham was perfect, full of rich, multi-layered flavours. The service is unfailingly polite and helpful.

Tito's
4-6 London Bridge Street, SE1 9SG (7407 7787). London Bridge tube/ rail. **Lunch served** noon-3pm Mon-Fri. **Dinner served** 6-11pm Tue-Fri. **Meals served** noon-11pm Sat, Sun. **Average ££**. **Set lunch** (Mon-Fri) £7.90 3 courses. **Map** p289.
Peruvian

Very much a cantina, Tito's is designed to offer London Bridge's office workers a break from chilled sandwiches and crisps. It's a bit basic for an evening excursion, but we gave it a go, and the combination of traditional ceviche (fresh raw fish marinated in lime, with onions and sweet potato) followed by rice, yucca pumpkin and fried prawns was impressive. The fish and vegetables were carefully spiced, and tastier than the maize-heavy dishes served in many Colombian cantinas. Both items were vast, so it's best to share. We even managed a fruit cocktail and ice-cream, and a glass of Inka Cola.

El Vergel
8 Lant Street, SE1 1QR (7357 0057). Borough tube. **Meals served** 8.30am-3pm Mon-Fri. **Average £**. **No credit cards**. **Map** p289.
South American
For the perfect lunch here, arrive late – when most of the local office workers have returned to work. Then, armed with a magazine or

book, indulge in a tortilla crammed with refried beans, spring onion, coriander and guacamole. There's even some feta cheese in there, proving the Chilean owners aren't bent on a purist Latino recipe. If you want a larger lunch, try one of the tender steaks smeared with avocado and tomato. Or a stew: the chicken broth is the light option, but the lamb stew is bolder and packs a peppery punch. The waitresses are among the sweetest and chattiest in town, and the coffee is strong enough to get you on your feet if you don't have the option of a siesta.

Meal deals

Georgetown 10 London Bridge Street, SE1 9SG (7357 7359/ www.georgetownrestaurants.co.uk). Set lunch (noon-2.30pm) £10 2 courses, £12.50 3 courses. **Map** p289. Malaysian

Kwan Thai The Riverfront, Hay's Galleria, Tooley Street, SE1 2HD (7403 7373/www.kwanthai restaurant.co.uk). Set lunch (11.30am-3pm Mon-Fri) £7.95-£8.95 2 courses. **Map** p289. Thai

In the area

Feng Sushi 13 Stoney Street, SE1 1AD (7407 8744). **Map** p289.

Frizzante@Unicorn Theatre 147 Tooley Street, SE1 2AZ (7645 0556).

Nando's 225-227 Clink Street, SE1 9DG. **Map** p289.

Paul The Vaults, London Bridge Station, Railway Approach, SE1 9SP (7403 7457). **Map** p289.

Pizza Express 4 Borough High Street, SE1 9QQ (7407 2995). **Map** p289.

Strada 2 More London Place, The Riverside, SE1 2JP (7403 8321). **Map** p289.

Tas 72 Borough High Street, SE1 1XF (7403 7200). **Map** p289.

Tas Café 76 Borough High Street, SE1 1LL (7403 8557). **Map** p289.

Wagamama 1 Clink Street, SE1 9BU (7403 3659). **Map** p289.

New Cross

★ 805 Bar Restaurant NEW

805 Old Kent Road, SE15 1NX (7639 0808). Elephant & Castle tube/rail then 53 bus. **Meals served** 2pm-midnight daily. **Average** ££. African
Considered by the capital's Nigerian community to be London's best Nigerian restaurant, this smart establishment on an insalubrious stretch of the Old Kent Road is an undiscovered gem for the rest of us. It's constantly abuzz with a dressed-up crowd of affluent Nigerians. The signature dish, Monika (the chef's own creation), comprises a whole marinated grilled fish drizzled with chilli sauce: it was impressive to look at, and exquisitely succulent. The popular accompaniment of moyin moyin (slabs of wobbly bean pudding flecked with dried fish and meat) was a good foil for the fish. Mashed Nigerian brown beans with chilli sauce, fried plantain and yam chips sounds pretty basic, but it was a hearty and flavoursome dish. Service from staff in black and white uniforms was efficient and swift.

Thailand

15 Lewisham Way, SE14 6PP (8691 4040). New Cross or New Cross Gate tube/rail. **Lunch served** noon-2.30pm Mon-Fri. **Dinner served** 5-11.30pm daily. **Average** ££. **Set meal** (lunch, 5-7pm) £3.95 2 courses. **Map** p290. Thai
This reliable Thai and Laotian canteen near New Cross station has been around for what seems an age, but its standards remain as high as ever. The dining room is tiny but the menu is vast, with pages of Thai and Laotian delights at prices that will leave change for the journey home. At lunchtime, most customers order the standards: green and red curries, pad kraprow (stir-fries with basil, chilli and green peppercorns) and

the like. We tucked into some deliciously tender pork spare ribs, which were marinated in honey and coriander and incredibly moreish. The follow-up, chicken stir-fried with cashew nuts, was also well seasoned, but a little dry and lacking in chilli punch. In all, this is a solidly authentic local Thai, but the food outweighs the atmosphere.

Peckham

Petitou

63 Choumert Road, SE15 4AR (7639 2613). Peckham Rye rail. **Open** 9am-5.30pm Tue-Sat; 10am-5.30pm Sun. **Average** ££. **Map** p292. Café
Great coffee, generous portions of good, fresh-cooked food and the gentle, unstinting courtesy of its staff has turned Petitou into the thriving, chocolate-sprinkled hub of Peckham's chattering classes. There's a quiet buzz from 10am on, as locals drift in for a coffee or one of the wide range of teas, fresh juices or gooey almond croissants. Huge slabs of toasted granary bread cost £1 for two slices with butter (40p extra for jam, Marmite or peanut butter). A choice of own-made quiches with salad, plus fresh soups, form the bulk of the lunch menu. The cakes are a must: a daily changing menu of moist, calorie-laden treats are homemade by a rota of three local domestic goddesses.

Meal deals

Ganapati *38 Holly Grove, SE15 5DF (7277 2928).* Set lunch £4.50-£5.50 1 course. **Map** p292. Indian

In the area

M Manze's *105 Peckham High Street, SE15 5RS.* **Map** p292.
Suya Express *43 Peckham High Street, SE15 5EB (7703 7033).* **Map** p292.

South Norwood

★ Mantanah

2 Orton Building, Portland Road, SE25 4UD (8771 1148). Norwood Junction rail. **Lunch served** noon-3pm Sat, Sun **Dinner served** 6-11pm Tue-Sun. **Average** ££. **Set dinner** £16 per person (minimum 2) 3 courses, £22 per person (minimum 2) 4 courses. **Set buffet** (lunch Sun) £7.95 adults, £3.50 children. Thai
No matter that Mantanah looks like any neighbourhood Thai, it serves better food than places charging three times as much. Vegetarians do particularly well: meat-free dishes are prepared with nuts, pumpkin, aubergine, tofu, or a very convincing mock-duck made from textured beancurd (just look for the quirky names on the menu). Pork satay was tasty, but it faded with the arrival of the yum lanna – an intoxicating mix of banana blossom, dried chilli and shredded chicken in a sweet, tart dressing, dusted with roasted coconut. We followed this with 'Copy Cat', a complex red curry with pineapple, cherry tomatoes and mock-duck, served with fragrant coconut rice (with the addition of lemongrass). A fabulous meal.

Tower Bridge

Meal deals

Le Pont de la Tour *Butlers Wharf Building, 36D Shad Thames, SE1 2YE (7403 8403/www.conran.com).* Set lunch (noon-3pm) £12.50 2 courses (bar & grill only). Modern European

In the area

ASK *Spice Quay, 34 Shad Thames, Butlers Wharf, SE1 2YE (7403 4545).*
Pizza Express *The Cardamom Building, 31 Shad Thames, SE1 2YR (7403 8484).*

EAST

Bethnal Green

Frizzante@City Farm

Hackney City Farm, 1A Goldsmith's Row, E2 8QA (7739 2266). Bus 26, 48, 55. **Open** 10am-4.30pm Tue-Sun. **Average £££. Unlicensed. Corkage** no charge. **Map** p294. Café

Being situated within Hackney City Farm might explain the noisy, child-heavy, 'herd of animals' atmosphere. Happily, the food is so good you won't care. There's own-made lasagne, pasta, herb-crusted chicken and – popular on Sundays – Frizzante's 'big farm' breakfasts. Prices are reasonable and portions large. Juicy burgers came with delicious roast potatoes and a big salad, while barbecued chicken had a tangy Thai dipping sauce. Orders are taken at the deli counter, where you can also buy goods such as olives, artichokes, cheese and salami, as well as scrumptious-looking cakes and own-made biscuits. Drinks include smoothies, tea, coffee and juices.

Jones Dairy Café

23 Ezra Street, E2 7RH (7739 5372). Bus 26, 48, 55. **Open** 9am-3pm Fri, Sat; 8am-3pm Sun. **Average £. No credit cards. Map** p294. Café

It's been almost 70 years since this dinky Dickensian-looking café last housed a cow, but it still pays homage to its roots with a fine selection of English and continental cheeses in its tiny shop. Regrettably, none of these is available in the attached café, which instead serves up huge bagels and excellent mugs of coffee during the Sunday Columbia Road flower market, when numbers dictate that only cold foods are available. Come on a Friday or Saturday and it's a very different matter. Then, the quietness of the old cobbled streets gives you an eerie sense of being on an empty film set, and it's delightful to while away an hour tucking into a hearty all-day breakfast or omelette, or a massive bowl of mixed salad, featuring egg, cheese, smoked salmon, olives and dressed organic leaves.

Laxeiro

93 Columbia Road, E2 7RG (7729 1147). Bus 8, 26, 48, 55. **Tapas served** noon-3pm, 7-11pm Tue-Sat; 9am-3pm Sun. **Average ££. Map** p294. Spanish

A visit to this bright café on Columbia Road is always a treat but on a sunny Sunday, when the flower market is in full swing, getting a table here is tough. We enjoyed our dinner, but this perhaps had more to do with the cosy, welcoming environs than the cooking, which was reasonable but could have been better. The albóndigas didn't taste freshly prepared and the calamares, though battered well, were a bit chewy. 'BBQ' marlin was a little dry, but the flavour was fine. On the other hand, chorizo in red wine was spot-on, as were the simple vegetable dishes, such as asparagus and pea revuelto (in other words, jazzed-up scrambled eggs). Portions are generous; advice not to order more than five dishes between two proved to be sound.

E Pellicci

332 Bethnal Green Road, E2 0AG (7739 4873). Bethnal Green tube/ 8, 388 bus. **Meals served** 6.30am-5pm Mon-Sat. **Average £. Unlicensed. Corkage** no charge. **No credit cards. Map** p294. Café

This classic East End greasy spoon café has been in the same family since Edwardian times, but the remarkable art deco marquetry interior – now grade II listed – was created in 1946 under the supervision of Elide Pellicci, the current owner's mother. Its friendly service and neighbourly feel made it

Mezedopolio.
See p184.

the favourite caff of the Kray twins. The same qualities now make it a popular spot for all manner of locals, plus the occasional visiting design student, slipping in to admire the primrose-coloured Vitrolite frontage. Yet with all that it's still a proper caff, serving fry-ups (including some unusual ones – you might have ham off the bone instead of bacon, say), salads, grills, chops and sarnies. A much-loved institution, and long may it remain so.

StringRay Globe Café, Bar & Pizzeria

109 Columbia Road, E2 7RL (7613 1141). Bus 8, 26, 48, 55. **Meals served** 11am-11pm daily. **Average** ££. **Map** p294. Pizza & Pasta
The dark converted pub interior will never garner any design awards, but this laid-back pizzeria wins over a young clientele with friendly, helpful staff, and cheap and cheerful prices geared towards providing an enjoyable night. A nicely varied menu includes an English breakfast (served until 5pm), braised rabbit, Basque-style cod, veggie risotto and 19 huge pizzas, from a simple margherita to a vegetarian calzone. Everything here is super-size; a

salad tricolore starter was big enough to be a hearty lunch; a plate of tender fried liver was turned into a Desperate Dan cartoon by a pile of creamy mash and perfectly cooked cabbage. About the only small thing is the selection of desserts, which we passed over with some relief, too stuffed to even debate the merits of white peach and redcurrant sorbet over cherry cheesecake.

Wild Cherry

241-245 Globe Road, E2 0JD (8980 6678). Bethnal Green tube/ 8 bus. **Meals served** 10.30am-7pm Tue-Fri; 10.30am-4pm Sat. **Average** £. **Unlicensed**. **Corkage** £1. **Map** p294. Vegetarian
This Buddhist-run vegetarian café is where E2's chattering classes come for weekend brunch. Tall windows spill light onto the monthly rotating art exhibitions lining the walls of the canteen-style interior, and the pretty courtyard's scattering of brightly-coloured flowers poking out of terracotta pots make this a serene location for a weekend fry-up or a breakfast pancake. You'll need to get here early for the grub as it goes quickly. No surprise: creamy free-range scrambled eggs with tangy cherry tomato and basil were excellent on our Saturday visit. During the week they offer a range of soups, curries and hearty baked dishes, and there's always one vegan option on the menu. If you're not a fan of crowds, midweek is probably the best time to pop your (wild) cherry.

Meal deals

Bistrotheque *23-27 Wadeson Street, E2 9DR (8983 7900/ www.bistrotheque.com).* Set dinner (6.30-7.30pm Mon-Fri) £12.50 2 courses, £15 3 courses. French
Winkles *238 Roman Road, E2 0RY (8880 7450/www.winkles seafood.com).* Set lunch £12.50 3 courses. **Map** p294. Fish

East

In the area

Nando's *366 Bethnal Green Road, E2 0AH* (7729 5783). **Map** p294.

Bow

Orange Room Café

63 Burdett Road, E3 4TN (8980 7336). Mile End tube. **Meals served** 8am-11.30pm Mon-Sat; 8am-10.30pm Sun. **Average** ££. **Set lunch** £4.95 1 course, £6.50 2 courses incl soft drink. Lebanese

In an area around Mile End station swamped with uninspiring kebab and chicken shops, the Orange Room Café is a treat: a charming, ramshackle Lebanese restaurant furnished with weary furniture and old movie posters. For diners hopeful of a more traditional Lebanese vibe there are a couple of low-to-the-floor sofas; perhaps the best place to enjoy a mango lassi or a shisha pipe. Kafta halabieh (minced lamb with parsley and onions on a skewer) was aromatic and delicious; the meze options all arrived in large, tasty portions. If you're waiting for the food to arrive and conversation runs a little dry, pluck a book from the shelf of oldies. A 1987 Berlitz guide to Milan anyone?

Brick Lane

Brick Lane Beigel Bake

159 Brick Lane, E1 6SB (7729 0616). Liverpool Street tube/rail/ 8 bus. **Average** £. **Unlicensed**. **Open** 24hrs daily. **No credit cards**. **Map** p294. Café

The competitor two doors down does better sausage rolls, but this charismatic, 24-hour East End institution – all human life is here – nevertheless wins out in every other regard: perfect bagels both plain and filled (egg, cream cheese, herring, mountains of salt beef), superb breads and magnificently moreish cakes. When the bars and clubs in the area begin to close, the queue for bagels curves round the shop and trails out the door. Even at 3am, fresh baked goods are being pulled from the ovens at the back of the tight interior; as you'd imagine, the smell is wonderful.

★ Story Deli

3 Dray Walk, The Old Truman Brewery, 91 Brick Lane, E1 6QL (7247 3137). Liverpool Street tube/rail. **Meals served** 9am-6pm daily. **Average** ££. **Unlicensed**. **Corkage** no charge. **Map** p294. Pizza & Pasta

With its distressed floorboards, huge butcher's block tables and cardboard packing case seats creating a strangely uncafé-like appearance, it would be easy to overlook this 100% organic café and pizzeria. But on a Tuesday evening, Story Deli was packed to its shabby-chic rafters, and on tasting the food it's easy to see why. The pizzas are amazing, a cross between classic thin Neapolitan dough and the delicate pastry of Egyptian fatirs, topped with an inventive range of ingredients – prawns and peppers; ham, aubergine and olive; and rosemary and garlic among them. Other dishes were equally good; a prawn kebab came laden with sweet, fat prawns, grilled with juicy chunks of courgette, aubergine and onion; and the small but excellent range of mains includes steak sandwich, the Story burger, roasted cod and aïoli chips, and huge bowls of salad.

Docklands

Meal deals

Royal China *30 Westferry Circus, E14 8RR (7719 0888/www.royal chinagroup.co.uk).* Dim sum (noon-5pm daily) £2.20-£4.50. **Map** p293. Chinese

Premises Café. See p184.

In the area
Carluccio's Caffé *Reuters Plaza, E14 5AJ (7719 1749).* **Map** p293.
Itsu *Level 2, Cabot Place East, Canary Wharf, E14 4QT (7512 5790).* **Map** p293.
Nando's *Unit 25-26, Jubilee Place, E14 4QT (7513 2864).* **Map** p293.
Paul *Promenade Level, Cabot Place East, Canary Wharf, E14 5AB (7519 1703).* **Map** p293.
Pizza Express *200 Cabot Place East, Canary Wharf, E14 4QT (7513 0513).* **Map** p293.
Prezzo *37 Westferry Circus, E14 8RR (7519 1234).* **Map** p293.
Tootsies Grill *Jubilee Place, 45 Bank Street, E14 5NY (7516 9110).* **Map** p293.
Wagamama *Jubilee Place, 45 Bank Street, Canary Wharf, E14 5NY (7516 9009).* **Map** p293.
Zizzi *33 Westferry Circus, E14 8RR (7512 9257).* **Map** p293.

Limehouse

In the area
La Figa *45 Narrow Street, E14 8DN (7790 0077).*

Shoreditch

Anda de Bridge
42-44 Kingsland Road, E2 8DA (7739 3863). Old Street tube/rail/ 26, 48, 55, 67, 149, 242, 243 bus. **Meals served** 11am-midnight Mon-Sat; noon-11pm Sun. **Average** ££. **Map** p271. Caribbean

Anda de Bridge was undergoing refurbishment when we last visited. Despite the fresh look, our meal wasn't as convivial as it might have been – perhaps a result of visiting early in the week. The thundering ragga music was very intrusive and our request for it to be turned down was ignored. The food however, ordered at the bar, was fine enough. Starters were limited, but olives and good-quality bread sufficed. For mains, tasty ackee and saltfish was well-seasoned and served with a generous side of rice and peas, while brown chicken curry was succulent, the meat sliding from the bone. Anda de Bridge best serves drinkers who fancy a quick bite, rather than anyone looking for the full Caribbean gastronomic experience.

Au Lac

104 Kingsland Road, E2 8DP (7033 0588). Old Street tube/rail/26, 48, 55, 67, 149, 242, 243 bus. **Lunch served** noon-3pm Mon-Fri. **Dinner served** 5.30-11.30pm Mon-Thur; 5.30pm-midnight Fri. **Meals served** noon-midnight Sat; noon-11.30pm Sun. **Average ££. Set dinner** £12-£15.50 per person (minimum 2) 7 courses. **Map** p271. Vietnamese

Isn't it always the way? Just when you feel like eating crispy eels with betel leaf, the waiter informs you that they've run out. This was the only disappointment of our meal at Au Lac, a classy standout among the Kingsland Road Vietnamese brigade. We ordered the set dinner for two and found it enough for four. The golden pancake was excellent, the filling bursting with fresh beansprouts, chicken and prawns. Grilled monkfish on noodles was equally accomplished. Among the mains, spicy chicken was packed with chilli yet wasn't so hot as to ruin our palate for the tender stir-fried beef with crunchy green vegetables. Service was friendly, reasonably prompt and unobtrusive, although we've also experienced total collapse on busy nights. The former branch in Highbury (82 Highbury Park, N5 2XE, 7704 9187) is now run entirely separately, even though it shares the same name.

Cantaloupe

35-42 Charlotte Road, EC2A 3PB (7613 4411). Old Street tube/rail. Bar **Open** 11am-midnight Mon-Fri; noon-midnight Sun. **Meals served** noon-11.30pm Mon-Sat; noon-5pm, 5.30-10.30pm Sun. **Average ££.** *Restaurant* **Lunch served** noon-3pm Thur, Fri. **Dinner served** 6-11pm Mon-Fri; 7-11pm Sat. **Average £££.** **Map** p271. International

This bustling DJ bar has a cosy dining room with red padded booths at the back. The menu has taken a few more steps towards Latin culture of late, but our most recent visit revealed a kitchen that had lost its groove. Marinated seafood salad had a taste and texture as if the raw cod and salmon had only just met their dressing – a crude assault on the senses. Moqueca is a Brazilian seafood stew; this version had only small pieces of meat and seafood, none of the advertised cashew nuts, and was overwhelmed by coconut milk. The best dish was the Uruguayan fillet steak: aged, tender, and cooked perfectly medium-rare as requested. Standards in the kitchen appeared to be at a low point on this visit, but we'll be happy to return for the fabulous selection of wines by the glass and the cool, easy vibe.

Cây Tre

301 Old Street, EC1V 9LA (7729 8662). Old Street tube/rail. **Lunch served** noon-3pm Mon-Sat. **Dinner served** 5.30-11pm Mon-Thur; 5.30-11.30pm Fri, Sat. **Meals served** noon-10.30pm Sun. **Average ££.** **Map** p271. Vietnamese

Bright little Cây Tre is set amid the hustle and bustle of Old Street. Its menu offers some rarely seen (even in Shoreditch) Vietnamese dishes that, to indicate their authenticity, are marked with small smiley faces. The speciality of the house, cha ca la vong (sliced monkfish with fennel and dill, marinated in galangal and saffron), was fried at the table for us by the happy waitress. Combined with rice vermicelli and fermented shrimp sauce (pungent and sour), this appetiser for two produced a luscious fusion of different, typically Vietnamese aromas. Unfortunately, the meal went downhill from there. Canh chua soup (spicy and sour soup with beansprouts, pineapple, celery and taro stems) was refreshing yet unspectacular in flavour, and the white fish had a rather unpleasant rubbery texture. A shame.

Pie eyed

As London's white working-class communities continue to sell up and shift to the outer boroughs, so the eateries that nourished them must change, relocate or die. London's boozers have gone down the transformation route, making the most of their Victorian interiors, yet jettisoning their pickled eggs for Parma ham.

No such compromise has, and perhaps can, be made by London's time-honoured caterers to the workers: the pie and mash shops. They stick resolutely to providing food that has altered little since the middle of the 19th century: potatoes (a wedge of glutinous mash), pies (minced beef and gravy in a watertight crust), eels (jellied and cold, or warm and stewed) and liquor (an unfathomable lubricant loosely based on parsley sauce). Escalating eel prices mean that many places only serve eel and mash. Vinegar and pepper are the preferred condiments, a fork and spoon the tools of choice.

A choice bunch of these establishments remains – resplendent with tiled interiors, marble-topped tables and worn wooden benches. The oldest and most beautiful pie and mash shop is **M Manze's** on Tower Bridge Road, established in 1902, though **F Cooke** of Broadway Market, the **Kellys'** and the **Harrington's** shops all date from the early 20th century. Visit these family-run businesses while you can, for each year another one closes,

and with it vanishes a slice of old London. Relish the food, the surroundings, the prices (you'll rarely pay more than a fiver) and also your dining companions: Londoners to the core, not yet seduced by the trashy allure of burger chains.

None of these shops serves alcohol or accepts payment by credit card; all offer takeaways. They're often family-friendly too.

WJ Arment *7 & 9 Westmoreland Road, SE17 2AX (7703 4974/ www.armentspieandmash.com).*
Bert's *3 Peckham Park Road, SE15 6TR (7639 4598).*
Castle's *229 Royal College Street, NW1 9LT (7485 2196).* **Map** p292.
Clark's *46 Exmouth Market, EC1R 4QE (7837 1974).*
Cockneys Pie & Mash *314 Portobello Road, W10 5RU (8960 9409).* **Map** p280.
F Cooke *150 Hoxton Street, N1 6SH (7729 7718).* **Map** p271.
F Cooke *9 Broadway Market, E8 4PH (7254 6458).*
AJ Goddard *203 Deptford High Street, SE8 3NT (8692 3601).* **Map** p290.
Harrington's *3 Selkirk Road, SW17 0ER (8672 1877).* **Map** p285.
G Kelly *414 Bethnal Green Road, E2 0DJ (7739 3603).* **Map** p294.
G Kelly *600 Roman Road, E3 2RW (8983 3552).*
S&R Kelly *284 Bethnal Green Road, E2 0AG (7739 8676).* **Map** p294.
L Manze *76 Walthamstow High Street, E17 7LD (8520 2855).*
Manze's *204 Deptford High Street, SE8 3PR (8692 2375).* **Map** p290.
M Manze's *87 Tower Bridge Road, SE1 4TW (7407 2985). Bus 1, 42, 188.* **Map** p289.

★ Furnace NEW

1 Rufus Street, N1 6PE (7613 0598). Old Street tube/rail. **Lunch served** noon-3pm Mon-Fri. **Dinner served** 6-11pm Mon-Sat. **Average** ££. **Map** p271. Pizza & Pasta

Tucked away off Hoxton Square, this neat, exposed-brick restaurant challenges Story Deli (*see p179*) for the title of east London's best pizzeria. We opted for asparagus salad with quail's eggs and asiago cheese sauce to start, a swanky combination that worked very well. For mains there are daily pasta specials such as spinach and ricotta tortellini, but the monster pizzas are what everyone comes for (including a constant stream of patient take-away customers). You could opt for gorgonzola with poached pears or a funghi feast of wild, porcini and large flat mushrooms on truffle paste. Our porchetta (pork roast) topping was thinly cut and generously piled on to a base topped with sour cream and fennel. The crusts are artfully thin and slightly crunchy rather than stretchy.

Hanoi Café

98 Kingsland Road, E2 8DP (7729 5610). Old Street tube/rail/26, 48, 55, 67, 149, 242, 243 bus. **Meals served** noon-11.30pm daily. **Average** £. **Set lunch** £3.80 1 course. **Map** p271. Vietnamese

The screeching soundtrack of a kung fu movie in the kitchen was soon turned down after our arrival at this unassuming café. It's decorated with arty photos and jaunty green table-tops and it attracts a steady stream of eager customers. So it should, for the food here is highly appealing. Most of our dishes (excepting a king prawn bun) sparkled with flavour. Three dainty sticks of prawn mousse on sugar cane made a great appetiser, leaving plenty of room for the huge serving of DIY lime chicken summer rolls.

Even better was caramelised ginger duck: tender chunks of meat in a luscious, yet not overly sweet sauce. The high point of our meal was a whole king fish, crisply fried to perfection, and covered with fresh mango slices and a tangy sauce.

Lennie's

6 Calvert Avenue, E2 7JP (7739 3628). Liverpool Street or Old Street tube/rail. **Open** 8am-3.30pm Mon; 8am-3.30pm, 7.30-10pm Tue-Fri; 7.30-10pm Sat; 9am-2.30pm Sun. **Average** £. **Unlicensed**. **Corkage** £1. **Map** p271. Café

On a sunny Sunday morning, Lennie's is the place to go for a fry-up. Set out along the pavement, its wooden tables soon fill up with hungry – and hungover – residents of Hoxton. Own-made chicken burger and chips is on the menu, but most customers come for the breakfasts – the four or five different combinations on offer all cost £5 and include tea or coffee. If you like your greens then go for the house special, which incorporates a portion of spinach and mushrooms alongside the more conventional components of toast, eggs, bacon, and bubble and squeak. On weekdays breakfast is served until eleven; after that a caff menu takes over (lasagne, shepherd's pie and the like). It's all change again in the evenings, morphing into a Thai restaurant (Tue-Sat).

Loong Kee

134G Kingsland Road, E2 8DY (7729 8344). Old Street tube/rail/ 26, 48, 55, 67, 149, 242, 243 bus. **Lunch served** noon-3pm Mon-Fri. **Dinner served** 5-11pm Mon-Thur; 5pm-midnight Fri. **Meals served** noon-midnight Sat; noon-11pm Sun. **Average** £. **Unlicensed**. **Corkage** no charge. **No credit cards**. **Map** p271. Vietnamese

Although Loong Kee has got somewhat run down (the toilet in particular was in a state), locals still

East

appreciate its northern Vietnamese specialities. Noodle soups, vermicelli dishes and salads make up the genuine Vietnamese section of the Sino-dominated menu. Banh cuon (steamed rice pasta filled with minced pork and cloud-ear fungus), served with lettuce and sweet-sour nuoc mam, was a treat for the taste buds. Chicken feet and lotus stem salad with herbs and peanuts, on the other hand, was over-dressed and less delightful. The unusually small and flappy goi cuon (rice-paper rolls filled with shrimp, lettuce and vermicelli) were also disappointing. However, bun bo xao xa, a rice vermicelli dish on a bed of shredded lettuce, beansprouts and deliciously lemongrass-flavoured beef, saved the dinner. The place could do with some money being spent on it.

Mezedopolio

14 Hoxton Market, N1 6HG (7739 8212). Old Street tube/rail/26, 48, 55, 149, 243 bus. **Meals served** noon-10.30pm Mon-Sat. **Average** £££. **Map** p271. Greek

Like the Greek equivalent to a tapas joint, Mezedopolio is a drink and nibble sort of place, offering a menu of small seasonal meze that give a funky twist to a traditional meal. The emphasis is on sharing: six to eight dishes are about right for two diners. But while the portions seem to have got smaller, prices haven't. Two small fingers of battered, flaky salt cod on a tiny mound of skordaliá (garlic sauce) cost a princely £6.25. Still, the food is delightful, and with careful ordering you can stay within budget. Fáva (puréed split peas) was rich, the tzatziki was thick, and the fluffy gigandes (butter bean stew) was comforting to eat. Though inaccurately described as tirópitakia (small cheese pies), the bite-sized spinach and feta filo triangles were pleasingly delicate. Service can be pushy, but this is a fun venue.

Premises Café/Bistro

209 Hackney Road, E2 8JL (7684 2230). Old Street tube/rail/26, 48, 55 bus. **Meals served** 8am-11pm Mon, Wed, Thur-Sun; 8am-5.30pm Tue. **Average** ££. **Map** p294. Café/Bistro

The music studios attached to this eaterie have seen everyone from Nina Simone to Spiritualized go through the mixing desk, though an appetite-dampening picture of Jamie Cullum features on the café's wall of fame. The rock 'n' roll ethos snakes through to the eating section, where breakfast is served until 5.30pm in a head-spinning number of combos. Choose from meaty or veggie sausages, bubble and squeak, hash browns and thick bacon on a man-sized platter surrounding a lake of beans, or have them fill a sandwich. It's predictably greasy grub, great for filling a hangover hole. In the evening a bistro menu is offered: a mixed, loosely Mediterranean bag of meze dishes, pastas and grilled meats. The dining space is titchy, though not overbearingly cramped, and service is chummily bustling.

Amitas. See p187.

Shish

*313-319 Old Street, EC1V 9LE
(7749 0990). Liverpool Street or
Old Street tube/rail.* **Meals served**
11.30am-11.30pm Mon-Fri; 10.30am-
11.30pm Sat; 10.30am-10.30pm Sun.
Average ££. Set meal (until 7pm
Mon-Fri) £6.95-£8.45 2 courses.
Map p271. International

This small chain markets itself as
serving Silk Road cuisine, with food
hailing from points along the old
trading route from Turkey to China
and Japan. This concept does make
room for some strengths: alongside
the Middle Eastern-style starters
(falafel, tabouleh and so on) are
delicate Tashkent (lamb) dumplings.
As one might guess from the place's
name, main courses are kebabs,
offered with rice, couscous, chips or
salad, and as wraps. All are made
fresh with good meat, but they can
taste rather bland. Sichuan chilli
beef, for example, was supposed to
be marinated in spices, though
any chilli flavour was indiscernible.
A nice touch is the sparkling or still
mineral water on tap for a fixed fee,
along with fresh fruit juice cocktails.

★ Sông Quê

*134 Kingsland Road, E2 8DY
(7613 3222). Old Street tube/
rail/26, 48, 55, 67, 149, 242, 243
bus.* **Lunch served** noon-3pm,
dinner served 5.30-11pm Mon-
Sat. **Meals served** noon-11pm
Sun. **Average £. Map** p271.
Vietnamese

The interior of Sông Quê may be
kitsch – flaky, pale green paint
covers the walls, along with plastic
lobsters and fake ivy – but don't be
put off. Here you'll find delicious and
authentic Vietnamese food. Bi cuon
were luscious rice-paper rolls with
lettuce, vermicelli, mint and chives.
Banh xeo was a bit greasy, yet still
delicious: coriander, sweet basil and
mint brilliantly complemented the
salty filling and the sweet and sour
sauce. Sông Quê is particularly good
for soups. Pho rice noodle soup was
full of aromatic nuances: hints of
star anise, cinnamon, coriander and
sweet basil unfolded in our mouths.
From central Vietnam, bun bo hue
(vermicelli topped with beef and
Vietnamese sausage) also proved to
be a scrumptious treat.

Tay Do Café

65 Kingsland Road, E2 8AG (7729 7223). Old Street tube/rail/26, 48, 55, 67, 149, 242, 243 bus. **Lunch served** 11.30am-3pm, **dinner served** 5-11.30pm daily. **Average** ££. **Set lunch** £3.30 1 course. **Unlicensed**. **Corkage** 50p. **Map** p271. Vietnamese

This little café on Kingsland Road is certainly a hit with Hoxton hipsters and Vietnamese locals – at weekends it can be hard to find a table. The popularity is understandable, as the food is simply outstanding. Rich minced eel and onions on crunchy prawn crackers had the sweet and spicy taste of Vietnamese curry, as well as a lovely velvety texture. To follow, we ordered gilthead snapper in fish sauce with mango. This deep-fried delicacy was extremely crisp and yet tender on the inside – the unripe mango strips harmonised wonderfully with the salty taste of the fish sauce. The only downside to Tay Do is the service: the waiters rush from one table to another, keeping conversations with the diners brusque and they often have trouble understanding food orders too.

Viet Hoa

70-72 Kingsland Road, E2 8DP (7729 8293). Old Street tube/rail/26, 48, 55, 67, 149, 242, 243 bus. **Lunch served** noon-3.30pm, **dinner served** 5.30-11pm Mon-Fri. **Meals served** 12.30-11.30pm Sat, Sun. **Average** ££. **Map** p271. Vietnamese

Outdoing the local Vietnamese competition in size and length of tenure, Viet Hoa doesn't quite reach their culinary standards. Apart from the usual rice vermicelli dishes and noodle soups, the main courses sound like Sino-Viet combos rather than Vietnamese specialities. Cha ca ha noi (Hanoi-style fried fish fillets), a northern Vietnamese recipe, arrived in a small iron dish still sizzling, the dill and turmeric producing an appetising aroma. The fish rested atop lettuce, cucumber, coriander and rice vermicelli, and was more evocative of the herbal experience that is Vietnamese cuisine. There's some authenticity in the drinks list as well: to quench your thirst, choose from a small selection of Asian beers, including Tiger, Tsingtao or Vietnamese Hue.

Zen Satori

40 Hoxton Street, N1 6LR (7613 9590). Old Street tube/rail. **Lunch served** noon-3pm Mon-Fri. **Average** £. **Set lunch** £7.25 3 courses. **Map** p271. Oriental

Set on a bland stretch of modern, residential Hoxton, not five minutes from the square itself, the on-site restaurant of the Oriental School of Catering is smarter and sassier than its institutional appearance first suggests. Attentive, all-in-black student waiting staff promptly present you with the limited lunch-only menu (£5.40 mains; £7.25 with a soup and accompaniment), which is changed every six months. You'll find Indonesian satay chicken, stir-fry Vietnamese beef and Malaysian mee goreng – concocted by the all-in-white student chefs in the long, open, central kitchen. Our meal was well presented and tastier than expected at such a price. There's also an underused bar area for a crafty glass of draught Cobra. Most visits are swift and functional.

Meal deals

Drunken Monkey *222 Shoreditch High Street, E1 6PJ (7392 9606/ www.thedrunkenmonkey.co.uk).* Dim sum (noon-11pm Mon-Fri; 6pm-midnight Sat; noon-11pm Sun) £2.50-£4.50. **Map** p271. Chinese

Hoxton Apprentice *16 Hoxton Square, N1 6NT (7739 6022/ www.hoxtonapprentice.com).* Set lunch (Mon-Fri) £9.99 2 courses, £12.99 3 courses. **Map** p271. Modern European

In the area

Apostrophe *42 Great Eastern Street, EC2A 3EP (7739 8412).* **Map** *p271.*
Miso *45-47 Hoxton Square, N1 6PB (7613 5621).* **Map** *p271.*
Pizza Express *49-51 Curtain Road, EC2A 3PT (7613 5426).* **Map** *p271.*
The Real Greek *15 Hoxton Market, N1 6HG (7739 8212).* **Map** *p271.*
Tay Do Restaurant *60-64 Kingsland Road, E2 8DP (7739 0968).* **Map** *p271.*
Viet Grill *58 Kingsland Road, E2 8DP (7739 6686).* **Map** *p271.*

Stratford

In the area

Nando's *1A Romford Road, E15 4LJ (8221 2148).*
Pizza Express *Theatre Square, Stratford East, E15 1BX (8534 1700).*

Upton Park

Amitas NEW

124 Green Street, E7 8JQ (8472 1839). Upton Park tube then 58 or 330 bus. Deli **Open** 10am-9.30pm Tue-Thur; 10am-10pm Fri-Sun. *Restaurant* **Meals served** noon-9.30pm Tue-Thur; noon-10pm Fri-Sun. **Average** £. **Set thali** £5.95-£7.95. Gujarati
This neat, spacious vegetarian eaterie, with glossy white marble floors, has a counter selling Gujarati snacks, savouries and sweets to one side, and a restaurant to the other. The menu encompasses savoury tea time snacks, chaats, south Indian dosas, and Indian-Chinese dishes. There are four thalis and all other items cost less than a fiver. A glass of wine, beer, or spirit is £2.25 or £2.50. So how's the food? Much better than similar restaurants. We can recommend khandvi (savoury

chickpea flour 'swiss rolls') and dhokra (steamed lentil cakes), both of which came with an abundance of mustard and sesame seeds, green and red chillies, and fresh coriander.

Saravanaa Bhavan NEW

300 High Street North, E12 6SA (8552 4677). East Ham tube. **Meals served** 10am-10.30pm Mon-Thur; 10am-11pm Fri-Sun. **Average** £. **Set thali** £4.99-£5.99. Sri Lankan
Saravanaa Bhavan majors in Tamil vegetarian cooking. The Wembley franchise closed earlier this year, but a flagship is due to open in Croydon in late 2006. This outlet is small and café-like at the front, but leads to a spacious dining area at the back. In the middle is a partially open kitchen and brightly coloured sarees run the length of the opposite wall. Adai (here made with chickpea flour) came with avial (vegetable curry). Beautifully soft idlis were served with exceptional chutneys. Most items cost less than £3, and the delicious, generously portioned thalis are excellent value.

Victoria Park

Mar i Terra

223 Grove Road, E3 5SN (8981 9998). Mile End tube then 277 bus. **Meals served** 6-11pm Mon-Thur; noon-11pm Fri, Sat; noon-10pm Sun. **Average** £££. Spanish
Aside from the addition of loud paint and cheapish furniture, this airy space looks much as it did when it was still an organic gastropub called the Crown, with windows looking towards Victoria Park and a few tables out front. The tapas menu, an appetising jumble of dishes ancient and modern, will be familiar to anyone who's visited any of the other restaurants in the Mar i Terra group. Pimientos de padron (small green peppers) were greasy and higadillos de pollo (chicken livers)

East

Namo

marinated in five-spice, smeared with sweet chilli jam and served on a bed of sweet, gingery pickles, vermicelli noodles and black-eyed beans. This was among the most imaginative Vietnamese cooking we've sampled in London, and service was zippy, even on a busy Sunday lunchtime.

Wapping

Il Bordello
81 Wapping High Street, E1W 2YN (7481 9950). Wapping tube/100 bus. **Lunch served** noon-3pm Mon-Fri. **Dinner served** 6-11pm Mon-Sat. **Meals served** 1-10.30pm Sun. **Average £££. Map** p294.
Pizza & Pasta
Il Bordello is a classy joint, its brushed copper walls far from the checked tablecloths of Italian restaurant cliché. The food, while not earth-shattering, was fresh and enjoyable: linguine with scallops in a cream and brandy sauce was a highlight, although too rich to finish. Luckily, the smoothly professional waiting staff ensured that our meal went off without a hitch on a surprisingly busy Sunday night. Prices are on the high side, but you get what you pay for – a typical 'that little bit extra' touch was the house wine, which is specially bottled for Il Bordello at their vineyard in Italy.

In the area
Pizza Express *78-80 Wapping Lane, E1W 2RT (7481 8436).* **Map** p294.

Whitechapel

In the area
Mirch Masala *111-113 Commercial Road, E1 1RD (7377 0155).* **Map** p294.
Nando's *9-25 Mile End Road, E1 4TW (7791 2720).* **Map** p294.

lacked texture, but everything else was good: we especially enjoyed a zingy portion of grilled chorizo, creamy arroz a banda (a rice and fish dish) and some quality boquerones. Service was in Spanish, but we pointed and mimed and eventually got what we wanted.

★ Namo NEW
178 Victoria Park Road, E9 7HD (8533 0639). Mile End tube then 277 bus. **Lunch served** noon-3.30pm Thur-Sun. **Dinner served** 5.30-11pm Tue-Sun. **Average ££.**
Vietnamese
Namo fits perfectly into the small cluster of shops and restaurants bordering Victoria Park. A moody black frontage opens on to a bright interior full of 1950s-style chrome chairs and Vietnamese bric-a-brac. Food-wise, Namo takes some Viet favourites and modernises them. We started with the traditional – a piping hot bowl of bun Hue noodle soup with tender beef, chilli and lemongrass – then moved on to an inspired creation of chargrilled pork,

NORTH EAST

Chingford

In the area
Pizza Express *45-47 Old Church Road, E4 6SJ (8529 7866).*

Dalston

CAM at Centerprise
136-138 Kingsland High Street, E8 2NS (7254 9632). Dalston Kingsland rail. **Meals served** 10am-8pm daily. **Average** ££. **Set buffet** (noon-8pm Sun) £5. **Unlicensed. Corkage** £2.50. **Map** p295. Caribbean

Although a little rough around the edges, this Caribbean eaterie (attached to the specialist Centerprise bookshop) serves up large portions of quality chow for a few pounds and pennies. Jerk chicken came in a piquant barbecue sauce with a huge pile of rice and peas, as well as a can of cream soda – all for the excellent price of £3.99. Vegetable curry was its equal in size and price. Those who want to add a little more pep to the moderately-spiced food can choose from a collection of chilli and hot pepper sauces from around the world. And, as if the food weren't cheap enough, there are further reductions for customers who spend money in the neighbouring bookshop before their meal. The £5.99 buffet on a Sunday makes the perfect prelude to a matinée at the nearby Rio cinema.

Faulkner's
424-426 Kingsland Road, E8 4AA (7254 6152). Dalston Kingsland rail. **Lunch served** noon-2.30pm Mon-Fri. **Dinner served** 5-10pm Mon-Thur; 4.30-10pm Fri. **Meals served** 11.30am-10pm Sat; noon-9pm Sun. **Average** ££. **Set meal** £13.90-£16.90 4 courses (minimum 2 people). **Map** p295. Fish & Chips

Faulkner's is one of the only joints in this gritty, some might say run-down, part of town at which you'll find tablecloths. And you don't only get a bit of linen: think fresh flowers, heavy well-polished cutlery, and beautifully groomed waitresses. Starters highlight the new Turkish ownership, with houmous, taramasalata and tender fried calamares; all are served in main-course portions. A specials board offers whole sea bass and halibut at reasonable prices. We enjoyed a fabulous fried lemon sole, the batter crisp in some places, moist in others. Only the chips let the side down, being pale in colour, soft and very dried out. Own-made desserts of cakes and cherry tart, and an impressive fish tank, provide the finishing touches.

★ Huong-Viet
An Viet House, 12-14 Englefield Road, N1 4LS (7249 0877). Dalston Kingsland rail. **Lunch served** noon-3.30pm Mon-Fri; noon-4pm Sat. **Dinner served** 5.30-11pm Mon-Sat. **Average** ££. **Set lunch** £6 2 courses incl soft drink. **Map** p295. Vietnamese

Tucked away behind the nondescript doors of the An-Viet Foundation, a charity devoted to the aid of Vietnamese refugees, Huong-Viet has been serving fabulous Vietnamese food since the early 1990s. The dining room is cavernous; tables are lit by tiny spotlights, and photos of south-east Asia hang in every spare space on the walls. The menu offers a huge selection of salads, stir-fries, grills, noodle soups and spring rolls, and the food more than lives up to its reputation. Spare ribs came bite-sized, encrusted with chilli, ginger and lemongrass. We also rated the crispy Vietnamese pancake, stuffed with beansprouts, onions and tender prawns, and served with a divine sweet dip. Soft noodles with chicken went perfectly with a giant slice of kingfish, grilled to smoky brilliance in a wrapper of banana leaves.

CAM at Centerprise

Istanbul Iskembecisi

*9 Stoke Newington Road, N16 8BH
(7254 7291). Dalston Kingsland rail.*
Meals served noon-5am daily.
Average £££. Set lunch (noon-
5pm) £7 2 courses. **Set dinner**
(after 5pm) £11.50 2 courses; £16 per
person (minimum 2) 2 courses incl
glass of wine; £18.50 3 courses incl
glass of wine. **Map** p295. Turkish
Once the flagship restaurant of the
area, Istanbul's main claim to fame
now is that it stays open until 5am;
there's permanently something of the
early hours about it. Starters of
mitite köfte were small meatballs,
overcooked so that the taste was
mostly of frying. They were
presented with wonderful pide,
though. Houmous kavurma (with
lamb and pine nuts) was superb, the
nibblets of lamb ultra-crispy. To
follow, the mixed grill showed that
the chefs still know how to cook
meat, with adana, tavuk and shish
all being fine. There are some nice
touches, such as the plate of
complimentary watermelon, yet
service was (literally) distant – the
staff congregated by the bar at the
far end of the restaurant.

Mangal Ocakbaşı

*10 Arcola Street, E8 2DJ (7275
8981). Dalston Kingsland rail.*
Meals served noon-midnight
daily. **Average ££. Unlicensed.
Corkage** no charge. **No credit
cards. Map** p295. Turkish
A queue could be seen emerging
from the door as we approached the
hidden side street entrance of this
Dalston institution. It says
something about its legendary
reputation that, amid London's
densest concentration of Turkish
restaurants, people are still prepared
to queue to squeeze past the
takeaway counter and be crushed
into a plain, grey-tiled café where
they will have to endure curt service.
There are no menus, so we chose our
dishes from the stacks of raw
kebabs on display at the front. Basic
starters such as houmous and lentil
soup are often available if you ask.
Our grills were wonderful, though
no longer exceptional – quality has
not fallen, but the competition has
caught up, particularly in the
provision of starters and other
comforts. Still, all fans of Turkish
food (other than vegetarians) should
visit Mangal at some point.

Mangal II

*4 Stoke Newington Road, N16 8BH
(7254 7888). Dalston Kingsland
rail.* **Meals served** noon-1am daily.
Average ££. Set meal £14.50 per
person (minimum 2) 2 courses.
Map p295. Turkish
The three related Mangal
restaurants in this area are so
different that their link isn't
immediately obvious. The original
(Mangal Ocakbaşı; *see above*) is a
café offering straightforward grills
and the third is a specialist pide
pizza stop, while Mangal II is a

DISCOVER MORE CITIES

Tell us what you think and you could win £100-worth of City Guides

Your opinions are important to us and we'd like to know what you like and what you don't like about the Time Out guides

For your chance to win, simply fill in our short survey at **timeout.com/guidesreply**

Every month a reader will win £100 to spend on the Time Out City Guides of their choice . With over 50 titles to choose from, it's a great start to discovering new cities and you'll have extra cash to enjoy your trip!

bustling high-street restaurant, popular with a broad spectrum of Stoke Newington and Dalston locals, including many Turkish families. We mixed a standard but very pleasant ispanak (spinach) salad with a less common dish of lightly fried lambs' kidneys. Both were very fresh and perfectly prepared. For mains, an adana kebab was top-notch; patlıcan kebab, alternating patties of minced lamb and slices of aubergine grilled on a skewer, was also very good. A constant stream of diners came and went during our meal, but friendly, eager staff put us under no pressure to leave.

Nando's

148 Kingsland High Street, E8 2NS (7923 3555). Dalston Kingsland rail.
Meals served noon-11.30pm Mon-Thur, Sun; noon-midnight Fri, Sat.
Average ££. **Map** p295.
Portuguese

This chain chicken emporium is an international brand that plays hot with spicy peri-peri sauce and a laid-back, brightly coloured cabin vibe. Offering fresh ingredients, a decent wine list, plenty of bonuses – endless soft drinks – and a spirited humour, it's very much at the top end of the fast-food spectrum. The Dalston branch is one of the biggest in London, catering well to the taste demands of the locals for spicy fried chicken. This is really an assembly operation, where you choose the part of the bird that you fancy, then add the extras (fries and so on), alongside the crucial element, the sauce and its degree of fire. For vegetarians, the beanburger is perfectly serviceable, and the coffee and tarts serve to make for a reliable finish.

★ 19 Numara Bos Cirrik

34 Stoke Newington Road, N16 7XJ (7249 0400). Dalston Kingsland rail.
Meals served noon-midnight daily.
Average ££. **Unlicensed**.
Corkage £3. **Map** p295. Turkish

Still our favourite on Stoke Newington Road, the original 19 Numara remains pretty much perfect. It's a small restaurant, with a café-like feel. The pale walls are decorated with reliefs of Egyptian and Greek scenes. Across the back runs the ocakbaşı grill. When a main course is ordered it comes preceded by a range of starters, usually including grilled onion in a sharp pomegranate and turnip sauce, and chilli onion. Portions are sizeable. A main course of spicy adana yoğurtlu came with a minty yoghurt sauce, as did tavuk yoğurtlu; both also featured succulent, well-grilled meat. Bıldırcın was outstanding, with ridiculously plump quail – tasty and tender. If grills don't take your fancy, try something from the wide range of Turkish pide pizzas.

Shanghai

41 Kingsland High Street, E8 2JS (7254 2878). Dalston Kingsland rail.
Meals served noon-11pm, **dim sum served** noon-5pm daily. **Dim sum** £2-£3.90. **Average** ££. **Set meal** £13.50-£15.20 per person (minimum 2). **Map** p295. Chinese

In recent years we've found the food at this local Chinese opposite the market on Ridley Road quite patchy, but two recent visits impressed. A well-executed broth of shark's fin and crab meat was thick with crab and egg white. We also enjoyed the braised stuffed scallops with crab meat sauce; tasty medallions of minced prawn were generously sandwiched between slices of fresh scallop. The dim sum is good too, and absurdly cheap during late afternoons. The pretty scallop dumplings with their spinach-green wrappers are definitely worth trying. Dating from 1862, the front dining room was once a pie and mash shop; now listed, it still boasts the original art nouveau features. A rear dining room is more conventional.

Sömine

*131 Kingsland High Street, E8
2PB (7254 7384). Dalston Kingsland
rail.* **Meals served** 24hrs daily.
Average £. Unlicensed no alcohol
allowed. **No credit cards.**
Map p295. Turkish

Locals come here for hearty staples
at bargain prices, choosing from a
changing selection of dishes
scrawled above the counter. The
dips were pleasant enough, if
slightly bland, while translucent
leaves of flavour-packed pickled
cabbage were the highlight of the
accompanying salad. Manti
(traditional Turkish dumplings)
were disappointing, the meat filling
overwhelmed by a sea of garlic
yoghurt and too much dough. A dish
of mevsim kizartma – fried
aubergine, mushrooms, tomatoes,
potato and courgette – was also
below par, with chunks of potato
tasting disconcertingly like damp
and ancient chips. This is more of a
quick in-and-out daytime joint than
an evening venue, given the bright
overhead spotlights, metal chairs
and sparse decor.

Suya Obalende NEW

*523 Kingsland Road, E8 4AR
(7275 0171). Dalston Kingsland rail.*
Dinner served 3pm-midnight Fri,
Sat; 2-10pm Sun. **Average ££. Set
buffet** (Sun) £9.95. **Map** p295.
Nigerian

The slogan in the window reads:
'We don't serve fast food. We serve
good food fast.' But it's easy to miss
the fact that Suya Obalende houses
a restaurant as well as a takeaway.
Hidden behind a door at the back lies
a sizeable area where grills can be
eaten in. The menu is limited, but
dishes are hearty and filling –
various grills with chicken, lamb,
beef, goat, fish and, apparently, the
occasional appearance of crocodile.
A buffet is sometimes also available.
Grills are served with jollof rice or

pounded yam and potato. Several
are offered with 'notorious' chilli
sauces. We tried suya chicken with
jollof rice, which came in a great
mound, along with a thick gravy.
Asaro lamb was a well-grilled
portion with a satisfying mix of yam
and potato. A good local café.

Hackney

Anatolia Ocakbaşı

*253 Mare Street, E8 3NS (8986
2223). London Fields rail.* **Meals
served** 11am-midnight daily.
Average ££. Unlicensed.
Corkage £3.50. Turkish

Both the somewhat barn-like
restaurant and the takeaway at the
front are usually busy, with a fast
turnover of customers. Haydari (a
mix of fresh yoghurt, garlic, chilli
and, in this case, grated carrot) made
an invigorating starter. For mains,
an enormous dish of halep kebab
was served bubbling hot. A thick,
buttery, tomatoey sauce –
containing a mix of peppers and
other vegetables – enveloped lamb
döner kebab and pide bread,
drenching the bread to the point of
disintegration. As ever, it was good
to see the kebabs and salad being
prepared behind the grill. Anatolia
could offer more for vegetarians, but
remains a decent local ocakbaşı.

Cilicia

*1 Broadway Market, E8 4PH (7249
8799). London Fields rail.* **Meals
served** 11am-11pm Mon-Fri;
10am-11.30pm Sat; 10am-11pm
Sun. **Average ££. Set lunch**
(11am-5pm) £7.50 2 courses,
£8.50 3 courses. Turkish

The day-glo orange-painted walls
are covered in Turkish ephemera,
with paintings, hubble-bubble pipes
and textiles dotted about, while
brightly decorated lights (made
from gourds) hang over wooden
tables. When the sun is shining, the

umbrella-covered terrace area at the back is usually filled with families and local shoppers. The Mediterranean-influenced menu covers the range from all-day breakfasts (featuring traditional fry-ups to a lovely Turkish version with halloumi cheese) to mixed meze and stuffed pide. Starters of broad beans in yoghurt, and tzatziki were both deliciously tangy, while a side of tabouleh was fresh and full of parsley. Service is friendly, if a little distracted when busy.

L'Eau à la Bouche

49 Broadway Market, E8 4PH (7923 0600). London Fields rail. **Meals served** 8.30am-7pm Mon-Fri; 8.30am-5pm Sat; 10am-4pm Sun. **Average** ££. Café
The range of goodies at this little French deli always means that you'll spend much more here than you ever intended to. Everything is tempting: breads, patisserie, meats (parma, serrano, merguez and a range of handmade sausages), cheese (plenty of lesser-known British and French varieties as well as goat's, camembert, brie and roquefort), olives, and salads. There's also a host of scrumptious-looking tinned and dry goods. Happily you can sample most of this produce sitting at one of the little tables within or without (on Broadway Market). Try an enormous filled ciabatta, a chunk of tortilla or quiche, or just some great coffee with a chocolate florentine. It's usually packed, especially on a Saturday when the market is in full swing, but it's worth waiting around.

Green Papaya

191 Mare Street, E8 3QE (8985 5486). London Fields rail. **Meals served** 5-11pm Tue-Sun. **Average** ££. Vietnamese
Green Papaya firmly targets the Hackney middle classes with Hoxton-style modernist decor and a thought-provoking menu, selected to appeal to adventurous western palates. All the Vietnamese favourites are here: pho, spicy stir-fries, meats and seafood encrusted in salt, pepper, garlic and chilli. Everything we tried was delicious. Tangy banana flower salad with shredded chicken was crisp and full of texture, while crispy-battered squid was brought to life by a zesty purple basil dip. A main of slow-cooked lamb was tender, with a complex lemongrass, coconut and galangal sauce, and stir-fried beef with asparagus had an almost Chinese quality – full of pepper and chilli punch and piled with tender asparagus spears. We ordered rice noodles with barbecued pork on the side, but it could easily have been a meal in itself. A feast.

Hai-Ha

206 Mare Street, E8 3RD (8985 5388). London Fields rail. **Lunch served** noon-3pm daily. **Dinner served** 5-11pm Mon-Fri; 5-11.30pm Sat, Sun. **Average** £. **Unlicensed. Corkage** no charge. **No credit cards**. Vietnamese
The extensive menu at this typically busy local canteen may look overwhelming but choose carefully and you'll be amazed at how fresh and flavoursome the food is here. Our advice? Avoid the Chinese dishes, which tend to be gloopy and oversauced, and stick instead to the traditional Vietnamese: deep-fried crispy squid with peppercorn and salt (£3) was delicious, and barbecued sugarcane prawn (moist pieces of prawn served with a spicy chilli and rice vinegar dressing) was just as impressive. The 'Hai-Ha special' of grilled whole fish (a type of bream on our night) was laced with sticks of ginger and garlic and fell off the bone. The place is BYO so pick up beers or wine from the off licence over the road.

North East

Café Larosh

LMNT

*316 Queensbridge Road, E8 3NH
(7249 6727). Dalston Kingsland rail.*
Meals served noon-11pm Mon-Sat;
noon-10.30pm Sun. **Average ££.**
Modern European

An urn-shaped dining pod, tables in
raised cubbyholes, stone sphinxes
and a candelit Zeus-like mask – the
boldfaced decor at LMNT is one of
its principal draws. The food,
however, is less reliable. Crisp-
skinned sea bream was
overpowered by badly judged, oddly
tangy braised fennel. Beetroot and
horseradish risotto was an
intriguing idea, but too watery.
Some of this was forgiven with the
arrival of a delectable pistachio
crème brûlée. At £8.95 for mains,
£3.45 for starters and desserts, too
much griping would be unfair –
especially given that on a repeat
visit everyone in the party was more
than satisfied with the food. LMNT
pulls off a surprisingly authentic
Mediterranean tourist-joint vibe, in
the nicest, most convivial way.

Tre Viet

*251 Mare Street, E8 3NS (8533
7390). London Fields rail.* **Meals
served** 11am-11pm daily. **Average
££. Unlicensed. Corkage** no
charge. **No credit cards.**
Vietnamese

Tre Viet serves Vietnamese food to
Vietnamese locals, using fresh
ingredients from the Vietnamese
wholesalers along Mare Street.
Diners eat at glass-topped tables
beneath a bamboo trellis hung with
faux leaves and red Chinese lanterns.
We started with a tasty plate of bo la
lot, a north Vietnamese staple of five-
spiced beef wrapped in peppery betel
leaves and grilled on skewers. Goi
cuon rolls were just as special: soft
steamed prawns, vermicelli,
coriander and mint, rolled up in
freshly steamed, semi-transparent
rice paper. Mains were more hit and
miss: a huge pile of soft noodles with
sliced chicken was delicious, perked
up by crisp pieces of water chestnut,
but sizzling lamb with coconut, chilli
and lemongrass had a distracting
medicinal flavour. Best to opt for
familiar Vietnamese standards over
exotic-sounding specials.

La Vie en Rose [NEW]

*2 Broadway Market, E8 4QG (7249
9070). Liverpool Street tube/rail then
26, 48 or 55 bus/London Fields rail.*
Meals served 9am-4pm Mon; 9am-
10.30pm Tue-Thur; 9am-11pm Fri,
Sat; 9am-10pm Sun. **Average £££.
Set lunch** (noon-4pm Mon-Fri)
£6.95 2 courses, £7.95 3 courses.
French

Occupying the site that used to be
home to Little Georgia, this easy-
going French outfit has settled in as
a decent local on a road with plenty
of options. The menu plays it safe in
a charmingly old-school way: the

likes of fish soup or goat's cheese salad followed by chicken stew, say, or lamb chops with ratatouille in the evenings; brunch means big cooked breakfasts, croque monsieur or pastries. At dinner the sure bet is steak frites, with either a creamy roquefort or green pepper sauce. The only real problem we've found here is that the relaxed vibe extends to the staff – service is friendly but sometimes verges on the clueless. Last time we were here, the coffee arrived quickly, but we had to wait almost an hour for a very simple brunch order of croissant plus scrambled eggs and smoked salmon.

Leyton

Café Larosh

7 Church Lane, E11 1HG (8518 7463). Leytonstone tube. **Meals served** 11.30am-11pm Mon-Thur; 11.30am-midnight Fri, Sat; 11.30am-11pm Sun. **Average** **££. Unlicensed. Corkage** no charge. Indian

A stylish new interior plus a chill-out room downstairs have moved Café Larosh up a few notches in the Leytonstone eating stakes. Where once it was a place to pop in for a takeaway, now more locals are taking time to enjoy the relaxed surroundings and decent north Indian cooking in which spicing has been tempered to western tastes. The food is still prepared in large metal tureens then heated to order, which helps the flavours of the curries and birianis to develop. The menu, however, has expanded with imaginative fish dishes such as mackerel curry, while the local South African population are enticed in with bunny chow – a loaf of bread with the inside scooped out and filled with curry. A selection of good-value set meals means two people can eat well here for less than £20.

Gastrodome

17 High Street, E11 2AA (8989 8943). Snaresbrook tube. **Meals served** noon-10pm Mon-Fri; 9am-10pm Sat, Sun. **Average £££.** International

This split-level diner remains a popular venue for a relaxed family meal that won't break the bank. The menu keeps things simple and relatively healthy. Spit-roast chicken and ribs, prepared in the galley kitchen that runs along one side of the restaurant, come with a choice of sauces, while salade niçoise appealed to a hungry teenager. Steak, burgers and superior pasta are decent alternatives, and even the most mouse-like appetite will be tempted by the Spanish and Greek-style starters. A plate of grilled bread, manchego cheese, roast peppers, smoked ham, grilled artichokes and olives is a colourful option for £8.50. Service is deft and smiling.

Swaad NEW

715 Leytonstone High Road, E11 4RD (8539 1700). Leytonstone tube/Leytonstone High Road rail. **Lunch served** noon-3pm, **dinner served** 6-11pm daily. **Average ££. Unlicensed. Corkage** no charge. Indian

This site used to be occupied by the south Indian vegetarian restaurant Chandni. New owners have brought a change of name, an upgrade to the decor and the appearance of standard (though well-made) curries on the menu, but enough regional specialities remain to please the connoisseur. There's a fresh ginger kick to both sag paneer (spinach with curd cheese) and rasam (thin, tomato-based Keralan soup), while deep-fried cashew nut pakoda (like a bhaji) is the best of the selection of farsan, or snacks. Among the more substantial dishes, fish moly – kingfish cooked in coconut milk with onion, chilli, ginger and tomato – is a snip for £4.25.

Leytonstone

Base Camp NEW

552 Leytonstone High Road, E11 3DH (8988 3904). Leytonstone tube/Leytonstone High Road rail. **Lunch served** noon-2.30pm Mon-Fri. **Dinner served** 6-10pm Mon-Sat. **Average** £. **Set lunch** (Mon-Fri) £3 1 course incl drink. **Unlicensed. Corkage** 50p. **No credit cards.** Nepalese

With only eight tables arranged around an open kitchen, this tiny restaurant has an understandably homely feel, and the restaurant adds a welcome touch of colour to an otherwise drab stretch of road. Influences from Mongolia, Persia and the Indian sub-continent are apparent on the menu, which opens with steamed lamb or vegetable dumplings known as momo and piquant pork choila (shredded meat cooked with ginger, garlic and spices). Main courses are spiced to order (children will have no problem with 'normal'); meat, tofu or seafood are selected to be stir-fried with a particular sauce: the pick of these are the intriguing kaju, with cashews, nutmeg and milk, and the light and tangy amilo. All except one main course costs less than a fiver which, combined with a BYO policy (50p glass charge), makes Base Camp a great place to explore the foothills of Nepalese cuisine.

Singburi

593 Leytonstone High Road, E11 4PA (8281 4801). LLeytonstone tube/Leytonstone High Road rail. **Dinner served** 6-11pm daily. **Average** ££. **Unlicensed. Corkage** no charge. **No credit cards.** Thai

A genuine welcome from owners Tony and Thelma Kularbwong, plus tasty home-style Thai cooking, are the hallmarks of this ever-popular caff, whose basic decor and location away from Leytonstone's main drag haven't prevented it becoming a staunch favourite in these parts. The menu is a roll call of familiar flavours, but the standard is high and there's no skimping on authentic ingredients such as pea aubergines in the gang keow-wan (green curry). Pad talay (stir-fried mixed seafood) was crammed with fishy morsels; all veg tasted fresh and crunchy. There's a small specials board from which one dish each year is added to the main menu – the kind of quirky touch which Singburi's devotees appreciate. Prices have risen slightly in the last year but the BYO policy remains.

Newington Green

Beyti

113 Green Lanes, N16 9DA (7704 3165). Manor House tube then 141, 341 bus. **Meals served** noon-midnight daily. **Average** ££. **Unlicensed. Corkage** no charge. **No credit cards. Map** p295. Turkish

In addition to Turkish restaurant food, Beyti offers Black Sea and northern Anatolian dishes. This is enough to make the restaurant worth finding, even though its location is far from the main drag of Green Lanes. Beyti also provides a varied range of fish dishes. For starters, we enjoyed some subtly spiced deep-fried meatballs (misket köfte). Kalamar arrived piping hot in fine batter, with well-flavoured squid that wasn't the least bit rubbery. As a main, we wolfed down tasty grilled salmon. Pirzola (grilled lamb chops) were also fine, though ours were too well done. It's also worth checking for the daily specials. Food is hearty rather than subtle, and the atmosphere is akin to that of a café – but these aren't criticisms. Beyti is a jolly place.

North East

Base Camp

★ Sariyer Balik

56 Green Lanes, N16 9NH (7275 7681). Manor House tube then 141, 341 bus. **Meals served** 5pm-1am daily. **Average** ££. **No credit cards. Map** p295. Turkish

First-time visitors must peer into the rather shabby, black-painted interior of Sariyer Balik and wonder if they have come to the right place. They shouldn't worry; it's got a little run down over the years, but the quality of food here is as high as ever. A new menu has been printed, but the basic dish is still char-grilled fish – the species dependent on what's fresh at the market. For starters, the mixed hot meze showed how much can be achieved without shooting too high: prawns in chilli sauce, calamares marinated in vodka, and mussels in batter and beer are all simple dishes, flawlessly executed. Lightly battered anchovies were a melting delight as a main course. True, the bass was full of bones, but the flesh was moist and just right. For those in the know, Sariyer Balik is a treasure.

Stoke Newington

Abi Ruchi

42 Stoke Newington Church Street, N16 0LU (7923 4564). Stoke Newington rail/73, 393, 476 bus. **Lunch served** noon-3pm Mon-Sat. **Dinner served** 6-11pm Mon-Thur; 6-11.45pm Fri, Sat. **Meals served** 1-10.15pm Sun. **Average** ££. **Set lunch** (daily) £4.50-£5.50 1 course, £5.95-£7.50 2 courses. **Map** p295. South Indian

With its focus on Keralan cooking, the menu departs from predictable curry-house standards. Deep-fried chicken kizhi set the benchmark: crunchy parcels filled with tender meat and spinach. To follow we chose lamb ulathiya masala: generous chunks of meat in an impeccably spiced tomato sauce, laced with roasted coconut, curry leaves, ginger and garlic. A bowl of rich chemmen alleppey (king prawns with onion, tomato, ginger and chilli) was deliciously spicy and satisfying – instead of rice, order a chewy, flaky keral paratha to mop up the sauce. Vegetarians are spoilt for choice with an impressively varied list of curries, and the inexpensive vegetable side dishes (such as the meltingly soft but deceptively hot aubergine with mustard seeds and spices) are well worth investigating. The small, peach-hued dining room is relaxed and dimly-lit, enlivened by an elephant statue and an irrepressibly jovial waiter.

Il Bacio

61 Stoke Newington Church Street, N16 0AR (7249 3833). Stoke Newington rail/73, 393, 476 bus. **Dinner served** 6-11.40pm Mon-Fri. **Meals served** noon-11pm Sat, Sun. **Average** ££. **Map** p295. Pizza & Pasta

Bring a good appetite to Il Bacio: the pizzas are seriously large, at least a foot and a half in diameter. We made

North East

the mistake of having one each – one with ham, rocket and asparagus, the other with parma ham, sweetcorn and mushrooms – and at around £9.50 each, they'd have been a steal if we'd shared. As it was it was up to the staff to cheerfully doggie-bag what we couldn't finish. Quality is high: bases were light and crisp, the toppings fresh, tasty and wide-ranging – including a special selection with extra buffalo mozzarella. The meat and fish dishes looked good too, and were almost as hugely-portioned. The atmosphere is authentically Italian (maybe too authentic – we had to repeat our orders) and the decor endearing, from classic prints to paintings of big-bottomed ladies climbing into baths.

Blue Legume

101 Stoke Newington Church Street, N16 0UD (7923 1303). Stoke Newington rail/73, 393, 476 bus. **Meals served** 9.30am-11pm Mon-Sat; 9.30am-6.30pm Sun. **Average** ££. **Map** p295. Café
If you want a cake that will brighten your day try the lemon cheesecake at this Stokey stalwart. It's fantastic. They also have an extensive and tasty selection of veggie food, as well as smoothies, a good range of teas and coffees, and breakfasts like organic honey waffles with fresh fruit, maple syrup and yogurt. At night, Blue Legume transforms into a restaurant, serving wine and Turkish-inspired food, such as their eponymous dish, an aubergine parcel of roasted vegetables topped with goat's cheese. The surroundings are very pleasant: green walls and a quirky cloud-covered ceiling in the front room, and an airy mini conservatory at the back. The attractive mosaic tables are somewhat crammed together, but if you've sampled the lemon cheesecake, you probably won't care.

Bodrum Café & Bar

61 Stoke Newington High Street, N16 8EL (7254 6464). Stoke Newington rail/73, 76, 149, 243 bus. **Meals served** 7am-11pm daily. **Average** £. **Set breakfast** (7am-noon) £1.99 incl tea/coffee. **Set lunch** (11am-6pm) £4.99 2 courses incl coffee. **No credit cards**. **Map** p295. Turkish
With its wooden tables and yellow-painted walls, dotted with black-and-white photographs and posters for local jazz evenings, Bodrum Café has a cheerily laid-back, welcoming feel. The menu ranges from Turkish and English breakfasts through to traditional caff fare (liver and bacon, gammon and chips) and tempting Turkish meze and mains. With the exception of a bland grilled aubergine salad, starters were excellent: grilled hellim cheese; crunchy, feta-filled filo parcels called signari boregi; spicy, garlicky chunks of suculi tava sausage and, best of all, a plate of tiny broad beans with yoghurt, sprinkled with dill. Mains, served up on huge white plates, were simple but satisfying; fresh, chunky igzara kofte (grilled lamb meatballs) and melt-in-the-mouth imam bayıldı, the aubergine cooked to perfection and piled high with tomato, onion and peppers.

Café Z Bar

58 Stoke Newington High Street, N16 7PB (7275 7523). Stoke Newington rail/73, 76, 149, 243 bus. **Meals served** 8am-11pm daily. **Average** ££. **Set meal** £4.95 2 courses. **No credit cards**. **Map** p295. Turkish
A standard café menu is complemented by a fair choice of Turkish mezes and grills. Muhamarra (a paste made from red peppers, walnuts and pomegranate syrup) made a very fresh, spicy starter. Our main course, juicy çop şiş, was served on wooden skewers, with a salad of grated lettuce, carrot and

red cabbage. Several vegetarian and fish dishes are available, as well as a selection of Turkish pizzas. You can also order Turkish all-day breakfasts, as well as freshly squeezed apple, orange and carrot juices. We've always found the service to be excellent. Mixing elements of café, bar, gallery and restaurant, Z Bar has become something of a local cultural centre, with occasional evening gigs and events in the basement.

Itto

226 Stoke Newington High Street, N16 7HU (7275 8827). Stoke Newington rail/73, 76, 149, 243 bus.
Meals served noon-11pm daily.
Average ££. Map p295. Oriental
The perfect little local to satisfy a craving for Asian cuisine. There are no surprises in the menu, which sticks to tried-and-tested Chinese, Japanese and Thai favourites. But everything we requested was freshly cooked to order. We started with agedashidofu that was nicely bathed in a soy and mirin sauce. A mild Thai green chicken curry was fine, while egg-fried rice was simple and faultless. Best of all was the Itto chicken noodle spicy soup: a large steaming bowl of rice noodles with slices of fried fish cake and beancurd, crab sticks, pak choi, eggs, prawns and soft juicy morsels of chicken. The lilac and deep pink interior has a DIY quality about it, but every neighbourhood should have a local like this.

Rasa

55 Stoke Newington Church Street, N16 0AR (7249 0344). Stoke Newington rail/73, 393, 476 bus.
Lunch served noon-3pm Sat, Sun.
Dinner served 6-10.45pm Mon-Thur, Sun; 6-11.30pm Fri, Sat.
Average £££. Set meal £16 4 courses. **Map** p295. South Indian
The original restaurant of a six-strong chain, Rasa has a striking cochineal-pink frontage which leads

to a traditional interior complete with hanging lamp stands and statues of Hindu deities. You'll find no modern interpretations on the menu; Rasa is resolutely true to its Keralan culinary heritage. Tempting own-made crunchy snacks work particularly well with the array of relishes. Afterwards, mysore bonda (deep-fried dumplings of mashed potato, spiced with mustard seeds and curry leaves) were all the more delicious for their crisp chickpea-flour batter. But idlis didn't measure up to expectation, having a dense (rather than light and spongy) texture. Our mood perked up with a marvellously fruity mango and green banana curry, which made a fabulous partner to lemon rice. Service, like the cooking, is homely.

Testi

38 Stoke Newington High Street, N16 7PL (7249 7151). Stoke Newington rail/73, 393, 476 bus.
Meals served noon-1am Sun-Thur; noon-2am Fri, Sat. **Average ££.**
Map p295. Turkish
'Less is more' isn't a concept that holds much truck here. Take the decor: orange walls, a red marbled ceiling (bedecked with jewelled lamps) and wooden beads, wicker sheep and other ornaments. The food, meanwhile, comes in giant portions: meat and offal, cooked on the ocakbaşı grill. Testicles *are* on the menu but the restaurant's name is actually the Turkish word for jug. Starters of mixed meze and light, crispy lahmacun were excellent, though a portion of liver was overpowering. To follow, grilled quail was salty and delicious; lamb and aubergine was good but the latter overdone. The main courses came with three complimentary side dishes: tomato and onion salad, a fierce onion and chilli concoction and, best of all, chargrilled onions in pomegranate juice.

In the area

Il Bacio Express *90 Stoke Newington Church Street, N16 OAD (7249 2344).* **Map** p295.

Fresh & Wild *32-40 Stoke Newington Church Street, N16 0LU (7254 2332).* **Map** p295.

Rasa Travancore *56 Stoke Newington Church Street, N16 0NB (7249 1340).* Branch of Rasa. **Map** p295.

Walthamstow

La Cafeteria

841 Forest Road, E17 4AT (8527 1926). Walthamstow Central tube/ rail then 212 or 275 bus. **Meals served** 7.30am-4.30pm Mon-Sat. **Average** ££. **No credit cards.** Café Bag a table at the back of La Cafeteria and you won't believe you're yards from the A503 in a down-at-heel swathe of east London. There's a bright, welcoming and civilised feel to this place, which turns out fine breakfasts and light, Mediterranean-inspired lunches – for which you may need to book, as seats are eagerly seized upon by workers from the nearby council offices. It's very family-friendly, non-smoking throughout, with a rack of newspapers and upmarket magazines encouraging you to linger. Quick to arrive and prepared with a keen eye for colour, the daily-changing menu may include roast vegetables with couscous or penne with bacon, spinach, olives and sun-dried tomatoes. Alternatively, baguettes and toasties are served with salad and fruit. There's a clamour for the owners to open in the evenings, but they've resisted so far.

★ Trattoria La Ruga

59 Orford Road, E17 9NJ (8520 5008). Walthamstow Central tube/ rail. **Dinner served** 6pm-midnight Tue-Sat. **Meals served** noon-11pm Sun. **Average** £££. Italian

Some people find the lack of a printed menu or wine list at La Ruga pretentious. Others find it shows a commitment to serve only fresh, seasonal, carefully-sourced and uncomplicated produce. We're in the latter camp. Half a dozen choices for each course are chalked up on boards, in Italian; then you wait for the friendly staff to explain the ingredients. Starters might include a simple rocket salad or spaghetti with prawns in a rich tomato sauce, while fish is given equal billing to meat among the mains. Roasted seabass and a swordfish steak served with a piquant lemon dipping sauce were recent standouts. Service is unhurried and the many regulars know that characterful owner Peter will simply pull up a chair for a chat if there's any delay.

Wanstead

Nam An

157 High Street, E11 2RL (8532 2845). Wanstead tube. **Lunch served** noon-2.30pm Wed-Sun. **Dinner served** 6-11.30pm daily. **Average** ££. Vietnamese

The fact that on our midweek visit the waiter was mopping the floor of a deserted restaurant indicates that lunchtime trade hasn't picked up since last year – though evenings are much busier. It wasn't long after our arrival before Vietnamese music parped into action, with the waiter not far behind. Ornate dark-wood screens, plastic bamboo and a carp pond provide an old-school oriental set-up. Soft-shell crab deep-fried with chilli and salt had a clean, nutty crunch; and a zingy soup with prawns and tamarind was crammed with crisp beansprouts and juicy straw mushrooms. An unctuous main course of duck with aubergine cooked in a clay pot was resplendent with subtle aromatic spices.

NORTH

Archway

The Archgate NEW

5 Junction Road, N19 5QT (7272 2575). Archway tube. **Meals served** 10am-midnight daily. **Average** ££. **Set meal** £13.95 3 courses (minimum 2). **Set meze** £9.95 per person (minimum 2). **Map** p298. Turkish

Slap-bang opposite Archway tube, on a grotty stretch of the very variable Archway Road, this is a welcome find: a small, friendly restaurant, prettily decorated with colourful Turkish tiles and hanging lanterns. Although the wide-ranging menu offers all-day breakfasts and burgers, Turkish food is the name of the game here. On our lunchtime visit, customers included local office workers tucking into charcoal grilled kebabs with relish, and a couple of OAPs eating a classic caff fry-up. Our selection of meze dishes, including crisp börek, lamb köfte, imam bayıldı and houmous, were well-made and satisfying, although the pan-fried squid was rather on the chewy side. Not only were the dishes freshly cooked, they were served out to us in noticeably generous portions and at bargain prices.

Charuwan

110 Junction Road, N19 5LB (7263 1410). Archway or Tufnell Park tube. **Lunch served** noon-3pm Mon-Fri. **Dinner served** 6-11pm daily. **Average** ££. **Map** p298. Thai

Though in the neighbourhood-Thai mould, Charuwan has built a reputation by steadfastly refusing to water down its food to appeal to the masses. This is Thai cooking the way Thais like it: homely, authentic and unashamedly hot. Walls are covered in oriental bric-a-brac, while framed portraits of the Thai king and queen hang proudly over the bar. Service is friendly but tends to the ponderous; things can slow to a

Lighthouse

crawl at busy times. To start, house laap was formidable – red hot and lemon-tangy with the flavour of coriander winning through. As on our last visit, pla lad prik stole the culinary show: crispy fried hunks of white fish with a scorching sweet sauce packed with bird's-eye chillies. Charuwan is a lovely little Thai, but not ideal if you're in a hurry.

Lighthouse NEW

179 Archway Road, N6 5BN (8348 3121). Highgate tube. **Dinner served** 5pm-midnight Mon-Fri. **Meals served** noon-midnight Fri-Sun. **Average** £££. **Set meal** (noon-5pm Sat; noon-midnight Sun) £8.95 2 courses. **Map** p298. Fish

This bright and airy fish restaurant is inspired by the sort of culinary establishments that you'd find on the Black Sea in Georgia – that's where the owners come from – and it's always packed to the rafters. A good selection of fish that's fresh from Billingsgate is cooked with simplicity and confidence by a chef comfortable with such a range of produce. A complimentary fish soup was light and tasty, sea bass was soft and subtle, and the wild salmon

North

steaks were unfatty and quite simply delicious. Also deservedly popular is Lighthouse's nod to prole food: good old-fashioned battered fish and chips. There are some great two course meal deals to be had which make this restaurant very reasonable, but don't expect a quick turnaround: service, when it comes, is friendly enough, though we had to do a lot of arm-waving.

Camden Town & Chalk Farm

Asakusa
265 Eversholt Street, NW1 1BA (7388 8533/8399). Mornington Crescent tube. **Dinner served** 6-11.30pm Mon-Fri; 6-11pm Sat. **Average ££. Set dinner** £5.20-£19. **Map** p296. Japanese
Combine your local pub with a sushi bar and this is what you get. With its flock wallpaper, swirly carpet, wooden bar and unpretentious atmosphere, you half expect to see Dot Cotton coming through the restaurant's doors carrying a menu. Ordering from this massive document, we kicked off with a nigiri platter, which included luscious portions of all the regulars: mackerel, tuna, salmon, prawn and ikura (salmon eggs). Unagi (grilled eel) was also a winner. Mackerel simmered in miso was similarly impressive, the nutty soy flavours infusing the flesh. Service was pleasant and unobtrusive and the final bill was extremely reasonable. On our visit Asakusa was packed to its mock-Tudor rafters with Japanese customers – who clearly know they're on to a good thing.

Bintang
93 Kentish Town Road, NW1 8NY (7813 3393). Camden Road rail/Camden Town tube. **Dinner served** 5.30-11.30pm Mon-Thur,

Sun; 5.30pm-midnight Fri, Sat. **Average ££. Set meals** (5.30-7.30pm Mon-Thur; 5.30-11.30pm Sun) £6.95 3 courses. **Unlicensed**. **Corkage** £2 wine, 50p beer. **Map** p296. Oriental
There aren't many places in London where you can buy an entire sea bass, cooked to perfection, for under a tenner – or dine in such surreal surroundings. Bintang's inimitable decor incorporates plenty of bamboo and a few tribal masks, topped off with what looks like a decrepit, fairy light-draped beach shack along one wall. The cooking is a revelation, from chanai puri puri – deliciously light discs of batter, with delicately-spiced lentil filling – to plump and spicy king prawns with lime leaf and galangal. But sea bass is the undisputed highlight, marinated and oven-baked in the sauce of your choice – rich, fragrant bintang sauce is perfect if you don't like things too hot. With warm and welcoming staff and candlelit tables, it's a romantic place to linger over a bottle of wine; on hot evenings, head for the garden.

Daphne
83 Bayham Street, NW1 0AG (7267 7322). Camden Town or Mornington Crescent tube. **Lunch served** noon-2.30pm, **dinner served** 6-11.30pm Mon-Sat. **Average £££. Set lunch** £7.75 2 courses, £9.25 3 courses. **Set mezédes** £13.50 meat or vegetarian, £17.50 fish. **Map** p296. Greek
Time seems to stand still in this homely, bustling little bolt-hole. Vintage black and white photos of the old country dot the walls, the bubbly proprietress welcomes diners from the bar, and Greek and Cypriot regulars chat loudly in the booths at the back. Even the daily specials board hardly seems to change. Lovely fresh squid was fried in a light, crispy batter. A portion of revithia (warm chickpeas with spinach, cooked in a smooth tomato

sauce), which was ordered on the recommendation of an amiable waiter, was excellent. A main course of hearty moussaká – a hefty portion, served in its own pot – was the purest sort of comfort food: rich and herby and topped with an inch of thick, fluffy white sauce. The desserts, such as rice pudding, are reassuringly traditional.

★ Haché NEW

24 Inverness Street, NW1 7HJ (7485 9100). Camden Town tube. **Meals served** noon-10.30pm Mon-Sat; noon-10pm Sun. **Average** ££. **Map** p296. Burgers

Haché eschews the utilitarian aesthetic of most of today's burger bars, instead resembling a bijou modern bistro with its fairy lights and fey art. The dishes themselves also take an approach that is slightly more sophisticated than you might expect: the Ayrshire steaks are chopped (*haché*, in French) and seasoned before being grilled medium, or cooked as requested. The toppings are excellent: bacon dry-cured in brine, proper cheese, huge portobello mushrooms. Haché also wins our best buns award: the ciabatta buns don't just look good, they also have an appealingly chewy texture. Chips are frites-style, skinny or fat (we preferred the latter, which are made on the premises). Non-beef burgers include tuna steak, chicken and three veggie variations. This is a restaurant that you can visit with a date, family or friends, while still feeling that you're treating yourselves – even if it is a burger you're munching on.

Jamón Jamón

38 Parkway, NW1 7AH (7284 0606). Camden Town tube. **Meals served** noon-11.30pm Mon-Thur, Sun; noon-12.30am Fri, Sat. **Average** £££. **Set meal** (noon-5pm Mon-Fri) 2 dishes for the price of 1. **Map** p296. Spanish

Haché

Although the updated decor of this comfortable, cheery neighbourhood tapas joint aspires towards the sophisticated, the menu itself promises nothing so spectacular (featuring, as it does, mostly the old standards like calamares and chorizo al vino). But reliable simplicity is precisely the appeal of this kind of cooking. We enjoyed jamón serrano (ham), its salty, succulent slices still glistening from fresh carving. Pollo al ajillo (chicken in white wine and garlic sauce) was also respectable, the meat tender, the broth assertive, while bacalao con tomate was fresh, flaky chunks of cod fillet in a straightforward but authentic sauce. There were, however, some quite notable let-downs in our meal – stuffed peppers and patatas bravas particularly. Still, the house Rioja was enjoyable, the service was attentive, and this remains a shrewd choice for a cheap, hearty meal.

Lemongrass

243 Royal College Street, NW1 9LT (7284 1116). Camden Town tube/Camden Road rail. **Dinner served** 5.30-11pm daily. **Average** ££. **Map** p296. Oriental

A flashing neon yellow sign hanging above the door marks out this quirky little Cambodian/Indo-Chinese local. We enjoyed leek cake to start, a fried glutinous rice pancake with chopped Chinese leeks sealed inside. Also good was a soft, sweet mango salad dressed with salty fish sauce, hot red onions and shreds of crunchy pickled cucumber and carrot. Other dishes were less successful. Garlic lemon mushrooms and fresh asparagus were both drenched in too much seasoning, and monivong whisky prawns suffered from a sickly-sweet sauce heavy with alcohol that hadn't been burned off. The meal was saved by tender lok luk beef: cubes of seared rare fillet in a black peppercorn sauce. A decent option if you're in the area.

Marine Ices

8 Haverstock Hill, NW3 2BL (7482 9003). Chalk Farm tube. **Lunch served** noon-3pm, **dinner served** 6-11pm Tue-Fri. **Meals served** noon-11pm Sat; noon-10pm Sun. **Average** ££. **Map** p296.
Pizza & Pasta
This gelateria/eaterie has been run by the same family since its inception, and occupies a soft spot in the heart of many locals, particularly the families who bring successive generations to continue dearly held traditions. You'll want to join in with the uninhibited nippers screaming for ice-cream – which has its own menu and is available in grown-up, liqueur-soaked combos. Or go with the kiddie flow and invent your own sundae with an assortment of sauces and teeth-aching toppings. The pizza and pasta aren't gourmet by any means, but they are immensely hearty, as our tomato and cream gnocchi and chilli scampi linguine coated in identical fluoro-orange sauces attested. Good feeling towards the place had already been

engendered with a starter of thick bruschetta topped with super-fresh tomatoes. The takeaway ice-cream hatch does a brisk trade too.

Melrose & Morgan NEW

42 Gloucester Avenue, NW1 8JD (7722 0011). Chalk Farm tube. **Meals served** 8am-8pm Tue-Fri; 9am-6pm Sat; 10am-6pm Sun. **Average** ££. **Set lunch** (noon-2.30pm Tue-Fri) £4.50 lunchbox. **Map** p296. Café
Nick Selby and Ian James's gorgeous deli employs three chefs and a baker. The open kitchen turns out freshly cooked pizzas, tarts, salads, sausage rolls, plus upscale hot dishes such as chard, goat's cheese and parmesan parcels, and Aylesbury duck with roast peaches and cherries. A daily changing lunchbox features one dish with salad for £4.50. Own-made cakes and tarts are also available.

★ El Parador

245 Eversholt Street, NW1 1BA (7387 2789). Mornington Crescent tube. **Lunch served** noon-3pm Mon-Fri. **Dinner served** 6-11pm Mon-Thur; 6-11.30pm Fri, Sat; 6.30-9.30pm Sun. **Average** £££. **Map** p296. Spanish
A full house by 7pm on a Monday night has got to bode well. The place isn't much to look at: the location is unremarkable and the decor is unassuming, although it's not unpleasant. It's only when you read the menu that things get interesting. The list of dishes and the choice of ingredients all reflect a grown-up, forward-thinking approach to tapas cooking that is painfully scarce in the capital. Things were good from the start: our bread was served with a wonderfully aromatic hot paste of broad beans, rosemary and roast garlic. And it got better: slow-roasted pork belly was thick and sticky; morcilla (black pudding) with chestnut mushrooms, green beans, feta and toasted pine nuts was

superb, and a roast beetroot, feta and rocket salad was a revelation. Virtually everything we tried was top-notch. Yes, a chicory salad was overdressed and our espressos weren't great, but by that point we were well and truly won over.

Trojka

101 Regent's Park Road, NW1 8UR (7483 3765). Chalk Farm tube. **Meals served** 9am-10.30pm daily. **Average ££. Set lunch** (noon-4pm) £9.95 2 courses. **Licensed. Corkage** £3 wine; £15-£25 spirits. **Map** p296. Eastern European
We've been disappointed by off-hand service at Trojka on occasion, but this time, on a cold, wet Sunday afternoon, the place was an oasis of warm fuggy hospitality. Red decor and dark-wood furniture relieved by bold artwork serve to create a Mittel-Europa vibe. A full menu of east European cuisine is served all day, along with grills, breakfasts, coffees and the like – all easy on the wallet, given the Primrose Hill location. The usual herrings, blini, Russian salad and borscht make reliable starters. Koulebiaka (puff pastry and salmon pie), bigos, golubtsy (stuffed cabbage) and latkes feature among the mains. Trojka works well for big parties on a budget; you can bring your own drink (though beware the expensive corkage on vodka) and by night a gypsy violinist is sometimes on hand to lure customers into a polka round the tables.

Viet Anh

41 Parkway, NW1 7PN (7284 4082). Camden Town tube. **Lunch served** noon-4pm, **dinner served** 5.30-11pm daily. **Average ££. Map** p296. Vietnamese
When we arrived for lunch, Viet Anh was packed – always a good sign. The light turquoise walls and the painted clouds across the ceiling provide an airy atmosphere and keep this compact place from feeling too cramped. The menu lists over 250 items (but no desserts), though many are variations on similar themes and the helpful waitress was happy to make recommendations. Starters of golden pancake with prawns and beansprouts, and minced beef wrapped in betel leaf, both came with quarters of crisp iceberg lettuce and sprigs of coriander for wrapping. All the ingredients couldn't have been fresher, and the own-made dipping sauce was a delightful sweet-sour accompaniment. Best of all was the galangal monkfish, meaty pieces of fish with a delicate ginger flavour. We were in, fed and out within the hour, making this an ideal pit-stop for a speedy lunch.

Meal deals

Belgo Noord *72 Chalk Farm Road, NW1 8AN (7267 0718/www.belgo-restaurants.com).* Set lunch £5.95 1 course incl drink. **Map** p296. Belgian
Kaz Kreol *St Martin's Tavern, 35 Pratt Street, NW1 0BG (7485 4747).* Set buffet (noon-3.30pm Mon-Sat) £7.99. **Map** p296. Seychelles

In the area

Chon Thong *5-6 Plender Estate, NW1 0JT (7380 1196).* **Map** p296.
Feng Sushi *1 Adelaide Road, NW3 3QE (7483 2929).* **Map** p296.
Fresh & Wild *49 Parkway, NW1 7PN (7428 7575).* **Map** p296.
Miso *30 Hawley Crescent, NW1 8NP (7482 5924).* **Map** p296.
Nam An *14-16 Camden High Street, NW1 0JH (7383 7245).* **Map** p296.
Nando's *57-58 Chalk Farm Road, NW1 8AN (7424 9040).* **Map** p296.
Pizza Express *83-87 Parkway, NW1 7PP (7267 2600).* **Map** p296.
La Porchetta *74-77 Chalk Farm Road, NW1 8AN (7267 6822).* **Map** p296.
Strada *40-42 Parkway, NW1 7AH (7428 9653).* **Map** p296.
Wagamama *11 Jamestown Road, NW1 7BW (7428 0800).* **Map** p296.

North

Crouch End

Aanya Wine Lounge NEW

*29 Park Road, N8 8TE (8342 8686).
Finsbury Park tube/rail then W7 bus.*
Lunch served 11am-3pm, **dinner
served** 5.30-10.30pm Mon-Fri.
Meals served 11am-10.30pm Sat;
noon-10.30pm Sun. **Average ££**.
Set lunch £6 1 course incl soft
drink. Indian

Although Aanya is a wine bar not a
restaurant, it deserves inclusion here
for the impressive selection of North
Indian snack food; it's the sort of fare
you might find at Mumbai's smart
cocktail parties. Reshmi ('silken')
chicken kebab and lamb chops were
tender and vibrantly spiced, while
paneer parcels were expertly made
filo pastry bags stuffed with spiced
cheese. We also liked the bread-
based canapés that come topped
with sweetcorn and peppers, but the
succulent tandoori prawns were
somewhat overwhelmed by their
coriander, mint and chilli marinade.
The menu can seem short and
repetitive if you're planning on
eating a full meal, but on our visits
Aanya has always been packed with
beautiful young people having a
good time, which goes a long way to
making up for its limitations as a
destination dining venue.

La Bota

*31 Broadway Parade, Tottenham
Lane, N8 9DB (8340 3082).
Finsbury Park tube/rail then W7 bus.*
Lunch served noon-2.30pm Mon-
Sat. **Dinner served** 6-11pm Mon-
Thur; 6-11.30pm Fri, Sat. **Meals
served** noon-11pm Sun. **Average
££.** Spanish

This is a paragon of the tapas genre.
The Spanish proprietor has opted
for authenticity, decorating the two-
tiered dining room with rustic
furniture and some repro Spanish
artwork. Service was exceptionally

attentive on a recent visit, even
though the place filled up quickly.
The food, though not dazzling,
ticked all the relevant boxes: what
we ate was hearty, fresh and tasty.
We couldn't fault our selection of
rape al pisto (monkfish in a tomato
and vegetable sauce), chistorra
(sausage in cider), tortilla de patatas,
and spinach with raisins and pine
nuts. Unusually, kidneys in sherry
was done well, while grilled sardines
were some of the best we've had on
these shores. If you don't expect
surprises or sophistication, just good
food, you'll leave satisfied.

Khoai Café

*6 Topsfield Parade, N8 8PR (8341
2120). Finsbury Park tube/rail then
W7 bus or Archway tube then W5
bus.* **Lunch served** noon-3.30pm,
dinner served 5.30-11.30pm daily.
Average ££. Set lunch £7.45 2
courses. Vietnamese

Khoai Café's pared-down, Formica-
happy interior is never going to win
any design awards, but that doesn't
bother the Crouch End locals who
have thronged to the place since it
opened early in 2005. The lure's easy
to understand: deftly handled
Vietnamese dishes at distinctly
wallet-friendly prices. A starter of
sautéed squid was tender, and
fragrant with chilli and garlic fried
to toffee-like nuggets. Main courses
displayed the same sense of flavour
balance: fried catfish was served
whole, with slivers of punchy
ginger; beef pho was assertively
spicy; and a side dish of just-wilted
greens came in a delicate, liquor-like
oyster sauce. Booking's a good idea,
but staff will happily take your
mobile number while you scoot over
to a nearby bar; they'll phone as
soon as a table's free.

Satay Malaysia

*10 Crouch End Hill, N8 8AA (8340
3286). Finsbury Park tube/rail then
W7 bus.* **Dinner served** 6-10.45pm

Mon-Thur, Sun; 6-11.45pm Fri, Sat. **Average ££. Set dinner £12-£14** per person (minimum 2). **No credit cards**. Malaysian

There are more than 120 dishes on the menu at this small, friendly Chinese-Malay restaurant, so perhaps it's not surprising that the cooking can be slightly patchy. Beef satay had a fine and appetising flavour but the accompanying peanut sauce was too sweet and sticky. A generous portion of sambol prawns in a sweet chilli sauce went down well, as did sayur lemak (spinach in coconut sauce). Our favourite dish was shien ba: tender aromatic pork in soy sauce gravy, but the pa tai mee (stir-fried noodles) was distinctly dull. Nonetheless, banana fritters with ice-cream and golden syrup rounded off the meal nicely. A homely and hospitable eaterie, Satay Malaysia makes for a relaxed venue offering good-value grub.

Meal deals

Les Associés *172 Park Road, N8 8JT (8348 8944/www.lesassocies. co.uk).* Set dinner (Tue-Fri) £11 2 courses. French
Bistro Aix *54 Topsfield Parade, Tottenham Lane, N8 8PT (8340 6346/www.bistroaix.co.uk).* Set lunch (noon-3pm Tue-Fri) £10 2 courses. French
Florians *4 Topsfield Parade, Middle Lane, N8 8PR (8348 8348/ www.floriansrestaurant.com).* Set meal £6.25 2 courses (wine bar only). Italian

Finchley

Orli

108 Regents Park Road, N3 3JG (8371 9222). Bus 82, 406. **Meals served** 7.30am-11pm. **Average ££. Unlicensed. No credit cards**. Jewish

Situated, as it is, near two Indian restaurants, an Italian pizzeria and a Chinese takeaway, Orli is quite

obviously not short of competition. To its credit, this large, airy café – simply decorated with modern paintings and taupe-coloured walls – pulls in the punters. On our visit, the place was filled with a wholly female clientele, ranging from teenagers enjoying coffee and cakes to parties of well-groomed older ladies. Food on offer ranges from breakfast fry-ups to substantial mains, such as grilled fish or pasta. Salads, too, feature heavily, with the Orli salad a huge platter of tomatoes and lettuce, generously topped with fried halloumi cheese (made from sheep, cow and goat's milk) and mushrooms. An ice-cold strawberry smoothie slipped down nicely; no problem here getting your five portions of fruit and veg.

Meal deals

The Ottomans *118 Ballards Lane, N3 2DN (8349 9968).* Set lunch £5.95 2 courses. Turkish

In the area

ASK *Great North Leisure Park, Chaplin Square, N12 0GL (8446 0970).*
Nando's *Unit 2, Great North Leisure Park, Chaplin Square, N12 0GL (8492 8465).*
Pizza Express *820 High Road, N12 9QY (8445 7714).*
Zizzi *202-208 Regent's Park Road, N3 3HP (8371 6777).*

Finsbury Park

Los Guaduales

53 Stroud Green Road, N4 3EF (7561 1929). Finsbury Park tube/rail. **Meals served** 2.30-10pm Tue-Fri; 1.30pm-1.30am Sat, Sun. **Average ££. Map** p297. Colombian

There still isn't much of a following for this Colombian restaurant just north of Finsbury Park. And we think we know why. It's not that the

Yayla

service isn't charming, nor that the food isn't decently prepared, but more that the restaurant is catering for cattle ranchers who've just rolled in from a week on the corn prairies rather than office workers who've spent their day sitting at desks. Portions are enormous: T-bone steak was not much smaller than the cow it came from and a fried plantain starter with shredded beef and melted cheese was the size of a pancake and four times as filling. Mains – mostly grills – come with cassava, potatoes, rice and beans, plaintain or a mixture of all four. For the rabbit-like eaters of north London, there isn't much in the way of lighter options or green stuff and a rather daunting amount of lumpen, dry-beige carbs. If you're a hungry person, pop along. Otherwise, prepare to be overwhelmed.

Hummingbird

84 Stroud Green Road, N4 3EN (7263 9690). Finsbury Park tube/rail. **Meals served** noon-midnight Mon-Sat; 1-11pm Sun. **Average ££. Set meal** £12 3 courses (minimum 4). **Map** p297. Caribbean

This has long been a favourite with Caribbean food fans. Lovers of Barbadian food, for example, will appreciate coo-coo (cornmeal mush) and stewed fish. A dish of creamy polenta with okra and coconut milk, with red fish cooked in a rich tomato, pepper and red herb stew, was sumptuous and almost perfect. Curry fanciers will be impressed by the dhalphouri rotis – delicate Trinidadian flatbreads stuffed with ground split peas and served with fillings such as curried chicken, goat, fish or vegetables. And it's refreshing to visit a Caribbean restaurant where under rated dishes like fried sprats (commonly known as 'fry dry'), Tobagonian curried crab and dumplings, and St Lucian lobster are at the heart of the menu. Service was not unfriendly, but it was quite slow. The bar is a bit cluttered and untidy, and could do with updating.

Jai Krishna

161 Stroud Green Road, N4 3PZ (7272 1680). Finsbury Park tube/ rail. **Lunch served** noon-2pm, **dinner served** 5.30-11pm Mon-Sat. **Average £. Unlicensed. Corkage** 30p beer, £1.25 wine. **Set meal** £6.75 1 course. **No credit cards. Map** p297. South Indian

Despite the competition on this stretch of Stroud Green Road – Turkish cafés, pizzerias, takeaways

North

– we still prefer this meat-free South Indian cheapie. Pricing counts, with most dishes being under £3, but choice matters too. Curries include red cabbage and apple, marrow, okra, radish and broccoli, the 'exotic' range featuring sabji bahar (potato, fresh spinach and mustard seeds) and jeeri aloo (potato, cumin seed, fresh tomatoes, coriander). Dosas and chutneys comprise the starters, kulfis (almond, mango, pistachio) and ice-creams (papaya, passion fruit) the attractive desserts. Presentation may be basic – orders are scribbled on a scrap of notepaper and taken to the desk – but the swift end result cannot be faulted. And this all takes place in pool-hall hush, amid necklaced images of Krishna.

In the area

Nando's 106 Stroud Green Road, N4 3HB (7263 7447). **Map** p297.
La Porchetta 147 Stroud Green Road, N4 3PZ (7281 2892). **Map** p297.

Harringey

Antepliler NEW

46 Grand Parade, Green Lanes, N4 1AG (8802 5588). Manor House tube. **Meals served** 11.30am-11.30pm daily. **Average** £.
Turkish

Antepliler comes across as more adventurous than most Turkish restaurants on this relatively conservative strip. For instance, çiğ köfte is among the cold starters – spicy raw mince balls served with lettuce leaves. In Turkey this is a popular dish in the home, but rarely found in restaurants (where it's harder to judge the freshness of the meat). A portion of lamb ribs was plentiful, though the meat was quite rare and the accompanying rice with chickpeas a little overdone. However, the pide was excellent, and useful for handling the hot bones.

The restaurant space is dominated by a large wall painting of food preparation; brick ovens at the front and rear provide more activity to watch. A Turkish pâtisserie is attached to the premises, which explains the restaurant's name (roughly meaning pâtisserie).

La Viña

3 Wightman Road, N4 1RQ (8340 5400). Harringay rail. **Meals served** 5pm-midnight Mon-Sat. **Average** £££. **Set meal** (Mon) £6.95 paella per person (minimum 2).
Spanish

This unpretentious and highly amenable neighbourhood tapas joint, tucked away just north of Finsbury Park, continues to do a successful line in classic Spanish comfort food. There's little to dislike: the trad two-tiered dining space, with the odd splash of decorative authenticity, is comfortable; staff are attentive; and the cooking, while not spectacular, is reliable. The menu is largely a line-up of old favourites, but what we ate was tasty and fresh: grilled sardines; a well-dressed salad of green beans with red onion and raw garlic; a fabada (stew) of chorizo and beans. Cod with chickpeas would have benefited from a bit more fish, but it was still good; estofado (lamb stew) could have been a little bit juicier. A sound choice should you find yourself in the neighbourhood.

Yayla NEW

429 Green Lanes, N4 1HA (8348 9515). Manor House or Turnpike Lane tube/Harringay rail. **Breakfast served** 6am-noon, **meals served** noon-midnight daily. **Average** ££. **Unlicensed.** Turkish

This higher class of sit-down Turkish diner blends in with the opposing pavements of oriental eateries, stalls and shopfronts leading from Harringay railway station. Find a spot in the spacious back room decorated with reproductions of Ottoman scenes, order up a 50p Dimes-brand fruit juice (Yayla is non-licensed) and consider quail, lamb ribs or lamb chops if the humble kebab, served in two sizes, seems too unadventurous. Everything comes with a mound of rice, salad and cacik – the soups (chicken, yoghurt, lamb or lentil) supported by a basket of warm Turkish bread and a plate of olives and chillies. The service is as friendly as the sign on the door – *hosgeldinis* (welcome) – promises, so to finish off it would seem downright churlish not to force down a couple of spoonfuls of rice pudding.

Highbury

Exquisito

167 Blackstock Road, N4 2JS (7359 9529). Arsenal tube/Finsbury Park tube/rail. **Dinner served** 5-11.30pm Mon-Fri. **Meals served** 11am-11.30pm Sat, Sun. **Average** ££.
Map p297. Latin American
Though not on a stretch of the street saturated with fine restaurants, it's worth hunting out this amiable Mexican joint on Blackstock Road. There's a something-for-everyone menu, the portions are colossal, and a litre of the house white comes at the can't-argue-with-that price of £9.95. What's more, there are plenty of herbivorous options too, since most of the main dishes are available with artichokes substituting for the meat. The artichoke fajitas arrived with no less than six artichoke hearts, so don't fill up on the complimentary nachos beforehand. Jennifer Lopez and Gloria Estefan had heavy rotation on the in-house stereo, but don't let that put you off. The service was attentive and if you enjoy a free post-meal tequila slammer (and who doesn't?) then Exquisito should suit perfectly.

★ Iznik

19 Highbury Park, N5 1QJ (7354 5697). Arsenal tube. **Lunch served** 10am-4pm, **dinner served** 6pm-midnight daily. **Average** ££.
Map p297. Turkish
This is a wonderful place to sample the wide range of Turkish dishes based on oven cooking rather than grilling. The atmosphere is cosy; the walls are cluttered with an array of tiles from the city of İznik, lamps, candles and even a finely embroidered Ottoman jacket. For starters, mücver was excellent, not in the least oily (as this dish can sometimes be), and served with chilli sauce. Fava beans came with rich, high-quality olive oil, a reminder that the simplest starters are often among the most flavoursome. For mains, kadin budu (literally 'ladies' thighs') was a dish of succulent lamb patties fried in egg and flour. Our other choice was a marvellous beykoz kebab: a soft hunk of lamb in aubergine. Both mains came with a small portion of rice with more aubergine, diced this time, and a very fresh salad with olives.

Olive Tree

177A Blackstock Road (entrance on Mountgrove Road), N5 2LL (7503 5466). Arsenal tube/Finsbury Park tube/rail. **Dinner served** 6.30-11pm Tue-Sat. **Average** ££. **Set meze** £9 per person (minimum 2).
Map p297. Greek
It's all about cooking like mamma used to at Olive Tree. Run by Athenians, this Greek restaurant does a nice line in the kind of experience you'd expect to get at a Hellenic family occasion. Mediterranean hospitality comes on tap, with the matron of the show almost falling over herself to ply us with a second helping of their excellent fluffy own-made pitta bread. The meze included a nicely spiced platter of pastourma (spicy

North

Café Mozart

cured beef) and loukanika (pork and lamb) sausages as well as a range of dips that was competent enough despite an oddly eggy houmous. Unfortunately, there was a strange lack of customers, meaning that there wasn't quite the jauntiness you'd hope for at a Greek restaurant.

Yildiz

163 Blackstock Road, N4 2JS (7354 3899). Arsenal tube/Finsbury Park tube/rail. **Meals served** noon-midnight daily. **Average ££. Set lunch** £6 2 courses incl soft drink. **Map** p297. Turkish

Though Yildiz's menu ranges all around the Mediterranean basin, Anatolian food remains very much its focus. Behind the ocakbaşı at the front of the restaurant, the lighting is subdued and the atmosphere scented by the smoke from the open grill. A starter of patlıcan kizartma (slices of fried aubergine with thick yoghurt and tomato) was hearty but unsubtle. It also proved unnecessary, as Yildiz will supply nibbles while the main course is being prepared. We were given grilled onion in spicy turnip and pomegranate sauce, onion with chilli, and a salad. All this came with

fine slim pide bread. The main itself – iskender (a base of pide with a layer of köfte kebab, covered in sauce and served with yoghurt) – was fine indeed. Yildiz remains a good, solid local restaurant.

In the area
Il Bacio Highbury *178-184 Blackstock Road, N5 1HA (7226 3339).* **Map** p297.

Highgate

Café Mozart

17 Swains Lane, N6 6QX (8348 1384). Gospel Oak rail/214, C2, C11, C12 bus. **Meals served** 9am-5pm Mon; 9am-10pm Tue-Sun. **Average ££. Map** p298. Café

A cosy wood-panelled outpost of Austrian cuisine that spills on to a wide pavement, Café Mozart is an institution. Thankfully the owner of neighbouring Kalendar took it over last year and arrested something of a decline in standards. Before, Mozart's cakes were dropping in quality and it had adopted a 'beans with everything' approach for its mighty breakfasts. Now the menu is shorter, fresher and features appropriate fare such as borscht, sausages, schnitzels and strudels, as well as hearty salads and fresh fish. Cakes are back on legendary form: juicy plum tarts, rich chocolate tortes and heavy baked cheesecakes, all made on the premises. Make sure you get here early for a table on a weekend lunchtime.

Kalendar

15A Swains Lane, N6 6QX (8348 8300). Gospel Oak rail/214, C2, C11, C12 bus. **Meals served** 8am-10pm Mon-Fri; 9am-10pm Sat, Sun. **Average ££. Map** p298. Café

Situated in the kind of affluent suburbia that provides the blueprint for Working Title film sets, Kalendar is an open-all-hours café that manages to be all things to all people. The menu, like the boho-country decor, is eclectic: along with a stellar all-day breakfast, there are fresh juices, chargrills, and sandwiches and salads with a Mediterranean bias. Much of the produce used is available from the on-site deli, and sourcing is careful: meat from Elite Meats next door, cakes from Konditor & Cook, cheeses from Neal's Yard (including, on our visit, an oozily ripe Brie the size of a hubcap). Come the evening, the line-up is gastropub in all but name – our salad of smoky duck breast came with a beautifully-judged dressing, and salmon fish cakes were crisp without, sweetly flaky within. Special.

★ Al Parco   NEW

2 Highgate West Hill, N6 6JS (8340 5900). Kentish Town tube/rail then C2, 214 bus. **Meals served** 8am-10pm Tue-Sun. **Average ££.** Pizza & Pasta

Brightly lit and sparsely occupied on our visit, Al Parco is a restaurant that puts some artistry into pizza production. The varieties we tried were delicious, and looked fantastic. Calzone with vine tomatoes and salami was a particular highlight:

carefully shaped, it wasn't the usual unsightly blob common in pizzerias. Elsewhere, huge salads were fine enough, but own-made tiramisu was heavenly. Tactical eaters may want to go easy on the mains. The restaurant itself has a cheery Italian vibe which never feels put on. Staff are attentive and chummy (they kindly didn't laugh when we mispronounced some of the pizza names). It may be small and a little far from the tube, but Al Parco is a real charmer.

In the area

dim T Café *1A Hampstead Lane, N6 4RS (8340 8800).*
Pizza Express *30 High Street, N6 5JG (8341 3434).*
Strada *4 South Grove, N6 6BS (8347 8686).*
Zizzi *1-3 Hampstead Lane, N6 4RS (8347 0090).*

Holloway

★ Tbilisi

91 Holloway Road, N7 8LT (7607 2536). Highbury & Islington tube/rail. **Dinner served** 6-11pm Mon-Fri; 6pm-midnight Sat, Sun. **Average ££. Map** p297. Georgian

We've always loved the relaxing, rather glam red decor, dark furniture and clever lighting here, as well as the strikingly fresh and subtly warm spicing, typical of Georgian cuisine. Starter plates are irresistible, combining dishes themed by region. Our kolheti, ample for two, comprised two salads (exquisite spicy walnut and spinach, and beetroot), accompanied by khachapuri – typical regional bread filled with crumbly soft cheese. Walnut, ubiquitous in the Georgian kitchen, features heavily in main courses too; try that most famous of Georgian dishes, chicken satsivi – the creamy ground walnut sauce countered by the blandness of satisfying, polenta-like ghomi (made from cornmeal). Walnut again figures

North

in the tarragon-infused soupy lamb stew, kharcho. Tbilisi's exotic cooking – using high-quality fresh ingredients, and served in smart surroundings – remains a genuine bargain, and the restaurant is still a well-kept secret. Don't tell.

Hornsey

Meal deals

Le Bistro *36 High Street, N8 7NX (8340 2116).* Set meal £10.95 2 courses, £12.95 3 courses. French

Islington

Afghan Kitchen

35 Islington Green, N1 8DU (7359 8019). Angel tube. **Lunch served** noon-3.30pm, **dinner served** 5.30-11pm Tue-Sat. **Average** ££. **No credit cards**. Map p299. Afghan
A tiny place, Afghan Kitchen has just a few tables at ground level and the first floor. Nevertheless, it's surprisingly easy on the eye, with soothing pastel colours and blond-wood furnishings making best use of the space. The homespun Afghan menu offers a limited range of pre-prepared dishes, akin to Indian curries, but milder and sweeter in nature. Banjon borani (squidgy fried baby aubergines, spiced with garlic and cumin) married well with the chill of a yoghurt topping – marvellous for mopping up with hot flatbreads. To accompany the food, try the doga, an Afghan take on Indian lassi made from churned yoghurt whisked with crushed mint and nutty-tasting toasted cumin – it's seriously thirst-quenching.

Candid Arts Café NEW

Candid Arts Trust, 3 Torrens Street, EC1V 1NQ (7837 4237). Angel tube. **Meals served** noon-10pm Mon-Sat; noon-5pm Sun. **Average** £££. Map p299. Café

Attached to the Candid Arts Trust theatre and gallery, this café still just about counts as a secret. In a dark, attic-like room, with battered floorboards and what seems like 100 years' worth of wax drippings, Islington's arty types lounge in red velvet chairs or sit and read at the stately communal table. Some rehearse plays over coffee, others whip out a drawing pad and sketch fellow customers while they eat. Candid is bohemian to a T; the only thing missing from the fit is bohemian-friendly prices. Homely meals of pasta, quiches, pies and curries are fine for what they are (own-made earlier, then heated to order and served with salad) but are very over-priced: expect to pay £8-£12 for a dish that should really cost half as much. Staff can either be very delightful or very curt, perhaps depending on the variable music. On our visit: languid French 1920s jazz, and they were lovely.

Flaming Nora

177 Upper Street, N1 1RG (0845 835 6672). Highbury & Islington tube/rail. **Meals served** 11am-midnight Mon-Thur, Sun; 11am-2am Fri, Sat. **Average** £. Map p299. Burgers
Here's a novel concept: seeing inside the kitchen of a kebab joint. Normally, the idea would have you running for the hills, but funky Flaming Nora is not your normal kebab house. From the arty decor on the walls to the 'lo-carb' options on the menu, it's a different beast to the average fast-food grease palace. The service is friendly, the burgers and kebabs come in wrappers saying things like 'luvvly lamb', and – as a boon for the health-conscious – the meat, from beef to salmon, is grilled. Nora is let down by not having quite enough seats for eating in, but then it is primarily a takeaway place. And, should you forget that, just

take a look at the ingenious 'extras' they sell: condoms and breath freshener. We're saying nothing.

Gallipoli

102 Upper Street, N1 1QN (7359 0630). Angel tube/Highbury & Islington tube/rail. **Meals served** noon-11pm Mon-Thur; noon-midnight Fri; 10am-midnight Sat; 10am-10.30pm Sun. **Average ££.** **Set lunch** £5.95 2 courses. **Set dinner** £14.95 3 courses. **Set meze** (lunch) £7.95, (dinner) £11.95. **Map** p299. Turkish

The Gallipoli restaurants remain the most popular Turkish eateries in Islington, despite stiff competition. This, the original branch, is relaxed and a great favourite. The standard of food is generally very high. We started with a mixed meze, which included cacik, a most enjoyable patlıcan salata and black-eyed beans. A large meze is also offered as a full meal and makes a good choice, especially for vegetarians. For mains we had delicious imam bayıldı: oven-baked aubergine stuffed with various vegetables and chickpeas. Sujuk kebab (spicy sausage, yoghurt and bread) was a bit heavy and monotonous as a main course on its own. There's a cluster of small tables on the pavement outside during the summer.

Gem

265 Upper Street, N1 2UQ (7359 0405). Angel tube/Highbury & Islington tube/rail. **Meals served** noon-11pm Mon-Sat; noon-10.30pm Sun. **Average ££.** **Set lunch** £5.95 3 courses, £7.95 4 courses. **Set dinner** £8.95 3 courses, £11.95 4 courses incl house wine or beer. **Map** p299. Kurdish

It is worth travelling further along Upper Street than the average punter to visit this charming Kurdish restaurant. Diners sit at heavy wooden tables with farming implements adorning the walls. The

Candid Arts Café
See p217.

complimentary qatme – Kurdish flatbread, made in the open restaurant – is beautiful. It came stuffed with cheese, though it's also available with other fillings, such as spinach. For good or ill, the portion was small enough for us to be eager to sample another starter, and we ordered an exceptionally fresh and tangy dolma with rice and pine nuts. A main course of minced beyti kebab was accompanied by dishes of fresh yoghurt and chilli sauce, as well as rice, bread and salad. There's also a reasonable selection of vegetarian dishes. A single complimentary baklava, served with ice-cream, made an ideal dessert.

Maghreb NEW

189 Upper Street, N1 1RQ (7226 2305). Angel tube/Highbury & Islington tube/rail. **Meals served** 6-11.30pm daily. **Average £££.** **Set dinner** (Mon-Thur, Sun) £9.95 2 courses. **Map** p299. North African

Maghreb's bright-yellow walls and glowing, jewel-rich silk lanterns against red and blue upholstery give

North

an opulent, exotic feel without any 'road to Morocco' overload. Traditional Moroccan fare is cooked with a delicate hand, along with some fusion-style dishes. Chicken tagine with olives and preserved lemons was tender and flavoursome, the liquor cooked just to the right point of reduction. Mixed grill couscous also impressed: tender char-grilled lamb and chicken with feistily spiced merguez sausages and kefta (meatballs) sat on a pile of light, fluffy couscous, with an aromatic vegetable stew. Lastly, there's a good range of puds: baghrir are rich, yeasty pancakes with an irresistible honey and butter sauce. We particularly enjoyed the friendly, attentive yet unobtrusive service from the owner.

Masala Zone

80 Upper Street, N1 0NU (7359 3399). Angel tube. **Lunch served** 12.30-3pm, **dinner served** 5.30-11pm Mon-Fri. **Meals served** 12.30-11pm Sat; 12.30-10.30pm Sun. **Average** ££. **Set thalis** £7-£11.55. **Map** p299. Indian

Making more accessible the Indian snacks and street food that are widely available in the restaurants of Wembley and Southall, Masala Zone tends to be abuzz with gorgeous, hip twentysomethings. This branch is a spacious venue decorated with colourful tribal-style murals, an open kitchen, outside seating and, in fine weather, a barbecue at the front. However, its standards are variable. On our last visit, the starters were good: gosht dabalroti and channa dabalroti – two signature dishes in which lamb and chickpeas are cooked in spicy gravy, combined with cubes of bread, and topped with tamarind sauce, minced onions, fresh coriander and chickpea-flour vermicelli. Both dishes were tangy, aromatic and deeply savoury. Sadly,

the meal went into something of a decline after this promising beginning: the vegetable thali lacked flavour and the accompanying rice was a soggy disgrace. Staff were inattentive. A shame, as Masala Zone is a real looker, and the kitchen is capable of more.

Mem & Laz NEW

8 Theberton Street, N1 0QX (7704 9089). Angel tube/Highbury & Islington tube/rail. **Meals served** 11.30am-11.30pm Mon-Thur, Sun; 11.30am-midnight Fri, Sat. **Average** ££. **Set meal** (11.30am-6pm) £6.95 2 courses, £8.95 3 courses. **Map** p299. Turkish

A 'Mediterranean restaurant' based on Turkish cuisine with a largely Turkish staff, Mem & Laz feels no great pressure from its heritage. Turkish dishes are offered, bizarrely, alongside Italian fare – but the decor is all Anatolian. Dark wood and clusters of lamps dominate. While we were ordering, sun-dried tomato bread and olive bread arrived: a nice touch, even if it marked another break from the traditional. Two large grilled sardines made an excellent starter. We also enjoyed an obviously freshly-made pepper dolma, with sweet rice and raisins stuffed in a green pepper. To follow, a sizeable portion of grilled halibut was served with boiled potatoes and a heavy salad. Köfte meatballs were well spiced (though arguably undercooked), and came with thick yoghurt and a salad. A separate menu offers daily changing specials. Service was friendly, if a little over-attentive at times.

Le Mercury

140A Upper Street, N1 1QY (7354 4088). Angel tube/Highbury & Islington tube/rail. **Meals served** 10am-1am Mon-Sat; 10am-midnight Sun. **Average** ££. **Map** p299. International

Situated as it is on the corner of Almeida and Upper Streets, the French-leaning Le Mercury is ideally suited for a meal before or after a show at the Almeida theatre opposite. The constant stream of patrons only lulled at curtain-up time. The wraparound windows give the welcome illusion of space, but once inside, tables are a little cramped. On the food front, aubergine pithivier resembled an upmarket version of a pie, though the pastry was a little burned. Mackerel with rhubarb, beetroot and lime was a sort of fishy fruit salad, but much more appetising than it sounds. A thoroughly British treacle sponge pudding with a continental blob of Chantilly cream made a comfortingly dense and syrupy finish. One price for all starters, one for all mains makes keeping the bill low especially easy.

Nam Bistro
326 Upper Street, N1 2XQ (7354 0851). Angel tube/Highbury & Islington tube/rail. **Lunch served** noon-3pm, **dinner served** 6-11pm Tue-Sun. **Average ££. Map** p299. Vietnamese
Don't expect culinary fireworks at this high street Vietnamese. The locals that jostle for position in the queue on a Saturday night do so for a pre-bar meal that'll leave them full with enough spare for a night out in Upper Street's bars. Starters are all around the £4 mark, and you can pick up a one-course meal for under £6.50. The pre-crawl nature of the place means that turnover is quick, and woe betide those who dawdle. 'What?' scowled our waitress, 'you aren't ready to order yet?'. The food is nonetheless competent enough, with our beef in chilli and lemongrass having a creamy nuttiness to it, even if it didn't taste particularly of either lemongrass or chilli. A reasonable quick-fix stop, but nothing more.

★ Ottolenghi
287 Upper Street, N1 2TZ (7288 1454). Angel tube/Highbury & Islington tube/rail. **Meals served** 8am-11pm Mon-Sat; 9am-7pm Sun. **Average £££. Map** p299. Café
The long, brightly-white room at this Upper Street diner looks wonderful, with long shared tables, white Panton chairs, clever art and nice design details. The entrance area doubles as a bakery shop and deli, with big, puffy meringues, colourful salads and sublime breads to take away or eat in. In the evening, Ottolenghi shifts emphasis from café to restaurant, with a daily changing menu. The imaginative food combinations are Ottolenghi's trademark: a plate of tender, marinated beef fillet with a herb crust and a smoky tomato sauce; or a salad of beetroot with red chard leaves, slivers of red onion and a fig relish. There is a modern Mediterranean slant in some dishes while others defy categorisation, such as pork belly on a purée of potato and salt cod. Shared tables encourage cross-party chat.

S&M Café
4-6 Essex Road, N1 8LN (7359 5361). Angel tube. **Meals served** 7.30am-11pm Mon-Thur; 7.30am-midnight Fri; 8.30am-midnight Sat; 8.30am-10.30pm Sun. **Average ££. Map** p299. Café
It somehow doesn't seem right to call Kevin Finch's business a chain (though there are three outlets with two more in the offing) as the vintage interior of each property has been meticulously restored to preserve individual character. This Islington branch, once the legendary Alfredo's, is particularly special, with its authentic art deco shopfront. Choose three key components (sausage, mash, gravy) from a simple menu plus a daily changing specials board. Decide whether you

want mash, whether you want peas, and the job's done. There are other options – a few pies, some sausage-themed salads and old-fashioned desserts such as spotted dick – but, unless opting for one of the excellent fried breakfasts, stick to the speciality sausage and mash as it's too good to miss.

★ Sedir

4 Theberton Street, N1 0QX (7226 5489). Angel tube/Highbury & Islington tube/rail. **Meals served** 11.30am-11.30pm Mon-Thur, Sun; 11.30am-midnight Fri, Sat. **Average ££. Set lunch** £6.50-£7.95 2 courses. **Map** p299. Turkish
Spread over two floors, Sedir's pastel walls are decorated with large Victorian orientalist images of the Ottoman Empire, favouring pictures of naked harem women. In good weather a few tables are also placed outside on the quiet street. Both our starters were first class on a recent visit: dolma were delicious, crisp on the outside and fresh; patlıcan salata, with puréed aubergine, had a pleasing rough texture. Main courses were excellent, too: Kilyos fish stew – named after the Black Sea resort near Istanbul – contained a delicious mix of squid, mussels, large unshelled prawns and hunks of salmon, their flavours blended together in a thick sauce. Külbasti (grilled fillet of lamb) came with good rice and a side salad. Sedir has found a good niche for itself in the market in offering variations on the traditional Turkish canon.

Viet Garden

207 Liverpool Road, N1 1LX (7700 6040). Angel tube/Highbury & Islington tube/rail. **Lunch served** noon-3.30pm daily. **Dinner served** 5.30-11pm Mon-Thur, Sun; 5.30-11.30pm Fri, Sat. **Average ££. Set lunch** (Mon-Fri) £6 2 courses. **Set dinner** £15 2 courses. **Map** p299. Vietnamese

Well away from Islington's main drag, and with suburban-style half-timber and plaster walls, Viet Garden is unlikely to stop trendsters in their tracks. We were charmed, though, by the friendly service from one of the two sisters who run the restaurant. She recommended the pork kho, and when it came we could see why the flavoursome, slow-cooked meat is a winner with regulars. The golden pancake starter, while obviously made with plenty of fresh ingredients, lacked flavour. Compensating, though, was the salt and pepper fish: crisply fried chunks of cod given ample zing by a sprinkle of dill and chilli. Bun xa noodles, tossed with salad and chicken, was also a winner, as was beef in tamarind sauce, which got the sweet-sour balance just right.

Zigni House NEW

330 Essex Road, N1 3PB (7226 7418). Essex Road rail/38, 73, 341, 476 bus. **Meals served** 6am-1.30am daily. **Average ££. Set buffet** (6-11pm Thur-Sat) £12. **Map** p299. Eritrean
Attractively conspiratorial and tattily bohemian from the outside, Zigni House provides an accommodating welcome once you step through its front bar and into the dining area. Said back room – decorated with Eritrean artefacts and bookended by a long couch for intimate comfort – is dimly lit, so bring a dining partner rather than reading material. You're soon perusing a menu of simple starters and a whole mass of meaty mains – though service will be slower thereafter. Lamb, beef and chicken are concocted with a delicious, semi-spicy, rich house sauce, scooped up with strips of filling, spongy injera bread – messy for non-initiates. There are a few pulse or chick-pea based vegetarian options too. Wash it down with Asmara beer and finish with a shot of fiery Eritrean sambuca.

Meal deals

The Fish Shop 360-362 St John Street, EC1V 4NR (7837 1199/ www.thefishshop.net). Set meal (noon-3pm, 5.30-7pm Tue-Sat; noon-8pm Sun) £13.50 2 courses. **Map** p299. Fish

Isarn 119 Upper Street, N1 1QP (7424 5153). Set lunch £5.90 3 courses. **Map** p299. Thai

Med Kitchen 370 St John Street, EC1V 4NN (7278 1199/www. medkitchen.co.uk). Set lunch (noon-5pm Mon-Fri) £10.95 2 courses, £12.95 3 courses. **Map** p299. Mediterranean

Sabor 108 Essex Road, N1 8LX (7226 5551/www.sabor.co.uk). Set lunch £10 2 courses, £12.50 3 courses. **Map** p299. Latin American

In the area

ASK Business Design Centre, 52 Upper Street, N1 0PN (7226 8728). **Map** p299.

Carluccio's Caffè 305-307 Upper Street, N1 2TU (7359 8167). **Map** p299.

Fine Burger Company 330 Upper Street, N1 2XQ (7359 3026). **Map** p299.

Gallipoli Again 120 Upper Street, N1 1QP (7359 1578). **Map** p299.

Gallipoli Bazaar 107 Upper Street, N1 1QN (7226 5333). **Map** p299.

Giraffe 29-31 Essex Road, N1 2SA (7359 5999). **Map** p299.

Hamburger Union 341 Upper Street, N1 0PB (7359 4436). **Map** p299.

Mem & Laz 170 Upper Street, N1 1RG (7288 9222). **Map** p299.

Miso 67 Upper Street, N1 0NY (7226 2212). **Map** p299.

Nando's 324 Upper Street, N1 2XQ (7288 0254). **Map** p299.

Pizza Express 335 Upper Street, N1 0PB (7226 9542). **Map** p299.

La Porchetta 141 Upper Street, N1 1QY (7288 2488). **Map** p299.

Sangria 88 Upper Street, N1 0PN (7704 5253). Branch of Jamón Jamón. **Map** p299.

Strada 105-106 Upper Street, N1 1QN (7226 9742). **Map** p299.

Thai Square 347-349 Upper Street, N1 0PD (7704 2000). **Map** p299.

Wagamama N1 Centre, 39 Parkfield Street, N1 0PS (7226 2664). **Map** p299.

Yo! Sushi N1 Centre, 39 Parkfield Street, N1 0PS (7359 3502). **Map** p299.

Kentish Town

Eatzone Noodle House

18 Fortess Road, NW5 2HB (7485 0152). Kentish Town tube/rail. **Meals served** noon-11pm Mon-Sat; noon-10pm Sun. **Average** £. **Unlicensed. Corkage** £1. **No credit cards. Map** p298. Oriental
The formula here is beautifully simple: bring your own booze, take a seat at one of the plain wooden benches, eat your fill of tasty, ludicrously inexpensive pan-Asian fast food and go. All perfectly straightforward – unless, that is, you're feeling indecisive, as the menu offers a bewildering array of more than 100 different dishes. Crispy won ton (dumplings) were deliciously more-ish, while red chicken curry was light and flavoursome, with unusually tender meat. A 'chef's favourite' special of mee hoon – stir-fried vermicelli with beancurd, king prawns, fishcake and beansprouts – was also pleasant enough, if a little salty. But all paled into insignificance beside the glorious grilled meat dumplings, served with red vinegar. Plump, seasoned to perfection and unbelievably succulent, they were an absolute steal at £3.50 for four.

Lalibela

137 Fortess Road, NW5 2HR (7284 0600). Tufnell Park tube/134 bus. **Dinner served** 6pm-midnight daily. **Average** ££. **Map** p298. Ethiopian

North

The capital's most beautiful Ethiopian restaurant, bedecked with east African artefacts, is set over two floors. From a lengthy menu, we chose doro wot – a classic hot and spicy stew that in Ethiopia would be made with a chicken and its own eggs. We also liked gomen (stir-fried spring greens) and mushroom shiro (spicy stew thickened with ground chickpeas). Tibs are strips of marinated items, sautéed with peppers, onions, tomatoes and chillies; the fish and tofu versions here were beautifully flavoured. Although Lalibela's cooking is very accomplished, dishes tend to be too oily and are not as hot and spicy as they could be – the flavours seem toned down for the restaurant's western customers. However, if you've never tried Ethiopian food before, this is a good place to start.

Mario's Café

6 Kelly Street, NW1 8PH (7284 2066). Camden Town tube/Kentish Town tube/rail. **Meals served** 7.30am-4pm Mon-Sat. **Average** £. **Set breakfast** £4.50 incl tea. **Unlicensed. Corkage** £1.50. **No credit cards. Map** p298. Café
Mario's has the heart and soul of a greasy spoon – its eponymous owner is on first-name terms with his customers, happy to dole out chatter alongside steaming mugs of tea and there was a lively inter-table debate about the football going on as we arrived. But this place has a definite sense of style. The white-painted walls are dotted with cool contemporary pictures, and the menu shows similar flair: poached eggs on toasted ciabatta with prosciutto is hardly your typical caff breakfast and it was delicious. Mario's standard fry-up also met with approval – only the sausage tasted cheap. Lunch options range from salads and focaccia to more substantial specials such as pasta and meatballs.

Pane Vino

323 Kentish Town Road, NW5 2TJ (7267 3879). Kentish Town tube/rail. **Lunch served** noon-3pm Mon-Sat. **Dinner served** 6.30-11pm Mon-Sat; 6.30-10pm Sun. **Average** £££. **Map** p298. Italian
A traffic-fume filled, nondescript stretch of Kentish Town Road isn't, perhaps, the most obvious of locations for a culinary gem. Nor do Pane Vino's dog-eared, cardboard menus and unremarkable decor inspire confidence. When it comes to what matters, though, this small Sardinian restaurant gets it right: a dish of gnocchi with aubergine, tomato and ricotta was outstanding, while pizza with tomato, taleggio cheese, parma ham and mushroom was thinly crusted and generously topped – not to mention at least twice the size of most chain offerings. Bruschetta paesana was one let-down – two curmudgeonly slices of bread, with burnt edges. Large parties planning to split the bill, beware; you have to pay on one card.

★ Queen of Sheba

12 Fortess Road, NW5 2EU (7284 3947). Kentish Town tube/rail. **Meals served** 1-11.30pm Mon-Sat; 1-10.30pm Sun. **Average** ££. **Map** p298. Ethiopian
A contemporary eating venue, Queen of Sheba is a small, cream-coloured room decorated with Ethiopian masks and other knick-knacks, and graced by stunningly beautiful, statuesque Ethiopian waitresses. Every item we tried was distinctly and individually spiced – a combination of great tastes. Minced beef stew was aromatic with garlic, ginger and cardamom. Vegetable stews made from spinach, lentils, mushrooms and butter-soft, own-made yoghurt cheese were, quite simply, amazing. Injera here, too, is better than in most British-Ethiopian restaurants: it had a

notably deep, sour tang, which made it into a perfect foil to the robustly flavoured food. The coffee ceremony wasn't as theatrical and elaborate as it tradionally should be, but that was our only possible gripe; the Queen of Sheba is one of London's best Ethiopian restaurants.

In the area
Nando's 227-229 Kentish Town Road, NW5 2JU (7424 9363). **Map** p298.
Pizza Express 187 Kentish Town Road, NW1 8PD (7267 0101). **Map** p298.

Muswell Hill

Café Loco
266 Muswell Hill Broadway, N10 2QR (8444 3370). Highgate tube then 43, 134 bus. **Meals served** 6-11pm Wed-Sat; 5-11pm Sun. **Average** ££. **Set tapas meal** (6-8pm) £8.95 (3 dishes). Spanish
Dining is only half the equation at this lively bar-restaurant: drinking and dancing are given just as much attention (half the floor space has bar seating rather than dining tables, and a DJ plays on most nights). So our culinary expectations were not especially high. Yet there were some pleasant surprises in store for us. Albóndigas were moist, expertly seasoned and dressed in a mellow tomato sauce. Calamares, so often either chewy or deep-fried to destruction, were very good, their tender flesh coated in a crisp and light batter. A surprise menu entrant – scallops with prawns in a rich fish sauce – arrived sans prawns, but was tasty nevertheless. Other menu items were more predictable: some serrano ham looked as if it came from a packet and a tapa of garlic chicken was unnecessarily oily. Ultimately, Café Loco is an unpretentious local hangout that is first and foremost about having fun.

Meal deals
Bakko 172-174 Muswell Hill Broadway, N10 3SA (8883 1111/ www.bakko.co.uk). Set lunch (Mon-Fri) £8.90 3 courses. Turkish

In the area
ASK 43 Muswell Hill Broadway, N10 3AH (8365 2833).
Fine Burger Company 256 Muswell Hill Broadway, N10 3SH (8815 9292).
Giraffe 348 Muswell Hill Broadway, N10 1DJ (8883 4463).
Maison Blanc 61 Muswell Hill Broadway, N10 3HA (8883 7520).
Pizza Express 290 Muswell Hill Broadway, N10 2QR (8883 5845).
Ultimate Burger 82 Fortis Green Road, N10 3HP (8883 6198).

Primrose Hill

Café de Maya
38 Primrose Hill Road, NW3 3AD (7209 0672). Chalk Farm tube. **Dinner served** 6-11pm Tue-Sun. **Average** ££. **Map** p296. Oriental
Memories of restaurants that cater to western travellers backpacking across Asia came rushing back as we pushed open the door of Café de Maya, and heard the wind chimes over the door and saw the bookshelves stuffed with all manner of travel memorabilia. The cooking itself is mostly Malaysian or Thai and the quality is hit-and-miss. We enjoyed our starters of spare ribs in a sweet sticky sauce, and spicy salty battered squid. Similarly, Singapore laksa was a good combination of thin silky rice noodles with strips of chicken and egg in a gentle coconut and chilli broth. Malay fish curry was less successful, featuring a sauce that tasted uncannily like the instant curries that are sold in Japanese supermarkets. Generous portions and friendly service made for a nice meal, but not really one to go out of the way for.

Southgate

La Paella

9 The Broadway, N14 6PS (8882 7868). Southgate tube. **Lunch served** noon-3pm Tue-Sun. **Dinner served** 6-11pm daily. **Average** ££. **Set lunch** £5.95 2 tapas & soft drink. Spanish

This long-standing tapas joint contrasts with the kebab shops and burger bars around Southgate tube station. The interior has an authentic Catalan feel (whitewashed walls and dark oak beams), if you'll forgive all the Arsenal football paraphernalia. Tapas dishes are decent and well-priced: pan-fried kidneys were cooked to perfection and Spanish tortilla was properly firm with robust flavour. If you remember to give your order 30 minutes in advance (best to call ahead), go for the eponymous, tasty paella. Service is attentive and the atmosphere pleasant enough for a linger.

In the area
Pizza Express *94 Chaseside, N14 5PH (8886 3300).*

Stamford Hill

Springfield Park Café

White Lodge Mansion, Springfield Park, E5 9EF (8806 0444). Clapton rail. **Open** *Apr-Oct* 10am-6pm daily. *Nov-Mar* 10am-4pm daily. **Average** £. **No credit cards.** Café

The outdoor seating – white plastic tables and chairs set on a lawn in front of the café – offers a quiet green panorama of north-east London, with willow trees and a pond close by. The interior is spacious and welcoming, with bright yellow walls crowded with photos. The service was lovely, and this alone would tempt us back. The menu is quite substantial, and includes panini, sandwiches, salads and breakfasts, with plenty of

options for kids. An 'absolute' Mediterranean platter was huge and delicious, containing stuffed vine leaves, houmous, olives, tomato salsa, falafel and flatbread. A huge chunk of thickly iced coffee and walnut cake was irresistible. Ingredients are organic where possible, and there's lots of choice for the health conscious.

Turnpike Lane

Penang Satay House

9 Turnpike Lane, N8 0EP (8340 8707). Turnpike Lane tube. **Dinner served** 6-11pm daily. **Average** ££. **Set meal** £11.90-£13.50 per person (minimum 2) 3 courses. Malaysian

With its bright green neon sign adding a dash of colour to a rather scruffy corner of Turnpike Lane, the veteran Penang Satay House has built up a firm local following. House special satay (consisting of chicken, prawns and beef) was rather dry, though, and our main courses were a let-down, too. Chicken curry in coconut milk was so salty as to be inedible, and yet flavourless. Twice-cooked pork turned out to be very dull indeed, complete with leathery strips of meat. Only the chinese spinach with blachan (prawn paste) was a pleasure to eat. In the past, the kitchen here has performed to a much higher standard, so we left disappointed, hoping our latest experience was a temporary glitch.

Winchmore Hill

In the area
Pizza Express *701-703 Green Lanes, N21 3RS (8364 2992).*

Wood Green

In the area
Nando's *Hollywood Green, Redvers Road, N22 6EN (8889 2936).*

Belsize Park

The Village Café

92 Belsize Lane, NW3 5BE (07951 022418). Belsize Park tube. **Open** 7am-5pm Mon-Fri; 8.30am-5pm Sat. **Average** £. **Set lunch** £5.50 1 course incl bottle of beer. **No credit cards**. **Map** p300. Café

More of a caff, perhaps, than a café, in that its menu is about Brit comfort food rather than continental sandwiches and salads. But this is no greasy spoon: the exposed brickwork, wood floors and furniture, and minimal decor create a bright and airy space in which well-heeled Belsize Park villagers can convene and refuel. Fried breakfasts are executed with panache; the inclusion of omelettes, with a wide selection of ingredients, is welcome. Main courses on a separate menu include burgers, fishcakes, pasta options, cottage pie and soup; specials are chalked on a board. The coffee is superlative, there's a small selection of wines, and a little garden out back for use when the weather is clement.

★ Zara

11 South End Road, NW3 2PT (7794 5498). Hampstead Heath rail. **Meals served** noon-11pm daily. **Average** £££. **Map** p300. Turkish

Cushioned benches run along the walls of Zara's compact interior, which is divided into smoking and non-smoking areas. The mixed cold meze gives a good idea of the range of starters, including houmous, tarama, börek, cacik and kısır. Each had a pleasing texture and was distinctly fresh. A basic lamb shish kebab made an excellent main course, accompanied by rice and salad. Kuzu firin consisted of a melting knuckle of lamb from the oven, cooked in a thick gravy with vegetables and potatoes, served with rice and salad. The pale walls

are decorated with beautifully patterned tiles, studded with summery paintings. Zara is popular with local diners and is usually busy with people ending their day out in Hampstead on a prandial note.

In the area

ASK *216 Haverstock Hill, NW3 2AE (7433 3896).* **Map** p300.
Gourmet Burger Kitchen *200 Haverstock Hill, NW3 2AG (7443 5335).* **Map** p300.
Pizza Express *194A Haverstock Hill, NW3 2AJ (7794 6777).* **Map** p300.
Tapeo *177 Haverstock Hill, NW3 4QS (7483 4242).* Branch of Tapas Brindisa. **Map** p300.
Tootsies Grill *196-198 Haverstock Hill, NW3 2AG (7431 3812).* **Map** p300.

Brent Cross

In the area

Wagamama *Brent Cross Shopping Centre, NW4 3FP (8202 2666).*

Cricklewood

Abyssinia NEW

9 Cricklewood Broadway, NW2 3JX (8208 0110). Kilburn tube. **Dinner served** 6pm-midnight Mon-Fri. **Meals served** 2pm-midnight Sat, Sun. **Average** ££. Ethiopian

One of the best restaurants in the Cricklewood area, this well-established venue is popular with Ethiopians and locals. It's a compact space that is simply decked out with plants, framed pictures and linen-dressed tables. We enjoyed sprightly spring greens cooked with ginger; the complex flavours of red lentils cooked in hot berbere sauce; whole green chillies stuffed with tomatoes and onions; and bulgar wheat dressed simply in Ethiopian aged butter (similar to Asian ghee).

North West

Din Café. See p231.

Spiced lamb with rosemary and white wine (a contemporary Ethiopian dish) was served very cold, so we had to send it back. Once heated through, though, it was tasty, and we had fun scooping it up with plentiful injera.

Golders Green

L'Artista
917 Finchley Road, NW11 7PE (8458 1775). Golders Green tube. **Meals served** noon-midnight daily. **Average** £££. Italian
Very much a Golders Green institution, L'Artista is a cheerfully unreconstructed eaterie, decorated with streamers of flags and framed photos of celebs. The menu offers traditional trattoria fare, majoring in pasta and pizza. On a hot summer's day, we opted to eat al fresco in front of the restaurant, rather than within its cavernous confines, but with traffic and trains rumbling overhead, this wasn't the quietest spot in which to dine. Enormous portions of pasta arrived promptly: linguine con gamberone and rucola (pasta with prawns and rocket) was

very good indeed, studded with juicy king prawns, while bucatini puttanesca packed a salty anchovy kick. We rounded off with crème caramel and a featherlight chocolate sponge. Great value food, efficiently served; this is why L'Artista has a loyal following.

Beyoglu
1031 Finchley Road, NW11 7ES (8455 4884). Golders Green tube/ 82, 160, 260 bus. **Meals served** noon-midnight daily. **Average** ££. **Set dinner** £12-£13.75 3 courses incl coffee. Turkish
While there is nothing especially noteworthy about the food at Beyoglu – though the ingredients and presentation are commendable – this is a fine local restaurant that deserves support. For starters, both patlıcan (aubergine) salata and fava beans were faultless, the quality of the olive oil being noticeable. Similarly, main courses did not disappoint: chicken shish were nice and tender, while inegol köfte were luscious lamb patties spiced with cumin, parsley and pepper. Accompanying rice was light and fluffy. The mock-Tudor beams that

cross the wide interior are decorated – like the walls – with patterned Turkish plates, bags and tiles, but the restaurant retains a light, spacious feel. Service was friendly and attentive.

Carmelli
128 Golders Green Road, NW11 8HB (8455 2074/www.carmelli.co.uk). Golders Green tube. **Open** 6am-1am Mon-Wed; 6am Thur-1hr before sabbath Fri; 1hr after sabbath Sat-1am Mon. **Average** £. **Unlicensed** no alcohol allowed. **No credit cards**. Jewish

Despite its long opening hours, you'll always find a few members of the area's Jewish community picking up treats in Carmelli. Selling kosher produce under the supervision of London Beth Din – the court of the Chief Rabbi – expect to find black-clad Orthodox Jews browsing the luminous, fruit-shaped marzipan sweets, while the friendly staff serve up dense, creamy cheesecake by the kilo. There's a good range of bagels on offer, with chollahs and rolls on the left, creamy gateaux in the centre, and hot boreka and pizza by the 'milky counter' on the right. The range is huge, including a good nutty baklava, flaky pain au chocolat and well-filled sweet cheese buns. In the evenings, Carmelli is popular with a young crowd.

Coby's Café & Flowers NEW
115A Golders Green Road, NW11 8HR (3209 5049/5054). Golders Green tube. **Meals served** 8am-11pm Mon-Thur, Sat, Sun; 8am-2pm Fri. **Average** ££. **Set breakfast** £6.80 1 course incl soft drink. Jewish

Golders Green is bursting with eateries, so a new one needs an angle; this one has flowers. Coby's is divided into two: a flower shop on one side and a café with an espresso machine and fresh juices on the

other. In the back are tables where you can enjoy an Israeli-style lunch – light food, nicely presented. The menu gives new meaning to the word 'inventive': dishes are named after flowers, with apparently little connection between the names and flavours. There's a lizzianthus omelette (new potatoes and mozzarella) served with a pyramid of Israeli salad and a ball of soft cheese; bonsai (fried mushrooms); and freesia pizza (sweet potato and leek). The bird of paradise sandwich boasted fried smoked salmon. There are crêpes, fresh fruit shakes and nice-sounding cakes too.

Daniel's Bagel Bakery
12-13 Hallswelle Parade, Finchley Road, NW11 0DL (8455 5826). Golders Green tube. **Open** 7am-9pm Mon-Wed; 7am-10pm Thur; 7am-1hr before sabbath Fri. **Average** £. **No credit cards**. Jewish

You can tell a place knows how to do its bagels when the smoked salmon variety comes with a chunk of lemon for you to squeeze on. The surly staff and clattering metal baskets can be a bit off-putting, and the boreka sometimes lack in flavour, but that doesn't stop car loads of locals stopping by to pick up their weekly baked goods. Don't miss the fresh breads behind the counter, especially the rye, although pitta purists will be disappointed by Daniel's overly leavened offerings. Crumbles and pies are also served to customers at affiliated Café Dan next door.

★ Din Café NEW
816 Finchley Road, NW11 6XL (8731 8103). Golders Green tube. **Meals served** 7.30am-6pm Mon-Sat; 9.30am-4pm Sun. **Average** ££. Café

Handily positioned for Temple Fortune shoppers, Din Café – on our Sunday morning visit – was buzzing with an assortment of diners,

Eat Tokyo

ranging from family groups to immaculately coiffured old ladies enjoying coffee and cake. The menu, which has a South African flavour, offers both snacks and mains. Once our food arrived the reason for Din's success was apparent. Star of the show was ranana: pitta filled with houmous and coriander-flavoured boerwurst sausage served with a generous, colourful salad – a great combination. Chicken burger hit the spot too, while the thin-cut chips had us nibbling even when we were full. With cooking this good, we couldn't resist sampling the carrot cake and chocolate marble cake – both exemplary. Every neighbourhood should have a café like Din.

Eat Tokyo NEW

14 North End Road, NW11 7PH (8209 0079). Golders Green tube.
Lunch served noon-3pm Tue-Sun.
Dinner served 5.30-11pm Mon-Sat;
5.30-10pm Sun. **Average** ££.
Set lunch £5.80-£13. **Set dinner**
£7-£25. Japanese
The food in this red, black and white eaterie – festooned with bright kimonos and pictures of geishas – is worthy of its new local Japanese following. Potato croquettes were little more than mashed potato patties (studded with peas, dipped in breadcrumbs), but packed more flavour than anything made with such prosaic ingredients had a right to. Steak teriyaki was as glossy, tender and muscular as a sumo wrestler. Agedofu was pale, delicate and quivery: like female characters in a Murakami novel. The only dud was stir-fried vegetables, which were reminiscent of something you'd get in a Chinese takeaway, and arrived with unannounced chicken and pork pieces that had less flavour than the expected tofu. Otherwise, Eat Tokyo is a reliable Japanese pit-stop.

Kimchee

887 Finchley Road, NW11 8RR (8455 1035). Golders Green tube.
Lunch served noon-3pm Tue-Fri;
noon-4pm Sat, Sun. **Dinner served**
6-11pm Tue-Sun. **Average** ££.
Set lunch £6.50 1 course incl soup.
Korean
Busy wallpaper covered with blocks of oriental line prints are a feature at

Kimchee, as are wall-mounted wooden cupboards with bamboo screens, and ceramic Korean masks. Of particular note are the distinctive wood, glass and rope dining tables with built-in barbecues. There was a hiccup when we ordered a meal on one of these: the waitress placed unmarinated mussels, squid and mixed vegetables on to the barbecue all at once and as these ingredients require different cooking times, the dish wasn't a success. Moreover, it was bland. Much more flavoursome was yuk hwe – here flecked with lots of parsley. The best dishes were vegetarian: ultra-delicate, spongy bindaedok (made from fermented yellow mung-bean flour batter) came studded with an array of colourful vegetables; and fried tofu cubes and seaweed squares added texture and interest to vegetable tolsot bibimbap.

Kinnor David NEW

119 Golders Green Road, NW11 8HR (8455 7766). Golders Green tube. **Meals served** noon-11pm Mon-Thur, Sun. **Average ££. Set lunch** £8.99 2 courses, £11.95 3 courses. Jewish
The bright, welcoming space at this recently opened restaurant was full on our visit, and a juicy looking shawarma (the meat on a rod you see in kebab shops) was rotating in the stainless-steel cooking area. Food is predominantly North African: harira soup, couscous served in terracotta tagines and merguez sausages. Other warmers include a spicy white bean soup or a traditional chicken broth with lokshen and kneidlach – the latter well-flavoured and served in deep chunky bowls. From the grill there's chicken with honey mustard sauce, fresh tuna or steaks. A veal escalope was crisply breaded and served with decent chips. Competing with three established kosher restaurants very nearby, Kinnor

David has attractively low prices: a salt beef sandwich for £4, main courses at £10. Service was swift, and complimentary pickles were brought with a smile.

Local Friends

28 North End Road, NW11 7PT (8455 9258). Golders Green tube. **Meals served** noon-11pm, **dim sum served** noon-10pm daily. **Average ££.** Set meal £11-£19 per person (minimum 2). Chinese
As the name suggests, this little local is indeed very friendly. The interior is simple and white, with dark wooden furniture and Chinese paintings on the walls. The menu has few surprises, but there's a list of dim sum available until 10pm (instead of the usual 5pm cut-off), which includes a selection of vegetarian options. From the main menu, we opted for shredded roast duck with celery and pickles (a nice balance of soft meat and crunchy celery) along with crisp red peppers and soft beancurd stuffed with well-seasoned minced prawns. Less successful was a bland dish of thick rice noodles, stir-fried with chewy pork and shredded dried scallops. If you're in the area, pop in for a quick bite and enjoy the warm welcome.

Madison's Deli

1-4 Belmont Parade, NW11 6XP (8458 8777). Golders Green tube. Deli **Open** 11am-10pm daily. *Restaurant* **Lunch served** noon-3pm, **dinner served** 5.30-10pm daily. **Average ££.** Jewish
This is a noisy place (during busy lunchtimes the sound bounces off the grey tables and plastic chairs) but service is fast and smiling. The menu has been extended to include ciabatta sandwiches, wraps and melts, however, the original selection of deli favourites remains, featuring the likes of reuben sandwiches (corned beef, cheese and sauerkraut on rye bread), gefilte fish

and burgers. The food was hit and miss on our visit: cold borscht resembled a beetroot cordial with little depth of flavour, but vegetable spring rolls were crisp and tasty. Main courses were similarly variable. An unexceptional plate of salt beef and a poor meat loaf with watery mashed potatoes came from the same kitchen as a fresh grilled sole with crisp, dry chips and a precisely-cooked liver and fried onions.

La Maison du Café `NEW`

20 Golders Green Road, NW11 8LL (8731 6661). Golders Green tube. **Meals served** 8am-10pm Mon-Thur; 8am-1hr before dusk Fri; 8am-10pm Sun. **Average** £. Café

La Maison is a kosher café that serves savoury and sweet crêpes, one or two hot dishes, sandwiches, a few salads and pastries, and a variety of soft drinks. There's some fish but no meat on the menu. 'Vegetable quiche' was effectively an old-fashioned leek and mushroom bake (but a light, well-flavoured version) topped with mashed potato on good, crumbly, rough-hewn pastry. Velvety dark chocolate and maple syrup crêpe topped with hazelnuts was delightful and staff are fantastically friendly. The most striking aspect of the café, however, is its interior. Owned by artist and designer Linda Cohen, the venue is decked out with crystal chandeliers, amazing wall art, gorgeously attired mannequins and pretty birdcages from her collection. Everything is for sale.

Meal deals

Café Japan 626 Finchley Road, NW11 7RR (8455 6854). Set lunch £8.50 bento box. Japanese

In the area

Pizza Express 94 Golders Green Road, NW11 8HP (8455 9556).

Hampstead

Brew House

Kenwood, Hampstead Lane, NW3 7JR (8341 5384). Archway or Golders Green tube then 210 bus. **Open** Apr-Sept 9am-6pm (7.30pm on concert nights) daily. Oct Mar 9am-dusk daily. **Average** ££. **Map** p300. Café

Set in the beautiful English-country-garden surroundings of Kenwood House, the Brew House is geared for the masses, rather than for the individual's enjoyment. The interior is self-service, but hovers on the brink of chaos with hot and bothered people milling about food islands piled high with savoury food and desserts. Farmhouse sausages, roasted veg and onion gravy was the special on our visit. Free-range produce is sourced locally. The cakes are fabulous – a lavender and orange sponge, and a gooseberry and elderflower cheesecake were imaginative options. There is little shade in the outdoor seating area, so it is best avoided on a busy day in high summer.

Fratelli la Bufala `NEW`

45A South End Road, NW3 2QB (7435 7814). Hampstead Heath rail. **Lunch served** noon-3pm, **dinner served** 6-11pm Mon-Fri. **Meals served** noon-11pm Sat; noon-10.30pm Sun. **Average** ££. **Set lunch** (Mon-Fri) £10 2 courses. **Map** p300. Pizza & Pasta

This friendly Italian offers good-value Neapolitan grub and has a pleasant local vibe despite being part of an international chain (with branches in Naples, Rome and Miami, among others). To start, il tortino (potato cake with aubergines and mozzarella) had a perfectly light, fluffy texture and oozed with cheese; la filatina (melted mozzarella with fresh tomato sauce) was plainer but tasty. Mains were less consistent: a pizza margherita was too oily and sauce-laden, although a buffalo burger arrived tender and rare as requested. Staff were friendly, but the star of the occasion was the flamboyant owner – a bit of a local celeb by all accounts – who spent the evening jollying up to the waitresses, guests and anyone else who happened to be passing by.

★ Louis Pâtisserie

32 Heath Street, NW3 6TE (7435 9908). Hampstead tube. **Open** 9am-6pm daily. **Average** £. **Unlicensed** no alcohol allowed. **No credit cards**. **Map** p300. Café

The fact that you might not even notice this splendid Hungarian pâtisserie on Hampstead's main drag is a testament to the restrained air which it maintains. In the sepia-toned, wood-panelled, leather-benched tearoom at the back, old fellows while away the day with their newspapers, oblivious to (or perhaps avoiding) the bustle beyond the door. Those who join them are shown an inviting platter of creamy confections from which they can choose creations such as chestnut slice, strawberry cheesecake, marzipan moon and many others, although the prosaic names do nothing to convey the cakes' magnificence. Good quality tea is served by the pot; there's also a range of uber-simple sandwiches ('ham'). There are no gimmicks; this is an operation run passionately – and successfully.

Maison Blanc

62 Hampstead High Street, NW3 1QH (7431 8338). Hampstead tube. **Meals served** 8am-7pm Mon-Sat; 9am-7pm Sun. **Average** ££. **Map** p300. Café

A recent refit has given this branch of Maison Blanc a new sparkle, and even its range of gateaux, rich mousse cakes and cheesecakes looks fresher than in previous years. On a Saturday morning visit, the baguettes were particularly quick to disappear off the shelves. A dense and seductive chocolate mousse cake flecked with the crunch of ground praline will satisfy any chocolate cravings, while lovers of fruity flavours will be buoyed by satisfyingly tangy lemon tarts. Savouries are less appealing. Tarte provençale, a pastry flan lined with mustard and Emmental cheese and topped with sliced tomatoes, had a soggy texture and tasted as if it had been reheated in a microwave.

Woodlands

102 Heath Street, NW3 1DR (7794 3080). Hampstead tube. **Dinner served** 6-11pm Mon-Thur. **Meals served** noon-11pm Fri-Sun. **Average** ££. **Set thali** (noon-3pm Fri-Sun) £7.50. **Map** p300. Indian

This burgeoning restaurant chain, with close to three dozen branches in India, has recently opened another London outlet in the genteel setting of Hampstead. It's a modern, glass-fronted restaurant, embellished with a soothing water feature near the entrance and wispy drapes across the windows. Inside a Zen-like calm prevails. Idlis were as good as they get: light, spongy, and a perfect complement to sambar (mouth-watering lentils, sharpened with tamarind and tomatoes and incorporating squishy aubergines). Uppama – a classic breakfast dish and anytime snack, made from creamed wheat cooked with chillies, vegetables, curry leaves and mustard seeds – was a little too meekly flavoured. This branch might benefit from raising the heat and spicing things up a little bit.

Meal deals

Safir *116 Heath Street, NW3 1DR (7431 9888/www.safir-restaurant. co.uk).* Set meal £12.95 2 courses. **Map** p300. North African

Gracelands

A branch of a well-known halal eaterie, this busy restaurant-cum-takeaway comes boasting good credentials won at its original outlet in the East End. The dapper dining area – complete with illuminated mirrors, Bollywood satellite screen and a signed photo of Gwyneth Paltrow – was bustling with diners, ranging from Asian families to a large party of Australians. Business here is run with notable efficiency, with popadoms and water placed on our table the minute we sat down. Once our friendly waiter had taken our order, dishes appeared with commendable speed: crisp samosas, seriously peppery minced lamb kebab roll, tasty karahi jeera chicken (chicken cooked karahi style with cumin), rich baigan burtha (roasted aubergine dish), freshly cooked roti and naan, all washed down with sweet mango lassi. In short, a feast for a tenner a head. A bargain. We'll definitely be back for more.

Oriental City Food Court

Oriental City, 399 Edgware Road, NW9 0JJ (8200 0009). Colindale tube/32, 142, 204, 303 bus. **Meals served** 10am-9pm Mon-Fri, Sun; 10am-6pm Sat. **Average ££. No credit cards.** South-East Asian
This spacious mall is similar to shopping centres you'd find in Tokyo. In the crowded food court, a dozen shops sell very cheap Japanese, Chinese, Malaysian, Indonesian, Korean, Vietnamese, Thai and even South Indian fast food. There are also two inexpensive Chinese restaurants, plus a café selling Japanese crêpes, ice-cream, cakes and tapioca 'bubble tea'. A small bakery stocks wonderfully fluffy Japanese bread, plus melon buns and a variety of sweet and savoury doughnuts. There's also a huge supermarket selling mainly Japanese food.

North West

In the area
Carluccio's Caffé *32 Rosslyn Hill, NW3 1NH (7794 2184).* **Map** p300.
dim T café *3 Heath Street, NW3 6TP (7435 0024).* **Map** p300.
Giraffe *46 Rosslyn Hill, NW3 1NH (7435 0343).* **Map** p300.
Hamburger Union *1 South End Road, NW3 2PT (7794 7070).* **Map** p300.
Paul *43 Hampstead High Street, NW3 1QG (7794 8657).* **Map** p300.
Pizza Express *70 Heath Street, NW3 1DN (7433 1600).* **Map** p300.

Hendon

Lahore Original Kebab House

148-150 Brent Street, NW4 2DR (8203 6904). Hendon Central tube. **Meals served** 11am-11.30pm daily. **Average £.** Indian

In the area

L'Artista *17 Central Circus, NW4 3AS (8202 7303).*
Carluccio's Caffé *Brent Cross Shopping Centre, NW4 3FN (8203 6844).*

Kensal Green

★ Brilliant Kids Café NEW

8 Station Terrace, NW10 5RT (8964 4120). Kensal Green tube/ Kensal Rise rail. **Open** 8am-6pm Mon-Fri; 9am-5pm Sat; 10am-2pm Sun. **Average** ££. **Unlicensed**. **Corkage** no charge. Café
Already a mummy magnet, the new Brilliant café and arts centre sits next to the children's clothing and equipment store of the same name. Crisply turned out, the bright, polished space – with airy art rooms at the back, beyond which blossoms a lovely garden – is a ray of sunshine among the dowdy, drab shopfronts of Kensal Rise. Ingredients are wholesome and locally sourced where possible. Baked goods come from various artisan bakeries in the vicinity. Savoury dishes might include balsamic chicken with lentils or tomato and mozzarella quiche, while own-made elderflower cordial should be ordered to complete a virtuous, good-value light lunch. It can be lovely eating out in the garden, watching a pair of toddlers demolishing flapjacks on the large, sunny deck.

Gracelands NEW

118 College Road, NW10 5HD (8964 9161). Kensal Green tube. **Open** 9am-5pm Mon-Fri; 9am-4pm Sat; 9.30am-3pm Sun. **Average** ££. **Unlicensed**. **Corkage** no charge. Café
For local parents, Gracelands is almost too good to be true. Children can entertain themselves in a designated play corner while their long-suffering parents drink coffee

and take advantage of the wireless internet connection to work on their laptops. There's a friendly community feel; art, clothes and jewellery by local designers are displayed for sale on the walls. The food is healthy and delicious. Creative quiches (goat's cheese and sweet potato is a favourite) and salads show a loving touch; we enjoyed generous helpings of lemon-infused courgettes and a herby lentil and beetroot combo. A good selection of sandwiches, panini and breakfasts is boosted by heftier daily specials such as meatballs. Staff are a tad chaotic, but in a charming way. The café shuts early, so don't leave it too late.

The Island NEW

123 College Road, NW10 5HA (8960 0693). Kensal Green tube/ Kensal Rise rail. Bar **Open** 5-11pm Mon; noon-11pm Tue-Sat; noon-10.30pm Sun. **Lunch served** 12.30-3pm Tue-Fri; 12.30-3.30pm Sat; 12.30-4pm Sun. **Dinner served** 7-10pm Mon-Sat; 7-9.30pm Sun. **Average** ££. *Restaurant* **Dinner served** 7-10pm Mon-Sat. **Average** £££. Modern European
It may be located on a nondescript residential road in Kensal Rise, but the Island was buzzing with locals on a midweek night. A huge bamboo-screened terrace runs around the sandy-coloured exterior; the ground floor and basement are now a bar (also serving food), while the first floor is a light, bright dining room with colonial-style dark wooden furniture. A starter of smoked salmon with baby beetroot, spinach and (undetectable) horseradish was generous if unremarkable. Large ravioli were stuffed with a tasty mix of ricotta, spinach and oyster mushrooms, but the pasta was tough. Sea bass (two nicely cooked fillets) came with ratatouille that had a charred aftertaste. So, flaws in the kitchen, but the operation is still a definite hit.

Kilburn

Kovalam

12 Willesden Lane, NW6 7SR
(7625 4761). Kilburn tube/98 bus.
Lunch served noon-2.30pm daily.
Dinner served 6-11pm Mon-Thur,
Sun; 6pm-midnight Fri, Sat.
Average ££. Map p283.
South Indian

Kovalam is every inch the
neighbourhood Indian, so the exotic,
unusual-for-London menu comes as
something of a surprise. Familiar
staples such as dosas and vadai are
joined by intriguing fish dishes from
the Malabar coast, served at linen-
covered tables in a long dining room
with mirrored walls. There are
numerous Anglo-Indian meat dishes
for the less adventurous, but we can
heartily recommend the fish: keralan
fish curry was swimming with
flavour – yellow mustard, chilli,
creamy coconut, curry leaves,
green mango, ginger and lime,
complementing a generous slice of
Indian Ocean kingfish. However, idli
sambar was more pedestrian – the
spongy rice-cakes were a little over-
moist, making them tricky to dip
into the well-spiced sambar sauce
and coconut chutney. Still, a solid
south Indian meal at a very fair price.

Small & Beautiful

351-353 Kilburn High Road,
NW6 2QJ (7328 2637). Kilburn
tube/Brondesbury rail/16, 32 bus.
Lunch served noon-3pm, **dinner
served** 6-11.30pm Mon-Fri. **Meals
served** noon-midnight Sat; noon-
11pm Sun. **Average ££. Set meal**
(Mon-Thur, Sun; noon-7pm Fri, Sat)
£5.50 2 courses. **Map** p283.
Brasserie

Bright and cheerily decorated, Small
& Beautiful comes close to living up
to its name with its stripped wood
furniture and intricately tiled foor.
The food – an international mishmash of dishes – is hit and miss, but

Tandoor

prices are incredibly low, especially
if you opt for the £5.50 lunch deal.
Roasted pepper paté and smoked
chicken salad worked well; deep-
fried squid was a little too rubbery
and chicken wings were soaked by
an over-sweet tomato-based sauce.
Mains of pork escalope, grilled
chicken breast and 'puffy duck'
(roasted duck in a tasty puff pastry)
were generously portioned but
middling in quality. Although not
the richest food experience out there,
a trip to Small & Beautiful will
provide you with a decent enough
meal, a reasonable bill, and friendly,
attentive service.

In the area

Little Bay *228 Belsize Road,*
NW6 4BT (7372 4699). **Map** p283.
Nando's *308 Kilburn High Road,*
NW6 2DG (7372 1507). **Map** p283.

Kingsbury

Tandoor NEW

*232-234 Kingsbury Road, NW9 0BH
(8205 1450). Kingsbury tube/83, 183,
302, 204 bus.* **Lunch served** noon-
3.30pm, **dinner served** 6-11.30pm
daily. **Average** ££. **Set lunch**
£6.99 1 course. Indian

Hurrah! A pub with a curry house
attached. Yet this is no mundane
tandoori joint, but a modestly priced,
high-quality source of North Indian
cuisine. Test its mettle by ordering
the tandoori non-veg platter: a
glorious, 15-piece ensemble of
fiercely seared cod chunks, lamb,
tandooried chicken drumsticks (one
of ours was a mite undercooked) and
chicken tikka. This huge helping left
us nearly full before main courses,
but we couldn't miss the likes of lal
maas (a rich dark-red Rajasthani
dish of strongly spiced tender lamb),
creamy dahl makhani or mellow
murgh shahi korma (lamb in a
creamy sauce, properly prepared
with ground cashew nuts). Staff are
gracious and prompt, swiftly
bringing a pint of cider from the bar,
which went a treat with the food.

Mill Hill

In the area
Pizza Express *92-94 The
Broadway, NW7 3TB (8959 3898).*

Queen's Park

★ Baker & Spice

*75 Salusbury Road, NW6 6NH
(7604 3636). Queen's Park tube.*
Open 7am-7pm Mon-Sat; 8am-5pm
Sun. **Average** ££. **Map** p283. Café
What a place. Brilliant breads, cakes
and pâtisserie, excellent coffee, a
counter spilling over with attractive
and interesting salads, and a big
communal table at which customers

loiter over colour supplements. The
dishes are excellent quality and hard
to resist, even at their inflated prices
(£5.50 for a croque monsieur – mon
dieu!). Behind the glass display case
is a cornucopia of Mediterranean-
style lunch dishes: artichoke hearts
in olive oil with fresh chives, garlic
and rosemary; grilled aubergine
with pomegranate sauce and
parsley; grilled courgettes filled with
bechamel sauce. All are available to
takeaway if you can't find a seat.

St John's Wood

Ambra

*59A-61 Abbey Road, NW8 0AD
(7328 8692). St John's Wood tube.*
Meals served 8am-9pm Mon-Sat;
9am-7pm Sun. **Average** ££. **Set
lunch** (11am-3pm) £6.80 1 course
incl soft drink. **Unlicensed.**
Corkage £2. **Map** p300. Italian
The biggest draw of this simple
Italian café-deli is its setting, on a
peaceful corner right in the leafy
heart of St John's Wood. The wide
pavements of Abbey Road afford
ample al fresco space, so the café
really comes into its own in summer
when locals convene for a leisurely
coffee and luncheon out front in the
sunshine. Inside, large dishes of
hearty Italianate standards are laid
out under the counter: lasagne,
pasta, risotto, meatballs, roasted
vegetables and the like – reheated
to order in generous portions.
Baguettes are on offer, too, making
use of a good selection of Italian
charcuterie, and pizzas are available
during the week.

Harry Morgan's

*31 St John's Wood High Street,
NW8 7NH (7722 1869). St John's
Wood tube.* **Meals served** 11.30am-
10pm Mon-Fri; noon-10pm Sat, Sun.
Average £££. **Map** p300. Jewish
The 'kosher style' (that is, not
kosher) food at Harry's is as reliable

North West

as ever: smooth, creamy chopped liver with sweet and sour cucumbers; and boiled gefilte fish that's soft and just-like-grandma-makes. On a cold day you might choose Hungarian goulash or fried chicken livers, but in summer a plate of tongue with coleslaw was more appealing. We've had perfect haddock in the past here – crisply fried and flaky inside – but choosing it grilled was a mistake, and it seemed less fresh this time. A smoked salmon bagel or mozzarella salad might have been better. Big-portioned desserts are a strong point, with good cheesecake and lokshen pudding.

Meal deals

Royal China *68 Queen's Grove, NW8 6ER (7586 4280/www.royal chinagroup.co.uk).* Dim sum (noon-4.45pm Mon-Sat; 11am-4.45pm Sun) £2.30-£4.60. Chinese

In the area

Carluccio's Caffé *St John's Wood High Street, NW8 7SH (7449 0404).* **Map** p300.
Maison Blanc *37 St John's Wood High Street, NW8 7NG (7586 1982).* **Map** p300.
Pizza Express *7 St John's Wood High Street, NW8 7NG (7449 9444).* **Map** p300.
Pizza Express *39A Abbey Road, NW8 0AA (7624 5577).* **Map** p300.
Zizzi *87 Allitsen Road, NW8 7AS (7722 7296).* **Map** p300.

Swiss Cottage

Camden Arts Centre Café

Corner of Arkwright Road & Finchley Road, NW3 6DG (7472 5516). Finchley Road or Hampstead tube/Finchley Road & Frognal rail. **Meals served** 10am-5.30pm Tue, Thur-Sun; 10am-8.30pm Wed. **Average** £. **Map** p300. Café

This serene café located off the main hulk of the Camden Arts Centre and just across the way from Finchley Road Station is a great place to sit, relax and bask in the surroundings for hours. Staff are quick to recommend items from a menu which consists mainly of sandwiches, salads and a home-made soup of the day. This is one of the most pleasant cafés in north London, especially if (weather permitting) you're able to dine outside in the gardens. There were some glitches, though, on our visit: our pastrami and dill pickle sandwich arrived without pickle, and with a chunk of tuna fish (!) instead. A rogue slip-up, no doubt.

★ Green Cottage

9 New College Parade, Finchley Road, NW3 5EP (7722 5305/7892). Finchley Road or Swiss Cottage tube. **Meals served** noon-11pm daily. **Average** £££. **Set meal** £12.50-£25 per person (minimum 2). **Map** p300. Chinese
After a lengthy closure for rebuilding work, Green Cottage is back in business, with the same old homely tiled floor and dark wooden ceiling – and, more importantly, the same old roast meat kiosk by the window, turning out truly delicious barbecued duck and pork. The steamed fish could hardly have been fresher, slipping easily off the bone and on to the chopsticks, looking and tasting spectacular in its moreish black bean sauce. Complementing this was a simple dish of dou miao (pea shoots) with garlic, and a delightfully complex creation of minced pork, preserved greens and braised beancurd. True, the staff were as curt as ever, but as we were told by the manager (whose father opened the place 34 years ago), you can't get this sort of food at a highstreet takeaway.

Meal deals

Eriki *4-6 Northways Parade, Finchley Road, NW3 5EN (7722 0606/www.eriki.co.uk).* Set lunch £12.95 2 courses. **Map** p300.
Pan-Indian

Globe *100 Avenue Road, NW3 3HF (7722 7200).* Set dinner (6-7pm, 10-11pm Mon-Sat) £12 2 courses. **Map** p300. International

Hellenic Restaurant *291 Finchley Road, NW3 6ND (7431 1001/www. gonumber.com/hellenic).* Set lunch £7.95 2 courses. **Map** p300. Greek

Wakaba *122A Finchley Road, NW3 5HT (7586 7960).* Set buffet (lunch) £6.60. **Map** p300. Japanese

In the area

Fine Burger Company *First floor, O2 Centre, 255 Finchley Road, NW3 6LU (7433 0700).* **Map** p300.

Hafez II *559 Finchley Road, NW3 7BJ (7431 4546).* **Map** p300.

Louis Hungarian Pâtisserie *12 Harben Parade, off Finchley Road, NW3 6JP (7722 8100).* **Map** p300.

Nando's *O2 Centre, 255 Finchley Road, NW3 6LU (7435 4644).* **Map** p300.

Pizza Express *227 Finchley Road, NW3 6LP (7794 5100).* **Map** p300.

Yo! Sushi *O2 Centre, 255 Finchley Road, NW3 6LU (7431 4499).* **Map** p300.

West Hampstead

Czechoslovak Restaurant

Czech & Slovak House, 74 West End Lane, NW6 2LX (7372 1193). West Hampstead tube. **Dinner served** 5-11pm Tue-Fri. **Meals served** noon-11pm Sat; noon-10.30pm Sun. **Average ££. No credit cards**. **Map** p300. Czech

Dating back far into the Cold War era (though under new management since late 2004), this is London's only Czech restaurant and bar. The main dining room is decorated in typical Czech café style, complete with heavy chandeliers, red velvet curtains and tiny tables. Sleek, efficient staff serve a varied mix of authentic dishes: roast pork with dumplings, goulash and even street food snacks such as sausage, mustard and rye bread. We began with a flavour-packed sauerkraut soup flecked with ham, and a satisfyingly greasy potato pancake. Portions are large. Main courses saw us wading through svickova na smetane (sirloin of beef in sour cream sauce) and vepro knedlo zelo (pork with sauerkraut and dumplings), both served with enormous dumplings the size of doorstoppers. If you have room after such fare, try belt-busting strudel for pudding.

Sushi Bar Gen

243 West End Lane, NW6 1XN (7431 4031). West Hampstead tube. **Open** noon-2.45pm, 6-10.45pm daily. **Average ££. Set lunch** £6.80 bento box incl miso soup. **Map** p300. Japanese

At this no-nonsense, compact canteen – just a spit from West Hampstead's three stations – reliable Japanese fodder is turned out by reassuringly solemn and efficient Japanese chefs working in a little open kitchen at one end of the dining space. Service is equally swift, as it has to be given so few tables. Sizeable noodle dishes are the more filling menu choices, but offer nothing different to the ubiquitous stomach-fillers you get elsewhere. For a little more refinement and authenticity, opt for à la carte nigiri, sushi rolls (we recommend the beautifully decorated dragon roll), and sashimi, or more sizeable 'main course' plates like tempura prawn and vegetables. Extras – like oshinko (pickled cabbage), wakame (kelp) and miso soup – are very good, and dirt cheap.

Little Star

On an unlovely stretch of traffic-congested road, this pleasant Sri Lankan café is a definite oasis. Although the menu is limited, the food is well cooked and tasty; the charming owner was happy to explain what was on offer and concerned that we might find the dishes 'too hot'. We opted for string hoppers, a classic Sri Lankan dish made from a leavened rice batter, which, on arrival, resembled little, white mop heads. With them came a seriously fiery dahl (laced with red chilli) and a tasty coconut sambol, flavoured with dried fish – both set off admirably by the light-textured, delicate hoppers. There are very few places in London where one can eat so well and so generously for under £3 a head. Highly recommended.

Little Star
26 Station Parade, NW2 4NH (8830 5221). Willesden Green tube. **Open** noon-3pm, 6-11pm Mon-Sat; noon-11pm Sun. **Average ££. Set meal** (lunch, 6-6.45pm Mon-Sat) £5.50 2 courses. **No credit cards.**
International

Little Star's charms are many – the cosy, café atmosphere, the friendly staff and the easy-on-the-wallet prices. It was therefore a shame that each of the dishes we ordered were, at best, middling and, at worst, rather poorly put together. Our mains arrived with alarming haste and the Italian sausage in red wine sauce with sauté potatoes and green beans was a huge disappointment – the sauce achingly sweet and the vegetables soggy. The seafood linguine was more successful, the pasta al dente and the mussels and prawns in healthy abundance. The meal was salvaged by a decent ownmade tiramisu and the miniscule bill that followed.

In the area
Gourmet Burger Kitchen
331 West End Lane, NW6 1RS (7794 5455). **Map** p300.
Nando's *252-254 West End Lane, NW6 1LU (7794 1331).* **Map** p300.
Pizza Express *319 West End Lane, NW6 1RN (7431 8229).* **Map** p300.

Whetstone

In the area
ASK *1257 High Road, N20 0EW (8492 0033).*
Pizza Express *1264 High Road, N20 9HH (8446 8800).*

Willesden

★ Galla Café
91 Dudden Hill Lane, NW10 1BD (8459 7921). Dollis Hill tube. **Open** 10am-10pm daily. **Average £. Set meal** £3.50 1 course. **No credit cards.** Sri Lankan

In the area
Shish *2-6 Station Parade, NW2 4NH (8208 9292).*

North West

OUTER LONDON

Barking, Essex

In the area
Nando's Unit 1, The Odeon, Longbridge Road, Barking, Essex IG11 8RU (8507 0795).

Barnet, Hertfordshire

Emchai
78 High Street, Barnet, Herts EN5 5SN (8364 9993). High Barnet tube. **Lunch served** noon-2.30pm Mon-Thur; noon-3pm Fri-Sun. **Dinner served** 6-11pm Mon-Thur; 6pm-midnight Fri, Sat; 5-10pm Sun. **Average** ££. **Set meal** £14.50 per person (minimum 2) 2 courses. Oriental

Emchai's reasonably priced menu offers both Chinese and Malay dishes, from crispy duck to mee goreng, cooked by industrious chefs on show in the open-plan kitchen. Our meal got off to a good start with sticky pork ribs, and some tasty salt-and-spicy prawns with a garlic and chilli kick. To follow, a delicate stir-fry of prawns with lily bulbs and asparagus; honey-roast duck; and gai lan (Chinese broccoli) with ginger were all nicely executed. Our sweet tooth was satisfied by melon pudding in palm sugar syrup and (a retro classic, this) banana fritters. Serving staff were excellent bringing us complimentary prawn crackers.

Meal deals
Dylan's 21 Station Parade, Cockfosters Road, Barnet, Herts EN4 0DW (8275 1551/www.dylansrestaurant.com). Set meal (lunch Mon-Sat, 6-7pm daily) £12.50 2 courses, £15.50 3 courses. Modern European
Loch Fyne 12 Hadley Highstone, Barnet, Herts EN5 4PU (8449 3674/www.loch-fyne.com). Set lunch £10 2 courses. Fish

Beckenham, Kent

In the area
Miso 132 High Street, Beckenham, Kent BR3 1EB (8658 4498).

Bromley, Kent

In the area
Miso 10 East Street, Bromley, Kent BR1 1QX (8466 4678).
Nando's 9 Widmore Road, Bromley, Kent BR1 1RL (8290 5010).
Zizzi 11-13 Widmore Road, Bromley, Kent BR1 1RL (8464 6663).

Croydon, Surrey

Malay House
60 Lower Addiscombe Road, Croydon, Surrey CR0 6AA (8666 0266). East Croydon rail then 1 97, 312, 410 bus. **Dinner served** 6-11pm Tue-Sat. **Meals served** 1-9pm Sun. **Average** ££. **Buffet** (Sun) £7. **Unlicensed. Corkage** £1 per person. Malaysian

This simple little caff is still going strong after nearly a decade in the restaurant business, despite its curious location on a corner site of a traffic-laden Croydon road. For most of the week there's a classically Malaysian menu; on Sundays there's a buffet of dishes kept warm on hot-plates. We enjoyed many dishes on our Sunday visit – it's clear someone in the kitchen is an excellent cook. A lamb stock soup was scented with cinnamon and star anise, among other deftly blended spices. Beef rendang was also a flavoursome dish, with a clear lemongrass flavour. Not suprisingly, the dishes that were least impressive were the ones that don't take that well to being kept warm for hours on end, such as vegetable stir-fries or fried chicken, which was drying out by our 8pm visit. This late arrival sent the staff scurrying into the kitchen to add some fresh banana fritters and a coconut milk and sweetcorn pudding to the selection.

In the area

Little Bay *32 Selsdon Road, Croydon, Surrey CR2 6PB (8649 9544).*

Miso *11-12 Suffolk House, George Street, Croydon, Surrey CR0 1PE (8681 5084).*

Miso *103-105 High Street, Croydon, Surrey CR0 1QG (8681 7688).*

Nando's *Unit 4, Valley Park Leisure Centre, Beddington Farm Road, Croydon, Surrey CR0 4XY (8688 9545).*

Nando's *26 High Street, Croydon, Surrey CR0 1GT (8681 3505).*

Wagamama *4 Park Lane, Croydon, Surrey CR0 1JA (8760 9260).*

Yo! Sushi *House of Fraser, 21 North End Road, Croydon, Surrey CR0 1RQ (8760 0479).*

Zizzi *57-59 Southend, Croydon, Surrey CR0 1BF (8649 8403).*

Eastcote, Middlesex

★ Nauroz NEW

219 Field End Road, Eastcote, Middx HA5 1QZ (8868 0900). Eastcote tube. **Meals served** noon-midnight Tue-Sat. **Average** £. **Set meal** (vegetarian) £4, (meat) £5. **Unlicensed**. **Corkage** no charge.
Pakistani

The family behind this Pakistani restaurant have been in the business for more than 20 years, and were the original owners of Karahi King in Wembley, Mirch Masala in Norbury and Five Hot Chillies in Sudbury, before selling each venue in turn and moving on. So they have quite a pedigree. The curries, freshly cooked to order, come in fiery sauces flavoured with onions, garlic, ginger,

tomatoes and green chillies. We liked robustly spiced deigi gosht (lamb curry cooked on the bone), Punjabi tinda (Indian baby squash), and butter beans with fresh fenugreek. Nan was soft, crisp and enormous; and malai kulfi (Indian ice-cream) was own-made. Portions are huge, prices rock-bottom and service excellent, which may explain why this cosy BYO eaterie (with framed pictures on pastel walls, and an open kitchen) is packed with raucous crowds.

Edgware, Middlesex

B&K Salt Beef Bar

11 Lanson House, Whitchurch Lane, Edgware, Middx HA8 6NL (8952 8204). Edgware tube. **Lunch served** noon-3pm, **dinner served** 5.30-9.15pm Tue-Sun. **Average** ££. **Unlicensed**. **Corkage** no charge.
Jewish

B&K has been going for years. Possibly the locals come as much for a chat as for the rib-sticking kosher-style food; the decor isn't much of a draw. On a recent visit, the owner was welcoming and cheerful, and quick to bring bread and a menu. The traditional starters were all good: chopped liver, a hearty bean and barley soup, and gefilte fish that were so good we ordered more. Worsht (salami) and eggs were competently cooked, but it's the salt beef that's the star: a massive, warming, comforting plate of tender slices. (If you can't finish all the meat, ask to take it home.) The mixed salad could be a course on its own, but the latkes, as so often in restaurants, were poorly cooked.

★ Penashe

60 Edgware Way, Mowbray Parade, Edgware, Middx HA8 8JS (8958 6008). Edgware tube. **Lunch served** noon-3pm, **dinner served**

Masa. See p249.

Outer

5-10pm Mon-Thur. **Meals served** 1hr after sabbath-11pm Sat (winter only); noon-10pm Sun. **Average** £. **Unlicensed** no alcohol allowed.
Jewish

While waiting for their food to arrive at Penashe, some of the regulars while away the time with a carton of 'Booba's homemade soup', which is as good a chicken soup with matzo ball as you'll find in any Jewish home. It takes time for orders to appear because each item on the small menu is cooked to order. Penashe doesn't offer many types of burger, just the one, but that (like each order of scrumptious barbecued chicken wings) is grilled and temperature-checked to ensure that it has been perfectly cooked. The salt

beef – cut in the American style with layers of thinly sliced meat piled into rye or white bread – was succulent and fresh. Try the grilled steak sandwich, with the meat cut from the ball of the rib: satisfying down to the last tender bite.

Zanzibar

113 High Street, Edgware, Middx HA8 7DB (8952 2986). Edgware tube. **Lunch served** noon-3pm Mon-Sat. **Dinner served** 5.30-11pm Mon-Thur; 6-11pm Fri, Sat. **Meals served** noon-10pm Sun. **Average** ££. **Set lunch** £6.95 1 course.
North Indian

Adding a much-needed touch of culinary liveliness to Edgware High Street, Zanzibar is a large, bustling

246 Time Out Cheap Eats

North Indian eaterie housed in the reasonably appropriate environs of a former pub. On our Saturday night visit it was positively heaving with a predominantly Indian clientele, mostly in large groups, tucking in with gusto to a background of Bollywood films on flatscreen TVs. Being asked for a credit card to put behind the bar for 'security' did, however, come as a bit of an unpleasant surprise. The food, though, hit the spot, even if the chilli sauce-drenched masala mogo chips (cassava chips) were overly sweet. Succulent tandoori lamb chops, Asli chicken curry and sarson da saag (creamy textured mustard greens that had a fine, piquant kick) were satisfyingly tasty, accompanied by methi (fenugreek) roti and peshwari naan. Verdict: gutsy Indian cooking in boisterous surroundings.

In the area

L'Artista 120 Station Road, Edgware, Middx HA8 7AA (8951 5533).
Nando's 137-139 Station Road, Edgware, Middx HA8 9JG (8952 3400).

Enfield, Middlesex

In the area

Nando's 2 The Town, Enfield, Middx EN2 6LE (8366 2904).
Pizza Express 2 Silver Street, Enfield, Middx EN1 3ED (8367 3311).

Greenhithe, Kent

In the area
Ed's Easy Diner *Bluewater, Greenhithe, Kent DA9 9SG (01322 380 939).*

Harrow, Middlesex

Blue Ginger NEW
383 Kenton Road, Harrow, Middx HA3 0XS (8909 0100/www.vijay restaurant.com). Kenton tube/rail. **Lunch served** noon-3pm Tue-Sat. **Dinner served** 6-11pm Mon-Sat. **Meals served** noon-10.30pm Sun. **Average** ££. North Indian
A glossy black granite bar, a plethora of flat-screen televisions, and an assortment of squishy sofas and seating arrangements are easily accommodated at this spacious venue. A selection of classic North Indian kebabs and curries is served, alongside Indo-Chinese choices. Amritsari fish, a popular Punjabi bar snack, raised battered fried fish to a different level with a delectable chilli-speckled batter hiding lemon-steeped white fillets. Main courses and accompaniments also delivered the goods: yellow lentils, simmered with spinach paste and ginger, made an earthy and wholesome treat – ideal for mopping up with a stack of rotis. In comparison to these North Indian delights, the Chinese dishes didn't get off the starter's block and were akin to mundane takeaway offerings. Service tends to be harried when the place fills up, but the staff remain friendly throughout.

Caribbean Choice
116 High Street, Wealdstone, Middx HA3 7AL (8427 3666). Harrow & Wealdstone tube/rail. **Meals served** 10am-9pm Mon-Thur; 10am-11pm Fri-Sat; noon-6pm Sun. **Average** ££. **Unlicensed. Corkage** no charge. **No credit cards**. Caribbean

This unassuming high street canteen could have been plucked straight from downtown Kingston. A cornerstone of the local Jamaican community, the kitchen cooks up all the dishes regulars miss from home – freshly crimped beef patties, meaty stews and curries, oxtail soup, salt fish with ackee and Caribbean juices. The menu changes every day according to what the chef feels like cooking and you can get a hearty meal for a tenner, with change. We came for the sweet, onion-rich brown stew with chicken, tender and tasty and served on a big pile of rice and peas, lubricated with a deliciously creamy fresh soursop (guanabana) juice. Most diners are Jamaican, but the welcome is just as warm if you don't speak patois.

★ Golden Palace
146-150 Station Road, Harrow, Middx HA1 2RH (8863 2333). Harrow-on-the-Hill tube/rail. **Meals served** noon-11.30pm Mon-Sat; 11am-10.30pm Sun. **Dim sum served** noon-5pm Mon-Sat; 11am-5pm Sun. **Average** ££. Chinese
Such is the popularity of this large suburban restaurant that the recently painted dining room is already showing signs of wear and tear. In contrast, the dim sum remain as fresh as ever. Soft beef belly with preserved cabbage woke us up with its spirited covering of cracked black pepper. Cuttlefish with 'dried garlic and fresh garlic' then blew us away; served with rice vermicelli, it had a taste and texture similar to (much more expensive) steamed razor clam. Steamed crystal prawn dumplings were handmade and sensitively seasoned, while oven-baked roast pork puff pastries arrived flaky and bursting with sweet filling. This wonderful meal was blighted only by hasty and abrupt service. The à la carte menu is as well prepared as the dim sum.

Outer

★ Masa NEW

24-26 Headstone Drive, Harrow,
Middx HA3 5QH (8861 6213).
Harrow & Wealdstone tube/rail.
Meals served noon-11pm daily.
Average ££. Unlicensed.
Corkage no charge. Afghan
The menu at Masa incorporates a
medley of the flavours to be found in
Afghanistan and the surrounding
region. Expect meaty kebabs with
strains of Middle Eastern character,
central Asian dumplings, Indian-
inspired curries, and a selection of
pastas and flatbreads. We plumped
for a delectably smoky platter of
well-marinated kebabs. Kobeda
(minced chicken kebab) was
deliciously subtle with coriander
and ginger spicing. Similarly, seared
lamb chops, devoid of cloying
masala, scored highly for simplicity;
we mopped up the flavoursome
juices with a super-sized naan. Next,
quabili palow (spiced basmati rice,
studded with tender lamb morsels)
won our plaudits for its fragrant
seasoning of toasted cumin,
cinnamon and cloves. Masa looks
smart and showy with its sparkling
open kitchen, oriental carpets,
glossy granite flooring and heavy
wood panelling. But despite this, our
final bill was small, kept that way
thanks to a BYO policy.

★ Ram's

203 Kenton Road, Harrow, Middx,
HA3 0HD (8907 2022). Kenton
tube/rail. **Lunch served** noon-3pm,
dinner served 6-11pm daily.
Average ££. Set thalis £4.99
(lunch), £8.99 (dinner). **Set meal**
£15 (unlimited food and soft drinks).
Indian
This venue has recently been
refurbished with purple and lilac
walls, colourful portraits of Hindu
gods, and torans (festive wall and
doorway hangings). Many authentic
Surti specialities have been added to
the very long, revamped menu.

Kand (purple yam fritters) and
khandvi (steamed chickpea-flour
spirals topped with mustard seeds
and finely grated coconut) were
scrumptious. Val ni dahl (spicy split
field beans) was authentically
mushy. However, kadhi, a chickpea
curry prettily presented in a copper
pail, was overwhelmed with the
tongue-numbing heat of black
pepper. Shrikhand (a sweet yoghurt
dessert) is a quintessential festive
accompaniment to Surti dishes; here,
it had a satisfyingly rich and dense
texture. The own-made pickles and
chutneys added to what was a
highly enjoyable dining experience.

In the area
Nando's *300-302 Station Road,*
Harrow, Middx HA1 2DX (8427
5581).
Nando's *309-311 Northolt Road,*
South Harrow, Middx HA2 8JA
(8423 1516).
Palm Palace *34 High Street,*
Harrow, Middx HA3 7AB (8574
9209).
Pizza Express *2 College Road,*
Harrow, Middx HA1 1BE (8427
9195).
Sakonis *5-8 Dominion Parade,*
Station Road, Harrow, Middx
HA1 2TR (8863 3399).

Hounslow,
Middlesex

In the area
Nando's *1 High Street, Hounslow,*
Middx TW3 1RH (8570 5881).
Pizza Express *41-43 High Street,*
Hounslow, Middx TW3 1RH (8577
8522).

Ilford, Essex

★ Mandarin Palace
559-561 Cranbrook Road, Gants
Hill, Ilford, Essex IG2 6JZ (8550
7661). Gants Hill tube. **Lunch**

Outer

served noon-4pm, **dinner served**
6.30-11.30pm Mon-Sat. **Meals
served** noon-midnight Sun. **Dim
sum served** noon-4pm Mon-Sat;
noon-5pm Sun. **Average** ££.
Chinese

The gaudy, faux-antique Chinese
decor that greets diners here belies
the mastery of the culinary art that
prevails in the kitchen. In fact,
Mandarin Palace provides a good
example of what Chinese cookery
should be like. We went for dim sum
and were delighted by our meal.
Prawn dumplings were fresh and
full of bouncy flavour, while pork
puff pastries were a mouth-watering
combination of tender sweet-
savoury roast meat and the lightest
layers of delicate pastry. To follow
taro croquettes featured meat and
mushrooms wrapped in softly
mashed taro, deep-fried to produce
an exterior as fragile as lace – crisp,

comforting and delicious. The only
disappointment was a chilli salt and
pepper squid (ordered from the main
menu) that proved to be chewy and
uninspiring. Nonetheless, the quality
of the dim sum to be found here is
among the best in London.

In the area
Nando's *Unit 1A, Clements Road,
Ilford, Essex IG1 1BP (8514 6012).*

Kingston, Surrey

Cammasan
*8 Charter Quay, High Street,
Kingston, Surrey KT1 1NB
(8549 3510). Kingston rail. Meinton
noodle bar* **Lunch served** noon-
3pm, **dinner served** 5.30-11pm
Mon-Fri. **Meals served** noon-
11pm Sat, Sun. **Average** ££.
Chaitan restaurant **Lunch**

served noon-3pm, **dinner served** 5.30-11pm Mon-Fri. **Meals served** noon-11pm Sat, Sun. **Average £££.**
Oriental

Ascend to the first floor of Cammasan for a little formality; here you'll find tasteful pastel walls (kitschy trinkets are kept to a minimum), starched tablecloths and sweet-tempered service. The menu is divided into 'little plates' and 'big bowls'. The former consist mostly of deep-fried titbits (Thai fish cakes with satay sauce; vegetable spring rolls with chilli sauce); the latter include curries (duck red curry, say), stir-fries (cod sweet and sour) and salads (gado gado). There's a Wagamama-style canteen on the ground floor that serves a shorter, simpler version of what's to be found upstairs. Eat there if you've a movie to head for later, as you'll always get a spot, the food is good, and service swift.

fish! kitchen NEW

58 Coombe Road, Kingston, Surrey KT2 7AF (8546 2886). Norbiton rail/57, 85, 213 bus. **Meals served** noon-10pm Tue-Sat. **Average £££.**
Fish & Chips

With expansive decking outside and shiny black tiles and uniformed staff inside, the new restaurant annexe to Kingston fish shop Jarvis certainly looks the part. Though fishy dishes such as king prawn kebab and fish pie appear on the menu, the main focus is battered fish: five varieties plus daily specials, served with chips, mushy peas and tartare sauce. The portions aren't too huge, and the tartare sauce is own-made, but otherwise there are few surprises. Nevertheless, our cod dinner was excellent: an enormous door-stop fillet, thinly layered with batter and beautifully fleshy within, served

fish! kitchen

atop ungreasy, hand-cut chips and decent mushy peas. A starter of 'smoked haddock rarebit' was an interesting combination of ideas, the smoked flavour of the fish well offset by a mustardy cheese topping.

Riverside Vegetaria
64 High Street, Kingston, Surrey KT1 1HN (8546 0609). Kingston rail. **Meals served** noon-11pm Mon-Sat; noon-10.30pm Sun. **Average** ££. Vegetarian
This cosy restaurant offers an unusual juxtaposition of substantial old-school winter fare and summery views of the river bedecked with ducks, swans and boats. Owned by Sri Lankan-born Ritchie Sakthivel, a follower of Indian religious sect Sai Baba, the venue prides itself on offering additive-free, mainly organic and vegan dishes. The selection of mostly spicy dishes could easily be entitled 'around the world in 80 stews'. We liked the hearty Jamaican stew; it was made with sweet potatoes, carrots, green and red peppers, and a plethora of freshly cooked (not tinned) beans, like black-eye, red kidney, butter and chickpeas, in chilli- and turmeric-flecked coconut sauce.

Terra Mia
138 London Road, Kingston, Surrey KT2 6QJ (8546 4888). Kingston rail. **Lunch served** noon-2.30pm, **dinner served** 6-11.30pm Mon-Sat. **Average** ££. **Set lunch** (Mon-Fri) £5.90 1 course incl soft drink; £6.90 1 course incl alcoholic drink.
Pizza & Pasta
Terra Mia retains the decor of the previous pizzeria that occupied this site, including knick-knacks on the walls, and an enormous mural of the Pont du Gard. The menu offers 20 or so pizzas, including all the classic versions you'd expect, plus some extras including the seafood-heavy Terra Mia, with prawns, anchovies and tuna. The pizzas are a touch smaller than you'd find in most of the chains, but that's no bad thing if you're saving room for a sorbet later. It's the pick-and-mix pasta choices that we like the best; there are ten or so pasta sauces and seven types of pasta available. So instead of spaghetti bolognese, for example, you can have the bolognese sauce with fusilli or penne instead. We went for the latter, and found it a simple, hole-filling satisfier. A cheery spot.

Meal deals

Blue Hawaii *2 Richmond Road, Kingston, Surrey KT2 5EB (8549 6989/www.bluehawaii. co.uk).* Set meal £8.95-£11.95 unlimited barbeque. Hawaiian

In the area
Carluccio's Caffè *Charter Quay, Kingston, Surrey KT1 1HT (8549 5898).*
Gourmet Burger Kitchen *42-46 High Street, Kingston, Surrey KT1 1HL (8546 1649).*
Jo Shmo's *4 Jerome Place, Charter Quay, Kingston, Surrey KT1 1HX (8439 7766).*
Nando's *37-38 High Street, Kingston, Surrey KT1 1LQ (8296 9540).*
Paul *3-5 Eden Walk, Kingston, Surrey KT1 1BP (8549 6799).*
Pizza Express *Unit 5, Kingston Rotunda, Kingston, Surrey KT1 1QJ (8547 3133).*
Strada *1 The Griffin Centre, Market Place, Kingston, Surrey KT1 1JT (8974 8555).*
Wagamama *16-18 High Street, Kingston, Surrey KT1 1EY (8546 1117).*
Zizzi *43 Market Place, Kingston, Surrey KT1 1JQ (8546 0717).*

Loughton, Essex

In the area
Loch Fyne *280-282 High Road, Loughton, Essex IG10 1RB (8532 5140).*

New Malden, Surrey

Hamgipak
169 High Street, New Malden, Surrey KT3 4BH (8942 9588).
New Malden rail. **Meals served** 11am-10pm Mon, Tue, Thur-Sun. **Average ££.** Korean
Only 12 people can squeeze into this tiny Korean café on busy New Malden High Street, but locals drift in all day for authentic Korean food served in double-quick time. Don't be put off by the Lilliputian dimensions of the dining room; the menu runs for pages and pages, with all the expected barbecues, hot-pots and stir-fries. Dishes are divided into plate meals (with rice or noodles) and main courses, which are normally big enough to share. Spicy fried chicken on rice melted in the mouth; it came with a thick, chilli-speckled sauce full of broccoli and beansprouts. In all, Hamgipak is best suited for a lunchtime snack rather than a slap-up dinner.

★ Jee Cee Neh
74 Burlington Road, New Malden, Surrey KT3 4NU (8942 0682).
New Malden rail. **Lunch served** noon-3pm, **dinner served** 5-11pm Tue-Sun. **Average ££.** Korean
Previously known as Jee's, this smart café has been refurbished. It now boasts stripy coloured panels running down one wall, framed Korean paintings, polished dark-wood furniture and a grey, tiled floor. In a match for the new decor, the food too was wonderfully fresh and exquisitely flavoured. The final element, service, was helpful. We were wowed by namul; Korean greens, beansprouts with shredded cucumber, and grated radish. Yet we needn't have ordered this; free kimch'i arrived unbidden (along with malted tea). Young yang sot bab was a 'healthy' casserole cooked in an earthenware pot, a wholesome and delicious dish crammed with white, black and brown rice, red millet, black-eye beans, red kidney beans, chestnuts, pine nuts, gingko nuts, whole ginseng, dried red dates, and cubes of sweet potato and kabachi pumpkin. What more could we want?

★ You-Me
96 Burlington Road, New Malden, Surrey KT3 4NT (8715 1079). New Malden rail. **Meals served** noon-10.30pm Mon, Wed-Sun; 6-10.30pm Tue. **Average £££.** **Set lunch** (noon-4pm Mon, Wed-Sun) £5.90-£8.90 (minimum 2) 2 courses.
Korean
This home-style family restaurant could have been plucked straight from a suburban street in Seoul. Game shows babble on a TV in the corner, Korean magazines lie in piles around the dining room, and families feast at low tables in the banquet room at the back. We kicked off with warm saké and a satisfying bean-flour pancake, stuffed with spring onions and tiny morsels of pork. We also enjoyed the hot chilli chicken, rolled in batter in a tongue-searing sauce infused with the flavour of dried chillies. One caveat is that the portion sizes vary; the prawn barbecue was big on flavour, but quite small for the money. Free namul (vegetables) and panch'an were provided without prompting, and a tin pot of Korean tea arrived as soon as we sat down. Delightful staff tripped over themselves to please.

Rayners Lane, Middlesex

Eastern Fire
430 Alexandra Avenue, Rayners Lane, Middx, HA2 9TW (8866 8386/www.easternfireonline.co.uk). Rayners Lane tube. **Meals served** 6-11pm Mon-Fri. **Average ££.**
South Indian/Sri Lankan

This contemporary, sparklingly clean, cream-coloured venue has had a makeover and is now under new management. The owners are Sri Lankans from Malaysia, and the head chef is South Indian. Consequently, the very long and ambitious menu offers an extensive selection of Sri Lankan, South Indian and Indian-Malaysian 'mamak' dishes (spicy Indian-influenced food that's unique to Malaysia's roadside stalls). South Indian sambar vadai was a substantial dish; urid lentil fritter (a little too hard) was soaked in an extraordinarily flavoursome sambar crammed with fresh tropical vegetables such as yams, bottle gourd and vegetable drumsticks. A hearty dish of crushed pittu was also packed with flavour and colour: scrambled with paneer cubes and vegetables such as aubergines, leeks, carrots and potatoes.

Richmond, Surrey

Chez Lindsay

11 Hill Rise, Richmond, Surrey TW10 6UQ (8948 7473). Richmond tube/rail. Crêperie **Meals served** noon-11pm Mon-Sat; noon-10pm Sun. **Average** *££. Restaurant* **Meals served** noon-11pm Mon-Sat; noon-10pm Sun. **Average** *£££.* **Set lunch** (noon-3pm Mon-Sat) £9.75-£14.50 2 courses. *French*

Chez Lindsay is a charming Richmond restaurant, with simple furnishings and yellow walls. As you'll have guessed from the name, it provides a welcome slice of regional France in the heart of south-west London's suburbia. A starter of mussels à la St Malo, served with white wine, cream, shallots and thyme, was incredibly moreish. The choice of galettes (a variant on the crêpe and a house speciality) runs from the classic (ham and cheese, egg and ham, cheese and onion) to the more culinarily complex, such as

a decadent option with onion and Roquefort sauce, celery and walnuts. Seafood enthusiasts will have plenty to get their teeth into with the mighty cotriade, a hearty Breton casserole of red gurnard, sea bream, mackerel, langoustines, lobster and mussels. To accompany the galettes, the drink of choice really has to be one of the selection of superior French sparkling ciders.

Stein's NEW

55 Richmond Towpath, west of Richmond Bridge, Richmond, Surrey TW10 6UX (8948 8189). Richmond tube/rail then 20-minute walk or 65 bus. **Meals served** (phone to check times). **Average** *££. Bavarian*

Bavarian-themed Stein's is one of several quaint eateries that are located along the Richmond riverside walkway. A summer-time only operation, it has outside seating of trestle tables and benches. If you're unfamiliar with Bavarian dishes, Stein's offerings may seem hilariously limited. It's basically just three sausages: bratwurst (veal, pork and spices, fried), currywurst (frankfurter coated in curry powder) or weisswurst (white veal sausage, boiled). These are then served accompanied by a sizable heap of sauerkraut, and sautéed potatoes. Dunk your wurst in sweet mustard and munch with a brezen (bready pretzel). There's also Wiener schnitzel and spetzl (thick noodles), served with bacon and sauerkraut. Unfortunately, Stein's isn't a beer garden – you can only have one alcoholic drink per meal, which is maybe why you'll see most punters going for a hefty litre of beer. *Prost*!

Meal deals

Canyon *The Towpath, nr Richmond Bridge, Richmond, Surrey TW10 6UJ (8948 2944/www.jamiesbars. co.uk).* Set lunch £12.50 2 courses, £15 3 courses. *North American*

Outer

In the area

ASK 85 Kew Green, Richmond, Surrey TW9 3AH (8940 3766).

Carluccio's Caffé 31-35 Kew Road, Richmond, Surrey TW9 2NQ (8940 5037).

Giraffe 30 Hill Street, Richmond, Surrey TW9 1TW (8332 2646).

Gourmet Burger Kitchen 15-17 Hill Rise, Richmond, Surrey TW10 6UQ (8940 5440).

Maison Blanc 27B The Quandrant, Richmond, Surrey TW9 1DN (8332 7041).

Nando's 2&4 Hill Rise, Richmond, Surrey TW10 6UA (8940 8810)

Paul 13 The Quadrant, Richmond, Surrey TW9 1BP (8940 5250).

Pizza Al Rollo 20 Hill Street, Richmond, Surrey TW9 1TN (8940 8951). Branch of Café Pasta.

Strada 26 Hill Street, Richmond, Surrey TW9 1TW (8940 3141).

Wagamama 3 Hill Street, Richmond, Surrey TW9 1SX (8948 2224).

Zizzi 4-5 King's Street, Richmond, Surrey TW9 1ND (8332 2809).

Ruislip, Middlesex

In the area

Pizza Express 86 High Street, Ruislip, Middx HA4 8LS (9562 5100).

Southall, Middlesex

Delhi Wala NEW

11 King Street, Southall, Middx UB2 4DG (8574 0873). Southall rail. **Meals served** 8.30am-10pm daily. **Average** £. Punjabi

There are only very few Punjabi vegetarian establishments in London, but Delhi Wala is one of them. It is a light, airy, spacious restaurant and snack shop, selling a mixture of dishes: the everyday meals that you'd find in Delhi households, the rustic fare of the Punjabi countryside, and the unpretentious grub of 'dhabas', roadside pit stops for truck drivers. We liked paneer samosas stuffed with finely diced paneer, peas and cumin seeds. Chana bhatura was dark chickpea curry pepped up with cinnamon, cloves and shredded ginger, accompanied by what seemed almost impossibly fluffy fried bread. Makki roti aur sarson saag (cornmeal flatbread with curried mustard greens – Southall's signature dish) was also delicious.

Madhu's

39 South Road, Southall, Middx UB1 1SW (8574 1897). Southall rail. **Lunch served** 12.30-3pm Mon, Wed-Fri. **Dinner served** 6-11.30pm Mon, Wed-Sun. **Average** £££. East African Punjabi

Outshining its surroundings on a scruffy shopping parade, Madhu's is one of Southall's best – and poshest – restaurants. Highly presentable young staff are professional if a mite over-attentive; customers are a well-turned-out multicultural bunch. Bold spicing and expert chargrilling characterise the cooking. Tandoori salmon was beautifully executed: succulent chunks, marinated in lemon and then given a thyme-like edge with carom seeds. To follow, king prawn masala featured big meaty crustaceans in a sauce zingy with fresh ginger; karela aloo juxtaposed the slightly chewy skin of the bitter gourd with chunks of potato in a rather too salty, dry-ish spice blend; but dahl makhani was splendidly creamy. Puddings are notable too: delicate mounds of gajar halwa left us smiling.

New Asian Tandoori Centre (Roxy)

114-118 The Green, Southall, Middx UB2 4BQ (8574 2597). Southall rail. **Meals served** 8am-11pm Mon-Thur; 8am-midnight Fri-Sun. **Average** ££. Punjabi Indian

This cream-and-terracotta coloured restaurant has become even buzzier since its recent refurbishment. The paneer kebab rolled in soft nan was smoky and substantial. The maize bread and mustard greens combo, a traditional Punjabi winter dish, was robustly flavoured with fresh ginger and green chillies. We also enjoyed the chicken and spinach curry, and a dahl made from chunky black urid lentils and split Bengal gram. Roxy showcases the rich, rustic, earthy fare of the Punjabi countryside. However, some dishes seem pre-prepared and standards are inconsistent. On a second visit a couple of days later, all the curries (lamb, chickpeas, spinach paneer, and so on) were insipid and watery, and appeared to have been cooked by a different chef.

Palm Palace

80 South Road, Southall, Middx UB1 1RD (8574 9209). Southall rail. **Lunch served** noon-3pm daily. **Dinner served** 6-11pm Mon-Thur; 6-11.30pm Fri-Sun. **Average** £. Sri Lankan/Indian

This long-established venue, with a polished wooden floor, biscuit-coloured wallpaper, and smart, high-backed wood, metal and maroon suede chairs, is a popular meeting place for young Sri Lankan men. A long menu lists Sri Lankan, South Indian and North Indian dishes, chef's specials, seafood delicacies and a variety of thalis. Devilled paneer was more like that contemporary Indian classic, chilli paneer: tender cubes of paneer were slathered in oriental-style sweet chilli sauce, rather than the more traditional chilli and vinegar combo, but the dish was tasty nonetheless. Egg hopper was served cold and had a brittle, dried-out texture; string hoppers made from Sri Lankan red rice were much nicer. Portions were hearty, and service was warm and chatty.

In the area

Mirch Masala *171-173 The Broadway, Southall, Middx UB1 1LX (8867 9222).*

Stanmore, Middlesex

In the area

Madison's Deli *11 Buckingham Parade, Stanmore, Middx HA7 4EB (8954 9998).*
Pizza Express *55 The Broadway, Stanmore, Middx HA7 4DJ (8420 7474).*

Sudbury, Middlesex

★ Five Hot Chillies

875 Harrow Road, Sudbury, Middx HA0 2RH (8908 5900). Sudbury Hill or Sudbury Town tube. **Meals served** noon-midnight daily. **Average** ££. **Unlicensed**. **Corkage** no charge. Indian

A no-frills community café, Five Hot Chillies is as much a magnet for local Pakistani and Punjabi residents as it is for London's far-flung and ready-to-travel curry aficionados. The kebabs and hearty curries are the dishes to go for from the menu. We've yet to taste a more impressive seared fish tikka: the firm-fleshed chunks of white cod, cloaked with yoghurt, red chilli flecks and thyme-like carom seeds, delivered a perfect balance of intensely smoky flavours combined with a tart lemony bite. Next, a generous helping of saag gosht had a beguiling aroma of pounded cardamom seeds and ginger, making it a fabulous base for some meltingly tender lamb. We recommend the admirable breads, which make a better accompaniment to the curries than the rice dishes. The restaurant is noisy, but no matter: the boisterous, feel-good vibe only adds to its many charm.

Dadima. See p259.

Surbiton, Surrey

In the area
Terra Mia *138 London Road, Kingston, Surrey KT2 6QJ (8546 4888).*

Sutton, Surrey

In the area
M Manze's *266 High Street, Sutton, Surrey SM1 1NT (8286 8787).*
Nando's *9-11 High Road, Sutton, Surrey SM1 1DF (8770 0180).*
Pizza Express *4 High Street, Sutton, Surrey SM1 1HN (8643 4725).*
Zizzi *13-15 High Street, Sutton, Surrey SM1 1DF (8661 8778).*

Teddington, Middlesex

In the area
Pizza Express *11 Waldegrave Road, Teddington, Middx TW11 8LA (8943 3553).*

Twickenham, Middlesex

Pallavi
Unit 3, Cross Deep Court, Heath Road, Twickenham, Middx TW1 4QJ (8892 2345). Twickenham rail. **Lunch served** noon-3pm daily. **Dinner served** 6-11pm Mon-Thur, Sun; 6pm-midnight Fri, Sat. **Average** ££. Indian
Upstairs, above a suburban shopping arcade, Pallavi offers a menu that digs deep into the regional cuisine of Kerala – half a dozen varieties of dosa and vadai, served with sambar and spicy coconut chutney, vegetarian thorans cooked in coconut milk and tangy fish curries, as well as meaty Anglo-Indian staples. Indian families come here to feast in a cosy dining room full of faded plastic topiary and colourful Keralan knick-knacks. We dived in with a chilli-laced, papery rava (semolina) dosa, followed by an excellent vellappam – a hopper-like fermented rice and coconut pancake served with Malabar-style chicken curry. Then came fish moilee, a sensation of tender kingfish, coconut, mustard seed, lime and tamarind. Service can be slow, but food this good is worth the wait.

Meal deals
Brula *43 Crown Road, Twickenham, Middx TW1 3EJ (8892 0602/www.brulabistrot.co.uk).* Set lunch £11.50 2 courses, £14 3 courses. French
Ma Cuisine Le Petit Bistrot *6 Whitton Road, Twickenham, Middx TW1 1BJ (8607 9849/www.macuisinetw1.co.uk).* Set lunch £12.95 2 courses. French

In the area
Loch Fyne *175 Hampton Road, Twickenham, Middx TW2 5NG (8255 6222).*
Pizza Express *21 York Street, Twickenham, Middx TW1 3JZ (8891 4126).*
Sagar *27 York Street, Twickenham, Middx TW1 3JZ (8744 3868).*
Zizzi *36 York Street, Twickenham, Middx TW1 3LJ (8538 9024).*

Uxbridge, Middlesex

Satya NEW
33 Rockingham Road, Uxbridge, Middx UB8 2TZ (01895 274250). Uxbridge tube. **Lunch served** noon-3pm, **dinner served** 6-11pm daily. **Average** ££. **Set buffet** (noon-3pm Mon-Fri) £6.50. South Indian
This is a spacious, smartly decorated venue, with two dining rooms, bare floorboards and a lively cream, maroon and purple colour

scheme. Masala dosa was a crisp pancake filled with some assertively spiced soya mince, which is popular in contemporary Indian home cooking, accompanied by a light tamarind-tart sambhar (lentil broth) and creamy fresh coconut chutney. The Keralite fish curry featured succulent pieces of pomfret in rich gravy suffused with cloves, cumin and coriander. Mathanga erissery (festive pumpkin curry, here cooked with black eye beans) is rarely seen on restaurant menus in this country, and even the more prosaic dishes like sizzling chilli paneer, vegetable pilau and coconut rice were notably fresh and sparkled with flavour, colour, texture and spice. Service from smiling Keralite waiters was efficient, if a little languorous.

In the area
Nando's *Unit 204, The Chimes Centre, Uxbridge, Middx UB8 1GE (01895 274 277).*
Pizza Express *222 High Street, Uxbridge, Middx UB8 1LD (01895 251222).*

Wembley, Middlesex

★ Dadima **NEW**
228 Ealing Road, Wembley, Middx HA0 4QL (8902 1072). Alperton tube/79, 83, 297 bus. **Lunch served** noon-3pm, **dinner served** 5-10pm Mon, Wed-Fri; 5.30-10pm Tue. **Meals served** noon-10pm Sat, Sun. **Average** £. **Set thalis** £4.99-£5.99. Indian
If Dadima (meaning 'grandmother') had a PR company to speak on its behalf, no doubt much more would be made of the three varieties of dadi ni thali ('grandma's thali') and little-seen items that are central to its menu. However, Dadima is an unassuming family-run restaurant, with cream walls and bright red and yellow furniture. We've enjoyed the thalis on our previous visits, so this year decided to try out the snacks. Khichi (two substantial steamed lentil flour dumplings) came with a separate container of oil (to keep the dumplings lubricated) and dried red chilli chutney. Samosa chaat was a dramatic combination of hot miniature samosas, cooling yoghurt and fruity tamarind sauce. However, best of all was methi bhajiya (fenugreek fritters), which were impossibly soft, fluffy and ungreasy.

Karahi King
213 East Lane, North Wembley, Middx HA0 3NG (8904 2760). North Wembley tube/245 bus. **Meals served** noon-midnight daily. **Average** ££. **Unlicensed**. **Corkage** no charge. Indian
Asian families with children in tow all seem to love Karahi King. The darkened glass frontage doesn't look terribly tempting, and the decor isn't particularly scintillating, but a warm welcome extended by staff soon puts newcomers at ease. Grab a ringside seat by the open kitchen and admire the cooks as they swirl sizzling masalas around capacious karahis, turn kebabs over glowing charcoal, and slap rotis into the tandoor. Meat kebabs are probably the best bet. We can recommend the garlicky lamb chops and the deliciously smoky tandoori chicken. Keema methi (lamb mince fried with mustard greens, green chillies, and heaps of ginger) was a resounding success, with every last bit being mopped up with an obliging mint-speckled paratha. The curries have a tendency towards the hit-or-miss, some good, others less so, but the kebabs and hot breads get top marks.

Sakonis
129 Ealing Road, Wembley, Middx HA0 4BP (8903 9601). Alperton tube/183 bus. **Breakfast served** 9-11am Sat, Sun. **Meals served**

noon-10pm daily. **Average** £. **Set buffet** (breakfast) £3.99, (noon-4pm) £6.99, (7-9.30pm) £9.99. Gujarati

Although the Green Street branch has closed, this chain of Gujarati vegetarian chaat houses (snack bars) is doing very well, having opened new branches in Leicester and Dubai. So why, then, the grim-faced, tight-lipped service? The black-and-white decor is largely unmemorable, so it's best to focus on the colourful food. Aloo papdi chaat is a typically vibrant dish: here, pastry-like strips of pooris were combined with diced potatoes, fresh chickpeas and onions, drizzled with sweet yoghurt, tangy tamarind and green coriander chutneys, and topped with hot red chilli powder and coriander leaves. Sakonis' crispy bhajiya is famous: wafer-thin potato slices fried in garlicky, herby, flavoursome chickpea-flour batter (the recipe is a well-guarded secret). Sakonis also offers Indian-Chinese dishes. Its buffets featuring Gujarati specialities are legendary.

★ Sanghamam `NEW`

531-533 High Road, Wembley, Middx HA0 2DJ (8900 0777). Wembley Central tube. **Meals served** 11am-11pm daily. **Average** ££. **Set lunch** (11am-4pm) £3.95 3 courses. **Unlicensed.** Indian

Once part of the Saravanna Bhavan restaurant chain, Sanghamam has changed its name and decided to go it alone. However, the menu is almost identical to what it was before, but a wide selection of chaats and a Gujarati thali have been added to appeal to the Gujarati locals. The decor – polished tiled floor, a vertical kitchen hatch, fresh juice bar – hasn't changed. We loved the South Indian thali, which, at £4.95 must be one of the best-value meals to be found anywhere in town. It contained 13 items, including fluffy rice, poori

(soft and crumbly, though slightly greasy), sambar, rasam, split pigeon-pea dahl, suran (a variety of Indian yam with a nutty taste), black chickpea curry, spinach and bengal-gram curry, moong (green gram) dahl and payasam (rice pudding).

In the area

Nando's *420-422 High Road, Wembley, Middx HA9 6AH (8795 3564).*

Woodford, Essex

Pizzeria Bel-Sit

439 High Road, Woodford Green, IG8 0XE (8504 1164). Bus W13, 20. **Lunch served** noon-2.30pm Tue-Sat, **dinner served** 6-11pm Mon-Sat. **Average** ££. **No credit cards.** Pizza & Pasta

At 6pm every evening, without fail, there's a queue outside this Woodford Green eaterie. The no-booking policy is one explanation, but chiefly it's because the sports-mad locals love the place. Every inch of wall and ceiling space is covered with memorabilia, mainly from Italian and English football teams (and regular Teddy Sheringham) but recently enhanced by a Jonah Lomu framed shirt – the challenge on each visit is to see who's been in recently and handed over another autographed item. The staff are always immensely good-humoured considering the hectic atmosphere and will always make a fuss of children, many of whom have parties here. The menu is a familiar litany of pizzas and pasta dishes, while the specials board offers more imaginative fare such as slow-cooked lamb shanks or linguine with seafood in a rich tomato sauce.

In the area

Pizza Express *76 High Road, South Woodford, E18 2NA (8924 4488).*

INDEXES & MAPS

Greater London

MILL HILL

BAR

STANMORE   EDGWARE

FINCHLEY

PINNER

WEALDSTONE   KINGSBURY

HENDON

HARROW   KENTON

GOLDERS GREEN

HAMPS

p300

WEMBLEY

CRICKLEWOOD

NORTHOLT

WILLESDEN

p283 ST JO
WO

PERIVALE

HARLESDEN

KILBURN

KENSAL RISE

MAIDA VALE

GREENFORD

WEST

See p264-265

PADDING

EALING

ACTON

A40(M)

NOTTING HILL

SOUTHALL   HANWELL

M41

KENSINGTON

C

SHEPHERD'S BUSH

HAMMERSMITH

EARL'S COURT

CHEL

HESTON   M4

CHISWICK

p282

BRENTFORD   KEW

BARNES

FULHAM

PARSONS GREEN

HOUNSLOW

RICHMOND UPON THAMES

PUTNEY

p293

WANDSW

p28

TWICKENHAM

HANWORTH

TEDDINGTON

WIMBLEDON

SUNBURY

KINGSTON UPON THAMES

MERTON

HAMPTON

EAST MOLESEY

262 Time Out Cheap Eats

MORDEN

SURBITON

NEW MALDEN

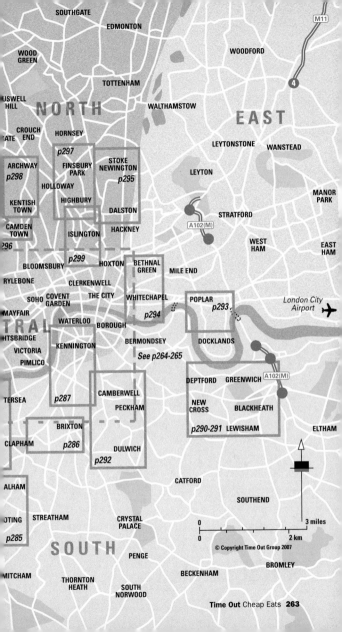

SOUTHGATE

EDMONTON

M11

WOOD
GREEN

WOODFORD

USWELL
HILL

TOTTENHAM

4

CROUCH
END

ATE

NORTH

WALTHAMSTOW

EAST

HORNSEY

ARCHWAY
p298

p297

FINSBURY
PARK

STOKE
NEWINGTON
p295

LEYTONSTONE

WANSTEAD

HOLLOWAY

LEYTON

MANOR
PARK

KENTISH
TOWN

HIGHBURY

DALSTON

STRATFORD

CAMDEN
TOWN

ISLINGTON

HACKNEY

A102(M)

WEST
HAM

EAST
HAM

296

p299

HOXTON

BETHNAL
GREEN

BLOOMSBURY

MILE END

RYLEBONE

CLERKENWELL

SOHO

COVENT
GARDEN

THE CITY

WHITECHAPEL
p294

POPLAR
p293

London City
Airport

MAYFAIR

WATERLOO

TRAL

BOROUGH

DOCKLANDS

HTSBRIDGE

KENNINGTON

BERMONDSEY

See p264-265

A102(M)

VICTORIA

PIMLICO

DEPTFORD

GREENWICH

TERSEA

p287

CAMBERWELL

PECKHAM

NEW
CROSS

BLACKHEATH

ELTHAM

CLAPHAM

BRIXTON
p286

DULWICH
p292

p290-291 LEWISHAM

ALHAM

CATFORD

OTING

STREATHAM

SOUTHEND

p285

SOUTH

CRYSTAL
PALACE

0   3 miles

0   2 km

© Copyright Time Out Group 2007

PENGE

MITCHAM

THORNTON
HEATH

SOUTH
NORWOOD

BECKENHAM

BROMLEY

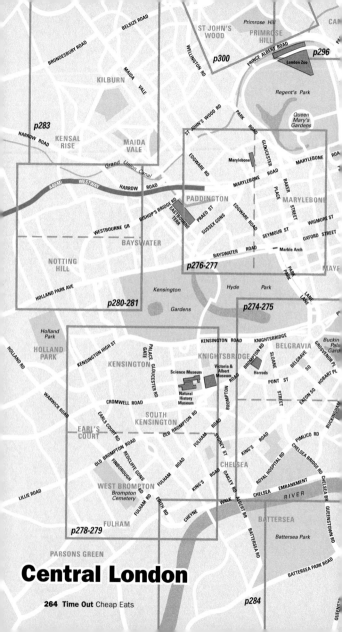

St John's Wood *p300*

PRIMROSE HILL

Primrose Hill

p296

CAM

BELSIZE ROAD

ST JOHN'S WOOD

WELLINGTON RD

PRINCE ALBERT ROAD

London Zoo

Regent's Park

BRONDESBURY ROAD

KILBURN

MAIDA VALE

ST JOHN'S WOOD RD

PARK ROAD

Queen Mary's Gardens

GLOUCESTER PLACE

p283

HARROW ROAD

KENSAL RISE

MAIDA VALE

Grand Union Canal

A40(M)   WESTWAY   HARROW   ROAD

Marylebone

MARYLEBONE   ROAD

BAKER STREET

MARYLEBONE

ROA

EDGWARE RD

MARYLEBONE

WESTBOURNE GR

BISHOP'S BRIDGE RD

EASTBOURNE TERR

PADDINGTON

PRAED ST

EDGWARE ROAD

WIGMORE ST

SEYMOUR ST

OXFORD STREET

SUSSEX GDNS

BAYSWATER

NOTTING HILL

p280-281

HOLLAND PARK AVE

BAYSWATER   ROAD

Kensington

Gardens

p276-277

Marble Arch

Hyde   Park

PARK   LANE

PARK LANE

MAYF

p274-275

Holland Park

HOLLAND PARK

KENSINGTON ROAD

KNIGHTSBRIDGE

Buckin Pala Gard

HOLLAND RD

KENSINGTON HIGH ST

PALACE GATE

GLOUCESTER

KENSINGTON

KNIGHTSBRIDGE

BROMPTON RD

SLOANE

BELGRAVE

BELGRAVIA

GROSVENOR PL

WARWICK ROAD

CROMWELL ROAD

Science Museum

Natural History Museum

Victoria & Albert Museum

BROMPTON

PONT ST

Harrods

CATON SQ

HOBART PL

SOUTH KENSINGTON

OLD BROMPTON RD

FULHAM   ROAD

ROAD

BUCKINGHAM

EARL'S COURT

EARLS COURT RD

SYDNEY ST

KING'S   ROAD

PIMLICO RD

CHELSEA BRIDGE RD

CHELSEA BR

OLD BROMPTON ROAD

REDCLIFFE GDNS

FINBOROUGH

FULHAM   ROAD

CHELSEA

ROYAL HOSPITAL RD

CHELSEA   EMBANKMENT

RIVER

LILLIE ROAD

WEST BROMPTON

Brompton Cemetery

FULHAM RD

EDITH RD

OAKLEY ST

ALBERT BR

KING'S ROAD

CHEYNE WALK

QUEENSTOWN RD

BATTERSEA

BATTERSEA RD

Battersea Park

p278-279

FULHAM

CHEYNE

PARSONS GREEN

BATTERSEA PARK ROAD

p284

Central London

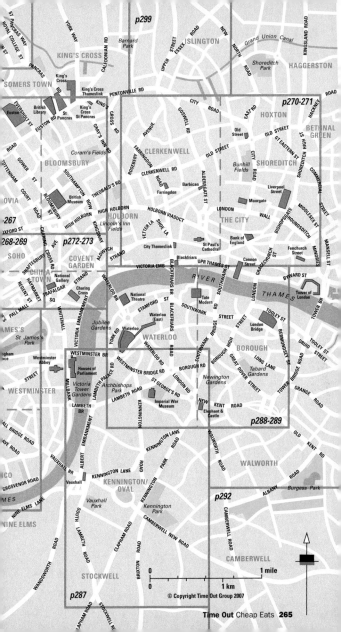

p299

p270-271

p272-273

p268-269

p288-289

p292

p287

ROYAL COLLEGE ST
ST PANCRAS WAY
PANCRAS RD
YORK WAY
CALEDONIAN RD
UPPER STREET
ESSEX STREET
LIVERPOOL ROAD
NEW NORTH ROAD
KINGSLAND ROAD
HACKNEY ROAD

KING'S CROSS
ISLINGTON
Barnard Park
Grand Union Canal
Shoreditch Park
HAGGERSTON

SOMERS TOWN
King's Cross
King's Cross Thameslink
PENTONVILLE RD
CITY ROAD
EAST RD
HACKNEY RD

Euston
British Library
St Pancras
King's Cross St Pancras
GRAY'S INN RD
GOSWELL RD
Old Street
OLD STREET
GT EASTERN ST
SHOREDITCH HIGH ST
COMMERCIAL STREET
BETHNAL GREEN

EVERSHOLT ST
EUSTON ST
GOWER ST
Coram's Fields
AVENUE
FARRINGDON
CLERKENWELL
CLERKENWELL RD
OLD STREET
CITY ROAD
Bunhill Fields
HOXTON
SHOREDITCH
MIDDLESEX ST
MANSELL ST

BLOOMSBURY
British Museum
SOUTHAMPTON ROW
THEOBALD'S RD
HIGH HOLBORN
Farringdon
Barbican
ALDERSGATE ST
Liverpool Street
Moorgate
LONDON WALL
BISHOPSGATE
HOUNDSDITCH

OVIA
COURT ROAD
TOTTENHAM
BLOOMSBURY ST
KINGSWAY
HOLBORN
HIGH HOLBORN
Lincoln's Inn Fields
HOLBORN VIADUCT
FETTER LA
SHOE LA
St Paul's Cathedral
THE CITY
Bank of England
Fenchurch Street
MINORIES

-267
268-269
OXFORD ST
SOHO
p272-273
CHARING CROSS RD
SHAFTESBURY AVE
COVENT GARDEN
ALDWYCH
City Thameslink
Blackfriars
UPR THAMES ST
Cannon Street
GRACECHURCH ST
BYWARD ST
Tower of London

CHINA TOWN
National Gallery
STRAND
WATERLOO BR
VICTORIA EMB
BLACKFRIARS BR
RIVER
SOUTHWARK
THAMES

HAYMARKET
REGENT ST
Charing Cross
TRAFALGAR SQ
Tate Modern
SOUTHWARK
London Bridge
TOOLEY ST
BERMONDSEY ST
DRUID STREET

AMES'S
PALL MALL
WHITEHALL
National Theatre
STAMFORD ST
Waterloo (East)
Waterloo
WATERLOO
STREET
SOUTHWARK BRIDGE
BOROUGH
Tabard Gardens
LONG LANE
TOOLEY ST
GRANGE ROAD

St James's Park
Westminster Abbey
Houses of Parliament
WESTMINSTER BR
Jubilee Gardens
YORK RD
WATERLOO RD
BOROUGH RD
Newington Gardens
GREAT DOVER STREET
TOWER BRIDGE ROAD

WESTMINSTER
MILLBANK
Victoria Tower Gardens
LAMBETH PALACE RD
WESTMINSTER BRIDGE RD
Archbishops Park
LAMBETH ROAD
ST GEORGE'S RD
LONDON RD
Imperial War Museum
NEW KENT ROAD
Elephant & Castle
OLD KENT ROAD

STREET
VAUXHALL BR
LAMBETH BR
KENNINGTON
BOROUGH RD
KENT ROAD
p288-289

BRIDGE ROAD
AVE ROAD
GROSVENOR ROAD
ALBERT EMBANKMENT
Vauxhall
KENNINGTON LANE
KENNINGTON ROAD
PARK ROAD
WALWORTH ROAD
WALWORTH
OLD KENT ROAD

AMES
NINE ELMS LANE
VAUXHALL BR
KENNINGTON/OVAL
Vauxhall Park
Kennington Park
CAMBERWELL NEW ROAD
ALBANY ROAD
Burgess Park
p292

WANDSWORTH ROAD
LAMBETH ROAD
CLAPHAM ROAD
BRIXTON ROAD
CAMBERWELL ROAD
CAMBERWELL

STOCKWELL
p287
CLAPHAM RD
STOCKWELL RD

0 — 1 mile
0 — 1 km

© Copyright Time Out Group 2007

Fitzrovia & Bloomsbury

0   300 m

0   300 yds

© Copyright Time Out Group 2007

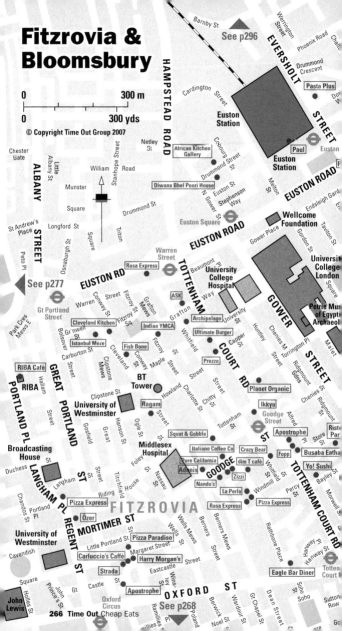

See p296

Barnby St

EVERSHOLT STREET

Wernington Street

Phoenix Road

HAMPSTEAD ROAD

Cardington Street

Drummond Crescent

Pasta Plus

Euston Station

Chester Gate

Netley St

Stanhope Street

African Kitchen Gallery

Cobourg Street

Drummond Street

Paul

Euston

Euston Station

ALBANY STREET

Little Albany St

William Road

Diwana Bhel Poori House

Gower St

Melton St

Euston St

Stephenson Way

EUSTON ROAD

Endsleigh Gard

Tavistock

Munster Square

Longford St

Euston Square

EUSTON ROAD

Gower Place

Wellcome Foundation

Gordon St

St Andrew's Place

Peto Pl

Osnaburgh St

Triton Square

Warren Street

TOTTENHAM

Beaumont Pl

University College Hospital

University Way

Universi College London

Gordon Square

See p277

Rasa Express

EUSTON RD

Fitzroy Square

Grafton Mews

Grafton

University

Huntley Street

Chenies M

Gower Place

Torrington Pl

Petrie Mus of Egyptia Archaeo

Gt Portland Street

Park Cres Mews E

Warren Street

Conway St

Cleveland Kitchen

ASK

Archipelago

Capper St

Gower

STREET

Ridgmount Gdns

Malet

Bolsover St

Grnwell St

Indian YMCA

Ultimate Burger

Carburton St

Istanbul Meze

Cleveland Mews

Fish Bone

Conway St

Maple Street

Fitzroy Street

Whitfield Street

Prezzo

Chenies Street

Ridgmount

RIBA Café

GREAT

Clipstone Mews

Hallam St

Clipstone St

BT Tower

Howland Street

Charlotte Street

Chitty St

Planet Organic

RIBA

PORTLAND PL

PORTLAND

University of Westminster

Ragam

Ogle St

Tottenham

Ikkyu

Alfred Pl

Store St

Riste Par

Apostrophe

PORTLAND

STREET

Gosfield

Hanson St

Great

Titchfield St

Squat & Gobble

Goodge Street

ST

Busaba Eatha

Broadcasting House

St

Langham St

Foley St

Nassau St

Middlesex Hospital

Italiano Coffee Co

Crazy Bear

Fopp

Whitfield Street

Fopp

Yo! Sushi

LANGHAM PL

Duchess St

Pure California

dim T café

TOTTENHAM COURT RD

Bayley St

REGENT

Chandos St

Portland St

Adonis

GOODGE

Zizzi

Percy St

Pizza Express

Nando's

La Perla

Windmill St

Pizza Express

Morwell St

University of Westminster

Pizza Express

MORTIMER ST

FITZROVIA

Wells Mews

Berners Mews

Rasa Express

Rathbone Place

Cavendish

Square

Özer

Little Portland St

Pizza Paradiso

Margaret Street

Berners Street

Hanway Pl

Hanway St

Totten Court

Carluccio's Caffè

Harry Morgan's

Eastcastle Street

Eagle Bar Diner

Strada

Wins ley St

Soho St

Soho Sq

Apostrophe

OXFORD ST

Poland

John Lewis

Holles St

Gt

John Prince's St

Castle St

Oxford Circus

See p268

Berwick

Gt Chapel St

Dean St

Sutton Row

Noel St

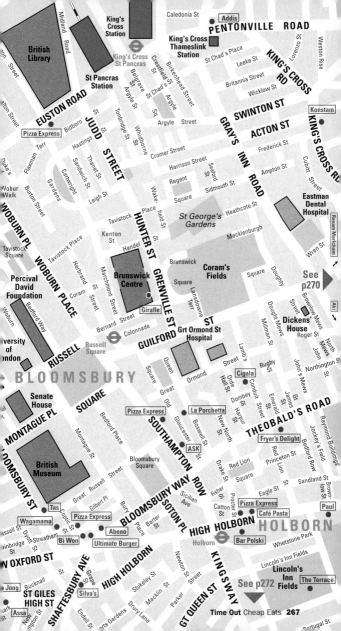

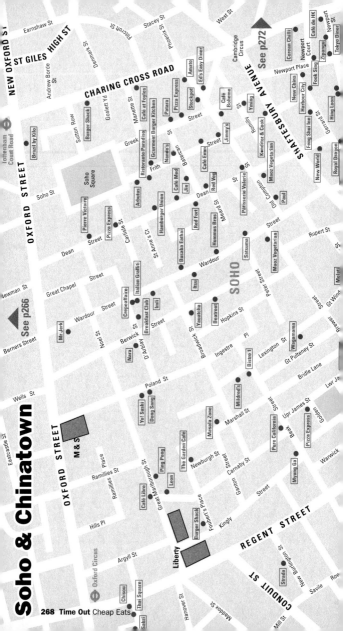

Soho & Chinatown

OXFORD STREET

NEW OXFORD ST
ST GILES HIGH ST

CHARING CROSS ROAD

SHAFTESBURY AVENUE

See p272

Cambridge Circus

Earnshaw St
Stacey St
West St
Newport Court

Andrew Borde St
Denmark St
Flitcroft St
Phoenix St
Newport Place

Sutton Row

Soho Square

Soho St

Dean Street

Great Chapel Street

Wardour Street

Newman St
Berners Street

See p266

Wells St

Eastcastle St

Ramillies St

Ramillies Place

Hills Pl

Oxford Circus

Argyll St

Hanover St

Maddox St

REGENT STREET

CONDUIT ST

New Burlington St

Savile Row

Mill St

Café de HK
Corean Chilli
Tokyo Diner
Zipangu
Fook Sing
New China
Harbour City
Feng Shui Inn
Ning Loon
New World
Royal Dragon

Greek Street
Frith Street
Bateman St
Dean Street
Old Compton Street

Amato
Ed's Easy Diner
Café Boheme
Yming
Jimmy's
Kendor & Cook
Maoz Vegetarian
Paul

Café at Foyles
Patara
Pizza Express
Stockpot

Burger Shack

Ristorante Paradiso
Gourmet Burger Kitchen
Nando's
Arbutus
Café Med
Jin
Hummus Bros
Red Veg
Pâtisserie Valerie

Pierre Victoire
Pizza Express
Hamburger Union
Red Fort

Busaba Eathai
Satsumi
Maoz Vegetarian

SOHO

Rupert St
Peter Street
Melati

Italian Graffiti
Crepeaffaire
Breakfast Club
Imli
Itsu
Yauatcha
Beatroot

Wardour Street

Hopkins St
Ingestre Pl

Bistro 1
Wagamama
Gt Pulteney St

Mr Jerk
Nara

Noel St
Berwick Street
Broadwick Street
D'Arblay Street

Lexington Street
Bridle Lane
Lwr Jar

Poland Street
Marshall Street

Yol Sushi
Dong Sang
Masala Zone
Mildred's

Great Marlborough St
Newburgh St
Carnaby Street
Ganton Street

Ping Pong
The Garden Café
Leon

Pure California
Beak St
Upr James St
Pizza Express
Myung Ga

Café Libre
Burger Shack
Foubert's Place
Kingly Street

Liberty

Golden
Warwick

Strada

Chisou
Thai Square
Sabri

Tottenham Court Road
Oxford Street
Berwick
Brewer Street
Gt Windmill St

268 Time Out Cheap Eats

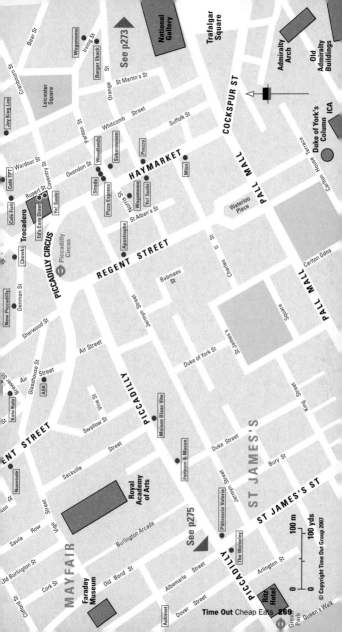

Bear St

Wagamama

Irving St

Burger Shack

St Martin's St

See p273

National Gallery

Trafalgar Square

Cranbourn St

Leicester Square

Orange

Street

Whitcomb

Suffolk Street

Admiralty Arch

Old Admiralty Buildings

COCKSPUR ST

Joy King Lau

Wardour St

Woodlands

Saharaween

Prezzo

HAYMARKET

Miso

Waterloo Place

Carlton House Terrace

Duke of York's Column

ICA

Café TPT

Oxendon St

Strada

Coventry St

Pizza Express

Yo! Sushi

Rupert St

Wagamama

Yo! Sushi

Norris St

St Alban's St

Apostrophe

PALL MALL

Café Fish

Edo Easy Diner

Trocadero

Chowki

PICCADILLY CIRCUS

Piccadilly Circus

REGENT STREET

Babmaes St

Charles II St

Carlton Gdns

PALL MALL

New Piccadilly

Denman St

Sherwood St

Jermyn

Street

Square

Air Street

Duke of York St

St James's St

NT STREET

Air

Street

Glasshouse St

ASK

Swallow St

Vine St

Vigo St

Sackville

Street

PICCADILLY

Maison Blanc Vite

Fortnum & Mason

Duke Street

Jermyn Street

Bury St

King

Street

ST JAMES'S

Kulu Kulu

Nouveau

Royal Academy of Arts

Burlington Arcade

See p275

Pâtisserie Valerie

ST JAMES'S ST

Savile Row

Old Burlington St

Clifford St

Cork St

MAYFAIR

Faraday Museum

Old Bond St

Albemarle Street

Dover Street

Automat

PICCADILLY

The Wolseley

Arlington St

Ritz Hotel

100 m

100 yds

0

© Copyright Time Out Group 2007

Green Park

Queen's Walk

Time Out Cheap Eats 269

The City, Clerkenwell, Shoreditch & Hoxton

See p299
See p267
See p272
See p288

CITY ROAD

City Road Basin

Coombs St

Graham Street

Moreland Street

Macclesfield Rd

Central Street

Wharton St

Lloyd Sq

Granville Square

Lloyd Baker Street

Margery Street

Spencer Street

ST JOHN STREET

Northampton Square

GOSWELL ST

Ashby St

Sebastian St

LEVER STREET

Fish Co

Dingle

King Sq

Central

Hardwick

Gloucester Way

Myddelton St

Wyclif

ROSEBERY AVE

ST JOHN STREET

Old China Hand

La Porchetta

Amwell Street

Merlin Street

Tysoe St

Whiskin St

Ambassador

Clark & Sons

SKINNER ST

Exmouth Market

PERCIVAL ST

Compton St

Woodbridge St

Agdon St

Cyrus St

Compton St

GOSWELL ROAD

Pear Tree St

Café Kick

Mount Pleasant Sorting Office

Corporation Row

House of Detention

Green La

Sekforde St

Seward St

Strada

Quality Chop House

The Eagle

Pear Tree Court

Bowling Green La

Clerkenwell Cl

Sans Walk

Aylesbury St

Compton St

Dallington St

Northburgh St

Gee St

Berry St

Bastwick Street

OLD STR

Little Bay

Farringdon Lane

The Real Greek Souvlaki & Bar

Great Sutton St

De Santis

Coach & Horses

Warner Street

CLERKENWELL

JOHN

CLERKENWELL RD

Cicada

ROSEBERY AVENUE

FARRINGDON ROAD

The Zetter

CLERKENWELL ROAD

Pizza Express

GOSWELL ROAD

Potemkin

Yo! Sushi

Xich Lô

Pho

St Barts Medical College

GRAY'S INN ROAD

CLERKENWELL RD

Anexo

Clerkenwell Grn

Museum of the Order of St John

St John's Sq

St John's La

Charterhouse

Fann St

Hatton Wall

Turnmill St

Britton St

Tinseltown

Charterhouse Square

HATTON GARDEN

Saffron Hill

Cross St

Kirby St

Pizza Express

Farringdon

Eagle Court

Charterhouse St

Barbican

BEECH

Portpool Lane

Leather La

Greville St

Cowcross St

Kurz & Lang

Verulam St

Baldwin's Gdns

Bleeding Heart Yd

Ely Pl

Tas

Smiths of Smithfields

LONG LANE

Kipferl

Ba

Gray's Inn

Konditor & Cook

Chancery Lane

Brooke St

Leather Lane

Le Comptoir Gascon

CHARTERHOUSE ST

Smithfield Market

Cloth Fair

Little Britain

Museum of London

Pizza Ex

ALDERSGATE ST

HOLBORN

Hatton Garden

Furnival St

CHANCERY LANE

New Fetter La

Fetter Lane

Cursitor St

Bream's Bldgs

SHOE LANE

Carluccio's Caffè

Hosier Lane

Cock Lane

Giltspur St

SMITHFIELD

St Bartholomew's Hospital

HOLBORN VIADUCT

Pizza Express

Stone La

Gough Sq

Dr Johnson's House

FARRINGDON ST

ST BRIDE ST

Fleet Lane

Old Bailey

NEWGATE

ANGEL ST

Goldsmiths Hall

Noble St

Gutter La

Foster Lane

Apostrophe

Paul

Leon

Warwick Lane

Paul

St Paul's

Paternoster Square

Paternoster Row

Pizz

CHEA

Carey St

Paul

Pizza Express

LUDGATE HILL

Wagamama

St Paul's Cathedral

ST PAUL'S CHYD

NEW CHANGE

Watling

Royal Courts of Justice

FLEET STREET

Prince Henry's Room

Inner Temple Lane

Middle Temple Lane

Crown Office Row

Whitefriars St

Bride La

Bouverie St

Dorset Rise

Bridewell Place

NEW BRIDGE ST

Pilgrim St

Ludgate Broadway

City Thameslink station

Strada

Carter Lane

Yo! Sushi

De Gustibus

St Paul's Chyd

Apostrophe

Godliman St

Watling

CANN

Essex St

Middle Temple

Inner Temple

Temple Ave

Temple La

Tudor Street

Carmelite St

John Carpenter Street

St Andrew's Hill

College of Arms

QUEEN VICTORIA ST

Mitford Lane

Temple

Blackfriars

Blackfriars Station

Castle Baynard Street

Castle Baynard St

White Lion Hill

UPPER THAMES ST

Painters' Hall

VICTORIA EMBANKMENT

BLACKFRIARS BRIDGE

Millennium Bridge

High Timber St

River Thames

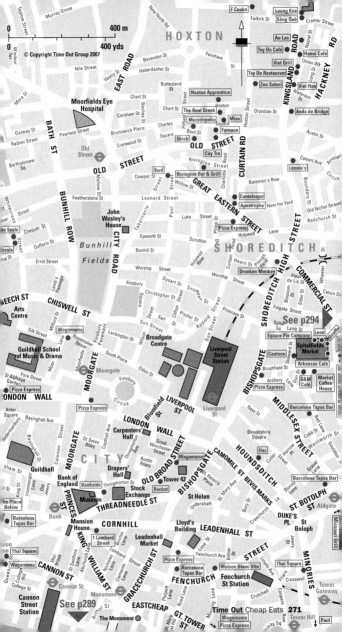

HOXTON

F Cooke
Loong Kee
Sông Quê
Falkirk St
Au Lac
Tay Do Café
Hanoi Café
Viet Grill
Tay Do Restaurant
Zen Satori
Viet Hoa
Anda de Bridge

Moorfields Eye
Hospital

Hoxton Apprentice
The Real Greek
Mise
Mezedopolio
Furnace
Shish
Boot St
Cây Tre
Lennie's

Yard
Rivington Bar & Grill

Cantaloupe
Apostrophe
Pizza Express

John
Wesley's
House

Bunhill
Fields

SHOREDITCH

Drunken Monkey

See p294

Arts
Centre

Wagamama

Guildhall School
of Music & Drama

Pizza Express

Square Pie Company
Leon
Spitalfields
Market
Canteen
Arkansas Cafe
S&M Café
Market
Coffee
House

Broadgate
Centre

Liverpool
Street Station

Pizza Express

Barcelona Tapas Bar

ONDON WALL

Pizza Express

Haz

Barcelona Tapas Bar

Carpenters'
Hall

Wagamama

Drapers'
Hall

Tower 42

CITY

Bank of
England
Bankside
Stock
Exchange
Rocket
St Helen
Lloyd's
Building

Museum

Barcelona
Tapas Bar
Thai Square
Mansion
House
1 Lombard
Street
Leadenhall
Market
Thai Square

Pizza Express
Barcelona Tapas Bar
Maison Blanc Vite
Fenchurch
St Station
Missouri Grill

he Place
Below

Cannon
Street
Station

See p289

Time Out Cheap Eats 271

The Monument

Wagamama
Pizza Express
Paul

© Copyright Time Out Group 2007

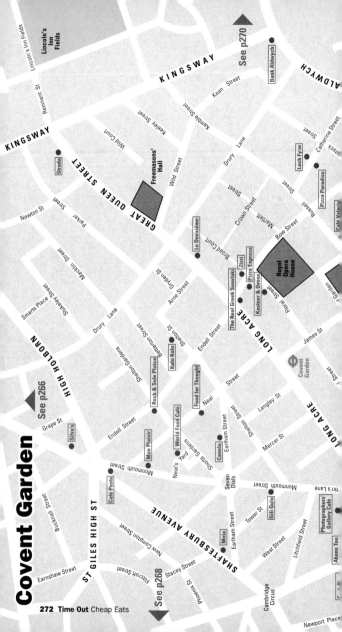

Covent Garden

272 Time Out Cheap Eats

Lincoln's Inn Fields

KINGSWAY

See p270

Bank Aldwych

ALDWYCH

Kean Street

Remnant St

Kemble Street

Keeley Street

Loch Fryne

Catherine Street

KINGSWAY

Wild Court

Drury Lane

Stock Street

Pizza Paradiso

Strada

GREAT QUEEN STREET

Freemasons' Hall

Wild Street

Crown Street

Russell Street

Café Valerie

Newton St

Parker Street

Macklin Street

Smarts Place

Stukeley Street

Drury Lane

Betterton Street

Shelton Gardens

Dryden St

Arne Street

Shelton St

Endell Street

La Deuxième

Broad Court

Zizzi

Pizza Express!

The Real Greek Souvlaki

Kastner & Ovens

Bow Street

Floral Street

Royal Opera House

LONG ACRE

James St

HIGH HOLBORN

See p266

Grape St

Silva's

Endell Street

Neal Street

Neal's Yard

Shorts Gardens

Mon Plaisir

World Food Café

Canela

Earlham Street

Rock & Sole Plaice

Kulu Kulu

Food for Thought

Langley St

Shelton Street

Mercer St

Covent Garden

LONG ACRE

I Street

Café Pasta

Buckhall Street

Monmouth Street

Seven Dials

Monmouth Street

tin's Lane

ST GILES HIGH ST

New Compton Street

SHAFTESBURY AVENUE

Mela

Earlham Street

Tower St

Gili Gulu

West Street

Litchfield Street

Photographers' Gallery Café

Abeno Too

Earnshaw Street

Flitcroft Street

Stacey Street

See p268

Phoenix St

Cambridge Circus

Newport Place

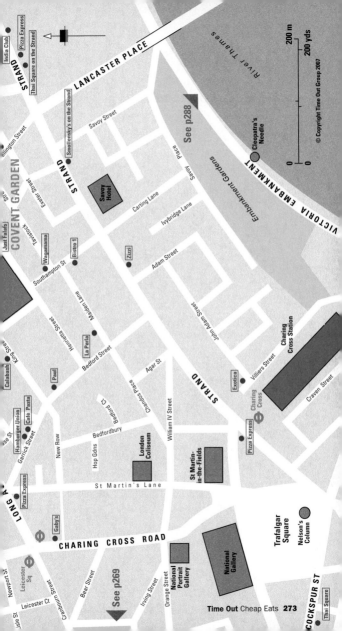

India Club
Pizza Express
Thai Square on the Strand

STRAND

LANCASTER PLACE

Smollensky's on the Strand

Wellington Street

Savoy Street

River Thames

See p288

Cleopatra's Needle

COVENT GARDEN

Exeter Street

Tavistock Street

STRAND

Savoy Hotel

Carting Lane

Ivybridge Lane

Savoy Place

Embankment Gardens

VICTORIA EMBANKMENT

200 m
200 yds

© Copyright Time Out Group 2007

Just Falafs

Wagamama

Bistro 1

Southampton St

Zizzi

Adam Street

Maiden Lane

Henrietta Street

La Perla

Bedford Street

Basil

Calabash

King Street

Agar St

Chandos Place

Bedford Ct

William IV Street

John Adam Street

STRAND

Villiers Street

Charing Cross Station

Charing Cross

Exotica

Craven Street

Hamburger Union

Café Pasta

Garrick Street

New Row

Bedfordbury

Hop Gdns

London Coliseum

St Martin's Lane

St Martin's-in-the-Fields

Pizza Express

LONG A

Pizza Express

Gaby's

CHARING CROSS ROAD

See p269

National Portrait Gallery

Newport St

Leicester Sq

Leicester Ct

Bear Street

Irving Street

Orange Street

National Gallery

Trafalgar Square

Nelson's Column

Lisle St

Cranbourn Street

Time Out Cheap Eats **273**

COCKSPUR ST

Thai Square

Knightsbridge, Belgravia, Victoria & Pimlico

Duke of York St
Jermyn Street
ST JAMES'S SQUARE
PALL MALL
King St
Bury St
Park Pl
St James's St
Marlborough Rd
St James's Palace
Clarence House
Stableyard Rd
Mall
ST JAMES'S PARK
Guards Museum
Home Office
Palmer St
Caxton St
Petty France
Vandon
Dilton
ARTILLERY ROW
Howick Pl
Pizza Express
Spencer House
Lancaster House
See p272
Arlington St
Ritz Hotel
Green Park
Queen's Walk
Birdcage Walk
See p288
Wellington Barracks
BUCKINGHAM GATE
Westminster City Hall
Wagamama
Zizzi
Pizza Express
VICTORIA STREET
Westminster
Dover St
Berkeley St
Stratton St
Bolton St
Clarges St
Half Moon St
White Horse St
Shepherd Market
Shepherd Street
Market Mews
Curzon St
Derby St
Brick Street
Down Street
Old Park Lane
Hamilton Place
Queen Victoria Memorial
Spur Road
Buckingham Palace
Queen's Gallery
Royal Mews
Buckingham Palace Gardens
Constitution Hill
BUCKINGHAM PALACE RD
Stafford Place
Victoria Square
Stag Place
Cardinal Place
BRESSENDEN PL
ASK
Pizza Express
Allington St
Sekara
Tiles
LWR GROS PL
GROSVENOR GDNS
GROSVENOR GDNS
Belgrave Mews
Lower Belgrave St
ECCLE
SQUARE
Dorchester Grill Room
MAYFAIR
Chesterfield St
Queen St
Waverton St
Hay's Mews
Charles St
Chesterfield Hill
PARK LANE
PARK LANE
Curzon Place
Pezzo
Apsley House
HYDE PARK
GROSVENOR PLACE
Chester Mews
Chapel Street
Groom Place
Wilton Street
Headfort Pl
Wilton Crescent
Montrose Pl
Upper Belgrave Street
BELGRAVE SQUARE
Eaton Place
Eaton Mews North
Eaton Square
BELGRAVE PL
CHESHAM PL
Lyall Mews
Lyall St
Chesham Street
Chesham St
Cadogan Lane
Cadogan
PONT ST
SLOANE
Hyde Park Corner
GROSVENOR CRES
Old Barrack Yard
Wilton Row
Wilton Pl
Belgrave Mews West
Kinnerton Street
Lowndes Square
William Mews
Harriet Walk
Morpeth Terrace
Pâtisserie Valerie
Yo! Sushi
KNIGHTSBRIDGE
Wagamama
SLOANE STREET
Pavilion Road
Hans Place
Hans Street
Lowndes St
Halkin place
Pavilion Road
Lowndes Place
South Carriage Drive
William Street
Serpentine Road
The Serpentine
Ranoush Juice Bar
Knightsbridge Green
Raphael St
Brompton Pl
KNIGHTSBRIDGE ROAD
Pâtisserie Valerie
Harrods
Basil Street
Hans Cres
Basil St
Hans Rd
Watton Pl
BEAUCHAMP PL
Brompton Gdns
Ovington Gdns
Pizza Express
PONT ST
Lennox Gdns
Clabor
HYDE PARK
Rotten Row
KENSINGTON
Trevor
Montpelier Terrace
Montpelier Street
Montpelier Place
Montpelier Walk
Rutland Gate
BROMPTON ROAD
Leon
See p278
Cheval Place
Rutland St
Brompton Square
Pâtisserie Valerie
The Oratory
Yeoman's Row
Egerton Terr
Ennismore

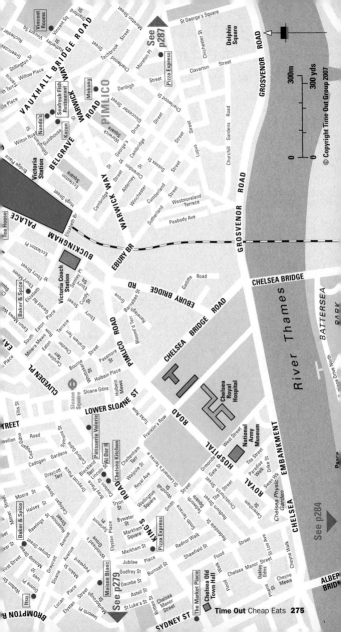

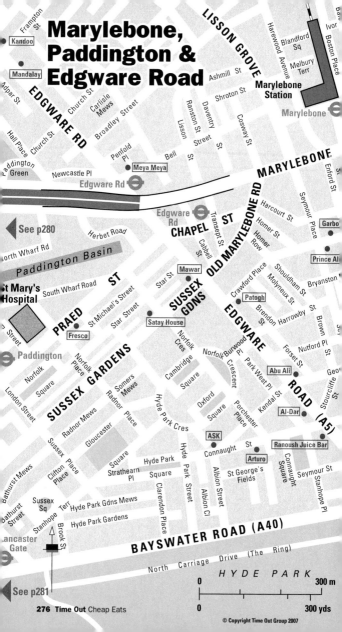

Marylebone, Paddington & Edgware Road

Frampton St

Kandoo

Mandalay

Adpar St

EDGWARE RD

Hall Place

Church St

Church St

Carlisle Mews

Broadley Street

Penfold Pl

Newcastle Pl

Paddington Green

Meya Meya

Bell St

Lisson Street

Ranston St

Daventry St

Shroton St

Ashmill St

LISSON GROVE

Harewood Avenue

Blandford Sq

Melbury Terr

Boston Place

Ivor

Marylebone Station

Marylebone ⊖

Cosway St

MARYLEBONE

Enford St

Edgware Rd ⊖

Edgware Rd ⊖

Transept St

CHAPEL ST

OLD MARYLEBONE RD

Harcourt St

Homer St

Homer Row

Seymour Place

Garbo

Prince Al

See p280

Herbet Road

North Wharf Rd

Paddington Basin

St Mary's Hospital

South Wharf Road

St Michael's Street

PRAED ST

Star St

Star Street

Fresco

Sussex GDNS

Mawar

Satay House

Norfolk Cres

Crawford Place

Patogh

Shouldham St

Molyneux St

Bryanston

Brendon St

Harrowby St

Brown St

EDGWARE

Nutford Pl

Forset St

Paddington ⊖

Norfolk Square

London Street

Norfolk Place

Somers Mews

SUSSEX GARDENS

Radnor Mews

Gloucester

Cambridge Square

Hyde Park Cres

Oxford Square

Norfolk Crescent

Burwood Pl

Park West Pl

Porchester Place

Abu Ali

Kendal St

ROAD (A5)

Stourcliffe St

Al-Dar

Ranoush Juice Bar

Geo

Bathurst Mews

Sussex Place

Clifton Place

Radnor Place

Square

Strathearn Pl

Hyde Park Square

Hyde Park Street

Connaught St

ASK

Albion Street

Albion Cl

Arturo

St George's Fields

Connaught Square

Seymour St

Stanhope Pl

Sussex Sq

Bathurst Street

Stanhope Terr

Hyde Park Gdns Mews

Hyde Park Gardens

Clarendon Place

Brook St

Lancaster Gate

See p281

BAYSWATER ROAD (A40)

North Carriage Drive (The Ring)

HYDE PARK

0   300 m

0   300 yds

© Copyright Time Out Group 2007

Ali Baba

Woodlands

Cornwall Terrace

York Terrace

Outer Circle

Upr Harley St

York Terrace East

Madame Tussaud's

Royal Academy of Music

London Planetarium

West

MARYLEBONE ROAD

Baker Street

ASK

Phoenix Palace

Pizza Express

Eat & Two Veg

University of Westminster

MARYLEBONE

Fresco

The Real Greek Souvlaki & Bar

Yo! Sushi

Original Tajines

Strada

Ishtar

Quiet Revolution

Pâtisserie Valerie at Sagne

Providores & Tapas Room

Le Pain Quotidien

Royal China Club

Giraffe

Paul

See p266

Royal China

Golden Hind

Woodlands

Maison Blanc

Pizza Express

Paul Rothe & Son

Levant

ASK

WIGMORE ST

Zizzi

Bistro 1

Grand Bazaar

Tootsies Grill

Eat-Thai.net

Pizza Paradiso

Wagamama

Carluccio's Caffè

Fine Burger Company

Bang! Sausage Bar & Grill

Apostrophe

Pizza Express

SEYMOUR ST

Selfridges

Busaba Eathai

Rasa W1

M&S

Yo! Sushi

Bond St

OXFORD ST

Square Pie Company

ASK

North Row

Marble Arch

Princess Gardens

CUMB'LAND GATE

Speakers' Corner

Grosvenor Square

See p268

PARK LANE

See p274

Time Out Cheap Eats **277**

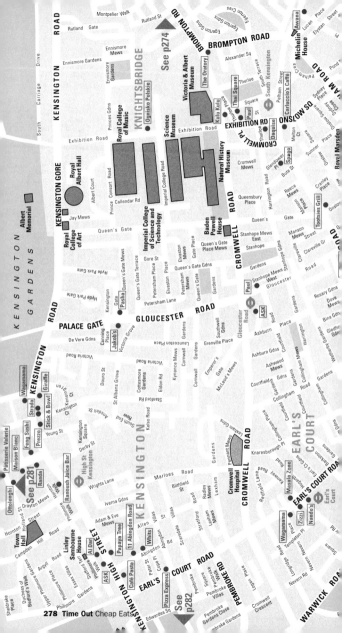

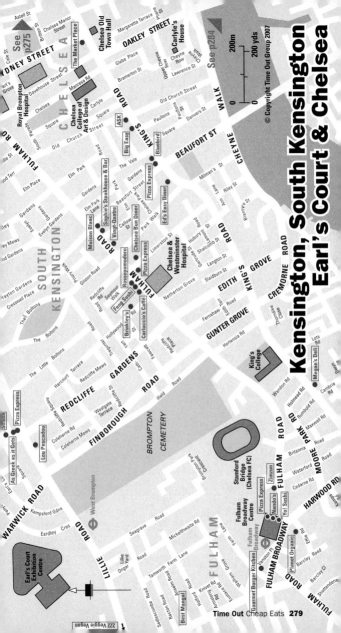

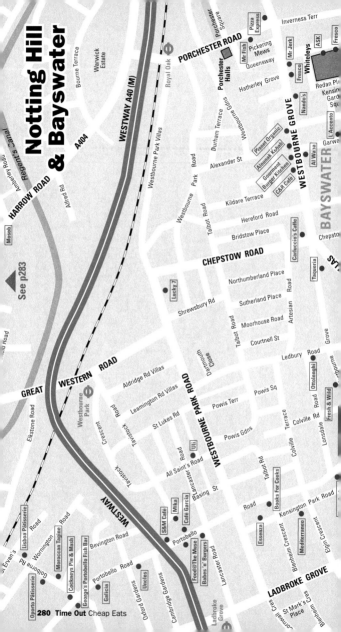

Notting Hill & Bayswater

Inverness Terr

Warwick Estate

Bourne Terrace

Porchester Terrace

Porchester Square

PORCHESTER ROAD

Mr Fish

Pizza Express

Pickering Mews

Queensway

Royal Oak

WESTWAY A40 (M)

A404

Mr Jerk

ASK

Fresco

Whiteleys

Hatherley Grove

Fresco

Porchester Halls

Nando's

Redan Pla
Kensin
Gard
Squ

L'Accento

Westbourne Park Villas

Durham Terrace

Westbourne Gdns

Planet Organic

Aloumak Kabab

Al Waha

Garwa

Alexander St

Gourmet Burger Kitchen

WESTBOURNE GROVE

BAYSWATER

C&R Café

Westbourne Park Road

Kildare Terrace

Hereford Road

Talbot Road

Bridstow Place

Carluccio's Caffè

Chepst

HARROW ROAD

Alfred Rd

Mosob

Aunqueley Rd

Regent's Canal

See p283

CHEPSTOW ROAD

Northumberland Place

Lucky 7

Shrewsbury Rd

Sutherland Place

Moorhouse Road

Artesian Road

Taqueria

Courtnell St

GREAT WESTERN ROAD

Elkstone Road

Aldridge Rd Villas

Leamington Rd Villas

Westbourne Park

Tavistock Road

St Lukes Rd

Crescent

Dartmouth Close

Powis Sq

Powis Terr

WESTBOURNE PARK ROAD

Powis Gdns

Colville Terrace

Ledbury Road

Ottolenghi

Fresh & Wild

Lonsdale Road

Colville Rd

WESTWAY

Golborne Rd

Wornington Road

Lisboa Pâtisserie

Moroccan Tagine

Cockneys Pie & Mash

George's Portobello Fish Bar

Galicia

Oporto Pâtisserie

Bevington Road

Portobello Road

Uncles

Oxford Gardens

Cambridge Gardens

S&M Café

Mika

Café Garcia

Basing St

All Saint's Road

Lancaster Road

Portobello

Fnod@The Muse

Babes 'n' Burgers

Blenheim Crescent

LADBROKE GROVE

Essenza

Books For Cooks

Kensington Park Road

Mediterraneo

Elgin Crescent

St Mark's
Place

Blenheim Cres

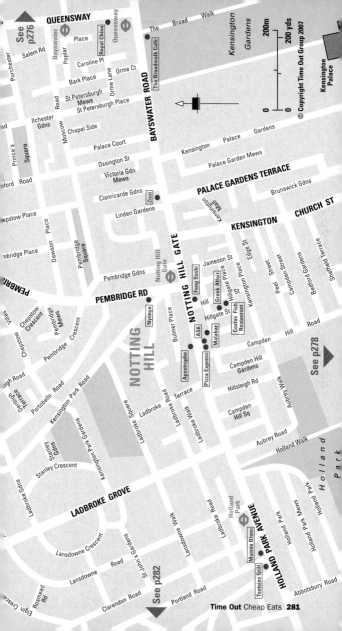

QUEENSWAY

See p276

Kensington Gardens

The Broad Walk

200m
200 yds

© Copyright Time Out Group 2007

Salem Rd

Porchester

Bayswater
Poplar
Place
Royal China
Queensway

Caroline Pl

Orme Ct

Bark Place
Orme Lane

Road
St Petersburg
Mews
St Petersburg Place

Moscow

The Broadwalk Café

Kensington
Palace

Ilchester
Gdns

Chapel Side

BAYSWATER ROAD

Prince's
Square

Palace Court

Kensington   Palace   Gardens

Ossington St

Victoria Gdn
Mews

Palace Garden Mews

eford   Road

Clanricarde Gdns

Zizzi

PALACE GARDENS TERRACE

Brunswick Gdns

hepstow Place

Linden Gardens

Kensington
Mall

KENSINGTON   CHURCH ST

mbridge Place

Dawson

Pembridge Square

NOTTING HILL GATE

Jameson St

Edge St

Peel   Street

Bedford Gardens

Sheffield Terrace

PEMBR

Chepstow Crescent

Pembridge Mews

Pembridge Gdns

Notting Hill
Gate

Feng Sushi

Hill

Greek Affair

Hillgate Place

Kensington Place

PEMBRIDGE RD

Nyonya

NOTTING HILL GATE

Hillgate St

Costas Fish
Restaurant

Camden

Hill

Road

See p278

Chepstow

Pembridge

Crescent

NOTTING HILL

Bulmer Place

ASK

Malabar

Camden   Hill   Gardens

igh Road

Portobello   Road

Kensington Park Road

Apostrophe

Pizza Express

Hillsleigh Rd

Camden
Hill Sq

ease   Terrace

Ladbroke Square

Ladbroke   Terrace

Ladbroke Walk

Aubrey Walk

Holland

Aubrey Road

Holland Walk

Park

Stanley
Gdns

Kensington Park Gardens

Ladbroke   Road

Stanley Crescent

LADBROKE GROVE

Ladbroke   Road

Lansdowne Walk

Holland
Park

Holland Park Mews

Holland Park

Ladbroke Gdns

See p282

Lansdowne Crescent

St John's Gardens

Maison Blanc

HOLLAND PARK AVENUE

Holland Park

Lansdowne   Road

Tootsies Grill

smead
Rd

Rosmead
Road

Clarendon Road

Portland Road

Abbotsbury Road

in Cres

Elgin

Time Out Cheap Eats **281**

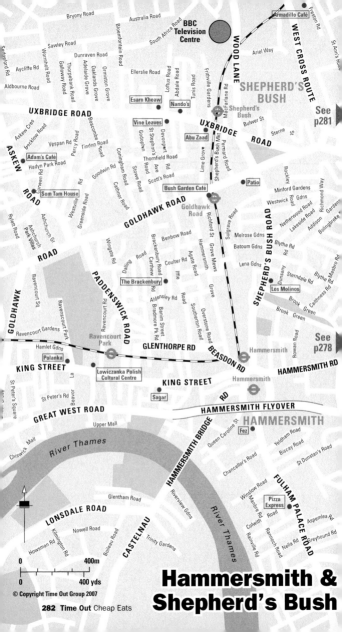

Hammersmith & Shepherd's Bush

Armadillo Café
Feston Rd
BBC Television Centre
WEST CROSS ROUTE
Bryony Road
Australia Road
South Africa Road
St Ann's Road
WOOD LANE
Ariel Way
SHEPHERD'S BUSH
Sawley Road
Wormholt Road
Dunraven Road
Bloemfontein Road
Ellerslie Road
Loftus Road
Addale Road
Frithville Gardens
MacFarlane Rd
Aycliffe Rd
Galloway Road
Thorpebank Road
Oaklands Grove
Adelaide Grove
Ormiston Grove
Esarn Kheaw
Nando's
Tunis Road
Shepherd's Bush
Bulwer St
See p281
Aldbourne Road
UXBRIDGE ROAD
Vine Leaves
St Stephen's
Godolphin
UXBRIDGE ROAD
Sterne St
Askew Cres
Crackbow Road
Percy Road
Boscombe Road
Findon Road
Devonport
Abu Zaad
Shepherd's Bush Mkt
Lime Grove
ASKEW ROAD
Adam's Café
Hadyn Park Road
Vespan Road
Coningham Road
Thornfield Road
Ave
Rd
Scott's Road
Goodwin Road
Patio
Minford Gardens
Rockley
Richmond Way
Som Tam House
Cathnor Road
Westville
Greenside Road
Stowe Road
Bush Garden Café
SHEPHERD'S BUSH ROAD
Westwick Gdns
Netherwood Road
Lakeside Rd
Addison
Bolingbroke
GOLDHAWK ROAD
Goldhawk Road
Richford St
Sulgrave Road
ROAD
Ashchurch Gr
Ashchurch Park Villas
Melrose Gdns
Batoum Gdns
Blythe Rd
Matbro Rd
Benbow Road
Brackenbury Road
Grove Mews
Hammersmith
Lena Gdns
Dunsany Rd
Sterndale Rd
Blythe Rd
Rylett Road
Wingate Rd
Dalling Rd
Carthew Road
Coulter Rd
Agate Road
Grove
Caithness Rd
PADDENSWICK ROAD
The Brackenbury
Iffle
Road
Hammersmith
Los Molinos
Brook
Green
Ravenscourt
Aldensley Rd
Banim Street
Bradmore Pk Rd
Southerton Road
Overstone Road
Brook Green
GOLDHAWK ROAD
Ravenscourt Gardens
Ravenscourt Park
Ravenscourt Sq
Rd
La
GLENTHORPE RD
BEASDON RD
Hammersmith
Rowan Road
See p278
Hamlet Gdns
Polanka
KING STREET
Lowiczanka Polish Cultural Centre
KING STREET
Sagar
Hammersmith
HAMMERSMITH RD
St Peter's Rd
GREAT WEST ROAD
St Peter's Square
RD
HAMMERSMITH FLYOVER
HAMMERSMITH
Upper Mall
Chiswick Mall
River Thames
HAMMERSMITH BRIDGE
Queen Caroline St
Fez
Yeldham Road
Chancellor's Road
Biscay Rd
St Dunstan's Road
Riverview Gdns
Glentham Road
LONSDALE ROAD
Winslow Road
Menteath Rd
Pizza Express
FULHAM PALACE ROAD
Aspenlea Rd
Nowell Road
Killington Rd
Boileau Rd
Colwith
Rannoch Road
Nella Road
Greyhound Rd
Howsman Rd
CASTELNAU
Trinity Gardens
River Thames
Rainville Rd

0   400m
0   400 yds

© Copyright Time Out Group 2007

Maida Vale & Kilburn

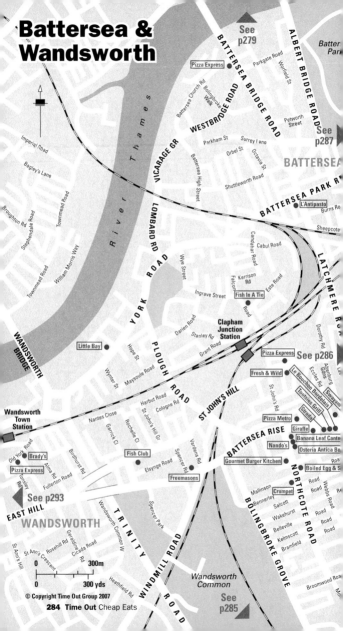

Battersea & Wandsworth

See p279

Pizza Express

BATTERSEA BRIDGE ROAD

ALBERT BRIDGE ROAD

Batter Park

Parkgate Road

Worfield St

Battersea Church Rd

Bolingbroke Walk

WESTBRIDGE ROAD

Petworth Street

VICARAGE GR

See p287

Parkham St

Surrey Lane

Orbel St

Octavia St

BATTERSEA

Battersea High Street

Shuttleworth Road

River Thames

BATTERSEA PARK R

L'Antipasto

Burns Ro

LOMBARD RD

Candahar Road

Cabul Road

Sheepcote

LATCHMERE R

Wye Street

Kerrison Rd

Este Road

Ingrave Street

Falcon

Fish In A Tie

Road

YORK ROAD

Darien Road

Stanley Rd

Clapham Junction Station

Imperial Road

Begley's Lane

Townmead Road

Broughton Rd

Stephendale Road

William Morris Way

Townmead Road

Wynter St

Hope St

Maysoule Road

Little Bay

PLOUGH ROAD

Grant Road

Dorothy Rd

Pizza Express

See p286

Fresh & Wild

Le Bouchon Bordelais

Eccles Rd

Falkirk Gdns

Swaine

St John's Rd

Footsee Grill

Strada

WANDSWORTH BRIDGE

Harbut Road

Cologne Rd

Wandsworth Town Station

Nantes Close

Garrick Rd

Rochelle Cl

St John's Hill Gr

Old York Road

Brady's

Pizza Express

Ainsty Rd

Horsley Rd

Fullerton Road

Birdhurst Road

Fish Club

Vardens Rd

Spencer Rd

Elsynge Rd

Freemasons

ST JOHN'S HILL

Pizza Metro

Giraffe

Banana Leaf Cante

BATTERSEA RISE

Nando's

Osteria Antica Bo

Gourmet Burger Kitchen

Boiled Egg & S

NORTHCOTE ROAD

Crumpet

Mallinson

Road

Webbs Rd

BOLINGBROKE GROVE

Bennerley

Road

Salcott

Road

Wakehurst

Road

Belleville

Road

Kelmscott

Road

Bramfield

Road

See p293

EAST HILL

WANDSWORTH

TRINITY

Spencer Park

WINDMILL ROAD

ROAD

St Ann's Hill

St Ann's Crescent

Rosehill Rd

Geraldine Rd

Cicada Road

0   300m

0   300 yds

Heathfield Rd

Wandsworth Common

See p285

Broomwood Roa

© Copyright Time Out Group 2007

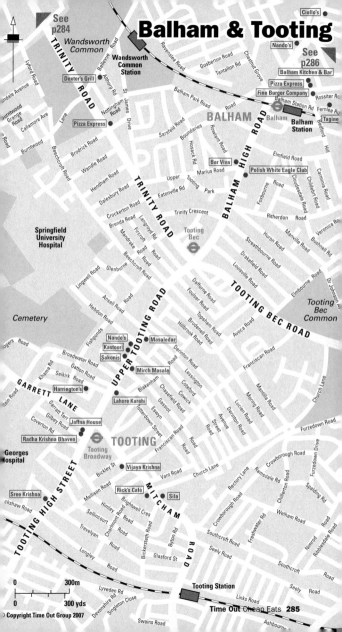

Balham & Tooting

See p284

Wandsworth Common

Ciullo's

Nando's

See p286

Balham Kitchen & Bar

Pizza Express

Fine Burger Company

Rossiter Rd

Wandsworth Common Station

Dexter's Grill

Balham Station Rd

Fernlea Rd

Tagine

Pizza Express

BALHAM

Balham Station

Bar Viva

Polish White Eagle Club

Springfield University Hospital

Tooting Bec

TOOTING BEC ROAD

Tooting Bec Common

Cemetery

Nando's

Masaledar

Kastoori

Sakonis

Mirch Masale

Harrington's

Lahore Karahi

GARRETT LANE

Jaffna House

Radha Krishna Bhaven

Georges Hospital

TOOTING

Tooting Broadway

Vijaya Krishna

Sree Krishna

Rick's Café

Sila

TOOTING HIGH STREET

MITCHAM ROAD

Tooting Station

0   300m
0   300 yds

© Copyright Time Out Group 2007

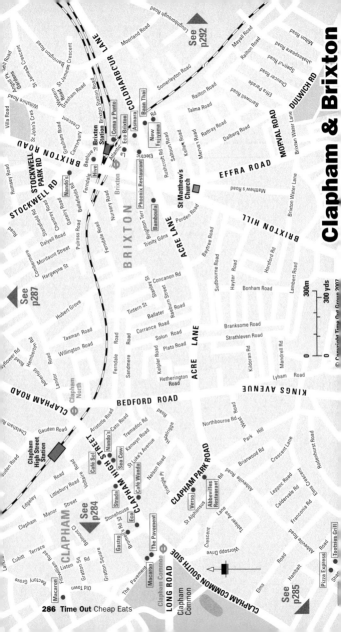

Clapham & Brixton

See p292

See p287

See p284

See p285

Loughborough Road · Moorland Road · Mayall Road · Milton Road · Shakespeare Road · Spenser Road · Chaucer Road · Effra Parade · Barnwell Road

Somerleyton Road · Railton Road · Talma Road · Rattray Road · Dalberg Road

BRIXTON STATION ROAD · COLDHARBOUR LANE

Baan Thai · Asmara · New Fujiyama

Coma y Punto · Eco Brixton

Brixton Station

Atlantic Rd · Electric Av · La Rd

Phoenix Restaurant

Bamboula

St Matthew's Church

Porden Road

EFFRA ROAD

MORVAL ROAD · DULWICH RD

Brixton Water Lane · Brixton Water Road

BRIXTON HILL

Matthew's Road

STOCKWELL PARK RD · BRIXTON ROAD

Nando's

Hive

BRIXTON

ACRE LANE

Wiltshire Road · St John's Cres · St James's Crescent · St James's Road · Kellett Rd · Gardens · Barrington Road · Gresham Road · Western Road · Crescent · Canterbury · Beehive Pl · Ferndale · Brixton · Nursery Road · Bellefields Rd · Gatieff Road · Chantry Road · Stanfield Road

Rumsey Road · Villa Road · Combermere · Mordaunt Street · Hargwyne St · Dalyell Road

Rushcroft Rd · Saltoun Road · Merva Rd

Baytree Road · Sudbourne Road · Hayter Rd · Horsford Rd · Lambert Road · Bonham Road

Concanon Rd · Stanley St · Raebun Road · Tintern St · Ballater · Corrance Road · Solon Road · Plato Road · Kelpler Road · Sandmere · Ferndale Road

Branksome Road · Strathleven Road · Mandrell Rd · Kildoran Rd · Lyham Road

Hubert Grove · Tasman Road · Willington Road

Trinity Gdns · Brighton Terr

300m · 300 yds

© Copyright Time Out Group 2007

ACRE LANE · Hetherington Road

KINGS AVENUE

Clapham North

BEDFORD ROAD

CLAPHAM ROAD

Gauden Road

Clapham High Street Station

HIGH STREET · CLAPHAM

Aristotle Road · Cato Road · Tremadoc Rd · Kenwyn Road · Nelson Road · Triangle Pl

Nando's · Café Sol · Strada · Sea Cow · Eco · Café Wanda

Northbourne Rd · West Rd · Park Hill · Briarwood Road · Crescent Lane · Leppoc Road · Calderdale Rd · Franconia Rd

CLAPHAM PARK ROAD

Versa · Abbevilles Restaurant · St Alphonsus · Tabbier Ave · Abbeville Rd · Abbeville Road · Rodenhurst Road · Elms Crescent · Abbeville Road · Hambalt Road · Elms Road · Abbeville Crescent

Pizza Express · Tootsies Grill

Chelsham Road · Venn Road · Littlebury Road · Edgeley · Manor Street · Belmont Cl · Bromell's Rd · Stonehouse · Liston Rd · Gratton Rd · Gratton Square

St Luke's Avenue

Gastro · Eco · The Pavement

CLAPHAM · Cubitt Terrace · Rectory Grove · Old Town · Liston Road · Larkhall Rise · Clapham

Macaron · Macaron · The Pavement

LONG ROAD · CLAPHAM COMMON SOUTH SIDE

Worsopp Drive · Einns Road

Clapham Common

286 Time Out Cheap Eats

Big Ben
Florence
Nightingale
Museum
WESTMINSTER
BRIDGE
ROAD
WATERLOO RD
See
p288
St. Thomas's
Hospital
LAMBETH PALACE RD
BAYLIS RD
Lambeth
North
St. George's
Circus
BOROUGH RD
LONDON RD
Houses of
Parliament
St Thomas's
Medical School
Lambeth
Palace
Gardens
LAMBETH ROAD
LAMBETH ROAD
LAMBETH ROAD
ST GEORGE'S ROAD
South Bank
University
NEWINGTON CAUSEWAY
Victoria
Tower
Gardens
The Courtyard
Café
Archbishop's
Park
Imperial War
Museum
Nando's
Lambeth
Palace
LAMBETH
Geraldine Mary
Harmsworth
Park
West
Square
Elephant
& Castle
LAMBETH
BRIDGE
See
p275
ALBERT
EMBANKMENT
Pratt Walk
High St
Old Paradise St
Newport Street
Lambeth Walk
Ravent St
Glasson Rd
Juxon Street
Walnut Tree Walk
Fitzalan Street
Lollard Street
St. Mary's
Gardens
Leisure
Centre
Elephant
& Castle
Pizzeria Castello
River Thames
Vauxhall Walk
Randall Rd
Black Prince Road
Newburn St
Salamanca St
Jonathan St
Tyers St
Wickham St
Market
Way
Hotspur St
Lollard St
Wincott
Street
Reedworth St
Chester
Way
Renfrew Rd
Dante Rd
Hampton St
The Lobster Pot
KENNINGTON ROAD
Madeira
Glasshouse Walk
Tinworth St
Orsett St
Sancroft
Street
Courtenay
Street
Cleaver St
Wheatley St
Cleaver
Sq
Kennings Way
Opal
Kennington
KENNINGTON LANE
KENNINGTON PARK ROAD
Alberta Street
Penton Place
Camberley Pl
Manor Place
Laud St
St Oswald's Pl
Tyer's Terr
Newburn St
Loughboro Rd
Pizza Express
Ravensdon St
Braganza Street
Doddington Grove
Westcott Rd
Lorrimore Square
Vauxhall
Station
HARLEYFORD RD
KENNINGTON LANE
Oval Way
Farnham Royal
KENNINGTON
De Laune Street
Sharsted Street
Harmsworth St
Cook's Rd
Fleming Rd
Lorrimore Rd
Lorrimore Street
Hillingdon Street
Grosvenor Terr
Bonnington
Centre Café
Langley Lane
Bonnington
Square
KENNINGTON OVAL
The Oval
Cricket
Ground
Kennington
Road
Clayton Street
Bowling Green St
Magee St
Kennington Park
Place
Royal Road
Otto St
Bolton
Cres
John Ruskin Street
Bethwin Road
Lawn Lane
Oval
Hanover Gdns
Claylands Road
Prima Rd
St Agnes Place
CAMBERWELL NEW ROAD
See
p292
VAUXHALL
FENTIMAN ROAD
Meadow
Mews
Rita Road
Heyford
Ave
Meadow
Road
Usborne Mews
Offley Rd
Richborne Terr
Place
Cranmer Road
Foxley Road
Wyndham Road
Bar Estrela
SOUTH LAMBETH ROAD
Dorset Road
Carroun Road
Oval Place
Palfrey
Place
Handforth Rd
Crewdson Rd
CLAPHAM ROAD
South Island Place
Mowll St
Vassall Road
Patmos Road
Liberty Street
Caldwell Street
Hackford Road
BRIXTON ROAD
Cancell Road
Hampson Way
Durand Gdns
Southey Rd
Cranworth Rd
Gosling Way
Cowley Road
300m
300 yds
© Copyright Time Out Group 2007
See
p284
Stockwell
See
p286
Guildford Road
Portland Grove
Aldebert Terr
thorne Road
sdowne Way

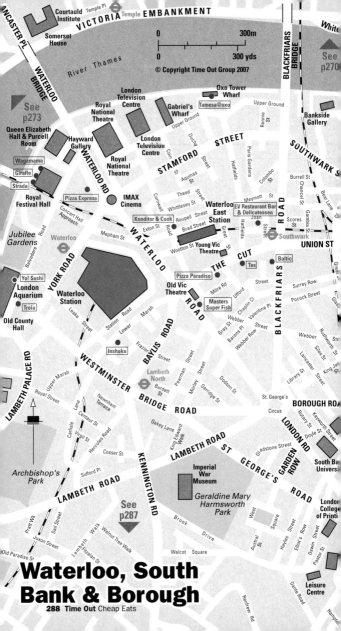

Waterloo, South Bank & Borough

Time Out Cheap Eats

See
p293 River Thames

Gosterwood Street
EVELYN STREET
Prince Street
Watergate St
DEPTFORD
Childers Street
Roll Street
CREEK ROAD
Thames St
Abinger Grove
Staunton St
Arklow Rd
Creek
West Lake
Edward St
Manze's
A.J Goddard
Copperas St
Greenwich Park
Bar & Grill
Roan Street
Straightsmouth
Deptford
Street
Crossfield St
NORMAN ROAD
Greenwich
Station
Amersham Vale
Deptford
Station
Creekside
DEPTFORD CHURCH ST
Beard St
Milton Court Rd
Tandoori Xpress
High
Street
GREENWICH HIGH ROAD
Circus St
Inside
Edward
Douglas
Way
Giffin St
Ashburnham Pl
GREENWICH SOUTH ST
Buenos
Café &
New Cross
Station
New Cross
Frankham St
Reginald Rd
Egerton Drive
Devonshire Dr
Blisset St
NEW CROSS ROAD
Thailand
BLACKHEATH ROAD
Guildford Gr
NEW CROSS
FLORENCE RD
Noodle King
Vanguard St
Coldbath Street
Morden
LEWISHAM WAY
Tanners Hill
Albyn Road
Cranbrook Rd
Friendly Street
BROOKMILL ROAD
Elverson Rd
LEWISHAM ROAD
Blackh
MALPAS ROAD
Rokeby Road
Upper Brockley Rd
Meze Mangal
Ashmead Road
St Johns Vale
Albyn Road
Barriedale Street
Shardeloes Road
Endwell Rd
Manor Avenue
Wickham Road
Breakspears Road
Tressillian Road
St Johns
Station
LOAMPIT HILL
Lewisham
Station
THURSTON RD
Ashby
Road
Everest
Curry King
LOAMPIT VALE
Upper Brockley Rd
Geoffrey Road
Tyrwhitt
Road
Shell Road
Algernon
Road
Elmira St
MOLESWORTH ST
Brockley
Station
Cranfield
Road
Brookbank
Road
Ermine
Embleton
Ellerdale St
Somethi
Fish
Harefield
Road
Wickham Road
BROCKLEY ROAD
Breakspears Road
Tressillian Road
Hilly Fields Cres
Clifaview Road
LEWISHAM
LEWISHAM HIGH ST
Montague Avenue
Marsala Road
Court
0   300 yds
ADELAIDE AVENUE
Veda Road
Vicars Hill
Algiers Road
Road
0   300 yds
Ivy Road
Ladywell Road
© Copyright Time Out Group 2007
LADYWELL ROAD
Ladywell
Station
Brockley Grove
290 Time Out Cheap Eats

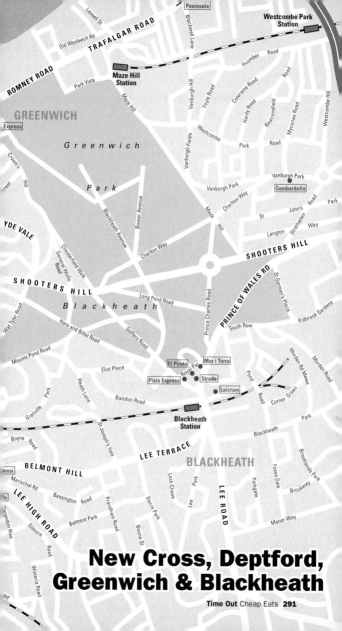

Peninsula

Westcombe Park
Station

Lassell St

Old Woolwich Rd

TRAFALGAR ROAD

Blackwell Lane

Humber Road

Romney Road

Park Vista

Maze Hill
Station

Vanburgh Hill

Foyle Road

Coleraine Road

Hardy Road

Beaconsfield Road

Mycenae Road

Westcombe Hill

GREENWICH

Express

Croom's

Greenwich

Westcombe

Park

Road

Vanburgh Park

Gambardella

Street

Hill

Park

Vanburgh Fields

Vanburgh Park

Charlton Way

St John's Road

Park

YDE VALE

Blackheath Avenue

Bower Avenue

Charlton Way

Maze Hill

Langton

Strathaden Way

SHOOTERS HILL

Chesterfield Walk

General Wolfe Road

PRINCE OF WALES RD

St German's Place

Kidbrook Gardens

SHOOTERS HILL

Long Pond Road

Prince Charles Road

South Row

Blackheath

Wat Tyler Road

Hare and Billet Road

Goffers Road

Morden Rd Mews

Morden Road

Mounts Pond Road

Eliot Place

Royal Par

Mar i Terra

El Pirata

Pizza Express

Strada

Baizdon Road

Laicram

Pond Road

Corner Green

Heath Lane

St Joseph's Vale

Blackheath
Station

Park

Granville Park

Blackheath

Boyne Road

LEE TERRACE

BLACKHEATH

Lock Chase

Lee Park

Foxes Dale

Parkgate

Brooklands Park

Brookway

BELMONT HILL

Mar i Terra

Marischal Rd

Bessington Road

Belmont Park

Prendham Road

Boone St

Dacre Park

Lee

LEE ROAD

Manor Way

LEE HIGH ROAD

Gilmore

Road

arendon Rise

Wisteria Road

ad

New Cross, Deptford, Greenwich & Blackheath

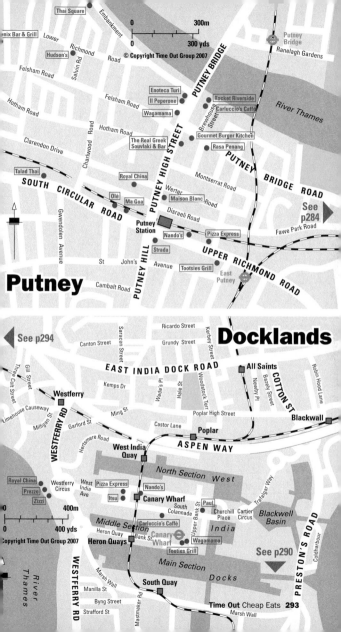

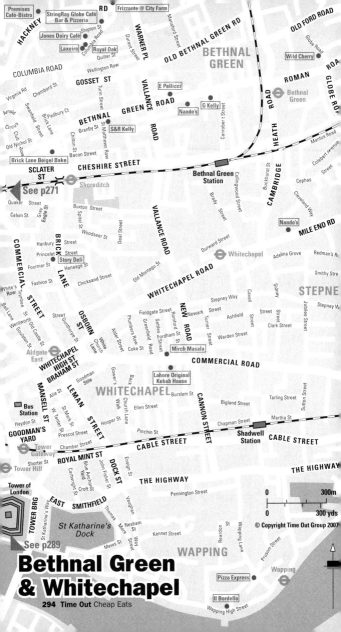

Premises Café-Bistro

HACKNEY

StringRay Globe Café Bar & Pizzeria

RD

Frizzante @ City Farm

Jones Dairy Café

Shipton St

Quilter St

Duran Street

Columbia Road

OLD FORD ROAD

OLD BETHNAL GREEN RD

Globe Road

WARNER PL

Royal Oak

Laxeiro

BETHNAL GREEN

Wellington Row

ROMAN ROAD

Wild Cherry

COLUMBIA ROAD

GOSSET ST

HEATH ROAD

GLOBE RD

Virginia Rd

Chambord St

Turin Street

VALLANCE ROAD

E Pellicci

ROAD

Bethnal Green

Arnold Circus

Swanfield St

Padbury Ct

BETHNAL GREEN ROAD

Nando's

G Kelly

Mantus Road

Brick Lane

Club Row

Granby St

St Matthews Row

Carrober t Street

Colebert Avenue

CAMBRIDGE

Old Nichol St

Chilton St

S&R Kelly

Cephas

Buckhurst St

Cleveland Way

Brick Lane Beigel Bake

Bacon Street

CHESHIRE STREET

SCLATER ST

See p271

Shoreditch

Bethnal Green Station

Collingwood Street

Brady Street

Quaker Street

Grey Eagle St

Buxton Street

Calvin St

Spital Street

Woodseer St

Deal Street

VALLANCE ROAD

Durward Street

Whitechapel

Nando's

MILE END RD

COMMERCIAL STREET

BRICK LANE

Hanbury Street

Princelet Street

Story Deli

Fournier St

Heneage Street

Fashion St

Chicksand Street

Old Montagu St

WHITECHAPEL ROAD

Adelina Grove

Redman's Rd

Smithy Stre

White Row

Toynbee

Bell Lane

Street

Wentworth Old Castle St

Coulston St

OSBORN ST

Gunthorpe St

White Church Lane

Aldgate East

Fieldgate Street

Plumbers Row

Greenfield Road

Settles Street

Romford Street

Fordham Street

Aldar Street

Coke St

NEW ROAD

Newark Street

Turner Street

Warden Street

Stepney Way

Ashfield Street

Cavell Street

Sidney Street

Clark Street

STEPNE

Jubilee Street

Stepney Wa

WHITECHAPEL HIGH ST

BRAHAM ST

Mirch Masala

COMMERCIAL ROAD

WHITECHAPEL

MANSELL ST

LEMAN STREET

Goodman Stile

Gower's

Baze

Church Lane

Alie St

St Mark St

W Tenter St

Prescot Street

Lahore Original Kebab House

Burslem St

Ellen Street

Hooper St

CANNON STREET

Bigland Street

Chapman Street

Tarling Street

Sutton Street

Martha St

Pinchin St

Shadwell Station

CABLE STREET

Bus Station

Haydon St

GOODMAN'S YARD

Tower Gateway

Chamber Street

CABLE STREET

Tower Hill

Shorter St

ROYAL MINT ST

DOCK ST

Ensign St

John Fisher St

Cartwright St

THE HIGHWAY

THE HIGHWAY

Tower of London

TOWER BRG

EAST SMITHFIELD

Blue Anchor Yard

Croft St

Vaughan Way

Thomas More

Nesham St

Pennington Street

Kennet Street

Reardon

Bewley Prusom Street

0   300m

0   300 yds

© Copyright Time Out Group 2007

See p289

St Katharine's Dock

St Katharine's Way

Mews St

Way

WAPPING

Wapping

Pizza Express

Bethnal Green & Whitechapel

Il Bordello

Wapping High Street

294 Time Out Cheap Eats

Stoke Newington & Dalston

Abney Park Cemetery

STAMFORD HILL

Stoke Newington Station

Cazenove Road

Alkham Road

Kyverdale Road

Osbaldeston Road

NORTHWOLD RD

Yoakley Road

Lordship Road

Bouverie Road

Il Bacio Express

Rasa Travancore

Abu Ruchi

Itto

Fresh & Wild

Arcora St

Stoke Newington Common

Jenner Road

RECTORY ROAD

STOKE NEWINGTON CHURCH STREET

Blue Legume

Il Bacio

Rasa

Dumont Rd

Brooke

Leswin

Darville Road

Baystone Road

Clissold Park

See p297

STOKE NEWINGTON

Defoe Road

Hawksly Rd

Kynaston Road

Chesholm Rd

Lavers Rd

Tyssen Rd

Rectory Road Station

Evering

Stoke Newington Church Street

Woodlea Road

Sandbrook Rd

Oldfield Road

Harcombe Rd

Nevill Road

Dynevor Road

Bodrum Café & Bar

STOKE NEWINGTON HIGH ST

Tin Phát

Café Z Bar

Testi

Clissold Road

ALBION ROAD

Barbauld Road

Londesborough Road

Nevill Road

Victoria Grove

Sydner Road

Rectory Road

Carysfort Road

Clissold Crescent

Beatty Road

Amhurst Road

Burma Road

Springdale Road

Arden Grove

Winston Road

Milton Grove

Shakespere

Walk

Allen Road

Spenser Grove

Wordsworth Road

Walford Road

Brighton Road

Palatine Road

Foulden Road

Farleigh Road

Shacklewell Road

Shacklewell Lane

Beyti

GREEN LANES

Leconfield Road

Sariyer Balik

Howard Road

Cowper Road

Prince George Rd

Belgrade Rd

Princess May Rd

STOKE NEWINGTON ROAD

Somerford Gr

Somerford Gr

Poets Road

Matthias Road

Barrett's Grove

Mangal Ocakbasi

Arcola St

Ferntower Road

Pyrland Road

Woodville Road

King Henry's St

Mildmay Road

Boleyn Road

Crossway

Istanbul Iskembecisi

Mangal II

Nando's

19 Numara Bos Cirrik

Alvington Cres

Downs Park Road

St Mark's Rise

Sandringham Road

Road

Beresford Terrace

NEWINGTON GREEN RD

Mildmay

Wolsey Rd

Queen Margaret's Gr

Sömine

Dalston Kingsland Station

Birkbeck Rd

Colvestone Crescent

Grosvenor Terr

Mildmay Grove North

Mildmay Grove South

Mildmay Park

King Henry's Walk

CAM at Centerprise

Ridley Road

KINGSLAND HIGH ST

Brampton Park

Bingham Road

Shanghai

PAUL'S RD

BALLS POND ROAD

DALSTON LANE

Dove Road

Culford Mews

Southgate

KINGSLAND

Roseberry Place

Beechwood Road

Laurel St

Buttermere Walk

See p299

ESSEX ROAD

Ockendon Road

Buckingham Road

Ardleigh Road

Culford Road

De Beauvoir Road

Stamford Rd

Hertford Rd

Tottenham Road

Suya Obalende

Forest

Richmond Road

KINGSLAND ROAD

QUEENSBRIDGE ROAD

Parkholme Rd

Road

LMNT

DALSTON

300m

300 yds

© Copyright Time Out Group 2007

Huong-Viet

De Beauvoir Square

Faulkner's

Englefield Road

Time Out Cheap Eats **295**

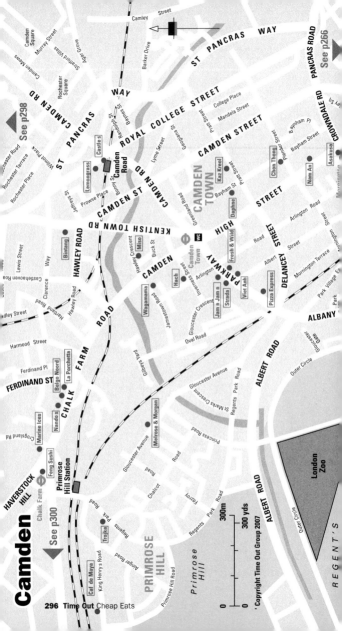

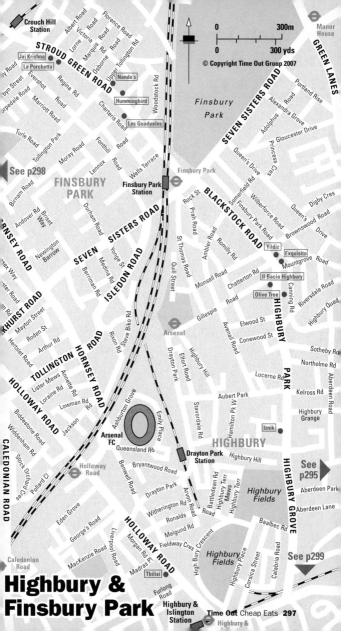

Highbury & Finsbury Park

Crouch Hill Station

Jai Krishna
La Porchetta
STROUD GREEN ROAD
Nando's
Hummingbird
Los Guadales

Albert Road
Florence Road
Victoria Road
Lorne Road
Marquis Rd
Osborne Road
Upper Tollington Rd
Woodstock Rd

Regina Rd
Charteris Road

Evershot Road
Marriott Road

Turle Road
Tollington Park
Moray Road
Lennox Road
Fonthill Road

Finsbury Park

SEVEN SISTERS ROAD
Portland Rise
Alexandra Grove
Adolphus Road
Gloucester Drive
Princess Cres
Queen's Drive
Digby Cres
Queen's
Brownswood Drive

See p298

FINSBURY PARK

Finsbury Park Station
Finsbury Park

Wells Terrace
Durham Road

Somerfield Rd
Finsbury Park Road
Wilberforce Road

Rock St
BLACKSTOCK ROAD

Prah Road
Ambler Road
Romilly Rd

Yildiz
Exquisito
Mountgrove Rd

Il Bacio Highbury
Olive Tree

HIGHBURY

SEVEN SISTERS ROAD
Yonge St
Medina Rd
Berriman Rd
ISLEDON ROAD
HORNSEY ROAD

St Thomas Road
Quill Street
Monsell Road
Chatterton Rd
Canning Rd
Riversdale Rd
Highbury Quad

Gillespie Road
Elwood St
Conewood St
Sotheby Rd
Northolme Rd
Aberdeen Road

Binsam Road
Andover Rd
Briset Way
Newington Barrow

Arsenal
Avenell Road
Lucerne Road
Kelross Rd
Highbury Grange

Mayton Street
Roden St
Arthur Rd
Hertslet Road

Steve Biko Rd
Rixon Rd
Drayton Park

Hamilton Pk W
Aubert Park
Iznik

TOLLINGTON ROAD
Lister Mews
Loraine Rd
Annette Rd
Lowman Rd
Jackson

HORNSEY ROAD
Ashburton Grove
Emily Place
Eltort Road
Highbury Hill
Stavordale Rd

HIGHBURY
Highbury Hill
See p295

Arsenal FC
Queensland Rd

Drayton Park Station

Highbury PARK
Aberdeen Park
Aberdeen Lane

HOLLOWAY ROAD
Biddestone Road
Widdenham Rd
Stock Orchard Cres
Pollard Ct

Holloway Road
Benwell Road
Bryantwood Road

Battledean Rd
Highbury Terr Mews
Highbury Terr

Highbury Fields
Baalbec Rd

CALEDONIAN ROAD
Eden Grove
George's Road
Liverpool Road
MacKenzie Road

Drayton Park
Witherington Rd
Ronalds Rd
Melgund Rd
Fieldway Cres

Arvon Road
Road

High Bury Crescent

Highbury Fields
Highbury Place
Corsica Street
Calabria Road

See p299

Caledonian Road

HOLLOWAY ROAD
Morgan Pl
Madras Pl
Tbilisi

Furlong Road

Highbury & Islington Station

© Copyright Time Out Group 2007

Manor House
GREEN LANES

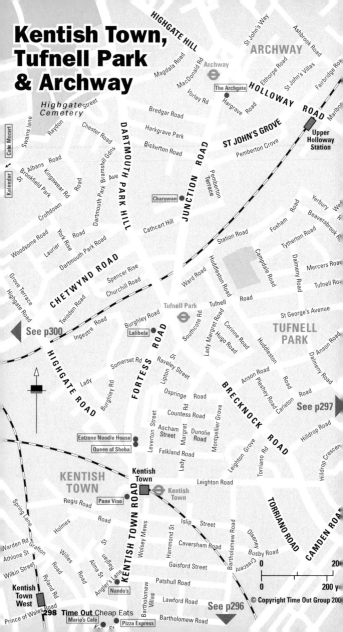

Islington

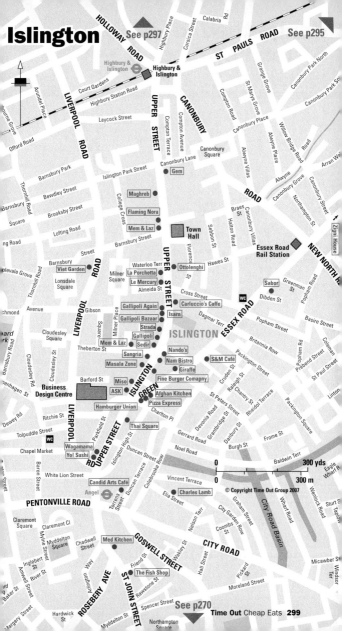

See p297
See p295

HOLLOWAY ROAD

Calabria Rd

Corsica Street

Highbury Place

ST PAULS ROAD

Canonbury Park North

Grange Grove

Canonbury Park South

Highbury & Islington

Highbury & Islington

Court Gardens

City Road

St Marys Grove

Willow Bridge Road

Alwyne Road

Canonbury Road

Highbury Station Road

Compton Road

Arundel Place

LIVERPOOL ROAD

UPPER STREET

Laycock Street

Compton Terrace

CANONBURY

Compton Avenue

Canonbury Place

Alwyne Villas

Alwyne Place

Arran W

Offord Road

Canonbury Square

Barnsbury Park

Islington Park Street

Canonbury Lane

Gem

ROAD

Braes St

Canonbury Villas

Alwyne

Canonbury Grove

Northampton St

Canonbury Street

Bewdley Street

College Cross

Maghreb

Halton Road

Brooksby Street

Flaming Nora

Barnsbury Road

Barnsbury Square

Lofting Road

Mem & Laz

Barnsbury Street

Town Hall

Sebbon St

Florence

Hawes St

Essex Road Rail Station

Zizzi House

NEW NORTH R

ng Road

Street

Barnsbury

Viet Garden

LIVERPOOL ROAD

UPPER STREET

Waterloo Terr

La Porchetta

Ottolenghi

Cross Street

Sabor

Greenman St

Popham Road

Lonsdale Square

Milner Square

Le Mercury

Almeida St

Dibden St

pevale Grove

Thornhill Road

Gibson

Gallipoli Again

Carluccio's Caffe

WC

Dagmar Terr

Popham Road

Basire Street

richmond

Avenue

Cloudesley Square

Milner Street

Gallipoli Bazaar

Isarn

Strada

Britannia Row

Prebend St

Coleman

ward

Park Road

Barnsbury Road

Sharens

Gallipoli

Mem & Laz

ISLINGTON

ESSEX ROAD

Packington Street

Cruden St

St Paul Street

Linton

Theberton St

Sedir

Nando's

Sangria

Nam Bistro

S&M Café

Raleigh St

Packington Square

Cloudesley Rd

Masala Zone

Giraffe

St Peters Street

Rheidol Terrace

enhagen St

Barford St

Miso

ISLINGTON GREEN

Fine Burger Comapny

Devonia Road

Danbury St

Frome St

Business Design Centre

ASK

Afghan Kitchen

Gerrard Road

Grantbridge St

Burgh St

Baldwin Terr

Eagle Wharf Rd

Dewey Rd

Hamburger Union

Pizza Express

Charlton Pl

Ritchie St

Parkfield St

LIVERPOOL RD

UPPER STREET

Thai Square

Noel Road

Vincent Terrace

0   300 yds

Tolpuddle Street

WC

Islington High St

Duncan Street

Gerrard Road

0   300 m

Chapel Market

Wagamama

Yo! Sushi

White Lion Street

Colebrooke Row

© Copyright Time Out Group 2007

Baron Street

PENTONVILLE ROAD

Candid Arts Cafe

Angel

Torrens Street

Duncan Terrace

Ella Street

Charles Lamb

City Garden Row

Graham Street

Wharf Road

City Road Basin

Wenlock Road

Claremont Square

Claremont Cl

Myddelton Square

Inglebert St

River St

Chadwell Street

GOSWELL STREET

CITY ROAD

Nelson Terr

Coombs St

Graham Street

Micawber St

Windsor Terr

Amwell St

Med Kitchen

Wakley St

Hall Street

Moreland Street

Sturt St

Baker St

ROSEBERY AVE

ST JOHN STREET

Friend St

The Fish Shop

Rawstone St

Spencer Street

Pickard St

Hardwick St

Myddelton St

Northampton Sq

Margery St

See p270

Menu glossary

a

accra saltfish cakes.
ackee a fruit tasting like scrambled eggs when it is cooked; often served with salt cod.
adai fermented rice and lentil pancakes.
adana a spicy minced lamb kebab.
agedashidofu fried tofu sprinkled with dried fish, in shoyu (qv) broth.
agedofu fried tofu.
aioli garlic mayonnaise.
albóndigas meatballs in a tomato sauce.
aloo potato.
arnavut ciğeri 'Albanian liver' fried then baked.
avial a mixed vegetable curry in a coconut and yoghurt sauce.
ayam the Malaysian word for chicken.

b

baba ganoush toasted aubergine purée.
bacalao or **bacalhau** salt cod.
baklava filo pastry with nuts, and served covered in syrup.
banh pho rice noodles.
banh xeo Vietnamese crispy filled pancake.
barszcz Polish borscht.
bastilla filo pastry filled with pigeon (or chicken), spices and almonds, and dusted with sugar.
béchamel sauce a white sauce made with flour, milk and butter.
bento meal served in a compartmentalised box.
beyti spicy mince and garlic kebab.
bhajee a 'dry' dish of vegetables cooked with various spices.
bhaji vegetables deep-fried in spicy gram flour.
bhaturas puffed discs of deep-fried bread.

bhel poori a snack of puffed rice, deep-fried vermicelli, pooris (qv) and assorted chutneys.
bhindi okra.
bibimbap rice, veg and meat with a raw or fried egg on top.
bifana marinated pork steak in a roll.
bigos hunters' stew.
bindaedok fried savoury pancake, made of mung bean flour, vegetables and (sometimes) minced beef.
biriani rice cooked with meat or vegetables.
blini a pancake made from buckwheat flour.
bocadillo a crusty roll that is filled with ham or cheese, etc.
boquerones anchovies.
börek or **böreği** filo pies with savoury fillings.
borekas Jewish filo pastries with fillings such as cheese or spinach.
borscht beetroot soup.
bresaola dried fillet of beef, sliced thinly.
brik a fried pastry parcel filled with egg and mince.
brinjal aubergine.
bruschetta garlic toast.
bulgogi marinated beef barbecued at table.
bun rice vermicelli.
burrito a filled cornmeal pancake.

c

cacik diced cucumber with garlic in yoghurt.
calamares squid.
caldo verde a cabbage, potato, olive oil and chouriço sausage soup.
calpis or **calpico** a sweet soft drink derived from milk.
calzone folded, stuffed and deep-fried pizza.
ceviche marinated seafood salad.
chaat snack.

cha gio spring rolls containing vermicelli and herbs.
chakchouka a spicy pepper and tomato stew.
channa chickpea.
chao tom minced prawns barbecued on a stick of sugar cane.
chapati flat bread.
char kway teow rice noodles wok-fried with meat and/or seafood and beansprouts.
char siu marinated barbecued pork.
chermoula a dry rub of herbs and spices.
cheung fun slithery rice flour pasta with various fillings; a dim sum dish.
chirashi sushi (qv) atop a bowl of rice.
cholent a stew of meat and beans.
chollah egg-rich, slightly sweet bread.
chorizo spicy sausage.
churros sugared dough-sticks.
ciger tava fried liver.
codornices quails.
çop şiş cubes of lamb.
concasse a pulp of tomatoes and garlic.
couscous semolina; couscous royale is a stew of lamb, chicken and merguez (qv).
crema catalana creamy custard dessert.
crostini savoury toasts.

d

dahi yoghurt.
dahl lentil curry similar to thick lentil soup.
dhansak spicy stew of meat, lentils and veg.
dim sum dumplings and other titbits.
dobrada tripe stew.
dolma stuffed veg (usually with rice and pine kernels).
dolmádes stuffed vine leaves.

donburi a bowl of rice with various toppings.
döner sliced lamb (or mince) kebab.
dosa or **dosai** crisp, filled pancakes.

edamame salted soy beans boiled in pods.
empanadillas small savoury pies.
enjera spongy flatbread.
escoveitched fish fish fried then pickled in a tangy sauce.

fajita grilled beef or chicken wrapped in warm flour tortillas.
falafel fried spicy chickpea patty.
falooda thick, sweet milk drink with vermicelli, nuts, etc.
fasólia plakí white beans in a tomato and herb sauce.
feijoada pork and black bean stew.
festival deep-fried, slightly sweet dumpling.
futomaki thick-rolled sushi (qv).
fuul brown broad beans, mashed with garlic, oil and lemon juice.

gado gado vegetable salad with a peanut-based sauce on top.
gajar halwa grated carrots cooked in cardamom milk.
galangal 'lesser ginger', a spice added to South-east Asian dishes.
gambas ajillo prawns with garlic.
garbanzos chickpeas.
gefilte fish white fish minced with onions and seasoning, made into balls and poached or fried; served cold.
gnocchi potato and flour pasta 'dumpling'.
goblaki cabbage parcels, usually stuffed with rice, kasha (qv) or meat.

gohan rice.
gosht lamb.
goulash rich beef soup.
gunkan round sushi wrapped with seaweed.
gyoza dumplings stuffed with pork and herbs, fried and steamed.

halep usually döner (qv) served over bread with a buttery tomato sauce.
har gau steamed mince prawn dumpling.
harira thick lamb and lentil soup.
harissa very hot chilli and garlic paste.
hollandaise a hot emulsified sauce of egg yolks and butter.
hoppers saucer-shaped rice-flour pancakes or (string hoppers) rice-flour noodles usually served steamed.
houmous creamy paste of chickpeas, sesame seed purée, oil, garlic and lemon juice.

idli steamed sponges of ground rice and lentil; eaten with sambar (qv).
ikan bilis tiny fish, often made into a dry relish with peanuts.
ikura salmon roe.
imam bayıldı aubergine stuffed with onions, tomatoes and garlic in olive oil.
incik slow-roasted knuckle of lamb.
injera Ethiopian flatbread.
iskender döner (qv) kebab with yoghurt, butter and tomato sauce.
ISO maki inside-out sushi (qv) rolls.

jalebis deep-fried spirals of batter, in syrup.
jerk spicy marinated then roasted meat.
jhingri prawns.
jollof rice spicy risotto, with tomatoes, onions and (usually) chicken.

kaburga spare ribs.
kadala black chickpea curry.
kaiten zushi 'revolving sushi' on a conveyor.
kalbi marinated beef spare ribs, wrapped in lettuce leaves with chilli sauce and sliced green onion.
kaleji liver.
karahi a wok-like utensil.
karela bitter gourd.
kasha buckwheat.
katsu breaded and deep-fried meat.
keftédes meatballs.
kenkey maize pudding, eaten with stews.
kheer thick rice pudding flecked with pistachios.
khoresh Persian stews.
kimch'i Korean pickles; often taken to signify the classic pickled cabbage.
kısır a mix of parsley, crushed wheat, olive oil, onions, tomatoes and lemon juice.
kléftiko knuckle of lamb, slow roasted.
knedliky bread dumplings.
kneidlach matzo meal dumplings.
köfte, kofta, kafta or **kufta** minced lamb or beef mixed with spices egg and onion.
ko sari na mool cooked bracken stalks with sesame seeds.
kothu roti strips of flat bread, pan-fried with vegetables and chicken or mutton.
kratong thong crisp batter cups filled with mixed veg and/or minced meat.
kueh Malaysian cakes.
kulfi ice-cream made from reduced milk.

laap minced meat flavoured with chilli, herbs and lime juice.
lahmacun a 'pizza' of minced lamb on pide bread (qv).

laksa rich and aromatic noodle soup.
lassi sweet or salty yoghurt drink.
latkes fried potato patties.
liquor milk-free parsley sauce served with pie and mash.
lokma fillet of lamb.
lokshen egg pasta noodles used in both puddings and soups.
lumpia spring rolls filled with meat or veg.

makhani cooked with butter and sometimes tomatoes.
maki sushi with the rice and filling inside a nori (qv) roll.
makki ki roti corn bread.
masala or **masaladar** 'with spices'.
massaman curry with coconut, peanuts, meat and potato.
masto musir yoghurt with chopped shallots.
mee goreng fried egg noodles with meat, prawns and veg.
mejillones mussels.
melanzane aubergine.
merguez spicy, paprika-rich lamb sausages.
meze or **mezédes** snacks, served either hot or cold.
miso a thick paste of fermented soy beans, used in miso soup and some dressings.
mogo cassava.
moussaká aubergines, minced meat and sliced potato, topped with béchamel sauce (qv) and baked.
moutabal aubergine and garlic purée.
mücver courgette and feta fritters.
mung kachori deep-fried spicy bean snack.

nabemono cooked in a pot at table.
nan or **naan** flatbread.
nasi goreng fried rice with shrimp paste.

nigiri lozenge-shaped sushi (qv).
nori dried seaweed.
nuoc mam fermented fish sauce.

ocakbası an open grill.
otak otak steamed mousse made of fish, coconut milk and egg.
ouarka pastry thin pastry, similar to filo pastry.

pad Thai fried noodles with shrimps (or meat), beansprouts, salted turnip and peanuts.
paella rice cooked with chicken and/or seafood.
pakora savoury fritters.
panch'an an assortment of little dishes holding pickles, such as bracken shoots, cucumber or perilla leaves.
paneer Indian cheese, similar to beancurd in texture.
pappa pomodoro Tuscan tomato soup made with stale bread.
papri chaat crisp pastry discs, dunked in yoghurt and doused in chutney.
paratha layered flaky fried bread.
parmigiana di melanzane aubergines baked with tomato sauce and parmesan.
pasteis de nata custard tarts.
pastel de feijão pastry with a filling of sweet creamed beans.
patatas bravas cubes of fried potatoes in a spicy tomato sauce.
patlıcan esme a puréed aubergine dip.
patlıcan salata aubergine salad.
paya curried trotters of lamb in a rich gravy.
pazham pori plantain fried in coconut oil.
pho rice noodle soup with a light, lemony and aromatic beef stock.
phoulorie Trinidadian fried dough balls.

pide flatbread; also the name for Turkish pizza.
pierogi ravioli-style dumplings.
pilau, pillau, pullao flavoured rice, usually with turmeric.
piliç chicken kebab.
piri piri or **peri peri** hot red pepper.
pittu rice flour and coconut steamed in bamboo to make a log.
piyaz white bean salad with onions.
platzel a type of white bread roll.
poh pia dumplings or spring rolls, deep-fried or steamed.
ponzu citrus fruit (ponzu) juice and soy sauce, used as a dip.
pooris puffed up deep-fried disks of dough.
popadom or **papad** thin wafers made with spicy lentil paste.
prosciutto cured ham, usually thinly sliced.
pulpo a la gallego octopus dusted with paprika.
pyzy potato and flour dumplings.

qatme flatbread.
quesadillas pancake stuffed with cheese.

r

raita a yoghurt mix, usually with cucumber.
raki an aniseed-flavoured spirit.
rambutan bright red, oval fruit.
rasam south Indian soup made with tomato and tamarind.
ras malai paneer cheese patties in very sweet, thickened milk.
rendang a 'dry' curry of beef cooked in coconut milk.
rice and peas rice cooked with kidney beans in coconut milk.
rojak raw fruit and veg in a spicy sauce.

Menu glossary

romesco a sauce of hazelnuts, almonds, red peppers and olive oil.
roti unleavened bread cooked in a tandoor.
roti canai layered fried flatbread with a dip of chicken curry or dahl.

saag or **sag** spinach.
sabzi fresh herb leaves (often mint and fennel).
saç thin, chewy bread.
saké rice wine.
salad olivieh a potato salad with chicken, eggs and mayonnaise.
salsa verde a sauce of parsley, garlic, olive oil, anchovies and vinegar.
sambar or **sambhar** spicy lentil gravy made with tamarind and veg.
sambol chilli-hot relishes, often served hot.
sambousek pastries filled with mince, onion and pine kernels.
sashimi sliced raw fish.
satay grilled skewers of meat or fish, served with a spicy peanut sauce.
seekh kebab grilled skewers of minced lamb.
shawarma döner kebab.
shoyu Japanese soy sauce.
şiş cubes of lamb.
soba noodles made from buckwheat.
soju a strong rice spirit.
som tam grated green papaya salad.
soon dae Korean-style black pudding, incorporating rice vermicelli.
sothi a coconut milk curry, used as a gravy.
sotong squid.
sujuk spicy sausage made with either lamb or beef.
sumac an astringent, fruity-tasting spice.
sunomono seafood or vegetables marinated in rice vinegar.
sushi raw fish, shellfish or veg on vinegared rice.
sütlaç rice pudding.
suya spicy meat kebab.

tabouleh a salad of parsley, tomatoes, crushed wheat, onions and lemon juice.
tagine meat stew, often with olives, almonds, lemon or prunes.
tandoor a clay oven.
tapas Spanish snacks.
tarama cod's roe paste.
tarator a bread, garlic and walnut mixture.
tavuk beyti spicy minced chicken.
temaki hand-rolled sushi (qv).
tempura fish or veg deep-fried in batter.
teppanyaki grilled on a hotplate (teppan).
teriyaki grilled meat or fish served in a spicy sauce of shoyu (qv), saké (qv) and sugar.
thali set meal with rice, bread, dahl (qv) and vegetable curries.
thoran vegetables stir-fried with curry leaves, mustard seeds, chillies and coconut.
tikka cubes of meat, fish or paneer (qv), marinated in a spicy yoghurt and baked in a tandoor.
tiramisu a rich dessert of sponge soaked in coffee and layered with brandy-flavoured cream.
tolsot bibimbap rice and vegetables, in a very hot stone bowl, mixed with raw egg yolk and chilli sauce at the table.
tom yam or **tom yum** hot and sour soup, with lemongrass.
tonkatsu breaded and fried pork.
tortilla a Spanish-style thick omelette.
twigim batter-fried seafood or vegetables.
tzatsiki yoghurt and cucumber dip.

udon fat noodles made from wheat flour.
uramaki inside-out sushi (qv) rolls.

uthappam a spicy, crisp pancake usually topped with tomato, onions and chillies.
uykuluk sweetbread.

vadai or **wada** a spicy vegetable or lentil fritter.
vindaloo a hot pork curry from Goa, containing garlic and vinegar; in Britain the term is often misused to signify very spicy dishes.

wasabi a fiery-hot green mustard.
wot a thick, dark sauce made from slowly fried onions, garlic, butter and spices; used in the aromatic stews of East Africa.

xacuti a Goan dish of lamb or chicken, coconut and spices.

yakimono literally 'grilled things'.
yakitori grilled chicken (breast, wings, liver, gizzard, heart) served on skewers.
yaprak sarma vine leaves stuffed with rice, lamb, tomatoes, onion.
yayla yoghurt and rice soup (usually) with a chicken stock base.
yoğurtlu meat (lamb) over bread and yoghurt.
yuk hwe shredded raw beef, strips of pear and egg yolk, served chilled.

zaalouk or **zalouk** a spicy dip of aubergine, tomato and garlic.
zabaglione a pudding of whisked egg, sugar and Marsala (dessert wine).
zensai appetisers.
zeytin olive
zrazy beef rolls stuffed with bacon, pickled cucumber and mustard.

Advertisers' index

Please refer to relevant sections for addresses / telephone numbers

Index by cuisine

For branches, see
Index A-Z p313.

Index by cuisine

Index by cuisine

Index by cuisine

Index by cuisine

Index by cuisine

Index by cuisine

Index A-Z

Index A-Z

Index A-Z

Index A-Z

Index A-Z

Index A-Z

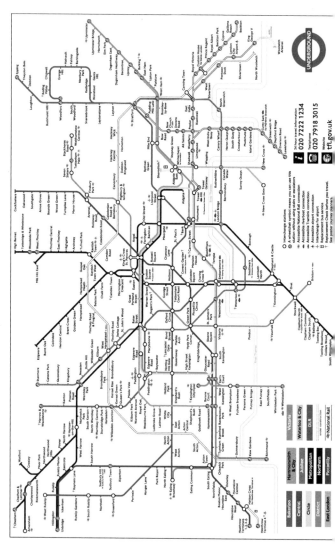